FROM

RELIGION

TO

SCIENCE

The Transition, Initiated by Copernicus and Galileo,

FROM
RELIGION
TO
SCIENCE

THE BECKONING BRIDGE MANY FIND DIFFICULT
OR
IMPOSSIBLE TO CROSS

LAWRENCE H WOOD

TRUE DIRECTIONS
AN AFFILIATE OF TARCHER PERIGEE

iUniverse®

FROM RELIGION TO SCIENCE
The Beckoning Bridge Many Find Difficult or Impossible to Cross

iUniverse books may be ordered through booksellers or by contacting:

iUniverse
1663 Liberty Drive
Bloomington, IN 47403
www.iuniverse.com
1-800-Authors (1-800-288-4677)

ISBN: 978-1-5320-2457-3 (sc)
ISBN: 978-1-5320-2458-0 (e)

Library of Congress Control Number: 2017908582

Print information available on the last page.

iUniverse rev. date: 07/07/2017

CONTENTS

LIST OF ILLUSTRATIONS

LIST OF TABLES

AUTHOR'S NOTE AND DEDICATION

Dear Reader,

Coming up with a book's title is among the more difficult tasks an author undertakes when a published book is the writing objective. I chose this book's title because I believe the beckoning bridge metaphor captures the essence of the fascinating story of how two diametrically opposite understanding of ourselves and our surroundings came to exist and currently coexist.

The initial explanation emerged thousands of years ago, as our evolving brain/mind "awoke" to an existence in a strange, perhaps terrifying place that longed-for explanation. Unfortunately, the only observation instrument available to attempt an explanation was the extremely limited human senses, particularly the eye and the ability to detect motion which produced five illusions, among them the apparent "sun around earth which placed us at the center of the universe." Illusions eventually led to a belief that:

> we live at the center of a very small, very young universe
> that revolves about us; a universe created by and controlled
> by an all-powerful, undetectable supernatural being.

This belief in its various forms is generally termed Religion: English speakers call the supernatural being God, while Native Americans, still living in the Stone Age, use the term Great Spirit

In the early 1600s, a second explanation developed as astute observers, equipped with two radically new, observation instruments: the telescope and the microscope, began to realize that the ancient illusion based explanations significantly conflicted with their new observations, resulting in a total revision of our understanding of ourselves and our surroundings – a revision that has become known as Science. The telescope revealed objects in the distant sky never seen before: e.g., the moons of Jupiter, while the microscope revealed infinitesimally small "animalcules" swimming in pond water and our bodies cellular structure.

We thus have this remarkable and totally unexpected finding –science is a "spin-off" from religion!

Unfortunately, the understanding revision resulting from illusion resolution, still in progress, has been so dramatic that many find the transition from the religious explanation to the scientific explanation, a transition from an approximately six-thousand-year-old universe created and controlled by an undetectable supernatural being to an 11.7-billion-year-old universe created by an incredibly violent explosion and controlled by the laws of physics difficult or impossible to accept.

To symbolize the transition, I invented the **Beckoning Bridge metaphor**, particularly for those who find themselves standing somewhere on the Bridge trying to decide whether or not to make the transition.

If you are one of those, **this Book is Dedicated to You,** since this book provides the answers you seek!

Lawrence H. Wood, PhD

PREFACE

It was mid-April 1543. In a darkened room in Frauenburg, Poland, the renowned polymath[1], Renaissance mathematician and astronomer Nicklaus Copernicus[2] *lay* dying. A few weeks previously, Copernicus' confidant and only pupil Georg Rheticus had sent a copy of Copernicus' last and most influential treatise, *'De Revolutionibus Orbium Coelestium (On the Revolution of the Celestial Sphere[3])* to a printer in Nuremberg. The treatise presented the astonishing and controversial results of Copernicus's observations at his astronomical observatory in Frauenburg -- observations that had led him to the inescapable conclusion that the sun's apparent motion around the Earth is an optical illusion *caused by the Earth's rotation – a motion undetectable by humans.* In reality the Earth (and the other planets) revolve around the Sun! Copernicus's treatise was published just before his death on May 24, 1543.

But why had Copernicus delayed publication of such an important discovery? The web site webexhibits.org[4] suggests that "Copernicus' delay until near death has been taken as a sign that he was well aware of the possible furor his work might incite[5]." A furor resulting from his *extremely controversial discovery* – Copernicus' conclusions clearly challenged an *ancient and revered Christian belief*[6] which placed the Earth at the center of the universe -- a geocentric (earth-centered) universe as opposed to the heliocentric (sun-centered) universe revealed by Copernicus's observations.

To place Copernicus's discovery in context, the belief in a geocentric universe, supported by thousands of years of "revealed truth" is enshrined in the *Book of Genesis* -- which forms a bedrock of the Western religious explanation of ourselves and our surroundings. As Vexen Crabtree remarks in his well-documented treatise regarding the struggle between religion and science, "It was deeply challenging to Christians to face the fact that the Earth wasn't the centre of the universe[7]."

Furthermore, hundreds of years before Copernicus's discovery, the sacred geocentric belief had been further *cast in concrete* by the esteemed Greek mathematician, astronomer, geographer and astrologer Claudius Ptolemy[8]. Ptolemy had cleverly devised a series of integrated circles, termed epicycles, which provided the ability to within reasonable accuracy predict the location of any of the five planets visible to the unaided eye, thereby *preserving the sacred position* of the Earth and its human inhabitants at the center of the "universe"!

Little wonder church doctrine was *harshly enforced* by ecclesiastical authority -- Copernicus's caution proved to be prescient as the Catholic Inquisition[9] cracked down viciously on followers of Copernicus' *heretical theory*[10]. The monk Bruno was burned at the stake and the esteemed Galileo was forced to listen as the Holy Edict of March 5, 1616, was read:

> "The view that the sun stands motionless at the center of
> the universe is foolish, philosophically false, and utterly
> heretical, because [it is] contrary to Holy Scripture."

Galileo was then forced to kneel and repudiate the Copernican theory and add: "...I will denounce him [Copernicus] to this Holy Office..."[11].

But the genie was out of the bottle -- the publication in 1543 of Nicolaus Copernicus's *On the Revolutions...* is often cited as marking[12] the beginning of the scientific revolution.

One could of course mark the scientific revolution's beginning with the invention of the telescope and microscope by Netherlands lens makers; however, Galileo's telescopic observations, occurring in 1610[13] sixty-seven years after the publication of *De Revolutionibus* merely confirmed Copernicus's observations – whereas Copernicus' observations challenged *thousands of years of revealed truth*! A much more fundamental threat to the church's authority.

Complimenting Galileo's telescopic observations, microscopic observations by Netherlands clothier, Antony Van Leeuwenhoek, beginning in 1674 revealed a heretofore unknown world "invisible" to the unaided eye swarming with strange animalcules, as Van Leuwenhoek first called them. Van Leuwenhoek was the first human to observe bacteria and human sperm!

Investigations enabled by these instruments and others developed from them have led to a *revolution in our understanding of ourselves and our surroundings! A total revision of what we thought we knew* -- still in progress and so dramatic that many persons are unable to accept it (I include an encounter with an individual in Appendix B who adamantly rejects the scientific explanation)

As the first four chapters of the book will demonstrate, the accepted understanding extant at the time of Copernicus' discovery, associated with the Catholic Church, had been formulated thousands of years ago, when the evolving human mind had attained the ability to make observations and attempt to formulate explanations of the observations.

Unfortunately, the five illusions listed below, created by *human observational capability limitations,* masked proper understanding development for thousands of years:

1. The apparent motion of the sun, moon, planets and stars around the earth is caused by the earth's rotation, a motion *undetectable* by humans.
2. The apparent same size and closeness of the sun, moon and stars is an illusion caused by an observer's *inability to judge distances* beyond a few feet without a reference to known objects.
3. The earth's apparently unchanging physical features: an illusion caused by the time scale of physical feature change – *millions of years* when compared with human lifetimes, *tens of years.*
4. The earth's apparently unchanging biological features: an illusion caused by the time scale of biological features change – *millions of years* when compared with human lifetimes – *tens of years.*
5. The earth's apparent solidness: an illusion produced by the atom's microscopic size – *invisible to the unaided human eye.*

The descriptions of Illusions 3 and 4 may appear quite similar, but the forces that cause physical change and the process that causes biological change are very different; hence, their separate description and explanation.

Illusion 1 led to the belief in a geocentric universe. Illusion 2 led to the belief that the universe is very small. Illusions 3 and 4 led to the belief that the universe is also very young. Finally, illusion 5, detected only recently, obscured the true material structure of the universe. The combined beliefs could logically have led to only one conclusion: *We live at the center of a very small, very young universe that revolves about us.*

Where did this universe come from? Examining the answers to this question that appear to have been formulated over thousands of years in many places on earth, *the universe was created by an all-powerful, undetectable supernatural being* with many names. As noted above, English speakers call this being God, Native Americans, still living in the Stone Age, use the term Great Spirit. As someone supposedly said: "God has many names." Thus, we have this (ancient) religious understanding of ourselves and our surroundings:

> We live at the center of a very small, very young universe that revolves about us; furthermore, everything in the universe including ourselves was created and is controlled by God.

Returning to Copernicus, his achievement becomes even more remarkable when one is informed that he didn't use a telescope! He didn't have one - the optical telescope wasn't invented until 1608 by German-Dutch optical instrument genius Hans Lippershey[14]. Copernicus's *contentious discovery* was based on years of observations with his unaided eye and mathematical calculation[15].

Many years after Copernicus' discovery, *observational technique and telescope technology improvements* would reveal that the light from some of the stars that entered Copernicus's eye each night had been traveling for *billions of* years -- the stars which had sent the light *had to be located billions of miles away*! Not only do we not live at the center of the universe, but the universe we live in is *unimaginably large* and *unbelievably old*! A significant *addition to the understanding revolution*!

It should be noted that to Copernicus goes the honor of recognizing and partially resolving illusion 1 (although he probably was unaware of the significant step he had taken). Resolving the remaining illusions occupies much of this book and answers these two central questions – *"Why were two diametrically opposite explanations of ourselves and our surroundings formulated*!? And more importantly, why do the two remain coexistent?

The answer to these questions involves an understanding of the transition from the religious understanding of ourselves and our surroundings to the scientific understanding: *literally an Understanding Revolution!*

As I will recount from personal experience, the transition from a religiously oriented understanding to a scientifically oriented understanding (crossing the beckoning bridge) is a mind wrenching experience and has had a significant negative impact on the development of correct (science) explanations which usually supplanted incorrect (religious) explanations.

A simple sketch outlining the approximate beginning of religion, its general development, and the "spin-off" divergence to science are captured below graphically illustrates the divergence of science in the 1600s leading to the coexistence of religion and science today plus the transition across the beckoning bridge. I will use expansions of this sketch in later chapters as it is the basic model for the relationship between religious and scientific development

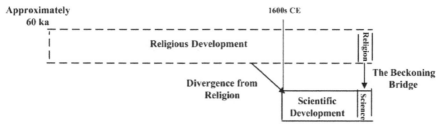

Relationship between religion and science
illustrating the divergence in the 1600s

The exact time of religion's appearance is indeterminate and not particularly important for this discussion – as will be demonstrated below religion definitely began thousands of years ago. However, a significant development time for the initiation of science can be established – the development of the microscope and telescope!

Anton van Leeuwenhoek (1632 - 1723), a "mere" fabric merchant founded microbiology by developing the first practical microscope that allowed him to accurately describe many human cells in1673, never before seen by the human eye.

Almost simultaneously Galileo, using his own improved telescope discovered the moons of Jupiter.

Initially, only the select few of the scientific community were aware of Van Leeuwenhoek's findings; however, as the findings became more widely circulated, many could not except animals that had not been described in genesis – again, thousands of years of revealed truth were being swept away! Furthermore, as mentioned above many individuals are apparently unable to make the transition from a religious based understanding to scientific based understanding. For example, a significant number of Americans are convinced the *Earth is only about six thousand years old*[16]; whereas, another group of Americans are equally convinced the *Earth is approximately 4.5 billion years old*. Obviously, only one age can be correct.

Clearly, this book discusses two very different explanations of ourselves and our surroundings. Which explanation is correct is perhaps less important than how the two explanations developed and why they coexist since their coexistence is a constant source of confusion and conflict. Wars are being fought today because of the differences and the differences color the political process in the United States.

Regarding the existence of religion and science; I have pondered the puzzling existence of the two diametrically opposite understandings for many of my eighty- plus years; the solution to this puzzle began to appear, almost as a present, for my eightieth birthday which I had decided to celebrate by joining a tour sponsored by the Archeological Institute of America, of which I am a member.

The tour's prime attraction was a visit to 17 of the more interesting prehistoric caves of northern Spain and Southern France dating from 10 ka[17] to 40 ka. The cave visits included discussions of those members of our genus who had inhabited the caves, particularly the magnificent cave paintings they had produced. Furthermore, information displayed at the various visitor centers provided insights into the journey from Africa that had brought the ancient residents to the cave area. I will discuss this further after a bit of personal history.

With respect to the development of my personal understanding of ourselves and our surroundings, as a member of the major religion in America, Christianity, my understanding began with indoctrination in the religious explanation based on the Bible. I went to church and Sunday school with my Bible "text book" concentrating on the New Testament and the book of *Genesis*. In public school, I don't remember any discussion regarding the Earth's age or anything else pertaining to the scientific understanding. In fact, I don't recall being acquainted with the term Science at the time.

My first encounter with the science understanding arrived in a red sleigh on my tenth Christmas: a book from an Uncle, *The Earth for Sam*[18]. *Sam* was written in 1928 by W. Maxwell Reed for his nephew Sam who "used to ask about the formation of rivers, mountains, etc." The first line in the book attempts to explain Earth's origin: "A long ... time ago, the Earth was hot[19]." No mention was made of specific time and the discussion continued with generalities. I recall enjoying reading about dinosaurs but not much else; although I remember the book fondly as it produced a lasting interest in science.

My religious indoctrination continued when I reached High School. I spent Sundays at church with an occasional class after school devoted to religious teachings. Some of my High School courses did begin to challenge my religious understanding such as an ancient history course which made no mention of the Biblical stories, but I recall nothing that seriously challenged the book of *Genesis*. Chemistry and Physics could easily be seen as explaining God's creation.

It was in graduate school that "the roof began to fall in." My physics courses presented undeniable facts regarding our surroundings such as the size, shape and age of the solar system, the structure of matter and related subjects. I began to realize that *the science and religious understandings were totally incompatible*. Moreover, it became clear that the *religious understanding, based upon a belief in supernatural causation was impossible*.

Furthermore, I was not alone; numerous people have apparently struggled with the religion-science dichotomy. One person, Dr. Stephen Godfrey even wrote a book about his experiences. Dr. Godfrey recounts his struggle with the *Genesis* creation story in his biography, "*Creationism, Paleontology and Biblical Interpretation*[20], lamenting, his strict young-earth creationist position began to seriously unravel when a year into his graduate studies he joined a fossil hunting group. The fossil record completely refutes Creationism but it took awhile for Godfrey to accept this. As in my case, his transition from the religious understanding to the scientific understanding was a mind-wrenching experience.

During my working career as an Electronic Program Manager I used some of my spare time to continue my investigations of the religion-science dichotomy, assembling a fairly large collection of books and scientific magazine articles related to the subject such as Carl Sagan's *The Demon-Haunted World: Science as a Candle in the Dark*[21].

Retirement in 2000 provided more time to investigate intriguing aspects of scientific understanding, particularly the history of science understanding's developments and the intellectual giants who made them possible. Furthermore, it enabled my establishment as a legitimate Science Historian and I joined the Pacific Division of the American Association of the Advancement of Science (AAASPD). Among the more rewarding features of AAASPD membership was the opportunity to present papers at their annual June meetings; a stimulating activity focusing my interest on topics that provided some of the motivation for this book. Two papers are of particularly interest:

"The Last of the Hominidae[22]*."* and
"Why is Creationism So Persistent?"[23]

The first paper addressed the question "Why are we the only surviving member of our genus?" An inspiration for the paper was the January 25, 2013 headline for a Wall Street Journal article: *"Neanderthals: Why Us and Not Them?"* plus the much-ballyhooed sequencing of the Neandertal genome[24] that involved the remarkable feat, at the time, of examining DNA that was more than forty thousand years old!

Because DNA is fundamental assumes a pivotal role in the development of life it is likewise central to an understanding of life's development. A detailed description of DNA is provided in chapter 16; however, for most of the book, DNA can be viewed as life's fingerprint. There are approximately 7.5 billion humans on earth. Each has a unique combination of DNA molecules known as genome. That's 7.5 billion unique genomes – no two people are alike. As you will see, this uniqueness allows scientists to trace human migration paths

Some of the material for the first paper referred to Dr. Ian Tattersall's seminal book *Masters of the Planet*[25], which suggested that our position as the planet's dominant species is the "result of the very unusual way in which our brains handle information[26]."

Further into his book, Tattersall reveals that "very unusual" refers to the attribute of symbolic thinking – viz. the ability to develop language and strategic thinking that Tattersall demonstrates is *totally unique to our species and a key to our success*. Details of our rise to prominence are included in the first four Chapters.

The second paper is based on a related article I published in the journal *Free Inquiry*[27], which addressed the controversial issue of creationism which is germane to this book:

> ...the religious belief that the Universe and life originated "from specific acts of a Supernatural being" For young Earth creationists, (those who believe the Earth is less than 10,000 years old) this includes a biblical literalist interpretation of the Genesis creation narrative and the rejection of the scientific theory of evolution[28].

As I was preparing the Creationism paper, I "connected some dots" and realized my personal transition from religious belief to science logically paralleled humanity's transitional development of an understanding of ourselves and our surroundings. Accordingly, as demonstrated above, religious explanation and development, driven by humanity's insatiable curiosity and clouded by five illusions clearly had to have *preceded* the development of a scientific explanation.

Contemplating my "discovery" of the parallel between my personal understanding development and humanity understanding development, I was frankly a bit excited. An explication of the understanding revolution from incorrect Religious understanding to correct Scientific understanding, had apparently *never been published; especially in a coordinated manner --* I set out to write this book; which presents, in an approachable form, what I believe is one of the most important and exciting mystery story's imaginable, -- the story of how and why we came to be: literally an understanding revolution!

After you have concluded this book, you will find that newspaper and magazine stories that previously seemed difficult to comprehend have suddenly become much clearer; moreover, you will have a well organized book that you can easily refer to.

INTRODUCTION AND GENERAL OVERVIEW

The quest for *an* understanding *of* ourselves and our surroundings is arguably one of the most significant and probably one of humanity's oldest pursuits. Satisfying this quest demonstrably began several thousand years ago, when evolving human cognitive ability had matured sufficiently to enable the first informed observations of ourselves and our surroundings which was followed by attempts to explain these observations.

As introduced in the Preface initial observation explanation attempts were frustrated by five illusions created by physical limitations of the human observation ability such as the eye's inability to observe the microscopic world of the atom or the cellular structure of life, or our bodies general inability to detect constant velocity motion.

Attempts to explain these illusion-clouded observations yielded a totally incorrect understanding of ourselves and our surroundings. The apparent motion of sun, moon and stars around the earth, the apparent closeness to the sun, moon, and stars plus the earth's apparently unchanging bio-physical features led to a belief that we inhabit the center of a small unchanging universe--a universe created and controlled by an all powerful supernatural being. *We call this understanding religion.*

About five hundred years ago, astute observers armed with vastly improved observational tools such as the telescope and microscope initiated a series of observational improvement developments leading to a series of ground-breaking discoveries disclosing that the illusion-clouded religious explanations were impossible to reconcile with their improving observations.

These development improvements and ground breaking discoveries eventually resulted in an explanation revolution. A continuing revolution *we call science.*

While all improvements and discoveries contributed to the explanation revolution, some were more important than others such as the development of microscope and telescope, mentioned above plus techniques for dating ancient objects which answers the question: "How can you know how old an ancient entity is, if no human was present?" Brief explanations of improvements and discoveries of particular importance, such as dating techniques, will be inserted as needed.

With respect to bizarre existence of two diametrically opposite explanations of ourselves and our surroundings: religion and science, one of this book's two objectives is tracing the historical evolution of our explanation of life's development, from the primordial cell to our dominant position on the planet. This historical examination will reveal how the religion-science dichotomy evolved and will demonstrate that the religious explanation which essentially culminates with *Genesis* (in the Christian religion) preceded scientific explanation development. Proceeding along this path will "automatically" establish which explanation is correct and the reason for the dichotomy.

The explanation of the dichotomy is followed by the second objective: an accessible, detailed "A-to- Z" historical tracing of science's development, organized by illusion resolution, introducing most of the brilliant individuals whose observation improvements and discoveries made illusion resolution possible.

A significant purpose of the detailed explanation is to address those individuals who are unable to accept the revised, scientific explanation by emphasizing "how do we know" the scientific explanation is correct? After all, the illusion based explanation persisted for thousands of years.

Achieving these two objectives has persuaded me to divide the book into two sections:

Section I: addresses the first objective in four chapters that trace life's development path in three phases, to the time, approximately three thousand years ago, when the *book of Genesis* was written. The discussion then moves to the time approximately five hundred years ago, when astute observers, employing new "game changing" observation instruments detected the illusions and began resolving them.

The new instruments were based upon "simple" pieces of glass developed by Netherland lens makers in the early 1600s. The pieces came in "two flavors" a convex lens thicker in the middle and a concave lens thinner in the middle. Experimenting with various lens combinations, two configurations emerged -- both involved placing the lens in a cylindrical metal tube: one configuration enabled the viewing of objects located at vast distances, the other enabled the viewing of infinitesimally small objects.

The first configuration became known as the telescope while the second became known as the microscope. These new instruments and their descendents enabled significantly improved investigations which branched off from the religious path, as introduced in the preface, onto an entirely new investigative path leading to the correct illusions explanations and the development of the understanding of ourselves and our surroundings we term science.

Finally, it should be noted that the explanations provided in Section I, covering almost four billion years were only achieved in the last few hundred years - attesting to the brilliance of those who were able to branch off the religious path onto the science path.

Section II: presents an overview of the historical development of science coordinated with the resolution of three illusion groups, introducing the brilliant investigators whose discoveries were responsible for illusion resolution:

Resolving the Solid Earth Illusions

Resolution of the apparent solid earth illusion explains in five chapters, the structure of matter, beginning with the study of electrostatic electricity, the first observable suggestion of matter's true structure to the discovery of the electron, the atom, the atom's nucleus and finally atomic fission (the source of the earth's internal heat) and the discovery of fusion, the source of the sun's energy. As will become clear, an understanding of the structure of matter underpins the understanding of all other illusion resolutions.

Resolving the Astronomical Illusions

Resolution of the astronomical illusions explains in three chapters, the determination of the correct shape of the earth's orbit and by extension the shape of all planetary orbits; the determination of the size of the earth's orbit and finally, using the earth's orbit as a baseline, the distance to the stars which ultimately led to the size and age of the universe.

Resolving the Unchanging Earth Illusion

Resolution of the two apparently unchanging earth illusions is explained in five chapters, beginning with the discovery after thousands of years that the earth does change. The explanation of how the physical features of the earth change is presented in two chapters by revealing the forces that cause the change. Biological property change is provided through the explanation of how the process that creates the phenomenon of evolution is the basic causes of biological features change.

Section II concludes with a discussion of the Earth's biogenic formation - an overview of how the lovely blue planet we inhabit and love came to be, plus an overview of the Life Cycle of the Universe from its fiery beginning billions of years ago to its absolute zero end uncountable billions of years in the future which places our Brief Shining Moment in proper context.

CHAPTER 1

LIFE BEGINS

Life appeared on planet earth in two phases

1. A single primordial cell.
2. Multicellular life, presumably a combination of primordial cells.

The primordial cell appears

> Analysis of 3.7-billion-year-old rocks in the Isua Greenstone Belt in Greenland, has serendipitously revealed relatively well preserved rocks that have survived geological time with some of their original sedimentary attributes intact extending the time of primordial life to 3.7 Ga[29].

The first primordial cell must have been created in the ocean; an ocean very different from today's ocean – it wasn't salty. Salt required millions of years of erosion to accumulate. Also, there were no predators, merely a concentration of the "molecules of life" carbon, hydrogen, oxygen and minerals which over millions of years "experimented" with various combinations until a combination that could be consider alive appeared.

Dating 3.7-billion-year old entities

We can have confidence in the age of the first cells thanks to reliable and accurate dating techniques developed in 1927 by British geologist Arthur Holmes.

Before we examine Holmes' technique, a simple definition of a "dating substance" should be understood: a dating substance must have these essential features:

1. Was present when the activity to be dated originated.
2. Has a sufficiently long life to be present at the time when the origin date is measured.
3. Must change in a measurable and detectable manner beginning with the origin of the activity to be measured.

British geologist Holmes was apparently the first person to recognize that the decay of an unstable atom has these features[30]. An in-depth discussion of atomic structure is provided in chapters 5 through 9; but a brief introduction to the structure of the atom necessary to permit an understanding of the important subject of ancient object dating using the decay or fission of unstable atoms is easily provided.

The atom can be "envisioned" as having the same structure as the solar system: the sun surrounded by rings of planets; where the atom consists of a nucleus (the "sun") surrounded by rings of negatively charged electrons ("the planets"). The nucleus in turn consists of positively charged protons and "neutral" neutrons

Regarding a dating substance, the tendency of an atomic nucleus with large numbers of neutrons, which is often unstable, to split or decay, a process known as fission is one of the atomic properties of interest[31]. Nuclear decay or radioactivity are the terms usually associated with the loss of particles from the nucleus due to fission which occurs at a constant measurable rate as exhibited in this figure:

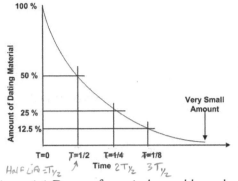

Figure 1-1 Decay of a typical unstable nucleus

Figure 1-1 reveals that the decay curve approaches the x-axis asymptotically, displaying less and less material until the right end of the decay curve is reached and the technique is no longer useful.

The essence of the technique, applied to items of interest, is exhibited in 1-1 where atoms with unstable nuclei such as Carbon 14 and Uranium are shown:

Item to be Masured	Descriptive term	Dating Substance	Half Life	Num. Useful Years	Decay Product
Ancient life	Radio-carbon	Carbon 14	5370 years	< 50,000 years	Nitrogen-14
Age of the Earth	Uranium-Lead	Uranium	4.47 Billion years	Several Billion yrs	Lead
Special Rocks	Uranium-Thorium	Thorium	75 kyrs	500 k yrs	Thorium
Volcanic Material	Potassium-Argom	Potassium	1.25 Billion years	Several Billion yrs	Argon

Table 1-1 Elements of the technique for dating ancient objects

Table 1-1 reveals a wide range of ages that can be measured with this technique from the age of ancient life to the age of the Earth. The primordial cell's age was measured by employing the decay of Uranium in the Greenland fossils.[32].

Regarding the evaluation of ancient entities, it is important to note that prior to the 1927 discovery of dating techniques, evaluation of new ancient discoveries was severely hampered by a lack of an understanding of earth's true age.

The primordial cell could reproduce and absorb energy from its environment

As introduced above, evidence of life's beginning appears in ancient rocks dated to over 3.7 Ga in the form of the single celled Cyanobacteria[33] -- bacteria are known as prokaryotes which have a very simple structure, particularly no nucleus[34]. The Cyanobacteria often form large structures known as stromatolites which can still be seen at Australia's Shark Bay[35].

Our knowledge of the first cell is perforce limited, but it definitely had two important features essential to life:

1. A finite life as do all current living cells; hence *it had to be able to reproduce itself* - otherwise you wouldn't be here reading this. The fist cells were primitive Prokaryotes – cells without a nucleus; hence they reproduced by fission.
2. Since the first primordial cell could reproduce itself, it must have been able to ingest the things it needed from its surroundings to survive: nutrients and at least oxygen eventually; although the *first cells were able to convert sunshine into energy.*

The first person to actually observe a cell was the remarkable investigator, Robert Hooke (1635-1703)[36]. In 1663, he detected cells in thin slices of wood christening the molecular combination the Cell[37] since the shape of cells in wood reminded Hooke of a Monk's cell-- the investigation into life's origins had begun!

Of particular importance, *only a single cell can reproduce itself!* Accordingly, all life including every living entity currently occupying space on earth began life as a single cell!

Multi-Celled life appears with Eukaryotic (cells with nucleus) and the "invention" of sexual reproduction

The most common form of life on earth is multi-celled; hence multicelled animals obviously appeared sometime:

> One of the oldest fossils identified as multicelled is red algae. These algae are also the oldest fossil eukaryotes (cell

with a nucleus), *Bangiomorpha pubescens*, a multicellular fossil from arctic Canada (probably Somerset Island[38].) strongly resembles the modern red alga *Bangia* despite occurring in rocks dating to 1.2 Ga.

Note that it required approximately 2.5 Gyrs for *B. pubescens* to evolve since the appearance of multi-celled life required the development through trial and error of multi-cell (sexual) reproduction which must ultimately involve the production of single cell since only a single celled entity can reproduce itself). I

Due to its importance, a brief description of the essential elements of the multicelled reproductive process is displayed in Figure 1-2:

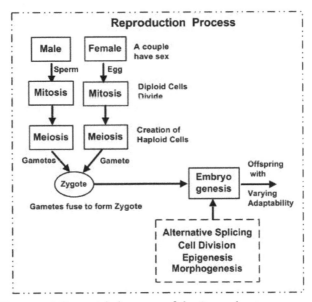

Figure 1-2 Essential elements of the Reproduction process

The diagram has been deliberately offset into two sections to emphasize that reproduction can be considered a two-step process: creation of the all-important beginning cell, termed a zygote (from the Greek word ζυγωτός *zygōtos* "joined[39]") followed by the creation of offspring via Embryogenesis. In many respects the zygote is the lineal descendent of the primordial cell introduced above.

Since Sperm and Eggs are cells, knowledge of some elements of cell structure is essential (more detail will be provided in chapter 16). All cells contain complex molecules termed chromosomes. Two different cell types have been identified based upon chromosome number. Diploid cells have two sets of chromosomes and Haploid cells have only one chromosome.

Creation of a Zygote, a distant ancestor of the primordial cell, requires haploid cells since a zygote is created by the joining of sperm and egg. Clearly, the fusing of a haploid sperm and a haploid egg will create a diploid zygote (whereas fusing two diploid cells would produce a nonsustainable cell). The creation of egg and sperm will be presented in chapter 16; however, as will be demonstrated, the creation of egg and sperm is completely random.

As shown in Figure 1-2, reproduction begins when a male and a female have sex at a time when the female can conceive. The male contributes multiple sperm while the female contributes, usually, one egg: sperm and eggs are officially termed gametes.

Figure 1-2 also shows that eggs and sperm go through two processes: Mitosis – simple cell division and Meiosis – cell division which produces the desired single chromosome haploid cell.

After sex, sperm go "racing" to the egg. One of the lucky sperms wins the race and fuses with the egg forming a zygote, another random event. Once formed, the zygote enters embryogenesis, a complex totally random process leading to an offspring.

The phenomenon of evolution develops from multcellular reproduction

One of the intriguing aspects of mult-cellular life is the appearance of the phenomenon of evolution. All the steps which produce an offspring are completely random; hence multicellular reproduction is a *completely random process* and, as will be demonstrated in chapter 17, the output of a random process is normal distribution usually termed a Bell Curve. Accordingly, *all human characteristics, particularly adaptability, conform to a bell curve.*

A typical bell curve is exhibited in Figure 1-3 where some of the numbers for IQ are shown.

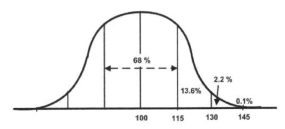

Figure 1-3 Some typical values for a bell-shaped distribution

the bell curve will be discussed in detail below – for now note the rather steep sides. The numbers on the horizontal axis refer to IQ scores: unsurprisingly there aren't many individuals with an IQ above 130 which we've all observed. The implications of the Bell curve are profound, but our interest here is just the adaptive characteristic which *is the key to evolution*; however, the Bell curve will appear many times throughout the book since the Bell curve is one of the book's more important leitmotifs (a recurrent theme throughout a literary composition, associated with a particular person, idea, or situation).

Regarding evolution, Charles Darwin was the first investigator to collect enough information to conclusively demonstrate that life has evolved, the first proof that life changes. Unfortunately, Darwin lacked enough information to explain how evolution occurred, but needing something, proposed Natural Selection:

> The process whereby organisms better adapted to their environment tend to survive and produce more offspring[40]".

However, Darwin was unable to define neither the process nor the mechanism of adaptation.

This simple graphic illustrates both. Note that the Bell-shaped adaptability selection process based upon the adaptability curve is added to the reproduction diagram from Figure 1-2 and we have this simple description of evolution's elements:

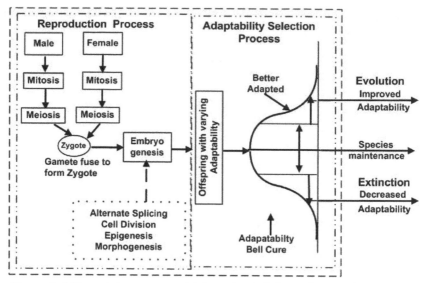

Figure 1-4 Essential processes which undergird the evolution phenomenon

- A couple has sex which results in a zygote.
- The zygote undergoes multiple cell divisions and the other processes associated with Embryogenesis, and outputs an offspring with varying characteristics.
- The adaptability Selection Process selects offspring according to their adaptability. Those better adapted survive, produce more offspring and life's improvement we call evolution continues. Of course, there are bell curves for all human characteristics hence there is variation in all human characteristics. Something we all observe – this is the reason for so much variability.

The details of reproduction will be presented in chapter 17.

Another important development that appeared with multicelled life is proteins

DNA gets all the press but, protein does the work. Proteins provide two important functions:

1. Proteins are essential for life
2. Protein manufacture is a source of new genes essential for evolution.

The importance of Protein is emphasized in Table 1-2 which presents some protein categories and the essential functions the proteins perform[41]:

Protein Category	Protein Function
Antibody	Helps protect the body
Enzyme	Performs almost all of the thousands of chemical reactions that take place in cells
Messenger	Transmits signals to coordinate biological processes
Structural Component	Provides structure and support for cells. On a larger scale, they also allow the body t move
Transport/Storage	Binds to and carries atoms and small molecules within cells and throughout the body

Table 1-2 Essential Protein Functions

In addition to the important functions listed in Table 1-2, the protein manufacture process is also a source of new genes -- of obvious value to evolution. In view of their importance, a brief description of protein manufacture will be provided here with details added in Chapter 17.

Proteins are an assembly of linked amino acids; however, while amino acids can self-assemble via the rules of quantum mechanics, assembly of amino acids to form a protein requires the assistance of a selection mechanism - this mechanism is assisted by genes positioned along a strand of the DNA molecule[42]. A simplified diagram of the basic protein manufacturing process is shown below:

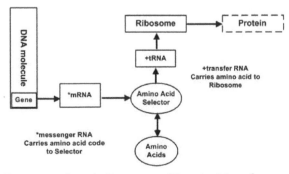

Figure 1-5 Simple Diagram of Protein Manufacture.

Genes are located along the entire length of the DNA molecule: for convenience, only one gene is shown in Figure 1-5. The basic process involves an amino acid selector that chooses the correct amino acid from a pool of amino acids in response to the correct amino acid code, termed a "codon[43]" transferred from the gene by a messenger element, mRNA[44]. The selected amino acid is then transferred to an entity known as a Ribosome via a transfer element, tRNA. The Ribosome then assembles the amino acids into a protein.

Due to the structure of the gene; the actual process is a bit more complicated. The correct "split-gene" structure exhibited in Figure 1-6 is a combination of coding and non-coding elements[45]:

Exon	Intron	Exon	Intron	Exon	Intron	Exon

Figure 1-6 Basic Split Gene Structure

Exons contain a portion of the gene where the code for an amino acid is stored while Introns contain supporting molecules.

This structure was *totally unexpected,* an "Oh My Gosh! "event (described in Chapter 2) earning the discoverers American geneticist Phillip Sharp (1944-)[46] and British biochemist Sir Richard Roberts (1943-)[47] a much-deserved Nobel Prize[48].

The extraction and combining of Exons to retrieve the amino acid code is termed splicing of which two types are known: simple and alternative[49]. Simple splicing is shown in Figure 1-7:

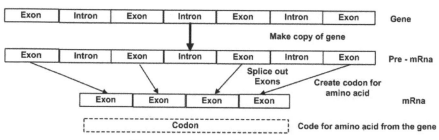

Figure 1-7 Simple Gene Splicing.

First a copy of the gene, termed a Pre-mRNA is created by a transcription process which avoids disturbing the gene's structure. Next the Exons are spliced out to create the mRNA which carries the codon for an amino acid to the selector, shown in Figure 1-8 which displays the complete protein manufacturing process:

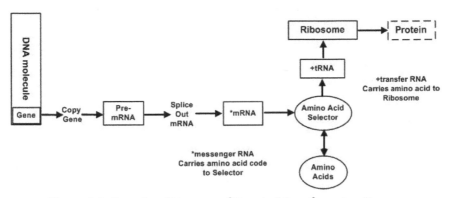

Figure 1-8 Complete Diagram of Protein Manufacturing Process.

In view of the involved splicing process required to assemble an amino acid code, the important question arises: "Why did this "split -gene" structure evolve?"

Although not fully confirmed, a logical conjecture can be found by examining the other type of gene splicing; alternative splicing which is shown in Figure 1-9:

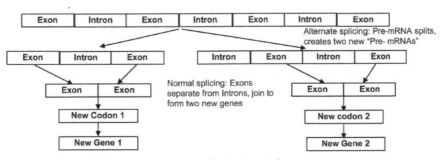

Figure 1-9 Alternative Splicing

Alternative splicing is a three-step process beginning in the same manner as normal splicing with a copy of the gene, however, instead of separating exons from introns as occurs in normal splicing, the Pre-mRNA is split into *two parts* creating *two new* "Pre-mRNAs"[50]! The new "Pre-mRNAs" shown on the second row of Figure 1-9 are then processed via normal splicing in which exons are separated from introns and joined to form new codons for two new genes, shown on the third and fourth rows.

Until August 2016, the possibility that new genes created by alternate splicing could select Amino Acids and create new proteins which may have significant new properties such as the beginning of a new species was only hypothesized[51]. But, in August 2016, the use of a novel gene-editing tool, the two-molecule combination CRISPR Cas (Clustered Regularly Interspaced Short Palindromic Repeats)[52] permitted the editing of genes during embryogenesis to cause "evolution related developments" such as zebra fish with legs as reported in the August 2016 Nature Magazine[53].

While CRISPR Cas may seem a mouth-full, the essential elements are fairly straight forward. CRISPR is a molecule discovered in the early 1990s and has proven to be a powerful tool for increasing our understanding of genetics. An interesting description of the investigation timeline leading to CRISPR Cas can be found in this reference *CRISPR Timeline*[54].

During gene editing with CRISPR Cas, the CRISPR molecule, a very sensitive detector of a gene on a DNA molecule, provides the ability for relatively easy identification of a single gene. The Cas molecule can then remove the gene for examination or replacement by another gene

Creation of a "fish with legs" involved the manipulation of a gene, known as HOX (which is responsible for structural development) using CRISPR Cas. The CRISPR molecule was used to find the appropriate HOX gene for fin development in the zebra fish embryo. Then Cas was used to remove the fin HOX gene and substitute the HOX gene for leg development in animals that have legs, and voila, *a fish with legs*!

As Axel Meyer, a biologist at the University of Konstanz in Germany who studies gene evolution in fish comments, "It's a very nice example of how changes in one or two genes can be responsible for a *huge evolutionary transition*" -- clearly demonstrating that *evolution can occur during embryogenesis*[55]. *Evolution in a Petrie dish!*

Surprisingly, the Nature article did not speculate how the new "leg gene" might occur. I offer the conjecture that Sherlock's Theorem suggests the source of the new gene would most likely be alternative splicing. In addition, Ian Tattersall's book *Masters of the Planet* introduced above contains this comment:

> Recent advances in molecular genetics are finally revealing what genetic development must have led …to our enlarged frontal lobes. Clearly, significant phenotypic changes must be accompanied by *equally significant genetic* changes - in particular new, unique genes and there is *no mechanism in the Modern Synthesis* that accounts for "Great Leaps Forward[56]."

Tattersall's comment was written long before the "evolution in a petrie dish demonstration" but was exceedingly prescient.

It is important to understand that, while DNA is the "code of life" it can also be viewed as the alphabet for life. Just as the 26 letters of the alphabet provides the ability to create millions of words, the four letters of the DNA alphabet (see Chapter 18 for details) which are combined to create the DNA molecule, can be combined into an almost infinite number of combinations, termed a genome. Accordingly, the genomes of all animals differ; the genomes of all humans differ slightly which accounts for our differences. Note, there are about 7 billion people on earth - that translates into 7 billion *unique genomes.*

Since no two genomes are the same, DNA is the ultimate human identifier. It is better than fingerprints and photographs of faces. Of particular interest, DNA has been used to free innocent people who were convicted based on eyewitness testimony which has been shown to be unreliable – obviously. Also, DNA has also begun to be used for improved understanding of our ancient ancestors as described in Chapter 3.

As we investigate the development of life, keep alternative splicing in mind – perhaps you will see the possibility that alternative splicing played a role. We will return to this subject in Chapter 17.

Prelude to modern life - The Ediacaran Period

The Ediacaran Period (635 Ma– 543 Ma) named after the Ediacaran Hills of southern Australia is the geological period immediately preceding a momentous period in life's journey[57]. The oxygen level in the oceans was so low that modern fish could not have survived. Animal life at this point was simple; but an evolutionary storm would soon upend this quiet world.

The Cambrian Period

About 504 Ma, a proliferation of life forms occurred when most of the phyla[58] present on earth today were created.

With the advent of the Cambrian[59], the simple Ediacaran system disappeared and gave way to a world ruled by highly mobile animals that possessed "modern" anatomical features. The Cambrian explosion, as it is called, produced arthropods with legs and compound eyes, worms with feathery gills and swift predators that could crush prey in tooth-rimmed jaws.

Biologists have argued for decades over what ignited this evolutionary burst. Recent research, reported in Nature reveals that the cause may have been a significant increase in the percentage of oxygen in the atmosphere[60].

However, it my conjecture that *the evolution phenomenon provides the mechanisms for the creation of the wide varieties of life forms with a plethora of complex body types and behaviors that fill the oceans today.* "This is the most significant event in Earth's evolution," says Guy Narbonne, a palaeobiologist at Queen's University in Kingston, Canada[61].

Life after the Cambrian

Over the millions of years since the Cambrian, life has developed in a generally regular pattern according to the evolutionary process, as displayed in figure 1-10 which exhibits an idealized composite sedimentary rock formation with each layer about a hundred million years "thick," displaying five classes per the Linnaean system – (see Appendix E. (The details regarding figure 1-10 will be presented in chapters 17 and 18) but the interrelation between adaptive improvement and reproductive improvement is a classic example of the evolution phenomenon:

Mya					
4.5	Fish	Amphibian	Reptile	Mammal	Primate	Homo
30	Fish	Amphibian	Reptile	Mammal	Primate	
100	Fish	Amphibian	Reptile	Mammal		
300	Fish	Amphibian	Reptile			
400	Fish	Amphibian				
500	Fish					

Figure 1-10 The ladder of life

The bottom layer contains the first significant animals: the fish, dominating the oceans for approximately one hundred Ma[62]. Fish reproduce via a rather inefficient system: the female lays eggs on the bottom of the body of water she is living in. Then several males squirt out sperm that settles onto the eggs and a few lucky sperm fuses with an egg. As anyone who has ever observed spawning knows, millions of eggs are laid with a small percentage hatching into small fish. Of course, enough egg-sperm combinations occur to maintain a stable (and actually growing) fish population.

One day, a "brave" fish, probably caught when the tide went out, struggled to **adapt** to breathing air and was successful. This fish was joined by others who could also adapt to breathing air. Eventually a new Class was formed – the amphibians (see Appendix F for a diagram illustrating the system that has been developed for organizing life.). Amphibians are found in the second layer. It should be noted that amphibian reproduction is essentially the same as fish.

Amphibians ruled the world until some amphibians developed the next **adaptive improvement**, the ability to remain out of water indefinitely, living on land continuously

The newly improved animals, known as Reptiles, developed a second **improvement** – a significantly advanced **reproductive** system in which the embryo is contained in an amniotic sack protected by a calcium based shell until the embryo could survive on its own.

Reptiles added one other **adaptive improvement** – an extension to the spinal cord forming a crude brain, termed the "Reptilian Brain" which controls basic life functions. Unfortunately, the Reptilian Brain is a double-edged sword – it can keep "brain dead people" alive – my Father almost suffered this fate until my mother and I stepped in and executed his Living Will.

The next **adaptive improvement** was also a **reproductive improvement** – the ability of females to retain their babies in their bodies until their babies could survive without the protection of the mother's body. Live birth was aided by another **adaptive improvement**, the modification of sweat glands on the female chest into organs, termed mammary glands, which produce a liquid that can nourish the newborn baby. Live birth supported by mammary glands is so important that the group was termed mammals. Mammals also developed an improved brain structure by the addition of a limbic cap which provided emotions for good (fear is a useful defense) and bad (anger and aggressiveness).

The next **adaptive improvement** was the "split-off" of the Primate Order from the mammals in which the two forelegs were converted into "arms." Arms enabled Primates to live in trees which provided protection from large ground animals.

Primates like Mammals **reproduce** by live birth. Further, they also developed an improved brain by adding another layer on top of the limbic, an enlarged cerebral cortex giving them the advantage of improved intelligence

Finally, in the top row in figure 1-10, our genus Homo appears. Recent study of genes demonstrates that our genus, the best **adaptive improvement** to appear (so far) diverged from the chimpanzee Pan, between five and seven Ma.

Homo sapiens, **adapted** for completely upright locomotion, has a considerably advanced cortex both in size and shape (see chapter 2). The skull shape has adapted to allow space for a new cerebral organ, the frontal lobes and reproduces with great abandon via live birth. As archeologist Ian Tattersall has eloquently written, we are "Masters of the Planet[63]."

Recent brain investigation reveals a brain structure considerably more complex than previously understood with one hundred eighty distinguishable areas[64], an obvious reason for the brain's amazing capability and, unfortunately, its complex problems.

I recently averred that the processes undergirding evolution contributed to the Cambrian explosion. The Ladder of life is a superb demonstration of the evolution phenomenon which chapter 17 will cover in more detail however, the biological developments accompanying the Cambrian involved considerable reproductive and adaptability improvement – *these are the hallmarks of evolution*

An important adjunct to the Ladder of Life is the Cycle of Life discussed below.

The Cycle of Life

As will be seen in later chapters, the concept of "life" can be generalized to include any entity that experiences this Life Cycle – the entity:

- Comes into existence, is born,
- Exists for a finite amount of time, and then
- Ceases to exist, i.e. "dies"

Thus, we can discuss the Life Cycle of our solar system, see chapter 12 and our universe, see chapter 19 since these chapters will demonstrate that both will pass through this cycle.

At this point in our discussion, we are principally interested in the biological life cycle which is illustrated in the simple diagram presented in figure 1-11.

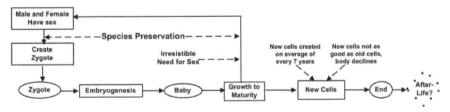

Figure 1-11 the cycle of life

The left side of Figure 1 - 11 contains a reduced reproduction diagram illustrating the "coming into existence" of any living entity via the formation of a zygote – every living entity begins as a zygote. Next the existence portion of the life cycle begins with embryogenesis and ends when cellular degradation leads to the failure of a vital organ and the entity ceases to exist or "dies.

The cycle of life provides the answer to three questions of interest to almost anybody: "Why am I here?" "Now that I'm here, why can't I stay?" and "While I am here, do I have any purpose for being here?"

Why Am I Here – the physiology of zygote production

The left side of figure 1-11 answers this question by providing a reduced version of the reproduction diagram, figure 1-2 demonstrating that you are here because your parents had unprotected sex when your mother could conceive.

Since reproduction is not required for individual survival, there is the related question: "Why did your parents engage in sexual activity?" The answer to this question is provided by an examination of the physiology of zygote creation. As the diagram in figure 1-2 reveals a zygote is created by the joining of male and female sex cells: an egg and a sperm.

No effort, of course, is required by the female to produce an egg. The female's hormone system periodically, monthly for humans, produces an egg - sometimes more than one. The egg is ejected from an ovary into a tube, the fallopian tube, which is connected to the uterus.

While the female does not have to exert effort to create an egg, the male must exert effort to provide sperm. This required effort consists of rubbing the male sex organ vigorously within the female genitalia a sufficient number of times to cause sperm to leave the testes travel up a duct termed the vas deferens to the urethra.

Of particular importance, continued rubbing creates an exceedingly strong muscular contraction, ejecting the sperm and creating the extremely exquisite sensation known as an orgasm. Thus, the irresistible urge for sex is actually an irresistible need to experience an orgasm –the reason your parents engaged in sexual activity.

While the creation of an egg requires no effort on the part of a woman, a woman also shares the ecstasy of an orgasm. This pleasure is provided by a small piece of tissue extending from the top of the vulva known as the clitoris. In addition to the woman's share in the joys of orgasm, stimulating the clitoris requires maximum male penetration; thereby enhancing the possibility of pregnancy assuring continuation of the species.

Regarding the vulva as a sex object, carvings of vulvas on the walls of prehistoric caves can logically have only one objective -enhance the enjoyment of sex. *It's truly an ancient need.*

Sperm is released into the uterus while the egg waits in the fallopian tube. There are two fallopian tubes; the one in which the egg awaits has a higher temperature than the other. Thus, the sperm is a "heat-seeking" missile. The sperm swims to the fallopian, enters it, fuses with the egg and a zygote is formed - the desired pregnancy has been achieved.

This is of the course the fundamental objective of sexual activity however there are grave consequences such as excessive population which will be discussed in chapter 19.

Do I have any purpose for being here?

In keeping with all living entities, you began life as a single cell created from your parent's sexual encounter as described above. As explained previously this cell divided an enormous number of times during Embryogenesis creating you, a baby.

After you were born, cell division continued until you reached mature size. After reaching mature size your purpose for being here became abundantly clear. An occasional overriding need for sex assumed a paramount position in your life. Heeding the same need for sex that motivated your parents, you found a mate, and engaged in sexual activity at a time when a baby could be created. In this way, you fulfilled your *main purpose for being here: the preservation of our species.*

There is an unfortunate downside to the preservation of our species: Population Growth. While climate change gets the headlines, perhaps a more serious problem confronting our species is Population Growth. The September 29, 2016 issue of Nature asks: "Where to put then next billion people[65]? Current estimates place the global population at 7.5 billion[66]. The current US population is slightly over 300 million. The Nature article suggests in fourteen years the world will add three more populations the size of the United States. The article is available via a Google search-- perhaps you should access it and see what kind of world your children or grandchildren might inhabit.

Why Can't I Stay?

After you have completed your main purpose, reproducing yourself, cell division continued. You get a new set of cells on average every seven years[67]. Unfortunately, each new set is inferior to the previous and the degradation we call aging, which leads to the end of your life, becomes increasingly apparent and you have completed life's cycle. In 2014, this cycle was traversed in the United States. 3,988,076 times.

Regarding our ultimate demise, there are a number of well documented causes. Latest statistics list these top three causes of death[68]:

Heart disease: (614,348)
Cancer: (591,699)
Chronic lower respiratory diseases: (147,101)

While heart disease is currently the most common cause of death, cancer is not far behind and, as the population ages, will probably move closer to first place.

Cancer is initiated when a "rogue" cell begins rapid cell division resulting in a multiplication of cells that damages tissue. The end result of this damage depends upon which tissues are being damaged. If it's breast tissue, there are a number of treatments including tissue removal - but your life is not threatened. However, if the cancer is allowed to spread to a critical organ, such as the lung, you may experience a premature death from cancer.

Concerning premature death from cancer, a recent study has shown that the "majority of cancers are due to 'bad luck,' that is, random mutations arising during very large numbers cell divisions in normal, noncancerous stem cells[69]." The implications of this study are unfortunately obvious -- the longer you live, the greater the probability of contracting cancer.

What happens after I die?

Discussions of the possibility of life after death are among the most controversial topics extant with a long history[70] -- I include it to complete the cycle.

The events following our death are well known. The support bacteria in our bodies lose out to the destructive bacteria and our bodies begin to decay - a repugnant, odorous process; a process that has compelled our species, when it had acquired the ability, to place our body in the ground. Some believe burial is a sign of religious development, but I submit it was invoked merely as a sanitation measure.

There is much "evidence" of an afterlife in the literature, among the most convincing are out of body experiences (OOBE). One web site[71] presents observations during an OOBE that are very difficult to explain unless the person experiencing an OOBE was "present." On the other hand an OOBE is apparently very rare – why are there only a "chosen" few?

Most people who experience an OBEE are physically sound - the OBEE usually occurs during an operation when a person is placed essentially in a state of "suspended animation." On the other hand, when we die, our organs disintegrate and return to the elements, mainly, carbon, hydrogen, oxygen and nitrogen, from which we came. For my part, I think the famous "tent maker" Omar Khayyam said it best in this quote from the Rubaiyat[72]:

> Strange, is it not? that of the myriads who
> Before us pass'd the door of Darkness through,
> Not one returns to tell us of the Road,
> Which to discover we must travel too.

Chapter Summary

- The appearance of life on planet earth in two phases is introduced:
  - o A single, primordial cell.
  - o Combinations of primordia; cells into multicellular life.
- Dating of ancient objects using nuclear decay is introduced
- The ability of a cell to reproduce and absorb energy from its environment was mentioned as important aspects of the first single cells
- The essential elements of multicelled reproduction accompanied by a diagram was provided

- A brief description, accompanied by a diagram of combining the reproduction process and the adaptability selection process which describes evolution was provided
- Some of the basic elements of proteins re introduced – their need for life and their source of new genes
- The Ediacaran and Cambrian periods were described
- The Ladder of Life, a prime example of evolution was described
- The all-important cycle of life which answers such questions as "Why am I here was introduced.
- Finally, the question *What happens after I die?* was addressed

Looking ahead:

We have followed life's progression from the primordial cell to appearance of our genus Homo with our species H. sapiens in the starring role. Chapter 2 extends our knowledge of our genus with unexpected Oh-My-Gosh discovery of three more members of our genus in Europe. which introduces the three phases of Anthropology. The discovery that three members of our genus actually evolved in Africa adds to the confusion and leads to an "out of Africa" diagram. Finally, a radically new investigation tool DNA analysis further muddies the waters by throwing serious doubt on the reality of one member of our genus necessitating a revision of the out-of-Africa diagram. Finally, an introductory discussion of cognition is presented.

CHAPTER 2

THE DISCOVERY OF THREE MORE MEMBERS OF OUR GENUS AND THREE PHASES OF ARCHEOLOGY

An unexpected discovery

August 1856 was oppressively warm. Sweaty miners were quarrying lime in the Feldhofer cave in Germany's Neander valley seven miles east of Dusseldorf. Suddenly, one of the miners saw something totally unexpected: the end of a human leg bone sticking out of the ground--someone had buried a body here! Soon other miners gathered around and it was agreed that the bones should be dug up.

The miners carefully removed the rock and soil from the bone gradually exposing the entire bone. But there was something wrong. The bone seemed too thick--perhaps the unfortunate person buried here had some form of bone disease.

After some effort, more bones were discovered. Being careful not to damage any, the miners eventually excavated twelve others. After a reasonably thorough search for more bones, no more were disclosed. Where was the rest of the body? Had some monster chopped up the body and spread the bones around?

Realizing that nothing more was to be gained at the mine, the miners took the bones to amateur naturalist Johann Fuhlrott (1803-1877)[73] who identified them as a skullcap, one more thighbone, three bones from the right arm, two from the left arm, part of the left pelvis, fragments of a shoulder bones and three ribs.

Other than identifying the bones, Fuhlrott was unable to do more to solve the mystery of the bones, so they were taken to anatomist Hermann Schaffhausen[74] for further investigation. Schaffhausen solved the mystery by deducing that due to the unusually massive bone structure, the bones were not human bones. They had to belong to another member of our genus, Homo[75]!

In view of the basic religious worldview extant, the impact of this discovery cannot be overemphasized! The discovery was totally unexpected. More importantly the discovery conflicted with the prevailing religious dogma which was inclined toward the *immutability of species* "--the concept which claimed that each individual species on the planet was specially created by God and could never fundamentally change[76]. Of note, Schaffhausen had previously declared that "the immutability of species... is not proven[77]."

The Three Phase of Archeology

The miner's discovery can be explained by viewing Archeology, the scientific study of prehistoric peoples, as divided into three phases:

- The "oh-my-gosh!" (OMG) phase.
- The pick-and-shovel scientific phase.
- The new technology DNA analysis phase.

The OMG phase as the name implies is associated with complete surprise, something totally unexpected. The pick and shovel scientific phase is associated with normal Archeological findings that are expected/hoped to be new but not shocking. The DNA phase is relatively new and is analogous to the addition of the telescope or microscope to scientific investigation--it is a *complete game changer*.

Clearly the unexpected discovery in the Neander Valley belongs to the "oh-my-gosh" phase. It is important to note three fundamental things about the discovery:

- The discovery was completely unexpected--the miners were not looking for anything unusual, especially bones.
- The bones were found in a river valley - no surprise now, members of our genus, homo, have always lived near rivers to obtain water.
- At the time, no one had any idea that other members of our genus existed.

It is important to note that "oh-my-gosh" reactions have accompanied other discoveries throughout scientific investigations in other fields, such as the Roberts and Sharp split-gene discovery, and will be highlighted as they appear.

One "oh-my-gosh" discovery related to the Neander Valley discovery, from the field of geology, is the completely unexpected discovery of spectacular prehistoric paintings on the ceiling of the Altamira Cave in Northern Spain, which is discussed below. So difficult was the acceptance of the paintings' antiquity that the cave's discoverer was actually accused of having the paintings fraudulently created!

The discoveries in the Neander Valley and the Altamira cave are summarized below:

Discovered Item		Disc. Date / Disc. Location / existence time	
H. Neandertal	1856	Neander River Valley, Gr.	400 ka – 40 ka
Altamira Cave	1868	Santillana, Del Mar, Sp	14 ka – 16 ka

Table 2-1 Summary of the first "oh-my-gosh" discoveries in Europe

Another important note: prior to the Neander Valley and Altamira discoveries, interest in the investigation of our species origins was nonexistent. As introduced above, lack of interest reflected the average person's worldview in the middle of the nineteenth century. "...the origins of mankind were assumed to be fixed, uncomplicated and divinely directed[78]." A world-view also supported by James Ussher's famous determination, from *Genesis,* of creation's date of 4004 BCE[79], published in 1658.

The discovery of three other members of our genus

Although more difficult to place in time than the "oh-my-gosh" phase, the pick and shovel Archeological phase possibly began after the excitement and disbelief associated with the discovery in the Neander Valley had sufficiently subsided such that enough people were able to take a more dispassionate reaction to the discoveries of three other new members of our genus is summarized in Table 2-2: Homo sapiens (at the time of discovery, no one realized the remains were our direct ancient ancestors), Homo erectus and Homo heidelbergensis.

Discovered Item		Disc. Date / Disc. Location / existence time	
H. sapiens	1868	Abri de Cro-Magnon, Fr	44 ka - present
H. Erectus	1891	Java, Indonesia	1.9 mya – 70 ka
H. heidelbergensis	1907	Heidelberg, Gr.	700 ka – 70 ka

Table 2-2 Summary of the second group of discoveries for our genus (Homo)

Note that H. erectus has been determined to have originated almost two million years ago, an antiquity totally incomprehensible to anyone at the time of the discoveries, but easily understood today with the dating techniques explained in chapter 1. We of course are the only surviving member of our genus. The reasons for our good fortune are detailed in chapter 3.

As a companion to tables 2-1 and 2-2, a diagram tracing our evolutionary path as understood, until another OMG discovery, in March 2016, is displayed in this figure:

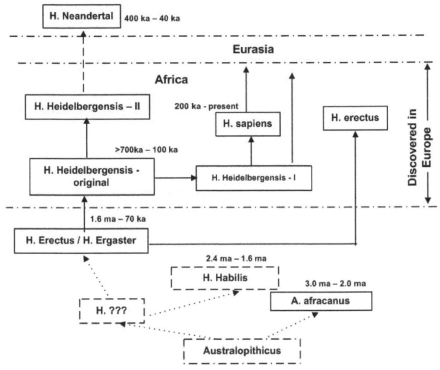

Figure 2-1 Our evolutionary path as understood until March 2016

The following paragraphs explain the findings listed in table 2-1 in their discovery order and the reaction to them. It should be emphasized that the initial discovery location of a species was purely serendipitous and has little bearing on the general understanding of each species' actual origin location, which as mentioned previously, with the exception H. Neandertal was confirmed in October 2016 as Africa[80].

H. Neandertal

Regarding the 1856 Neandertal discovery - it was not the first discovery for this member of our genus. In 1829, an apparently human skull was discovered in a cave near Engis Belgian[81], when Belgium was part of France. However, this child skull (found thirty years before Charles Darwin published "On the Origin of Species") was not recognized as an early human fossil until decades later[82]. A second discovery occurred in

Forbes' Quarry, Gibraltar in 1848[83], but again the discovery's importance escaped the discoverers.

Finally, as described above, in August 1856 the German Neander River Valley discovery occurred[84] and anatomist Hermann Schaffhausen[85] had deduced that they were not human bones. He suspected that "these bones are ante-diluvial (before the biblical flood) forms of fossil human remains[86]."

It remained for William King, professor of geology at Queens College in Galway, Ireland[87], to successfully argue, in a paper presented in 1864, that the Neander Valley fossils belonged to an extinct species of early humans he named *Homo Neanderthalensis*. When referring to this species, I will use the more recent designation *Neandertal*, which is closer to the pronunciation of the name.

H. sapiens

Frenchman Louis Lartet had the honor of the first discovery of an ancient fossil of our species, H. Sapiens, in southern France in 1868[88] a mere nine years after the publication of *The Origin of Species*. Asked to conduct excavations in a rock shelter, abri (French for rock shelter) de Cro-Magnon near the French village of Cro-Magnon, Lartet discovered the partial skeletons of four prehistoric adults and one infant. These Cro-Magnon humans were soon identified as a new prehistoric human race distinct from the *Neandertal* fossils discovered previously in Germany. As indicated above, knowledge of the antiquity of life was nonexistent until Arthur Holmes' 1927 dating technique development; accordingly, no one could have realized that they were actually our ancient ancestors.

Today we would obviously recognize the skeletons. Moreover, it should be noted that one of the more proper designations of our species is *anatomically modern humans* (AMH).

H. erectus

Eugene Dubois, a Dutch Surgeon set out for Asia, then believed to be humanity's cradle, in search of our ancestors. In 1891, Dubois's team apparently confirming the "Out of Asia" origin dug a human-like fossil from the bank of the Solo River on the Island of Java Note that the Java discovery occurred on a riverbank (same as the *Neandertal* discovery). Since knowledge of our genus' ancestry was essentially nonexistent, Dubois named his discovery *Pithecanthropus erectus* – Java man[89].

However, evolutionists (believers in the phenomenon of evolution) pushed for the revised name, "Homo erectus" (erect man) since the evolutionists believed that man evolved slowly (and directly) from the apes and would therefore have initially begun with a curved posture, gradually becoming erect[90]. On the other hand, evolution, as described above, is not necessarily a slow phenomenon and we did not evolve directly from the apes. Accordingly, throughout much of the twentieth century anthropologists debated the role of H. Erectus in human evolution.

During excavations in 1923–27 at Zhoukoudian near Peking, China, a group of fossil specimens identified at first as Peking man, but eventually as erectus was discovered.[91] In 2009, the finds were dated from roughly 750,000 years ago.

Several fossils resembling erectus have been discovered in many parts of the world confirming the existence of H. erectus and the various erectus migrations.

Homo heidelbergensis

On October 21, 1907, in a sand mine near Mauer, Germany, workman Daniel Hartmann spotted an unusual mandible (jawbone) in one of the sandpits. Hartmann gave the fossil to Heidelberg University Professor Otto Schoetensack (1850-1912)[92] who identified and named the fossil *homo heidelbergensis*[93].

Due to the scant material (only a jawbone) used to suggest a new species, reaction to the finding and interpretation was met with skepticism. The celebrated author H. G. Wells regarded this jawbone as: "One of the most tormenting objects in the world to our curiosity[94]."

After all, as you will see a single mandible is a risky piece upon which to base a new species. To date at least ten pieces of the *heidelbergensis* skeleton have been found in various places on the planet[95]. Examples include a fossilized skull near Stuttgart, Germany in 1933, a tibia plus many ancient hand axes at the English Boxegrove quarry in England in 1994 and a skull designated enigmatic found in the Petraloa Cave in Greece in 1997.

For many years archeologists seemed to have grudgingly agreed with the veracity of heidelbergensis with comments like "It is now fairly certain that *H. heidelbergensis* is an ancient extinct member of our genus[96]."

While these fragments do not fully buttress the case for *heidelbergensis*, twenty-eight skeletons found in a large cache of fossils in northern Spain which were associated with *heidelbergensis*, significantly strengthened the case for *heidelbergensis*. However, as will be disclosed below, the identity of the fossils in northern Spain have recently been revised by the DNA analysis archeology phase placing *Heidelbergensis's* identity in doubt.

Summarizing genus Homo discoveries

From 1856 to 1907, fossils representing four members of our genus, including our species, were discovered in Europe and Asia. Moreover, in 1907, our origin in Africa was unknown! The picture of our evolution will become clear in the following pages. A wealth of additional information regarding any of our extinct ancestors can be found on the web.

The Cave at Altamira – the OMG event of caves

The cave at Altamira is not only one of the most spectacular prehistoric caves, it was the first major cave discovered.

Discovered by a hunter in 1868 (the same year we were "discovered"), the first visitor was amateur archaeologist Marcelino de Sautuola in 1876[97] who returned a few years later after his eight-year-old daughter Maria had discovered the paintings (Sautuola had apparently missed the paintings since one must venture quite a distance into the cave to see them).

The cave was examined by Sautuola and archaeologist Juan Vilanova y Piera from the University of Madrid, resulting in a controversial publication in 1880 that interpreted the paintings as the work of ancient artisans. However, French specialists, led by French expert Emile Cartailhac, who, at the time, believed prehistoric man was intellectually incapable of producing any kind of artistic expression, vigorously rejected Sautuola's and Piera's hypothesis.

The supreme artistic quality, and the exceptional state of painting preservation "had to be recent creations" thus, Sautuola was accused of forgery. A fellow countryman even went so far as to claim that "the paintings had been produced by a contemporary artist, on Sautuola's orders[98]."

Of course, the reaction to the discovery is not unreasonable; as mentioned above, in the late 1800s, modern dating techniques had not been invented and knowledge of our prehistory was almost nonexistent. 19th Century Europe was just emerging from the medieval view of creation as presented by *Genesis* which led to the belief that creation occurred 6 ka. As I disclose below, after several years Cartailhac recanted.

The Pick and Shovel Scientific phase: African Genesis

As mentioned above, the beginning of the OMG and DNA analysis phases are easy to date, but the transition time between the OMG Phase and the pick and shovel Phase was necessarily a bit indistinct. Possible transition times include the development of reliable dating by Arthur Holmes in 1927[99] or the South African discoveries of Raymond Dart, (discussed below), beginning in 1924.

In this Pick and Shovel phase we explore the activities of important investigators and three of their finds that occurred in Africa beginning in 1924. The three finds in the order of their discussion are summarized in table 2-2. However, it should be noted that ergaster may be merely an older version of erectus:

Species	Disc. Date / Disc. Location / Species existence time		
A. Afarensis	1978	Ethiopia	3.9 mya – 3.0 mya
H. ergaster	1949	Lake Turkana, S. Africa	1.6 mya – 500 ka
H. Habiis	1960	Olduvai Gorge	2.3 mya – 1.8 mya

Table 2-3 Three important fossil finds in Africa

Raymond Dart-one of the first African Anthropologists

Raymond Dart (1893 -- 1988) an Australian anatomist and anthropologist, was appointed head of the anatomy department at the University of Witwatersrand, Johannesburg, South Africa, a position he had reluctantly assumed feeling that he was being assigned to the "outback." Little did Dart realize that he had been placed in a position that would ultimately give him considerable fame as it turned out to be a front row seat in the unfolding drama of the origins discovery of many members of our genus.

Dart had become interested in fossils found at a limestone quarry near Kimberley Africa. In 1924 he discovered the first fossil ever found of Australopithecus africanus (southern ape of Africa) an extinct hominin[100] closely related to humans. In addition, a colleague, Professor Young, had sent Dart two crates of fossils from the small town of Taung in South Africa.

Dart immediately recognized one of the fossils in the crate as appearing to be an early "human" because its brain dimensions were too large for a baboon. Dart had recently been studying 2 million-year old fossilized baboon remains, whose lives had obviously ended by a deadly blow to the head. Each head bore the same indentation which Dart eventually demonstrated was created by the humorous bone of a small antelope. The obvious question, "What animal had administered a blow logically intended to kill?"

Further study led Dart to unknowingly invoke Sherlock's theorem*, which allowed him to conclude that an intelligent animal must have been the culprit. But, the baboon's demise had occurred hundreds of thousands of years before the appearance of humans (who are well known killers). Again, Dart had to invoke Sherlock's theorem as his studies led to only one conclusion: the culprit had to be Australopithecus africanus. "The use of weapons had preceded man!"

> Australopithecus afarensis is one of the longest-lived and best-known early hominin species—Paleoanthropologists have uncovered remains from more than 300 individuals! Found between 3.85 and 2.95 million years ago in Eastern

Africa (Ethiopia, Kenya and Tanzania), this species survived for more than 900,000 years, more than four times as long as our own species has been around[101].

Dart arranged a presentation of his findings at the 1930 meeting of the Pan-African Congress in Prehistory[102]. Dart was allotted twenty minutes of a five-day congress and was roundly dismissed.

The reaction to Dart's discovery has, unfortunately been duplicated many times. We have difficulty accepting painful truths. However, continued progress toward an understanding of our origins in Africa was provided by the famous archeological team of Louis and Mary Leakey[103].

The unique idea of Sherlock's Theorem:

If you Google one of Sir Arthur Conan-Doyle's most famous books, The Sign of the Four, you will be presented with[104]:

> The Sign Of the Four – Wikipedia, the free encyclopedia
> https://en.wikipedia.org/wiki/The_**Sign_of_the_Four**
> *How often have I said to you that when you have eliminated the impossible, whatever remains, however improbable, must be the truth?* Sherlock Holmes, Chap. 6, pg 111
> Summary-Publishing history-Film adaptations-References

The italicized words are arguably Conan-Doyle's most famous lines:

> **After the impossible has been eliminated, whatever remains, however improbable, must be the truth**

While this admonition was of considerable assistance to Doyle's famous consulting detective, it is doubtful that Conan-Doyle realized how applicable this admonition would be to scientific investigation. As you will see, these words have been unknowingly applied to numerous scientific puzzles; hence, I will term Doyle's famous lines - Sherlock's theorem.

Louis Leakey-archeologist and ladies' man

Louis Leakey (1903-1972) was born in Kenya to British missionary[105] parents Harry and Mary Leakey[106]. Although Louis, like Robert Ardrey would ultimately achieve great fame, his earliest home had an earthen floor. The facilities slowly improved over time. The mission, a center of activity, set up a clinic in one of the tents, and later a girl's school for African women[107].

Leakey's interest in the past was stimulated by Arthur Loverage, the first curator of the Natural History Museum in Nairobi who Leakey encountered in 1914. In 1924, while a student at Cambridge, Leakey learned that the British Museum was sending a fossil-hunting expedition to South Africa and joined his first archaeological expedition.

Leakey's decision to search in Africa was fortuitous. At that time, as introduced in the Preface and the first section of this chapter, most authorities believed that Asia was the premier hunting ground for humanity's origins[108]. In 1927, Louis received a visit from Frida Avern who had done some course work in archaeology. It was apparently love at first sight; they married in 1928 and set off together for Elementia and Gamble's Cave[109]. While examining the cave, he discovered the Acheulean stone tool site of Kariandusi, Kenya, an area with a well established tourism industry including the Kariandusi prehistoric site.

The Acheulean discovery was indeed a stroke of luck. The Acheulean is an archeological industry of stone tool manufacture characterized by distinctive oval and pear-shaped "hand-axes[110]." Acheulean tools, originally discovered near the French town of Saint Acheul; (hence the name), were produced during the time period 3.3 Ma to 300 ka across Africa and much of West Asia, South Asia, and Europe, and are typically found with *Homo erectus* remains. Acheulean tools were the dominant technology for the vast majority of human history[111].

Louis Leaky was an attractive man and one day Louis met Mary Nichol with whom he had an affair, which led to a divorce from Frida and a second marriage for Louis. Louis and Mary made an excellent team, becoming instrumental in extending the story of modern human development in Africa, particularly through several discoveries made at Olduvai Gorge in Tanzania.

Olduvai Gorge is a steep-sided ravine in an area of Africa known as the Great Rift Valley, which is rich in fossils. Louis and Mary established and developed the excavation and research programs at the Gorge which achieved great advances of human knowledge and world-renown status for the Leakey's. One of their more important finds was *Homo habilis*

Homo habilis - oldest member of our genus?

Possibly the oldest member of our genus, H. habilis is one of the first important discoveries made in Olduvai. The specimen discovered became the specimen that led to the naming of this species. Interestingly, H. habilis is described as a well-known, but poorly defined species[112].

This specimen and its designation were the subject of much controversy through the 1970s. Louis Leakey was convinced habilis was the Olduvai toolmaker he had spent his life looking for, since habilis was the slightly larger-brained early human that made the thousands of stone tools also found at Olduvai Gorge.

Habilis has often been thought to be the ancestor of the more slender and sophisticated H. ergaster (see below) which in turn gave rise to the more human-appearing species, H. erectus[113]. In fact, as mentioned above, the two species are probably the same.

Richard Leakey (1944-) the famous duo's second son joined them on December 19, 1944. As he matured, Richard participated in his parent's field expeditions and was therefore well-placed to inherit their legacy. however, an independent personality brought him into conflict with his father and they parted ways[114].

Earliest known remains of H. sapiens

One of the most important discoveries associated with Richard Leakey are bones recovered by a scientific team from the Kenya National Museums directed by Richard and others[115]. The remains from Kamoya's *Hominid* Site (KHS) were called *Omo I* and those from Paul Abell's *Hominid* Site (PHS) *Omo II*. The Omo II fossils have more archaic traits. "Studies of the postcranial remains of Omo I indicate an overall modern human morphology with some primitive features.[116]

Parts of the fossils are the earliest to have been classified by Leakey as *H. sapiens*. In 2004, the geological layers around the fossils were dated, with the age of the Kibish *hominids* estimated at around 195 ± 5 ka [thousand years ago]. This would make the fossils the oldest known *Homo sapiens* remains[117]. Since this discovery is the earliest thus far, Ethiopia is among the main proposed locations for the cradle of *Homo sapiens*[118]. The recent realization that *H. sapiens* evolved in Africa and migrated from there to the rest of the world, is discussed below.

Leakey and associates noted that the skull material associated with H. sapiens showed definite modifications in skull shape, particularly the frontal lobes. The difference between H. sapiens and H. Neandertal skulls is clearly demonstrated in this crude sketch:

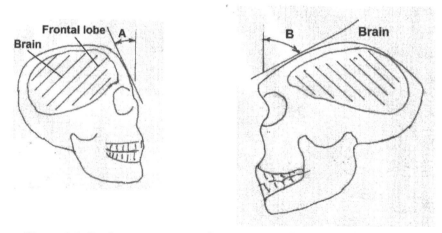

Figure 2-2 Outline comparison of H. sapiens and H. Neandertal skulls

The H. sapiens skull has a remarkably different shape – note that angle A, the forehead slope is much less for H. sapiens allowing for a much larger frontal lobe, the requisite for symbolic thinking.

Among the significant finds of Richard Leakey's expeditions was the discovery of a *H. erectus* skull in 1975. In 1978 Leakey "hit the jackpot" with one of his most important discoveries supposedly related to *H erectus:* Turkana Boy[119], discovered at lake Turkana, Africa in 1984. Turkana Boy, *a nearly complete skeleton of a youth,* has been dated to between 1.5 and 1.6

million years old. An excellent discussion with photos will be found in this web site: en.Wikipedia.org/wiki/Turkana_Boy.

This is one of the more remarkable archeological finds in Africa and ranks in the Oh-My-Gosh area of archeology with the Neandertal finding – the first non-human member of our genus. Regarding the find, as part of a National Geographic special, Ric_hard Leakey placed this skeleton in context, particularly with respect to evolution[120]:

I think [the Turkana Boy] is remarkable because it's so complete, but perhaps another aspect that is often overlooked is that many people who don't like the idea of human evolution have been able to discount much of the work that we've done on the basis that it's built on fragmentary evidence. There have just been bits and pieces, and who knows, those little bits of bone could belong to anything. To confront some of these people with a complete skeleton that is human and is so obviously related to us in a context where it's definitely one and a half million years or even more is fairly convincing evidence, and I think many of the people who are fence-sitters on this discussion about creationism vs. evolution are going to have to get off the fence in the light of this discovery.

Confirming the Origin of H. Erectus as Africa.

It is now generally accepted that *H. erectus* eventually migrated to Asia where one of its members lay waiting for Eugene Dubois. The earliest fossil evidence of H. erectus has been dated to 1.9 Ma and the most recent to 70 ka.

The discovery of Lucy

Donald Carl Johansson (1943 -) is another American Paleoanthropologist known for discovering a famous fossil, the fossil of Lucy, a female Australopithecine in the Afar Triangle region of Ethiopia[121]. The name "Lucy" was supposedly coined as Johansson was listening to the Beatles' "Lucy in the sky with Diamonds" while examining his find. As mentioned before, the official name is A. afarensis. Lucy has been dated to about 3.2 million years ago.

Interest in Lucy continues. A paper in the 22 September issue of *Nature* describing Lucy's probable demise

> Lucy has been at the centre of a vigorous debate about the role, if any, of arboreal locomotion (travel in trees) in early human evolution. It is therefore ironic that her death can be attributed to injuries resulting from a fall, probably out of a tall tree, thus offering unusual evidence for the presence of arborealism (tree travel) in this species[122].

Homo ergaster

Meaning "working man," ergaster is an extinct member of the genus Homo that lived in eastern and southern Africa between 1.9 million and 1.4 million years ago[123]. H. ergaster, generally assumed to be related to H. erectus, was discovered in 1949 by South African archeologist John Robinson (1923 –2001), head of the Department of Vertebrate Paleontology[124], on the shores of Lake Turkana. Turkana boy was found after Robinson's discovery but they are obviously related.

Ergaster played a significant role in stone tool development having inherited a very early stone technology and then going on to develop the first Acheulean bifacial axes. However, the line of H. erectus apparently diverged from H. ergaster some 200,000 years before the general innovation of Acheulean technology and erectus was the ultimate developer the Acheulean.

More recent finds - Discoveries at Pinnacle Point S. Africa

One of the more important recent finds, reported by two articles in the November 2012 issue of Nature, discusses a complex stone tool technology in the Pinnacle Point region of South Africa. Authors Kyle Brown and Curtis Marean describe:

> ...a previously unrecognized advanced stone tool technology from Pinnacle Point Site 5–6 on the south coast of South Africa, originating approximately 71,000 years ago. This technology is dominated by the

production of small bladelets (microliths) primarily from heat-treated stone [known as silcrete]. There is agreement that microlithic technology was used to create composite tool components as part of advanced projectile weapons[125].

In a companion article, Sally McBreaty suggests that:

> ... the humans making them (the microliths) had developed the capacity for complex thought, and passed this knowledge down the generations[126].

Hence the Pinnacle Point site represents one of the first firm evidences of cognition. Moreover, examination of the Pinnacle Point artifacts may also aid our understanding of modern human's development and spread as postulated by Grafton-Smith's innovation/origin axiom. Possession of a bow and arrow confers a significant advantage over people employing only hand-held weapons in both hunting and interpersonal conflict[127]. Human populations migrating out of from Africa armed with a bow and arrow would have been formidable foes.

The new technology DNA analysis phase:

As introduced in the Preface, in September, 2015, my wife and I had the privilege of visiting the Atapuerca Mountain in northern Spain where railroad workers blasting through the mountain in the nineteenth century had exposed cross sections of bone-filled limestone caverns[128].

Of particular interest was Side los Huesos ("The Pit of Bones"). I will describe atapuerca in greater detail along with other caves a bit further on; for now, only the important elements such as a superb archeological display plus information about the remains of twenty-eight members of our genus found in the pit are provided. At the time of our visit the accepted identification of the Side los Huesos specimens was *heidelbergensis* which provided considerable support for the existence of *heidelbergensis*[129].

Since our visit, the association of the bones with *heidelbergensis* has been shown to be incorrect and the true identity of the fossils has emerged - an informative story of scientific detective work.

When researchers first discovered the bones from the Side los Huesos in the mid-1990s, they noted that the fossils looked a lot like primitive Neandertals[130], but at the time other factors suggested *heidelbergensis* as the most reasonable choice.

In 2013, the fossil's identity became more complex when a study of the mtDNA (maternally inherited mitochondrial DNA) from one of the bones revealed that it more closely matched the mtDNA of a Denisovan, an elusive member of our genus. Puzzled researchers realized a complete DNA sequence was essential to properly establish the bones' identity.

Investigators at the Max Planck Institute for Evolutionary Anthropology in Leipzig, Germany, who had obtained the mtDNA, announced they would try to sequence the complete nuclear DNA of the fossils to solve the mystery.

After 2 years of intense effort, paleogeneticist Matthias Meyer from the Institute finally sequenced enough nuclear DNA from fossils of a tooth and a leg bone in the pit to solve the mystery[131].

> ...we find that 87 percent and 68 percent, respectively, of the positions on the common Neanderthal and Denisovan branch carry derived alleles (protein variations); that 43 percent and 39 percent, respectively, of positions on the Neanderthal branch carry derived alleles; while [only] 9 percent and 7 percent, respectively, on the Denisovan branch do so.

This indicated that the Pit of Bones skeletons are related to the ancestors of Neanderthals, and in particular not to *heidelbergensis*. As Paleoanthropologist Chris Stringer of the Natural History Museum in London, lamented[132]:

> That would mean that the ancestors of humans were already wandering down a solitary path apart from the other kinds of archaic humans on the planet 100,000 to 400,000 years earlier than expected. "It resolves one controversy—that they're in the *Neandertal* clade[133], (family)" Stringer says. "But it's not all good news: From

my point of view, it pushes back the origin of *H. sapiens* from the Neandertals and Denisovans." The possibility that humans were a distinct group so early shakes up the human family tree, promising to lead to new debate about when and where the branches belong [in particular our branch].

This of course includes origin. On the other hand, one thing is certain; about 44 ka we arrived in Europe.

Reflecting on *H. heidelbergensis*, the atapuerca DNA study results should have almost been predictable. Determining that *heidelbergensis* was a new species based on only a jaw bone was an amazing stretch. Furthermore, as time passed, just "bits and pieces" of the *heidelbergensis* skeleton have been found. Most tellingly, *heidelbergensis* is the only member of our genus for which at least one almost complete skeleton has not been found. The Mauer find was most likely an Asian *H. erectus*.

Since the bell curve guarantees variability, some of the fossil "bits and pieces" identified as *heidelbergensis* were likely variants of Neandertal as the early discoverers noted. Since no evidence of Neandertal has been found in Africa, the African remains could possibly be H. erectus remains or perhaps H. ergaster.

Adjusting our evolutionary path to align with Homo antecessor

In 1994, the remains of a boy and five other early humans were discovered by paleoanthropologist Antonio Rosas of the National Museum of Natural Sciences in Madrid[134] and his colleagues at another site in the Atapuerca Mountain called Gran Dolina[135]. The remains consisted of fragments of more than eighty fossils, including skulls, jaws, teeth and other parts of the skeleton.

The layers bearing these fossils were dated by using a rather bizarre characteristic of the Earth's magnetic field, periodic reversal. The last reversal occurred 781 ka[136] and is marked by a distinctive sedimentary layer known as the Matuyama-Brunhes geomagnetic polarity reversal. The layers containing the fossils are below this layer; hence they are at least 781 ka.

Today only part of boy's face remains, comments Rosa, but this part is stunning, because despite its antiquity, it "is exactly like ours." Rosa further avers that "the boy's modern face set between a primitive jaw and brow—shows that [antecessor] probably gave rise to both modern humans and Neandertals." as shown in figure 2-3:

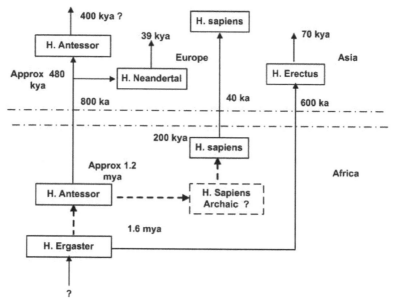

Figure 2-3 Our evolutionary path as understood after March 2016

Beginning with Antecessor, the preceding pages have established the reasonable hypothesis that antecessor evolved from Ergaster, who in turn evolved from habilis. Since habilis is the oldest known member of our genus, his ancestor must have been a member of the Australopithecus genus and due to its prevalence, afarensis is the logical candidate.

While we know that antecessor appeared before 780 ka, it is not yet known if antecessor was still present close enough to 200 ka. to allow antecessor to be our ancestor.

An alternative path is shown in Figure 2-3, suggesting the existence of an archaic version of H. Sapiens was supported by a recent discovery, reported in the June 8 issue of Nature, of fossil H. Sapiens remains found in eastern Africa dated to approximately 300 ka. This fills in half of the path from H. Ancestor to the oldest previously known H. Sapiens remains.

Regarding erectus, the preceding discussion deliberately blurred the line between erectus and ergaster since Sherlock's theorem suggests that the only difference between ergaster and erectus is few letters and a couple of hundred thousand years.

Development of Cognition:

The explanation of our development in Africa is not complete without the important subject of cognition. It's what makes us human.

Cognition has many definitions – a central definition is a reference to the mental processes involved in gaining knowledge and comprehension of ourselves and our surroundings from observations. These are higher-level functions of the brain and encompass language, imagination, perception, and planning. It encompasses processes such as knowledge, attention and memory in addition to problem solving[137].

The development of cognition obviously paralleled the development of the brain which is exhibited in figure 2-4:

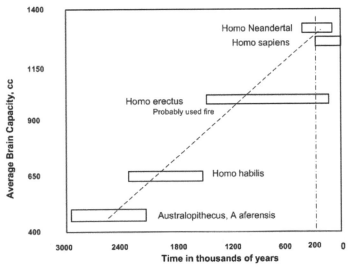

Figure 2-4 cerebral development in genus homo

The figure reveals a basically linear average brain size growth from the relatively small *A. afarensis* to the *Neandertal* brain which was actually slightly larger than ours.

In 1995, Leslie Aiello and Peter Wheeler developed the *expensive tissue hypothesis* to explain how our huge brains evolved …Aiello and Wheeler reasoned that the nutritionally dense muscle mass of other animals was the key food that allowed the evolution of our large brains. Without the abundance of calories afforded by meat-eating, they maintain, the human brain simply could not have evolved to its current form[138].

Lacking writing, symbolic archaeological evidence which can be used to determine the time and pattern of the emergence of modern human thought and behavior comes from an assessment of: the production of microliths (small stone tools); the use of ochre (hematite) as a pigment for paintings; the decoration of objects with incised motifs; and the creation of shell beads.[139]

The investigations by Brown et al in the Pinnacle Point area of South Africa (introduced above), presented compelling evidence for the development of cognition and language approximately 71 ka[140]:

> To resolve the timing of prehistoric human events for which there is no fossil evidence, Scientists rely on symbolically specific proxies, such as artistic expression to document the origins of complex cognition. Advanced technologies with elaborate chains of production are also proxies as these often demand high-fidelity transmission and thus <u>language</u>. This [Pinnacle Point] technology was dominated by the production of small bladelets (microliths) primarily from heat treated stone. There is agreement that the microlith technology was used to create composite tool components for advanced projectile weapons. Microliths were common by the Holocene[141], but rarely before 40 Ka. … Our research extends the record to ~ 71 Ka, shows that microlith technology originated early in South Africa evolved over a vast time span (~11,000 years) and was coupled to complex heat treatment that persisted for 100,000 years[142].

It is important to note that Pinnacle Point "tool" technology included the important fabrication of projectile weapons, perhaps among the first our species made, dating to ca 71 ka. As is discussed below, thrown weapons have made an important impact on our success.

Geological investigations at Pinnacle Point attempting to improve the date of activities at Pinnacle Point were reported at the 2013 meeting of Pacific Division of the AAAS[143].

Finally, Ian Tattersall eloquently explains our acquisition of cognitive ability in this passage from his book:

> Although it is in Africa that we find the earliest stirrings of the modern mind, it is only when we contemplate the astonishing cave art of Ice Age Europe [35 ka – 10 ka] that we encounter the first [conclusive] evidence of human beings who thought as we do, who left behind an overwhelmingly powerful body of evidence to prove it[144].

Regarding the development of cognition, we must distinguish between cognition and cognitive ability. In general cognition is defined as: "the mental action or process of acquiring knowledge and understanding through thought, experience, and the senses[145]." However, cognitive ability varies between individuals according to the bell curve distribution (introduced earlier) of cognition.

Evidence such as the Pinnacle Point microlith manufacture provides reasonable evidence that human cognition was fairly well developed 71 ka. Furthermore, those with superior cognitive ability probably contributed to continued improvement in stone tools (discussed in Chapter 3) and continued improvement of artistic ability described above. Finally, while developments attributed to human cognition continue today, there is little evidence that our brains in general are much different for those who created microliths at Pinnacle point – this idea will be explored more in later chapters.

In addition, the "Sage of Omaha, Warren Buffet offers this pithy comment regarding the difference between cognition and cognitive ability:

> Recently,… economic rewards flowing to people with specialized talents [greater cognitive ability, those on the right side of the cognition bell curve] have grown

dramatically faster than those going to equally decent men and women possessing more commonplace skills [median cognitive ability].

...Think back to the agrarian America of only 200 years ago. Most jobs could then be ably performed by most people. In a world where only primitive machinery and animals were available to aid farmers, the difference in productivity between the most talented among them and those with ordinary skills was modest[146].

Chapter 2 Summary

The apparent lack of interest in our species origins due to religious orientation is introduced.

- The three phases of archeological development understanding have been presented:
  - o the "oh-my-gosh!" phase.
  - o the "pick-and-shovel" scientific phase.
  - o the new technology DNA analysis phase.
- The discovery of four "new" members of our genus beginning with Neandertal was presented.
- Following *Neandertal,* the discovery of ancient remains of our species, then *H. erectus* and finally *H. heidelbergensis* was presented.
- The surprise discovery of Altamira rounded out the OMG phase.
- The "pick-and-shovel" phase was initialed in South Africa by Raymond Dart's discovery of *A. afarensis.*
- Next Louis Leakey was introduced as the discoverer of our oldest remains at 195 ka.
- Leakey also is credited with the discovery of *H. Habilis.*
- Richard Leakey's discovery of the complete skeleton of a *H. erectus* follows.
- Next the discovery of "Lucy," a member of the genus *Australopithecus* and then *H. Ergaster,* most likely a variant of H. erectus is disclosed.

- The discovery of a complex stone tool technology in the Pinnacle Point region of South Africa, shedding evidence on human cognition development is discussed next.
- The chapter is capped by the new technology DNA analysis phase which demonstrated that the bones at Atapuerca were *Neandertal*, not *Heidelbergensis* provided a complete surprise – upending much of what we thought we knew about our evolution.
- Finally, the important development of cognition and cognitive variability due to the cognition bell curve was introduced.

Looking ahead:

- Chapter 3 begins with the arrival from Africa of three members of our genus and the cultural/civilization "evolution" of the hunter-gatherers in prehistoric Europe: Aurignacian, Gravettian, Solutrean and Magdalenian.
- *Neandertal's* evolution in Europe and ultimate demise will be chronicled
- The significant role that caves played in human culture, especially the creation of magnificent paintings is described.
- The populating of Europe in three waves rather than one, plus the final confirmation of our ancestor's journey from Africa is described.

CHAPTER 3

OUR CULTURAL MATURATION IN ICE-AGE EUROPE AND THE MIDDLE EAST

Introduction

Chapter 2 was devoted to the identification of our ancestors and the path three of them: *H. Antecessor*, *H. erectus* and *H. sapiens* (our species) initiated from Africa to Europe and Asia.

This chapter addresses our cultural maturation in Ice-Age Europe and the Middle East and our ultimate domination of the planet plus recent findings due to advances in DNA detection in ancient *Homo* bones. To properly present this material, I have divided the chapter into four parts:

- The arrival from Africa of three members of our genus, *Neandertal's* evolution in Europe and the ultimate demise of all members of our genus except us, leaving our species the planets dominate primate.
- Cultural/civilization "evolution" of hunter-gatherers in prehistoric Europe: Aurignacian, Gravettian, Solutrean and Magdalenian.
- The first incorrect explanation of the five illusions and science's first faltering steps.
- The populating of Europe in three waves rather than one, plus the final confirmation of our ancestor's journey from Africa.

Migration from Africa.

The confusion caused by the initial discovery in Europe of the four species, (summarized in table 1-1) was discussed in chapter 1. Also mentioned was the fact that initial discovery locations of a species were purely serendipitous having little bearing on the general understanding of each species' actual origin location, which with the exception *H. Neandertal* was most likely South Africa.

However, at the outset, the migration out of Africa was controversial - some believed we came from Asia since two paths for our arrival in Europe were possible: a direct route skirting the eastern end of the Mediterranean and a more general route that shows our species arriving from the east[147].

More about this after a brief examination of the changes accompanying the findings at Atapuerca, which largely removed *heidelbergensis* from consideration as a member of our genus. Prior to the DNA findings at Atapuerca, the considered opinion of our evolutionary path resembled Figure 3-1 which is an extension of Figure 2-1 showing details of the migration in to Europe. *H. erectus* and *H. ergaster*, generally considered to be the same species which evolved around 1.6 Ma and migrated into Asia. *Heidelbergensis* evolved from erectus/ergaster and split into two groups:

1. *Heidelbergensis* I remained in Africa from which *H. sapiens* diverged about 200 ka. Then *Heidelbergensis* I migrated to Europe with one member expiring in Mauer, Germany.
2. *Heidelbergensis* II migrated to Europe where *Neandertal* diverged from *Heidelbergensis* II about 400 ka becoming the dominant primate in Europe.

About 44 ka later, H. Sapiens entered Europe and four kyrs later, Neandertal had become extinct as determined by Atomic spectroscopy DNA analysis

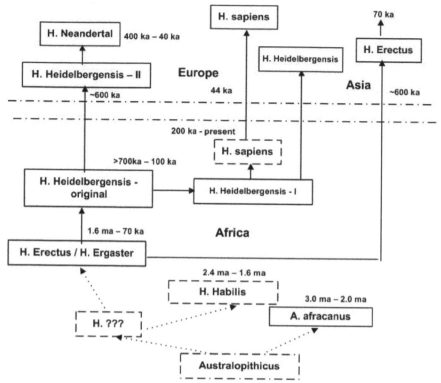

Figure 3-1 Out of Africa paths for our Genus
prior to March 2016 DNA discoveries

But as discussed in chapter 2 this story changed dramatically in March 2016 with the discovery that the remains thought to be *heidelbergensis* were actually *Neandertal.* An adjusted diagram partially explaining our evolution with *Antecessor* replacing *heidelbergensis* was presented in figure 2-4. A more complete modification of the Out of Africa diagram is provided in figure 3-2 with the introduction of *Homo Antecessor* in place of *heidelbergensis*[148] plus the important recent findings that Europe was actually populated in three waves.

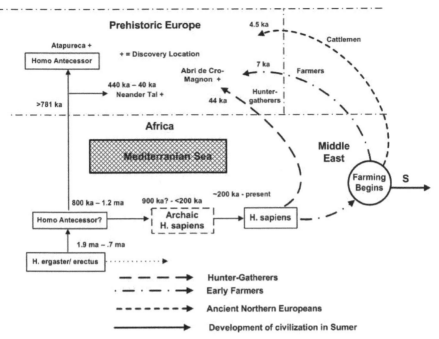

Figure 3-2 Three possible Out of Africa paths for our Genus.

Regarding figure 3-2, a few facts: our species clearly arrived in Europe; representatives of our species are found everywhere. The path in Figure 3-2 showing our arrival 44 ka has been the generally accepted path until the addition of the two other groups was discovered.

Erectus definitely arrived in Asia and some believe the fossil jaw bone found at Maurer comes from an eastern branch of erectus.

Confusion arises with the placement of *antecessor*. *Antecessor* seems to have been reasonably well identified at Atapureca, but the connection to *sapiens* is not clear. As Chris Springer mentioned, a possible intermediary, *archaic sapiens,* might fill in the blanks, but more data is needed; however, an educated guess regarding what must have happened based upon data available at present can be prepared and has been presented by a person who is probably as familiar with the discoveries at atapuerca as anyone, Antonio Rosas.

Rosas avers that "the [(antecessor) boy's remains has a] modern face set between a primitive jaw and brow— [this] shows that [antecessor] probably gave rise to both modern humans and *Neandertals*[149]."

It is important to note that Figure 3-2 presents some additional migration paths for our species as will be discussed below in particular, the path that leads to the development of Farming which will be discussed toward the end of this chapter. As with everything about our evolution, reality is often considerably more complex.

The European "welcoming party" for our ancestors and other members of our genus is illustrated in Figure 3-3; a rough approximation of the average European temperature over the last 60 kyrs. The trip from Africa to Europe must have resembled a modern trip from Florida to Maine in the winter. Our ancestors and other members of our genus were met by the Last Glacial Maximum, otherwise known as the Last Ice Age (any average temperature below 20° F). As will be discussed in detail in chapter 14, the existence of the Ice Age, along with other ancient Ice-Age events discussed in chapter 2 was considered preposterous until Louis Agassiz deduced its existence in the nineteenth century[150].

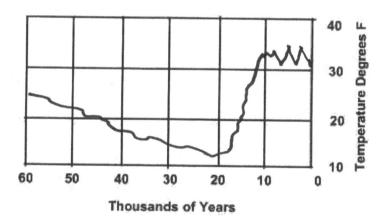

Figure 3-3 Average Annual Temperature, (past 60,000 years)

Who were the Cro-Magnon? As introduced previously, the first physical evidence of our species in Europe was five skeletons discovered in 1868 in the Abri de Cro-Magnon by Louis Lartet (1840 – 1899) a French Geologist and paleontologist. Since little was known about human evolution in the late nineteenth century, the term Cro-Magnon became associated with our species. Today, Cro-Magnon is too restrictive and as mentioned previously it is customary to use the term Anatomically Modern Human (AMH) or just the association with a particular culture, such as American.

The type specimen from the site Cro-Magnon 1 has been radiocarbon dated to about twenty-eight ka,[151] which places Cro-Magnon at the end of the Aurignacian culture described below; hardly the first members of our species in Europe.

The Evolution and ultimate extinction of H. Neandertal

The evolution of *H. antecessor, H. erectus*, and *H. sapiens* was described in chapter 2; we come now to the fourth member of our genus: *H. Neandertal*[152].

As illustrated in Figure 3-2, around 600 ka, the enigmatic *H. antecessor* migrated into Europe most likely over a land bridge spanning what is now the Strait of Gibraltar, settled in Atapuerca and other sites not yet discovered. At least 480 ka, *Neandertal* diverged from H. antecessor and populated Europe[153].

Due the controversy surrounding the demise of Neandertal, the time periods *Neandertal* and AMH resided in Europe have been measured with considerable accuracy thanks to the prowess of Tom Higham with the Atomic Mass Spectrometer (AMS) explained in chapter 1. The last evidence of *Neandertal* presence in Europe[154] and the first evidence of AMH in Europe[155] is presented in table 3-1:

Species	Earliest	Latest	Average
AMH - Arrival	43 ka	45 ka	44ka
H. Neandertal - Demise	39 ka	41 ka	40 ka

Table 3-1 Timing of the arrival of Anatomically Modern Humans and last evidence of *Neandertal*.

As emphasized in Table 3-1 four thousand years after the arrival of AMH no evidence of *Neandertal* can be found. The geologically rapid (four thousand years is a blink) disappearance has puzzled and bothered many individuals since most evidence regarding *Neandertal's* disappearance points to us. Table 3-1 conclusively demonstrates the timing of the Neandertal's disappearance, and there is ample evidence of our involvement.

Regarding our first encounter with Neandertal, to put yourself in the Neandertal's "shoes" or whatever they wore, imagine what it will be like if we ever encounter an individual from another world. Despite the three eyed cartoons, they will resemble us, but, if they have the technology to cover the vast distances involved, they will have the equivalent of the thrown spear, which must have frightened the Neandertal the same way the rifle frightened the Native Americans.

We can never know for sure what caused the Neandertal's demise but here are five possible causes:

- *Neandertal* was "out-gunned."
- The *Neandertal* DNA was impaired by "Epigenesis."
- The *Neandertal* was outnumbered 10-1.
- The *Neandertal* were intellectually inferior - we alone enjoy "Symbolic Thinking."
- Our species has an inherent propensity for violence.

As mentioned earlier, small stone blades dating to around seventy-one ka, fabricated by our species, have been discovered in South Africa[156]. They were probably used to make tools or projectile weapons such as thrown spears.

The Thrown spear is one of the greatest inventions involving the conflict between AMH and any other animal that has ever been invented: for the first time, injury or death could be delivered from a distance. Early humans wandering out of Africa armed with darts and arrows, were "armed to the teeth," which made them formidable hunters and deadly competitors for any *Neanderthals* that stood in their way[157].

Even if *Neandertal* could have obtained throwing spears, they couldn't have used them. Studies of the *Neandertal* shoulder demonstrate that *Neandertals* lacked this ability[158]. The fact that a small percent of our DNA comes from interbreeding with *Neanderthals* is generally well known; however, there is another aspect of our genomes that makes a significant difference between us. Archeologist Zach Zorich pointed this out in the June 9, 2014 issue of *Archeology*[159]. *Neandertal* DNA was adversely affected by epigenesis (introduced in chapter 1). In one type of epigenesis, molecules termed methyl groups, when attached to DNA in general disable the genes[160]. Research has shown that thousands of *Neandertal* genes, compared with corresponding portions of the modern human genes, had methyl groups attached much to the detriment of *Neandertal*.

With respect to the small amount of *Neandertal* DNA in our DNA, a study reported in the May 2, 2016 issue of Nature[161] demonstrated that over time, the amount of *Neandertal* DNA declined as shown in Figure 3-4.[162] This decline can be viewed as a "reverse evolution" since the decline is most reasonably due to diminished interbreeding:

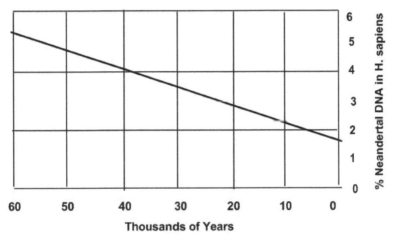

Figure 3-4 Decline of Neandertal DNA in H. sapiens over time

Another advantage our species enjoyed was greater fecundity. According to Paul Mellars, AMH population outnumbered the Neandertal 10 to 1[163]. As Mellars surmises, "we buried them ---"

Regarding intellectual comparisons, there is a significant difference between the *H. Sapiens* and the *Neandertal* skull sizes and shapes as outlined in Figure 2-3 The *H. Neandertal* skull was larger implying larger brain size which is true. The average *Neandertal* brain size deduced from the skull interior is 1600 cc, while the average H. Sapiens brain is approximately 1450 cc.

Much has been made of this difference; however as with many things size doesn't always matter. In the case of intellectual ability shape is much more important than size[164]. The *H. Sapiens* skull has a remarkably different shape than the *H. Neandertal* as demonstrated by the forehead slope of each skull indicated by angles A and B: Angle A is much less than angle B. Obviously the much more vertical *H. Sapiens* forehead allows for our enlarged frontal lobes – the seat of our considerable reasoning ability and symbolic thinking[165]. The *H. Neandertal* brain, lacking a frontal lobe, was incapable of symbolic thinking.

Another possible cause of the Neandertal's demise was the fundamental nature of our species - we are basically violent. One can enumerate several examples, but the "Native American Holocaust" which occurred when Europeans "invaded" North America is one of the worst. It is not clear how many Native Americans were in North America; perhaps as many as 100 million; however, between disease and violence, only 5 million remain. The genocide of Native Americans is considered by many to be the worst of any in history -- outstripping the later Jewish demise in the holocaust by as much as an order of magnitude[166].

Adios H. erectus and H. antecessor:

As shown in Figure 3-1 the last evidence of *H. erectus* dates to approximately 70 ka.[167] Regarding the last days of *H. antecessor*, it is highly probable that antecessor disappeared around 400 ka; however, so far, the only remains have been found at Atapureca.

With the passing of the *Neandertal*, we became the dominant primate on the planet.

Cultural/civilization "evolution" in prehistoric Europe:

Chapters 1 and 2 presented the long path life had traveled since the first cell appeared, propelled by the basic reproduction process, in particular the bell curve output of reproduction which provides the adaptive ability necessary for the evolution phenomenon to progress.

Soon after our arrival in Europe, we began the development of four identifiable cultures/civilizations in the first thirty-thousand years of our presence in Europe, summarized in table 3-2 in order of appearance in the archeological record:

Culture	Type Site/ Discovery Date/Culture Duration		
Aurignacian	Aurignac	1860	44 ka – 29 ka
Gravettian	La Gravette	1934	29 ka – 22 ka
Solutrean	Solutre	1870	22 ka – 17 ka
Magdelenian	La Madeleine	1875	17 ka – 12 ka

Table 3-2 Principal Prehistoric Human Cultures

Note that the cultures are named for the first place that evidence of the culture, termed a Type Site, was found, where a Type Site is defined as:

> An archaeological location, termed a Type Site[168], regarded as definitively characteristic of a particular culture is often applied to the culture. For example, the first site discovered to have been occupied by the Aurignacian culture was located near the town of Aurignac in western France.

There is of course no correlation between the Type Site and the place where the culture originated. For example, evidence indicates that the Aurignacians came from the east[169]. Accordingly, little information can be gleaned from the discovery site other than the site is the first location where evidence of the culture was found.

On the other hand, the Type Site is important because, unfortunately, the use of fossils to determine which of our ancient ancestors occupied a particular cave is difficult bordering on the impossible due to the simple fact that fossilization is a rare phenomenon; therefore, remains of our ancestors are not often found in a cave that was definitely occupied by a particular culture. Cultures developed all over Europe. Type Sites have been used to determine with reasonable accuracy which culture was associated with a particular cave. In addition, DNA is rapidly becoming an important tool.

Regarding culture, a definition of culture provided by Charles Starr in his superb *A History of the Ancient World*[170] is useful for this discussion and asserts that the term civilization may have many meanings, but will generally be characterized by:

1. The presence of firmly organized states that had definite boundaries and systematic political institutions under political and religious leaders who directed and also maintained society.
2. The distinction of social classes.
3. The economic specialization of "men" as farmer, trader, or artist, each dependant on his fellow.
4. The conscious development of the arts and intellectual attitudes,

It is unclear how many of these characteristics the four cultures that arose in prehistoric Europe possessed; however, the cultures could not have formed without Item 1, and humans are class conscious, so Item 2 would have been present. Since they were hunter-gatherers, some economic specialization must have arisen, if nothing more than male hunters and female hearth tenders.

Regarding Item 4, the prehistoric cultures are renowned for their paintings; hence, it is safe to assert that prehistoric humans had a modicum of civilization. Starr lists one more characteristic:

> … the use of writing to keep accounts or to commemorate deeds, and elaboration of religious views about the nature of the gods, their relations to man, and the origin of the world.

Clearly, Prehistoric humans lacked writing, but through oral traditions, they could have:

> …shared religious views about the nature of the gods, their relations to man, and the origin of the world.

General life style of the hunter-gatherer prehistoric humans

Before discussing specific cultures, a few words concerning what can be known about the prehistoric life-style. During a visit to Lascaux, I obtained the excellent official Lascaux book[171]. Combining information contained in the Lascaux book written by authors Brigette and Giles Delluc, two individuals who have spent their live studying Prehistoric humans, with other information available on the web, I offer this description of prehistoric human life style:

Prehistoric people were generally just like you and me. Anatomically they resembled us, being well built and about six feet tall. They had the same degree of intelligence as we have; only lacking acquired knowledge. They used language and were subject to tears and laughter like us, and lived active lives in the natural environment dwelling in simple structures located near caves.

Prehistoric people were nomadic hunter- gatherers who lived in groups and followed the seasonal migrations of the wild animals they hunted over vast distances. Similar to modern hunter- gather groups, the prehistoric groups had a leader, an exceptional individual who was guided by a council of elders.

Prehistoric cultures fashioned refined, sharp tools, and easy to handle light blades out of limestone, bone, reindeer antler and ivory, which allowed them to cut and prepare the meat of the large herbivores, mainly reindeer, they captured. Tool development was characterized by the progressive miniaturization over time, culminating in tiny blades termed microliths around 12,000 BCE (This aggregation of development over time mirrors what happened many times in history as will be seen chapters to follow.) These microliths were easily carved flakes and carried over long distances.

The pigments cave drawing artisans required were in the ground –yellow ocher, red iron oxide and black manganese dioxide provided all they needed. The limestone on the hillside could be split into small flakes that held lamps, pallets and crushers for pigments. Flint was fairly common everywhere

Thanks to the Ice-Age ice sheet which drove animals south, there was animal life in abundance – large herbivores: big cats, small animals and birds. Yet it was the reindeer that was most important to Prehistoric man, providing him with food and various materials. This was, indeed, the age of the reindeer. Reindeer antlers were carved into spears. Thin bones were used to regarding make sewing and a horse's skin with its close knit covering of hair, was tanned before being cut to make warm clothing.

Regarding the lifespan of prehistoric individuals, Historian Chester Star points out that life was short for ancient humans, examples of early modern man showed 54 percent died between twenty-one and forty. If one considers just those people of the *Neandertal* and early *Homo sapiens* periods who lived past twenty most women were dead by thirty while most men lived past that age[172].

An important feature of prehistoric life was the possibility of religion. Lacking written records, identifiable human behavior that is apparently a religious experience is not found in written history; hence, archeologists must acquire most of their knowledge about pre-historic religion from the archeological record[173] and other indirect sources; e.g., objects and architecture prehistoric people made, structures they built, especially their garbage and mortuary practices - did they bury their dead? Development of religious concepts obviously required the development of brains large enough to make possible the kind of abstract thought necessary to formulate religious and philosophical concepts.

Concerning the subject of religious history, during research for another AAASPD paper *Natural, a Code Word For I/We Don't Know*, designed to demonstrate that Natural Selection does not explain the evolution phenomenon, I had the immensely good fortune of an Internet meeting with a person of considerable renown, Professor Marcel Otte[174]:

> Président de la Commission « Paléolithique Supérieur d'Eurasie"
> Union Internationale des Sciences Préhistoriques et Protohistoriques - UISPP
> Conseil International de Philosophie et des Sciences Humaines – CIPSH

Our first e-mail exchange involved the history of religion. Professor Otte stated, rather emphatically:

> Our minds 'need' explanations by any way possible, so if these crucial needs are satisfied by any socially accepted system, then we are satisfied at least for a moment. Regarding religion, *there has never been any humans in the world, now or at any time before, without religion, never, nowhere*[175].

Clearly Professor Otte expresses the universality of the need for religion.

With respect to the lack of written history for religion, something that can offer significant assistance exists in North America today. When Europeans arrived in the "New World" they encountered humans, mistakenly termed Indians, still living in the Stone Age. This Native American culture has been partially preserved in many remote regions of the US – for example Glacier National Park (GNP). Currently, the Blackfeet tribe occupies a reservation on the edge of GNP.

Originally, the Kootenai tribe occupied the GNP area. Then many years ago, the Blackfeet tribe pushed the Kootenai out of the area, similar to what happened in Europe as will be discussed below.

One person intimately familiar with the Blackfeet, George Bird Grinnell (1849 –1938) lived with the Blackfeet for many years and wrote *Blackfeet Indian Stories* [176] recounting his first-hand experiences:

> Like many native people, the Blackfeet have stories and legends that originated centuries ago, perhaps thousands of years ago, and were passed down from generation to generation through oral tradition. Early explorers [like Grinnell] heard the stories directly from the Blackfeet and wrote them down[177].

With respect to the spiritual life of Native Americans, there was a reverent interrelationship between hunters and hunted. When a Native American hunter killed an animal for food, the hunter prayed to the animal's spirit for forgiveness, apologizing for taking the animal's life as the hunter needed food to live – such was the closeness the Native Americans felt with the spiritual world[178].

Regarding the association with the spiritual world, the Blackfeet have a ceremony resembling the Christian Eucharist. The ceremony is held in a sacred building. During the ceremony:

> A group is seated in a circle.
> A Spiritual Leader stands in front – holding a "Thunder Pipe": emblem of the Great Spirit – "God."
> The Thunder Pipe is kept in a sacred place in the sacred building,
> The Spiritual leader retrieves the pipe from the sacred place and displays it to the group.
> The Spiritual leader retrieves a sacred blanket - covers Thunder Pipe and chants a ceremonial Prayer to the Great Spirit.
> The pipe is passed to each person who takes a puff.

It is important to note that: the Blackfeet aren't the only Native Americans who display religious tendencies. This general religious tendency was termed Animism, a concept developed by anthropologist Sir Edward Tylor. In his 1871 book *Primitive Culture*, Tyler defined Animism as:

> "the general doctrine of souls and other spiritual beings in general and often includes an idea of pervading life and will in nature; i. e., a belief that natural objects other than humans have souls - even inanimate objects—possess a spiritual essence[179].

Also, of particular importance, the belief in a supreme being "The Great Spirit" mimics beliefs found in prehistoric humans in Europe indicating that the need to associate with and appease a higher being is universal.

These various pieces of information regarding Prehistoric human spiritual/religious life indicate that, with these caveats in mind, evidence of human behavior possibly associated with religious beliefs is arguably thousands of years old[180]. Moreover, invoking the origins axiom, religion obviously had to begin sometime-somewhere. In view of the fact that religion involves indirect supernatural phenomena, a slow growth would also be logical.

At least four indirect indications of the emergence of religious beliefs have been identified:

1. Possible evidence of ceremonial burial. Several sites located throughout Eurasia may represent the beginning of ceremonial rites.
2. Cremation is another indicator of ceremonial burials associated with belief in either a supreme being or other supernatural entity. One of the oldest cremations, dating to ca. 25 ka has been found in Australia[181].
3. Carving of "zoomorphic" combined animal and human forms in a statue is a third indicator of possible religious beliefs. These sculptures can also be interpreted as "anthropomorphic" attributing human characteristics to an animal, although it may have represented a deity.
4. Direct observation of Native American religious practices.

The possible development of religion will be discussed in greater detail in chapter 4. We turn now to a brief overview of the four cultures listed in table 3-2 beginning with the Aurignacian.

Aurignacian

The name originates from the type site of Aurignac, a town in southwestern France. Evidence of the culture indicates a time span from ca. 45 ka to 35 ka[182].

The Aurignacian tool industry was characterized by worked bone or antler points. Their tools included fine stone blades and bladelets struck from prepared cores rather than crude flakes. In addition, they made perforated rods, thought to be spear throwers. The people of this culture also produced some of the earliest known cave art, such as the animal engraving at Trois Freres and the paintings at Chauvet cave. In addition, they made pendants bracelets, ivory beads, and three dimensional figures.

The best dated association between Aurignacian industries and human remains are those of at least five individuals from a Type Site in the Czech Republic, radiocarbon dated to at least 31 ka.

With respect to religion, the oldest undisputed example of human figurative art (the *Venus of Hohle fels*[183],) comes from this culture and was discovered in September 2008. The production of ivory beads for body ornamentation was also important.

Gravettian

The Gravettian culture spanned 32 ka to 22 ka and is named for the Type Site La Gravette[184].

The Gravettian stone tool industry was an improvement over the Aurignacian, with small pointed blades used for hunting bison, horse, reindeer and other large mammals. Also, Gravettian people used nets to hunt small game -- the first time this technique is known to have been used.

A defining trait distinguishing Gravettians was their ease of mobility compared to *Neandertals* who preceded them. Gravettians developed the technology and social organization that enabled them to migrate with their food source, such as reindeer, whereas *Neanderthal* were not adept at traveling, even with relatively sedentary herds.

Artistic achievements of the Gravettians include hundreds of Venus figurines scattered throughout Europe.

Solutrean

The Solutrean culture spanned 22 ka to 17 ka[185]. The name derives from the type site Roche de Solutré, a dominant rock formation located in East Central France. The base of the Roche is littered with the bones of horses. A first explanation for the accumulation was a tactic used by Native Americans who drove buffalo over cliffs, but subsequent investigation demonstrated that the Roche was used as a meeting place for butchering animals. Solutrean tool making employed techniques not seen before. The Solutrean technique exhibits relatively fine working of bifacial points made with a method termed "lithic reduction percussion" and pressure flaking instead of cruder flint napping. Large thin spearheads and scrapers with an edge on the end (not the side) allowed fabrication of knives and saws.

Magdalenian

Magdalenian culture is one of the last of the ice-age prehistoric cultures dating from approximately 17 ka to 12 ka[186]. The culture is named for the type site the le Madeleine, a rock shelter in the Dordogne Valley. The first systematic excavation of the type site occurred in 1875. The Magdalenian were basically reindeer hunters, and the culture was widespread from Portugal in the west to Poland in the east. The Magdalenian period was dry and quite cold as shown by Figure 3-3. The Magdalenians were fearless hunters, hunting the mammoth to extinction (one of the first human caused extinctions)

Regarding Magdalenian religious beliefs, similar to other cultures, they are hard to discern; however, the Lascaux cave, frequented by the Magdalenians is embellished with numerous magnificent painting, many located far into the cave. As pointed out earlier, these paintings were difficult and dangerous to create - some strong force must have encouraged the painters.

The selection of Lascaux by the Magdalenian was apparently quite deliberate[187]. There were many caves in the area to choose from, but the Magdalenians selected Lascaux since this cave provided opportunities for the many techniques Magdalenians selected to suit the existing state of the cave walls.

Since much of what we know about the cultures has been gleaned from prehistoric caves, the culture/civilization investigation will be interwoven with cave exploration.

Homes for the Planet Masters

This discussion of prehistoric caves is partly based upon material gathered the September 2015 tour of prehistoric caves I introduced previously when I visited seventeen caves inhabited by *Neandertal, antecessor* and other members of our species at various times over the last million years, but mostly during the time period from 40 ka to 10 ka.

As mentioned in the preface, it is surprising but sad that these caves and the magnificent paintings in them vanished from the historical record until the nineteenth century when as introduced in chapter 2 they were serendipitously discovered by adventurous spelunkers.

The Prehistoric Caves

In the interest of brevity, only four caves will be discussed in detail: Altamira, Chauvet, Lascaux and Maz-d'Azil. (Altamira was introduced previously.) Basic cave information is summarized below:

Cave	Discovered By	Discovery Date	Location	Approx Dates For Paintings	Cultures
Altamira	Unknown Hunter	1868	Near Santillana Del Mar	18 ka: 16 ka and 14 ka	Solutrian - Magdellanian
Chauvet	Deschamps, Hillaire and Chauvet	1994	Vallon-Pont-d'Arc	32 ka – 30 ka	Aurignacian
Lascaux	Marcel Ravidat.	1940	Dordogne River	17 ka	Magdellenian
Mas-d'Azil	Uknown	Unknown	Vallon-Pont-d'Arc	32 ka – 30 ka	Aurignacian

Table 3-3 Summary of Four Important Prehistoric Caves.

Before discussing individual caves, let us begin with a basic question: "why were the adventurous first members of our genus welcomed by a land pot-holed with caves when they arrived?" It was indeed most fortuitous.

Cave Formation

The caves were formed in the layer of limestone that covers Spain and France, created during the Cretaceous Geological Period, beginning 145 Ma to 66 Ma[188]. During this period France and Spain were covered by a shallow inland sea. The sea was populated with now extinct mollusks (minute animals with calcium-rich shells). As the mollusks died, their shells accumulated on the sea floor. Over millions of years, the deposits were transformed into limestone, a relatively porous, cave forming rock.

About twenty million years ago, geological forces associated with plate tectonics (see chapter 15) raised the limestone sea floor and the limestone surface rocks of Spain and France were formed. Cave formation begins when rainwater absorbs carbon dioxide either by falling through the atmosphere or from ground absorption and becomes carbonic acid (HCO_3). The carbonic acid dissolves limestone which is mostly calcium carbonate ($CaCO_3$) and slowly hollows out a cave. This process, operating over millions of years resulted in multiple caves in northern Spain and southern France. Only a small percentage has been found.

The next sections will describe four specific caves exploring art related questions such as: what kind of art was created, when was the art created, and most interesting and important, why was the art created?

The Cave at Altamira

As mentioned previously, the initial reaction to the Altamira paintings was derisive. It was eventually determined that a rock closed the opening around 13 ka. Then in 1860 a nearby tree fell and disturbed the fallen rocks enabling the discovery. But, it was not until 1902, when several other findings of prehistoric paintings demonstrated that the Altamira paintings must be as old as Sautuola and Piero had claimed that the scientific society retracted their opposition to the Spaniards. That year, Emile Cartailhac emphatically admitted his mistake in a famous article, "Mea culpa d'un sceptique[189]" published in the journal *L'Anthropologie*. Sautuola, having died fourteen years earlier, did not live to enjoy his vindication.

Further cave excavation work proceeded and the cave was opened in the early 1950s. The main passage varies from six to twenty feet in height. Rich deposits of artifacts from the Solutrean and the Magdalenian cultures have been discovered.

It is important to note that human occupation was basically limited to cave entrances since caves were deep, dark and potentially dangerous due to possible collapse or cave bears. Despite the dangers, paintings were created throughout the length of the cave; which leads to an obvious question: "Why did the cave artists apparently ignore the risks to create the art?" As will be seen in the discussions of the other caves, the incredible effort required to reach the caves depths suggests that the caves were more than the equivalent of contemporary art galleries. The paintings must have had a *sacred or ritual significance*, revealing a universal, deeply felt need for satisfactory explanations of ourselves and our surroundings.

The artists used charcoal, and ochre, pigment containing ferric oxide, typically with clay, varying from light yellow to brown or red to create the images, often diluting these pigments to produce variations in intensity and creating strong contrasts between light and dark images. They also exploited the natural contours in the cave walls to give their subjects a three-dimensional effect.

The Chauvet Cave[190]

Discovered on December 18, 1994, the Chauvet cave in southern France is ironically the cave most recently discovered, but a study published in 2012 supports the placement of the art in the Aurignacian period[191], approximately 30 ka–28 ka. Chauvet contains the earliest known and best preserved figurative cave paintings in the world[192] as well as other evidence of Prehistoric life. It is located near the commune of Vallon-Pont-d'Arc (Arched Bridge). Considered one of the most significant prehistoric art sites in the world, it is perched on a limestone cliff above the former Ardèche River.

The cave was first explored by a group of three spelunkers: Éliette Brunel-Deschamps[193], Christian Hillaire[194], and Jean-Marie Chauvet[195] for whom it was named in 1996. In addition to the paintings and other human evidence, the three also discovered fossilized remains, prints, and markings from a variety of animals, some of which are now extinct.

The original cave entrance was a large hole in the cliff which has since completely vanished. Geological investigations determined that twenty-two thousand years ago, the weight of the rock above the overhang caused it to collapse and obscure the cavity. In 1994, the cave was rediscovered by geologist Jean Marie Chauvet searching for caves with his two colleagues. They gained access to the cave by crawling through a narrow passage above the original cave entrance.

Based on radiocarbon dating, the cave appears to have been used by humans during two distinct periods: the Aurignacian and the Gravettian. Most of the artwork dates to the earlier, Aurignacian, era 30,000 to 32,000 years ago. The later Gravettian occupation, which occurred 25,000 to 27,000 years ago, left little but a child's footprints, the charred remains of ancient hearths, and carbon smoke stains from torches that lit the caves. After the child's visit to the bull cave, as mentioned above, the cave entrance was blocked until it was discovered in 1994. The footprints may be the oldest human footprints that can be dated accurately. Fossilized bones are abundant and include the skulls of cave bears and the horned skull of an ibex.

Hundreds of animal paintings have been catalogued, depicting at least thirteen different species, including some rarely or never found in other ice-age paintings. Rather than depicting only the familiar horses, cattle and mammoths that predominate in Paleolithic cave art, the walls of the Chauvet Cave feature many predatory animals, (cave lions, panthers, bears, and cave hyenas.)

Typical of most cave art, there are no paintings of complete human figures, although there is one partial "Venus" figure composed of a vulva attached to an incomplete pair of legs[196]. Above the Venus, and in contact with it, is a bison head, which has led some to describe the composite drawing as a Minotaur, the mythical beast discovered in Crete with the head of a bull and the body of a man[197].

There are also two unidentifiable images that have a vaguely butterfly or bird-like shape to them. As with other caves, this combination of subjects has led some students of prehistoric art and cultures to believe there was a ritual or shamanic aspect to these paintings[198].

The Lascaux Cave[199]

One of the most recognized of the prehistoric caves, the entrance to Lascaux Cave was discovered by eighteen-year-old Marcel Ravidat On September 12, 1940[200]. Sometime later Ravidat returned to the scene with three friends, Jacques Marsal, Georges Agnel, and Simon Coencas. The friends entered the cave via a long shaft into a hall where they discovered the magnificent animal depictions covering the cave walls.

The cave is located in the beautiful Dordogne valley and contains some excellent Prehistoric art. These Magdalenian paintings are estimated to be 17,300 years old and primarily consist of images of large animals especially in the famous Hall of the Bulls, most of which are known from fossil evidence to have lived in the area at the time.

The cave complex was opened to the public in 1948. However, by 1955, contaminants, such as exhaled carbon dioxide, produced by 1,200 visitors per day, had visibly damaged the paintings. The cave was closed to the public in 1963 to preserve the art. After the cave was closed, the paintings were restored to their original state and were monitored daily. As with Altamira, a replica of the Great Hall of the Bulls and the Painted Gallery Lascaux II, located close to the original, was opened in 1983.

The most famous section of the cave, the Great Hall of the Bulls displays four black bulls, or aurochs, the dominant figures among the thirty-six animals represented there. One of the bulls is seventeen feet long, the largest animal painting discovered so far in cave art.

A painting referred to as "The Crossed Bison," found in the chamber called the Nave, is often submitted as an example of the skill of the Magdalenian cave painters. The crossed hind legs create the illusion that one bison is closer to the viewer than the other. This visual depth in the scene demonstrates a primitive form of perspective that was particularly advanced for the time.

Interpretation of cave images

Although their main prey was the reindeer, among the almost one thousand animals painted, only one reindeer painting exists. In addition to all that we can see in the cave, there was no attempt to picture any landscapes. Moreover, with two exceptions, the few animals which seem to have been wounded by spears, do not seem to be in pain.

Lascaux, considered by many to have been a place of worship, was understandably very popular, as revealed by numerous objects left behind such as more than one hundred rock bowls that held animal fat which could be burned to provide light in the dark caves. The ground has been trodden down, seeming to suggest the artists made themselves comfortable before beginning the work. They had poles and scaffolding to reach the ceilings; traces of seven have been discovered.

All these elements demonstrate that they appear to have been designed to serve a veritable religious cult[201] (as suggested above).

A similar hypothesis proposed by David Lewis-Williams and Jean Clottes following work with similar art of the San people of Southern Africa[202] suggests that certain cave art images imply that these paintings are shamanic in nature, a type of cave art [that] is spiritual in nature relating to visions experienced during ritualistic dancing[203]. Shamanism is also suggested by Clottes's 2012 book "Pourquoi l'art prehistorique?[204]" ("Why the prehistoric art?")

The Cave at Mas d'Azil[205]

The cave at Mas d'Azil is included in this chapter since the Mas d'Azil culture is intermediate between the European Aurignacian-Magdalenian cultures and the Middle East Neolithic cultures. Mas d'Azil is a commune in southwestern France, containing a cave that is the type-site for the prehistoric Azilian culture. The *Grotte du Mas d'Azil* a "supersite" with rich remains of human usages beginning about 30 ka is actually a tunnel large enough for a highway to pass directly through the cave.

The Azilian probably dates to around twelve thousand ka, representing the tail end of the Magdalenian as the warming climate (see Figure 3-2) which resulted in a melting of the ice sheets, caused reindeer to drift back north diminishing the Magdalenian food supply undoubtedly impoverishing the previously well-fed Magdalenians. As a result, Azilian tools and art were cruder and less expansive than their Ice-age predecessors - or simply different.

Diagnostic artifacts from the culture include Azilian points (microliths with rounded retouched backs), crude flat bone harpoons and pebbles with abstract decoration.

Innovation and Diffusion of Innovation in Prehistoric Europe

As introduced above, our species is very innovative. An excellent illustration of innovative prehistoric man is toolmaking improvement--a likely driver of cultural improvements. Since stone tool fabrication was a major activity, innovative improvements in stone tool fabrication would be a logical measure of general improvement.

One the better measures of toolmaking improvement is the relative lengths of usable stone cutting edge obtainable from a kilogram of flint. This measure of toolmaking improvement from different Paleolithic cultures, is captured in figure 3-5. This figure is adapted from figure 64, page 136 in André Leroi-Gourhan's excellent dissertation[206].

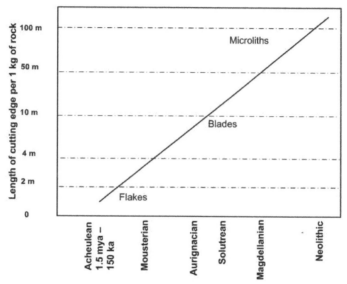

Figure 3-5 Continuous development of Prehistoric stone technology

Note that the horizontal axis is essentially linear and the line tracing the increase in cutting edge length in Figure 3-5 is straight. But the vertical axis is not linear; it is semi-logarithmic, indicating that more tools could be cut from the same amount of stone in the same time, or less stone material is needed to produce a tool. These gradual improvements spanned thousands of years. Prehistoric man was continually improving as a stone tool maker, but it is important to note that his brain was not changing; the improvement was a learning and innovation process.

This graph is particularly important as improved tool making was one of the hallmarks of Prehistoric innovations that delineate the separation between various cultures. However, unless an innovation becomes widely known, it is of relatively little value. As explained in chapter 1, the spread of knowledge regarding an innovation is termed diffusion. Since numerous cultures were involved with the steady increase in improved stone technology created by individuals in six cultures, it is hard to believe that this could have happened unless innovations in the various cultures were passed on to other cultures via some form of diffusion. During prehistoric times, the interaction between migrating hunter-gatherers was probably the main mechanism for diffusion.

The Neolithic Revolution - from hunting and gathering to farming

The life style change known as the Neolithic Revolution refers to one of the more dramatic transitions in human behavior -- from hunting and gathering to farming. The significant of the transition was discussed by Jared Diamond in his celebrated *Guns, Germs and Steel*, regarding European superiority:

> The first step toward civilization is the move from nomadic hunter-gatherer to rooted agrarian society. Several conditions are necessary for this transition to occur: access to high-protein vegetation that endures storage; a climate dry enough to allow storage; and access to animals docile enough for domestication and versatile enough to survive captivity. Control of crops and livestock leads to food surpluses [which allow development of sophisticated states] ...although agriculture arose in several parts of the world, Eurasia gained an early advantage due to the greater availability of suitable plant and animal species for domestication. In particular, Eurasia has barley, two varieties of wheat, and three protein-rich pluses for food; flax for textiles; and goats, sheep, and cattle. Eurasian grains were richer in protein, easier to sow, and easier to store than American maize or tropical bananas[207].

Archaeological data demonstrates that a wide variety of plants and animals became domesticated at different times in different parts of the world, beginning about 12 ka[208] as our species gravitated from the migratory world of the hunter-gatherer to the settled life of the farmer. This drastic change in life style is generally termed the Neolithic (Latin for new Stone Age) and represents the "world's first historically verifiable revolution in agriculture[209]."

Figure 3-2 exhibits the path followed by our ancestors out of Africa into the Middle East --in particular Mesopotamia preceded by the curiously named Levant (the place where sunrises "levants" if you are standing in France).

The earliest farming in the Middle East began with the domestication of triticum wheat. The process is described in one reference as "Cultivation plus repeated harvesting and sowing of the grains of wild grasses eventually led to the creation of domesticated strains"[210].

While "repeated harvesting and sowing" occurred, I believe the domestication process was not quite this "hit-or-miss". this composite Bell Curve diagram illustrates the interaction between plant variability and human intelligence variability – both produced by a reproduction process. One plant and one human.

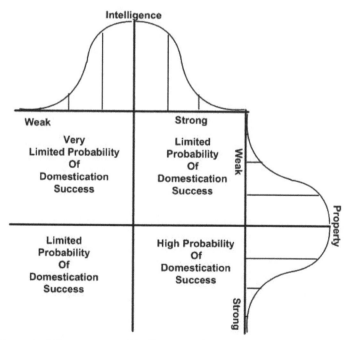

Figure 3-6 Superimposed bell curves depicting plant domestication

The plant bell curve would certainly have resulted in a distribution of plant varieties, some better than others indicated by Weak and Strong. Moreover, those investigators from the intelligence bell curve "right side" who were more strongly observant than others, would reasonably have noticed that some plants that appeared in the spring were superior to other plants and would thus have made an effort to separate them from others, "wheat from chaff" so to speak.

Over a number of years, there would be a tendency for the more intelligent "farmers" to gain increasing control over the superior plants and develop monopolies of plant production. This combined with reproduction's mutational magic would have created large farms with superior plant varieties in perhaps less than a century or two in some places.

Historically this is exactly what is observed. Some strong individuals began to dominate the production of food.

The geologic epoch associated with the transition from hunter-gathering is known as the Holocene[211], which continues to the present. However, a new geologic epoch is being suggested - the Anthropocene[212]: a period when our species began to overwhelm the Earth's carrying capacity. I will have more to say about this troubling development later -- stay tuned.

Ultimately, the Neolithic introduced other, important changes such as established villages, improved farming techniques -- irrigation and other changes that would infuriate modern environmental warriors. Relative to the current world situation, alluded to above, farming enabled the production of reliable food surpluses which supported population increases which continue today.

Furthermore, farming is still experiencing significant improvements. Genetic modifications of staple items such as corn which enable the genetically modified corn to resist such devastating problems as the corn borer have greatly improved corn agriculture. The modified entities are termed Genetically Modified Organisms (GMO). The October 4 2016 Wall Street Journal reported that: *GMOs Are a Necessity—for Farmers and the Environment.* After twenty years, the data are in: Genetic modification boosts crop yields by 21 percent and cuts pesticides by 37 percent[213].

GMO improvements are unfortunately resisted by those who either do not understand genetics or whose livelihoods are threatened – organic farmers. Perhaps, after reading this book you will be better informed regarding GMO crops.

The probable status of spiritual or religious beliefs

Nothing in the last two chapters could have led to a significant change in the basic beliefs introduced previously,

> We live at the center of a very small, very young universe that revolves about us; moreover, everything in the universe including ourselves was created and is controlled by God.

Chapter 4 will introduce some of the changes that occurred due to the Bronze Age.

Recent information pertaining to the populating of Europe

We conclude this chapter with recent information pertaining to the populating of Europe. Ironically, three different scientists, published three independently written, complimentary articles, in three separate scientific publications demonstrating that DNA analyses had identified three different groups populating Europe between 44 ka and 4 ka.

We begin with an article published in the July 1, 2015 issue of *New Scientist*, Colin Barras' discussion of *the three ancestral tribes that founded Western Civilization*[214]. An overall title for the three groups might be, borrowing from a spaghetti western: *The Good, the Bad and the Ugly*:

> First came the hunter-gatherers. Then the farmers. Then the cattlemen on horseback. Ancient DNA is now revealing how a very different group from the east [the cattlemen] joined the hunter-gatherers and farmers to lay Europe's foundations[215].

Note that DNA is the villain upsetting the "Pick and Shovel" apple cart:

...an explosion of studies is using fragments of DNA [extracted from] ancient bones to probe Europe's genetic make-up. Together they tell a more detailed, colorful tale: that [encounters with the *Neandertal*] marked just the first of three waves of *Homo sapiens* that shaped the continent. Each came with its own skills and traits. Together they would lay the foundations for a new civilization[216].

As emphasized earlier, Europe became the center of Western Civilization for many reasons, Jared Diamond provided one. Another, of particular interest to this book, is the fact that most of modern science originated in Europe or with European descendants especially in the United States.

The successes Europeans have enjoyed in many fields of endeavor could of course lead to accusation of Euro-centrism. However, it is difficult to avoid and I have made no attempt to sway the discussion in one way or the other.

The following diagram provides an overview of the migration of the three groups:

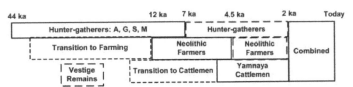

Figure 3-7 Time-line of three groups of H. sapiens entering and occupying Europe as shown by DNA Analysis.

Figure 3-2 reveals how the hunter-gatherers migrated relatively directly from Africa, appearing in the archeological record about 44 ka. 4 kyrs after this group arrived; the *Neandertals* disappeared leaving Europe to the hunter-gatherers who, as shown in Figure 3.7 developed 4 cultures: Aurignacian, Gravettian, Solutrean and Magdalenian. Of interest, recent DNA analyses demonstrate that modern Europeans still carry traces of the early hunter-gatherers in their DNA[217].

Figure 3-2 also traces the path of the second group discussed in the *New Scientist* paper. They probably left Africa about the same time as the hunter-gatherers, but migrated east and learned to become farmers. The transition from hunter-gathering to Farming that occurred in the Middle East is also shown in Figure 3-7.

Then about 7 ka, DNA data traces their return to Europe. Regarding this group, a second paper published in the Oct. 2009 issue of *Science*[218] poses this question:

> Were the ancestors of modern Europeans the local hunter-gatherers who assimilated farming practices from neighboring cultures, or were they farmers who migrated from the Near East in the early Neolithic?

The *Science* paper[219] does not reveal the identity of the "neighboring cultures" from whom the hunter-gatherers could have received "farming practices from neighboring cultures" were; however, when the authors compared DNA (mtDNA) sequences from late European hunter-gatherer skeletons with those from early farmers and from modern Europeans, they found large genetic differences which could only be explained if the farmers displaced the hunter-gatherers[220] (of course this is our common modus operandi).

In addition, early farmers also looked more like modern Europeans. DNA extracted from seven thousand-year-old bones from an early farmer revealed pale skin, dark hair and brown eyes.

Warfare comes to Europe

The third paper, published in the September 2014 issue of *Nature magazine*[221], describes a third group arriving from the north east astride horses towing wheeled vehicles carrying corded ware pottery and herding cattle[222]. Corded ware is a distinctive style of pottery due to its surface pattern. These were the Yamnaya; a culture identified with the late Proto-Indo-Europeans and the strongest candidate for the homeland of the Proto-Indo-European language[223]. Previously the origins and dispersal of Corded Ware[224] culture had been one of the pivotal unresolved issues of the Indo-European culture[225].

The arrival of the Yamnaya might whimsically be described thusly: Anticipating Spanish Conquistador Juan Pissarro and a small contingent of armed soldiers on horseback who defeated the mighty Incan warrior chief Atahualpa and an army of 200,000 soldiers thousands of years later[226], a powerful group of men on horseback, the Yamnaya, towing wheeled vehicles quickly subdued remnants of the hunter-gatherers plus the farmers and Europe was never the same. The success of the Yamnaya in conquering Europe, mirroring their Spanish ancestors is indicated by the large percentage in Europe of DNA from the third arrivals [Yamnaya] in modern European DNA[227].

While details of the Yamnaya are unclear, they had a significantly different demeanor - a group of people able to *inflict injury* on animals in order to domesticate them - then *slaughter them* to eat them - a drastic departure from the more reverent, thousands of years old approach to killing and eating animals that preceded them.

The arrival of the Yamnaya had a clear and profound effect on Europe – *the Yamnaya brought war! Things would never be the same as a perusal of European history demonstrates.* In the famous 1066 Battle of Hastings a Norman-French army defeated an English (actually Anglo-Saxon) army. This decisive Norman victory[228], *changed the course of European history,* or the two 20th century World Wars, which *changed the course of world history.*

The language the Yamnaya spoke, Proto-Indo-European is the common ancestor of all modern European languages[229], further establishing the Yamnaya as the dominant genome in Europe.

DNA once again adds a footnote to history

The preceding two paragraphs were written 2 months before the final first draft of this book was completed. During the final editing phase, more "late breaking news" arrived. I add this for as much completeness as possible but also to emphasize that science is a continually evolving subject.

On October 13, 2016, an article listing three very recent studies appeared in Nature firmly establishing our evolutionary birthplace in Africa, a concept that has been controversial:

> In the past decade, the maturation of whole-genome sequencing technology has enabled data to be generated on a scale that was previously difficult to imagine. Three studies reported on by Malaspinas *et al,* Mallick *et al,*

and Pagani *et al*) describe 787 new, high-quality genomes of individuals from geographically diverse populations, providing opportunities to refine and extend current models of historical human migration[230].

Between 40 ka and 60 ka our ancestors swept out of Africa, eventually inhabiting "the four corners of the Globe", becoming Master's of the Planet as Ian Tattersall revealed.

The Development of Farming

A final note relative to Figure 3-2: a group on the portion of our path into the Middle East, especially Mesopotamia, that founded the first city, Sumer, is designated by the solid arrow. I submit that this path and all paths that lead to the Middle East reflect the obvious choice individuals made regarding the development of farming. Would you choose the laborious task of clearing forests in Europe, or the relatively easy task of planting along the banks of tree-less rivers such as the Tigris Euphrates or Nile? I think the answer is obvious and history proves it.

One of the "advantages" of farming is food surplus which then leads to population growth (a problem still extant as discussed above and in chapter 18). Eventually the farmers had to find other places to live and they returned to Europe.

Summarizing the intergroup interactions in Europe after Homo sapiens left Africa. Violence seems to have been a major interaction factor as shown by the bell curve dedicated to intergroup violence shown in 3-8 which offers a relatively simple explanation of intergroup intersections:

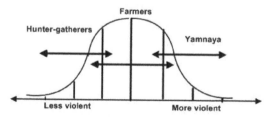

Figure 3-8 Violence/aggression distributions in
three groups that settled in Europe

The Hunter-gatherers, on the left side were the least violent. In the middle are the Farmers and on the right side, the most violent are the Yamnaya. A timeline of interaction reveals:

- 44 ka, spear throwing, arrow shooting improved brain hunter-gatherer H. *sapiens* arrived in Europe – 4 kyrs later the *Neandertal* was gone, they never had a chance.
- 9 ka, farmers arrived and overwhelmed the hunter-gatherers.
- 4.5 ka, the "cavalry" arrived on horses and soon both hunter-gather and farmer were gone.
- Five hundred years ago, another "cavalry" (Spanish soldiers on horseback) arrived in the New World, Iron Age meets the Stone Age.
- Today a fraction of the original New World residents remain, they never had a chance.

We are an interesting species. Our storey continues in the next chapter.

Chapter 3 Summary

- Chapter 3 begins with the arrival of three members of our genus: H. Antecessor, H. erectus and H. sapiens in Europe.
- Next, excerpts from Jared Diamond's treatise "Guns, Germs and Steel" are introduced to explain European domination.
- The rather severe climate awaiting our arrival was presented next.
- The evolution and final demise of Neandertal was then discussed.
- The General life style of prehistoric humans came next.
- Next the "evolution" of four cultures: Aurignacian, Gravettian, Solutrean and Magdalenian was discussed.
- Homes for the Planet Masters – and the description of four caves: Altamira, Chauvet, Lascaux and the Cave at Mas d'Azil came next.
- A discussion of Innovation and diffusion of innovation in prehistoric Europe was then presented.
- Finally, the latest information revealing that three groups of humans have contributed to the modern European gene pool was

presented. Hunter Gatherers who arrived 44 ka, Farmers, migrants from Africa who first went to the Middle East developed Farming and traveled to Europe 9 ka and last, cattlemen, also migrants from Africa who first went to the North and East, learning herding before entering Europe 4.5 ka. Some migrants from Africa went to the Middle East, remained and founded the City of Sumer.

- A "last minute" addition confirming that our species originated in Africa.

Looking Ahead:

In the next chapter, we follow the religious development path of the group who migrated into the Middle East, founding religions in places like Egypt and India but more importantly for this story -Judaism, the basis for the Hebrew religion which produced *the Book of Genesis*.

Next a short-termed branch from the main religious development path in the Aegean area of Greece is visited where the Greek civilization produced two renowned Philosopher/scientists.

Finally, a second, main branch from the religious development path, initiated by Copernicus which led to the development science in Europe and the religion/science dichotomy is presented.

CHAPTER 4

DEVELOPMENT OF RELIGION
AND THE PRELUDE TO SCIENCE

From Prehistoric mythology to Science:

This chapter picks-up our story from chapter 3, employing the timelines illustrated in Figure 4-1, briefly introduced in the Preface illustrating a fundamental feature of the religion-science understanding developments - science "spun-off" from religion and the two proceeded on separate, parallel paths:

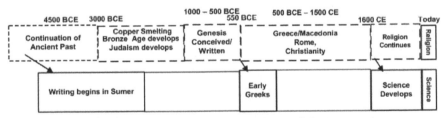

Figure 4-1 Time-line from the beginning of the Bronze Age
to the coexistence of religion and science today

The dashed line path depicts the continuation of the ancient path of understanding leading to modern religion. The solid line paths descending from the dashed path depicts three ground breaking intellectual developments related to the transition from religion to science:

1. The group who migrated into the Middle East (the arrow labeled S in Figure 3-2) founding the first city, Sumer approximately 5000 BCE.
2. The invention of writing.
3. A "false start" by two Greek Philosophers Aristarchus and Democritus approximately 550 BCE[231].
4. The occurrence of a significant transitions ca 1450 CE from the ancient belief in the apparently unchanging earth to the realization that the earth changes began the resolution of illusions 3 and 4.
5. Science, as we know it, is generally considered to have begun with Copernicus's discovery in the mid 1573 which challenged thousands of years of revered belief.

Some of the other significant developments illustrated by the dashed line in Figure 4-1 are:

- Copper smelting appears, with the earliest current evidence of copper smelting, having been found in Serbia [232]. Copper was quickly displaced by bronze, created by the addition of tin, known since ancient times, ushering in the Bronze Age approximately 3000 BCE[233]..
- With the advent of writing, the Book of Genesis, based upon oral traditions, was written down between 1000 BCE and 500 BCE. Regarding oral tradition, as George Grinnell remarks in his book about the Blackfeet: "…the Blackfeet have stories and legends that originated centuries ago, perhaps thousands of years ago, and were passed down through oral tradition[234].,
- Between 500 BCE and 1500 CE, first Greece/Macedonia under Alexander the Great, then the Roman Empire and finally Christianity buried the early Greek developments except for a few surviving bits.

The development of writing

Writing emerged in many different cultures in the Bronze age (ca 3600 BCE to 600 BCE) Examples are the cuneiform writing of the Sumerians,

Egyptian and Cretan hieroglyphs, Chinese logographs, Indus script and the Olmec script of Mesoamerica[235].

Sometime before 750 BCE, the Greeks adopted the Phoenician alphabet, an adaptation that included the innovation of the use of symbols for vowels. The Greek adapted alphabet eventually consisted of 24 characters each representing a consonant or vowel and played a central role in Greek culture development; and is the basis of most alphabets in use today. *It is one of mankind's greatest achievement* remarked Wisconsin classicist Barry Powell who heralds use of vowels as central to the achievement[236].

Recently started excavations in Northern Greece are providing a new look at the earliest days of writing. At the ancient city of Mehon, archeologists found troves of very early Greek alphabetic inscriptions on ceramics between 730 BCE and 690 BC that were created just as the alphabet was coming into widespread use and shows how quickly it went mainstream. Newly discovered inscriptions by John Papadopoulos, who also excavates at Mehon, shows how we transformed from a Greek world without witting in ninth century to its use in transcribing poetry 100 yrs later[237].

Powell further avers that the Greek alphabet was originally developed for the sole purpose of recording Homer's poems. According to Powell's theory, one person, probably a Greek, was commissioned by a wealthy patron to take dictation from the famous poet in Greece and preserve what even then must have been the most celebrated poems of the age.

But the phonetic alphabet was not up to the task of transcribing Homer's words so the scribe needed to invent vowels from existing Greek letters. Per Powell, it was a stroke of genius. In order to capture Homeric verse, the scribe created *one of the greatest innovations of all time* -- Homeric Verse

The development of organized religion:

Similar to language, organized religions developed in many places like Egypt and India. Most importantly for this story was the development of Judaism, the basis for the Hebrew religion, in the Middle East about 1000 BCE.

An examination of the human condition discussed in chapter 3 reveals a universal, deeply felt need for satisfactory explanations of ourselves and our surroundings. Pertaining to these needs, Professor Marcel Otte, who I introduced previously, offered these comments:

> Our minds 'need' explanations by any way possible, so if these crucial needs are satisfied by any socially accepted system, then we are satisfied at least for a moment. Regarding religion, there has never been any humans in the world, now or at any time before, without religion, never, nowhere![238]

Concerning the development of belief systems, as mentioned above the slow development of cognition must have allowed early humans to establish some understanding of their surroundings. In addition, there is no evidence this developed cognition progressed beyond the "We live at the center of the universe" stage.

The development of the concept of God is central to the development of belief systems. Evolutionary psychologist David Barash provides an "answer" in his whimsical treatise, "Is God a silverback [gorilla][239]?" Prior to the cultural homogenization that came with Western colonialism and missionary coercion, more than 80 per cent of traditional human societies were preferentially polygynous (The form of polygamy where a man has more than one wife at one time[240]).

Thus, in this scenario, the protective, omnipotent, scary and very territorial monotheistic God is modeled on the basic prehistoric family structure: dominant, protecting male at the head, subservient wives and children. Moreover, everything they had, they either made themselves or obtained from their surroundings. For example, they made their clothing, weapons cooking tools, etc. Therefore, it is reasonable to postulate that, some of the more perceptive and intelligent prehistoric humans conceived of a being, similar to themselves, but with vastly greater powers:

> An all powerful but undetectable supernatural Spirit, God or Gods had created everything and had then exerted control as needed.

This belief, in some form, is fundamental to all religions. Per the Origin concept it had to develop somewhere and I submit that prehistoric humans first conceived this belief.

Furthermore, to account for rainfall, the growth of plants and animals and other phenomena, perhaps other perceptive and intelligent Prehistoric humans added additional subordinate beings with the ability to control the environment, such as Fertility Goddesses, or Rain Gods. Finally, since these beings could not be observed doing things like making it rain; they also had the power to remain invisible.

A chief God plus multiple subordinate Gods were common in places where civilization was developing such as the Middle Eastern City-state Sumer - the chief deity was Marduk[241], while Greece and Rome "shared" Zeus who became Jupiter in Rome. Greece and Rome also shared Aphrodite and Venus, Goddesses of love[242].

Belief in these subordinate beings is still active; e.g., the belief in a Fertility Goddess is currently prevalent in many ancient cultures in addition to ours. The Easter Sunday celebration originated with Saxon fertility goddess Astra or Éostre a descendent of the Proto-Indo-European language, who was evidently worshiped for bringing the earth to life in the spring[243].

An interesting proposal for the development of religion was advanced by Duke University Anthropologist Weston La Barre, who made a case for religion being *The Ghost Dance* of the Roman Empire. La Barre's principal anthropological interest was the Native American cultures who developed a Ghost Dance as a mechanism to defeat the "White Man"[244].

Finally, the origination location for this belief system, a powerful intellectual innovation, is uncertain, but it had to have developed somewhere. Prehistoric Europe and the Middle East are logical origination locations, especially Europe since it enjoyed distinct evolutionary advantages as explained in the extract from Jared Diamond's treatise *"Guns, Germs and Steel"* provided previously. But religions are ubiquitous; the specific origin location is not that important.

The Writing of Genesis and its connection with the five illusions

For members of the dominant religion on Earth, Christianity with 2.2 billion adherents, *Genesis* enjoys a privileged position.:

This position was emphasized during the first ever manned trip to another space object, while orbiting the Moon for the very first time by human beings, on Christmas Eve 1968 the crew of Apollo 8: astronauts Frank Borman, Jim Lovell and Bill Anders appropriately decided to send a special message to Earth by reciting the first 10 verses from Book of *Genesis* (English King James Bible version)[245].

The reading of a three-thousand-year-old religious passage from a twentieth century spacecraft is indeed ironic, but it does underscore the importance of *Genesis* to many people. Furthermore, *Genesis* is still a significant part of many Bible study groups.

In view of this position, as mentioned previously, I selected *Genesis* as it is the religious explanation of ourselves and our surroundings most easily compared with the scientific explanation.

Regarding the writing of *Genesis*, there is considerable discussion available on the web pertaining to the subject, but as one source emphasizes: there is much disagreement[246]. However, the Documentary Hypothesis seems the most reasonable explanation of the writing of Genesis[247]. By the end of the nineteenth century, it was generally agreed there were four main *Genesis* sources, combined into their final form by a series of redactors, who wrote from 950 BCE to 500 BCE[248].

These four sources for Genesis have been identified:

Who	When	Where
Yahwist	950 BCE	Kingdom of Judah
Elohist	850 BCE	Kingdom of Israel
Deuteronomist	600 BCE	Jerusalem
Priestly source	500 BCE	Kohanim

Table 4-1 Sources for *Genesis*.

Concerning the four sources[249]:

- Jawist or Yawist (or simply J) is ....probably the oldest of the four sources, and gets its name from the term Yahweh, Hebrew YHWH for God in *Genesis*. - YHEH is viewed as an anthropomorphic figure, forming, with his own hand, man from the dust.
- Elohist (E) is identified through textual criticism as one of four sources of the *Torah* together with the other three sources. Elohist comes from Elohim, the term used in the Hebrew and Canaanite languages for *the Gods*.
- The Deuteronomist, (D), is one of the sources identified through source criticism as underlying much of the *Old Testament*. Seen by most scholars more as a school or movement than a single author.
- The Priestly source (P) is one of the hypothesized *Torah* sources together with the other three. P was written to show that even when all seemed lost, [e.g., during Babylonian captivity][250] God remained present with Israel.

As pointed out above, writing had developed about 3.2 ka BCE; hence, *Genesis* was able to develop in written form which facilitated combining the sources. However, there appears to be little or no information pertaining to *how the four sources arrived at the creation story* contained in the first thirty-one verses of *Genesis* provided in Appendix A. On the other hand, *Genesis* does exist in the form exhibited in Appendix A which contains the Vatican imprimatur. Note that I have partitioned the verses into logical sections.

If we compare the five illusions observable three thousand years ago with the first thirty-one verses of *Genesis,* we can align a list of apparent illusions with the possible corresponding *Genesis* verse as shown in table 4-2:

Illusion	Gen. Verse
1. Apparent motion of Sun, Moon, stars around Earth	3,4,5,16
2. Apparent same size and closeness of the Sun, Moon and stars	6, 7, 8
3. Earth's apparently unchanging physical features	9, 10?
4. Earth's apparently unchanging biological features	11, 12, 20, 21 24, 25
5. The apparently solid Earth	N/A
Deduction: Must have been a creator	All verses

Table 4-2 Correlation between illusions and verses in *Genesis*.

Regarding illusion 1, *Genesis* only states, in verse 3: "God said, "Let there be light"; and there was light." Later in verse 16: "God made the two great lights - the greater light to rule the day and the lesser light to rule the night - and the stars."

In general, what Genesis doesn't say is as interesting as what it does say. For example, there is no mention of the motion of the "two lights" or their apparent closeness. Although the presence of a dome added in verse 6 could imply the recognition of illusion 2.

Concerning illusions 3 and 4, *Genesis* discusses the origin of life in several verses: five are identified in table 4-2. However, there is scant mention of physical features, especially anything related to time except the six days of creation.

Genesis does get the creation sequence partially correct: first a formless earth and then an earth having dry land and water followed by the origin of life.

Actually, the sun came first but the *Genesis* authors could not have known that. Also, as has been pointed out by others, the order of the verses is incorrect - verse.16 should be closer to verse.3. The improper ordering of *Genesis* most likely reflects the fact that *Genesis* is a composite of four authors.

In view of all this I propose that it is reasonable to postulate that *the writers of Genesis were to some extent influenced by beliefs, based upon illusions* that had developed over thousands of years in Ice Age Europe and the Neolithic; such as the fundamental belief, that:

> An all powerful but undetectable supernatural Spirit, God
> or Gods had created everything in a short time and had
> then exerted control as needed[251].

In addition to *Genesis*, Christianity adopted some of the myths that had been created by the Greeks and the Egyptians; in particular, as mentioned above the Christian church adopted the astronomy of the Greek astronomer Ptolemy[252]. It was these findings that led to the problems that Copernicus wrestled with as mentioned in the preface.

Answers in Genesis?

The tenacity of *Genesis* is a testimonial to its power to provide answers to those receptive to a religious explanation, but close unemotional inspection reveals relatively little substantive information in *Genesis*. (Relative to Genesis tenacity, I have provided a relevant personal interview with a Genesis believer in Appendix A.)

The creation sequence is reasonable. The earth had to be created first and then water was added which is needed for life. Then a dome was put in place to define the heavens/sky - possibly "modeled" on the Celestial Sphere of other ancient religions. With the dome in place, the sun and moon were just hung in the dome. There is no mention of their motion and no mention the star creation. Then plants and animals were created followed by humans.

A fair start, but if we paraphrase verse 1 using the date established from the *Genesis* genealogy by the good Bishop, we have "Approximately six thousand years ago, an undetectable, all powerful being (God) created the universe in six days." A bit of a stretch, but many believe it.

In addition, no mention is made of the physical features of the earth such as mountains. The creator should have known about the forces of change such as plate tectonics discussed in chapter 15. Also, microscopic items such as our cells, the atoms that constitute matter or fossils are things the creator would have known. Therefore, there are **no answers in *Genesis***. However, many people continue to study *Genesis*, the flood is offered as an explanation of change--little wonder that many find it difficult/impossible to cross the beckoning bridge from religion to science.

The lure of Religion

Despite the fact that the religious explanation of ourselves and our surroundings is controversial, religion exerts a powerful attraction. Religion offers comfort, something science often lacks. However, the religious comfort is unfortunately often misleading. One of the major lures is life-after-death. The quest for the afterlife has a very long history. Prehistoric societies appear to hold some belief in an afterlife as is evidenced by burial material. Today the belief continues. I mentioned the afterlife previously supported by out of body experiences. I have a friend who had an out of body experience in which he apparently "visited" heaven. Oblique conversations with him the convinced me that he firmly believes he will reunite with friends and family after he dies.

Of particular import, a noted Neurosurgeon experienced an out of body experience. His apparent trip to heaven convinced him that heaven exists, to the extent that he wrote a book *"proof of heaven"*[253]

Cartoonists occasionally find humor is possible in the afterlife. A recent cartoon character worried that he would go to heaven without any clothes. Besides nudity, there is the logistic problem of finding your loved ones and also "housing" the heavenly multitude if that's the correct term

Science's False Start

Having introduced the basics of the *Genesis* explanation, our discussion proceeds to the tenuous beginning of science.

Identified in Figure 4-1 as the "Early Greeks" are two amazing Philosophers: Leucippus ca five hundred BCE and his pupil Democritus (470-380) BCE, and Aristarchus of Samos (310-230) BCE[254].

Leucippus is reported to have originated the concept of invisible objects termed atoms. On the other hand, there is some question about Leucippus's reality and a "pupil" of Leucippus[255], Democritus, whose existence can be confirmed[256], in 500 BCE, probably observing a pan of water evaporate, deduced that water had "disappeared" into the air. Since, water in the atmosphere must be an invisible vapor, water particles must be too small to be observed by the human eye. This deduction led to the realization that all matter was made of invisible particles termed atoms (Greek for indivisible). Amazingly, nothing new was added to our understanding of matter, until 1897 when JJ Thomson discovered the electron.

Aristarchus was apparently the first individual to realize that the apparent motion of the sun around the earth is an illusion. That the best explanation for all the observations of the sun, moon and five planets that were visible to the unaided eye was a heliocentric solar system with all planets, including the earth, revolving in circles about the sun. Aristarchus verified his deduction using triangulation which was limited by the observational equipment he had and his unaided eye, but which did allow him to determine the radius of the sun as many times the Earth's radius. The impossibility of a giant sun revolving about the earth became obvious.

Regarding the extraordinary contributions of the Greeks, Bertram Russell provided this trenchant observation in his History of Western Philosophy[257].

> In all of history, nothing is so surprising or so difficult to account for as the sudden rise of civilization in Greece. Much of what makes civilization had already existed supernatural for thousands of years in Egypt and in Mesopotamia, and had spread thence to neighboring countries. But certain elements had been lacking until the Greeks supplied them. What the Greeks achieved in art and literature is familiar to everybody, but what they did in the purely intellectual realm is even more exceptional. They invented mathematics (Arithmetic and some geometry had existed among the Egyptians and Babylonians, but mainly in the form of rules of thumb – deductive reasoning from general premises was a Greek innovation) and science.

Other discussions of religion and science

It is not my objective to ignore the writings of other individuals pertaining to the religion – science controversy. Of note: most speak of science and religion; when one should speak of religion and science since religion did develop first and the development order is crucial to an understanding of the current coexistence of the two opposite explanations.

The belief in a supernatural creator or being that overlooks and protects us permeates our culture in many places. Our currency contains the phrase "In God we Trust", our Anthem contains the phrase "Under God" and we sing "God bless America" at many athletic and other events attests to a general attitude inconsistent with religion-science compatibility.

An excellent compendium of articles pertaining to the religion-science controversy was published by Paul Kurtz, professor emeritus of philosophy at SUNY Buffalo New York. Professor Kurtz has organized twelve articles written by leading authorities in an anthology entitled *Science and Religion – Are They Compatible?* [258] Although well written and interesting, the book is inconclusive.

Regarding compatibility, the dictionary defines compatibility as:

> Capable of existing or performing in harmonious, agreeable, or congenial combination with another or others:

Considering the history of similar religion's incompatibility, for example the continuing conflict between Sunni Arabs and Shia Arabs over what a non-Arab would consider a trivial matter. Also consider the conflict between the Catholic and Protestant and branches of Christianity. In both cases the two sides of the religious conflict involve more with each other than with other religions.

I believe it is axiomatic that if two similar religions are incompatible, the likelihood of religion and science compatibility is nil.

There are those who think good things have happened because of God's interference with the laws of physics however no experiment has ever been conducted which demonstrates a divine supernatural presence.

Religion and Science are demonstrably incompatible

As introduced in the Preface, when I set out to write this book, my objective was the presentation of an answer to the question: "Why had two diametrically opposite explanations of ourselves and our surroundings: Religion and Science been formulated?" Moreover, why did they continue to coexist? One of the more bizarre dichotomies in human history -- a topic that, as far as I could discern, *had never been properly addressed.*

A few thousand hours of research later, as attested by over 800 references, I had the answer. Considering the previous examinations of religion and science, the reason for the dichotomy appears to be obvious:

- Religion was formulated first, thousands of years ago, by individuals who unfortunately labored under the restrictions of five illusions, which led to the belief that: we reside at the center of a small, young universe, revolving around us that was created by a supernatural entity.
- Science diverged from religion about five hundred years ago when improved observation instruments and techniques began to reveal the flaws in this religious explanation especially the implausibility of an all-powerful entity.
- Unfortunately, many were, and some still are, unable or unwilling to accept the scientific explanations.

As I mentioned in the Preface, believing this to be an interesting story, I decided to begin by presenting the development of life from the first primordial cell. This would allow me to include some other interesting facets of the development of an explanation of ourselves and our surroundings such as reliable methods for dating ancient objects, and the proper explanation of life's overall development -- evolution.

In addition, I would have the pleasure of tracing life's development to the present; in particular, the path of religious development from prehistoric Europe to a Bronze Age religion, Hebrew, where the *Book of Genesis* was written. A key feature of this development was the connection between five illusions that initially confused even the most brilliant individuals.

Tying *Genesis* to the illusions permits the development of an introductory explanation to the resolution of the religion-science dichotomy organized according to the illusions.

In view of the preceding chapters, I believe that I have demonstrated that religious explanation development began thousands of years prior to scientific explanation development. In addition, the science explanation was initiated when improved observations revealed flaws in the religious explanation. However, many found the developing science explanation difficult/imposable to accept establishing the reason for the bizarre coexistence of the two diametrically opposite explanations – Religion and Science.

However, while I believe that I have successfully demonstrated that Religion is not a correct explanation of ourselves and our surroundings, I am reminded of the closing remarks of Dr, Francis X Noble, narrator of the excellent Great Courses series, "*The Foundations of Western Civilization*[259]."

> We should not be too harsh on the defenders of the faith who harshly treated non-believers, after all the non-believers were viewed as upstarts who were challenging thousands of years of revealed truth - a significant challenge when relatively little proof was available initially.

I believe I have tried to keep this in mind while preparing this text.

Chapter4 summary Development of Religion and the Prelude to Science.

- Chapter 4 begins with a continuation of chapter 3 with a diagram illustrating the parallel development of religion and science – an extension of the simple Preface diagram.
- The development of organized religion follows.
- The writing of *Genesis* is explained by noting by the end of the nineteenth century, it was generally agreed there were four main sources for Genesis, combined into their final form by a series of redactors, who wrote from 950 BCE to 500 BCE.
- Comparing the five illusions observable 3 ka, with the first thirty-one verses of *Genesis* we can construct the comparison presented in table 4-2.

- Answers in Genesis are examined next demonstrating the lack of answers in Genesis
- Sciences' "False Start" which began in Greece in 500 BCE was described next,
- Followed by the conclusion that the book's main objective, resolving the religion-science dichotomy had been achieved.

Looking Ahead:

the A-Z introductory explanation of science –resolving the three main illusions:

We proceed now to the "A-Z" explanation of ourselves and our surroundings termed Science, organized around the resolution of the illusions which began when16th century Europeans initiated a "search for the correct understanding of ourselves and our surroundings" to replace the mythology of religion, through the development of new observation equipment and techniques and new explanation methods." In these chapters, you will encounter approximately 600? remarkable members of the right side of the bell curve.

These chapters are followed by a concluding chapter which "wraps everything up" by describing the life cycle of the universe: from its well-known beginning to its completely predictable end.

Having concluded Section I, we proceed to an the "A-Z" introductory explanation of science which explains the development of science coordinated with the resolution of three illusion groups, and the outstanding far right side investigators whose discoveries were responsible for illusion resolution. Of particular importance, I have organized the discussion historically so you can travel the twisting paths of discovery in the footsteps of the discoverers.

Resolving the apparently solid Earth Illusion: Chapters 5 -9.

Chapter 5: begins with the earliest observations of electricity and magnetism and discusses Electricity and Magnetism (E&M) phenomenon investigations prior to discovery of the electron in 1897 since, until the discovery of the electron, E&M phenomenon were believed to be separate from the "solid" Earth.

Chapter 6: discusses "Solid" matter investigations prior to 1897, beginning with the earliest understandings.

Chapter 7: discusses some empirical explanations of the "solid" Earth illusion that were developed between 1897 and 1911 via five breakthrough experiments aided by Sherlock's theorem.

Chapter 8 explains the mind-bending concept that the "visible rules" do not apply to the microscopic world.

Chapter 9 finalizes the resolution of the solid earth illusion ending with the so-called "Standard Model," recently completed with the discovery of the Higgs Boson at the huge CERN accelerator.

Resolving the Astronomical Illusions: Chapters 10-12.

Chapter 10 explains the determination of the solar system's shape which resolved the apparent motion of the sun and planets around the Earth illusion.

Chapter 11: explains the determination of the solar system's size which resolved the apparent same size and closeness of the sun, moon and stars illusion.

Chapter 12: explains the use of earth's position on opposite sides of its orbit to provide a platform for measuring the distance to the nearer stars which ultimately led to the correct explanation of the size and age of the universe.

Resolving the Unchanging Earth Illusion: Chapters 13 – 17

Chapter 13 addresses the question: "How had the illusions identified in chapter 1 escaped detection for thousands of years by individuals of great intellect?" A combination of serendipity plus the recognition, by one of history's greatest intellects, Leonardo da Vinci, that viewed properly, fossils are a window into the past, begins the unmasking of the unchanging earth illusion.

Chapters 14 and 15 will explain the resolution of Earth's unchanging physical properties illusion and explain the forces that cause change.

Chapters 16 and 17 will explain the resolution of Earth's unchanging biological features illusion and explain the process that causes biological change.

Putting it all together

Chapter 18 will assemble all the pieces developed in the earlier chapters to show how they provide the correct explanation of Earth's creation, the preparation for life's appearance, its initial appearance with the primordial cell, then simple multi-celled life, next the Cambrian Explosion, followed by sequence of steadily improving life forms: fish, amphibians, reptiles, mammals and finally primates our immediate ancestors.

Chapter 19 concludes the book with an explanation of the life cycle of the universe from its fiery beginning to its frozen absolute zero end with our "brief shining moment" in the middle.

CHAPTER 5

ELECTROMAGNETIC PHENOMENON INVESTIGATIONS PRIOR TO 1897

At the risk of excessively dividing this discussion, it is necessary to recognize that, initially, early investigators didn't realize that electricity and magnetism were related. Hence, investigations occasionally were separate and sometimes combined.

Earliest observations and explanations of the effects of electricity

It is reasonable to assume that the first observation of electrical phenomena was the observation of lightning, jagged streaks of bright light followed by a loud bang and usually accompanied by hard rain. Early humans, of course, had no idea what lightning is, often attributing it to the anger of gods. In the *Aeneid*, Virgil explains how Jupiter, king of the Roman gods, throws lightning bolts as a weapon to kill humans or cause destruction[260]. As will be discussed below, the belief that God is involved in lightning persisted into the 1800s with often disastrous consequences[261].

In addition to lightning, which is actually "current" or "flowing" electricity, another form of electricity, static electricity, which is produced when cloth or fur rubs a solid object, was undoubtedly known to early humans.

Early observers might have detected two "forms" of static electricity, one associated with amber. Amber, a fossilized resin, can be an item of beauty, often used as jewelry for millennia[262]. We can never know who was the first person to rub amber with fur and observe that small bits of material, such as straw, are attracted to the amber, but the Greek philosopher Thales (625-546) BCE[263] was apparently one of the first record the effect[264]. But, as with lightning, no one understood what it was.

Another "form" of static electricity can be made by rubbing a glass rod with silk. Since the earliest man-made glass objects, mainly non-transparent glass beads are thought to date back to around 3500 BCE[265] this form of static electricity was probably known at least by the time of Thales, although no record of this seems to exist. This other form would have been detected if amber rubbed by fur was brought close to glass rubbed by silk as one would have attracted the other; whereas, two pieces of rubbed amber or two pieces of rubbed glass would repel each other.

While early investigators had no idea exactly what was happening when a rubbed object acquired the ability to attract or repel, they probably reasoned that something was being transferred between the rubbing material, fur, silk, etc. and the rubbed object and they eventually called the something a "charge." Hence, an amber piece or glass rod became "charged."

The Electrostatic effect produced by rubbing dissimilar materials together is now termed tribo-electricity, from the Greek word for friction.

Earliest observation of the effects of magnetism

Just as lightning and static electricity were probably the first observations of electrical effects," naturally" formed magnets, created primarily by the iron based mineral, magnetite, the most common mineral displaying magnetic properties[266], were probably known for thousands of years. Often called lodestone[267], pieces of this material must have been found from time to time and careful observers noted that, depending upon orientation, pieces of lodestone would either repel or attract other pieces.

Early records, dating to the second century CE, show that the Chinese had discovered that lodestone, placed on a piece of wood floating in a bowl of water, would always point to the pole star and hence created the first practical compass[268].

The first organized investigations of electricity and magnetism, before 1897:

Early, somewhat ineffective investigations of E&M ended about 1500 CE. While a number of interesting phenomena had been observed, e.g., the existence of static electricity and magnetism, there were few realistic explanations of these phenomena, e.g., how the effects were produced. Accordingly, serious investigation began with Girolamo Cardano.

Girolamo Cardano (1501-1576) distinguishes electricity from magnetism:

Girolamo Cardano was an Italian Renaissance physician, astrologer and gambler[269]. He apparently led quite a life. While, early observers had undoubtedly "discovered" electricity and magnetism, Cardano was apparently the first to write a formal paper discussing the two phenomena. His most famous work was "De subtilitate" published in Nuremberg, by Johann Petreius in 1550 in which Cardano explains that this

> ...was his great encyclopedia of scientific knowledge. This was the most advanced presentation of physical knowledge up to its time. It contains many remarkable observations and ideas; including Cardano's distinction between the attractive powers of rubbed amber (electric) and the lodestone (magnetic), his pre-evolutionary belief in creation as progressive development, and the premise that natural law was unified and could be known through observation and experiment[270].

As stated above the fact that lodestone had two "magnetic poles," one at each end of a magnet, whereas rubbed amber has only one "pole," must have been known long before Cardano, but he gets credit for being the first person to formalize this knowledge.

William Gilbert (1544 – 1603), the first organized investigations of electricity and magnetism[271]

English physician, William Gilbert and Sir Thomas Browne are credited with the origination of the English word electricity. Gilbert coined the term electricus from the Latin electricus meaning "Amber like attractive properties" which Browne Anglicized into electricity[272].

Since the tendency for two pieces of lodestone to attract or repel each other depending upon orientation must have been known for thousands of years, Gilbert would also have known of this property of magnetic materials. Hence, his experiments must have easily led him to conclude that the Earth is a giant magnet which correctly explains the functioning of a compass. It was then natural for Gilbert to apply the term North and South poles to the ends of a magnet.

Gilbert observed that like poles: N-N or S-S repel each other, while unlike poles, N-S attract. One of the more mysterious aspects of the magnetic attraction/repulsion force is that it exerts its effect when magnets are merely brought next to each other – touching is not required.

The same is true of the force generated when amber is rubbed. Gilbert studied these electrostatic effects and employed the term *"electric force"* to describe the effects. Gilbert summarized his work in De Magnete[273], a thorough exposition that was highly influential. A copy of the book is available at this site[274].

Creating a practical means for creating and storing electricity

As mentioned above, a significant impediment to the establishment of a correct explanation of electricity is that, unlike "solid" matter, electricity is invisible and only detectable by its effects. Compounding the difficulty is that one of the principal detectable effects, forces generated by electrical entities, act at a distance. Thus, in order to study electricity, practical means for laboratory creation of electricity as well as a practical means for detecting it had to be developed. These two pursuits form a large part of the establishment of a correct explanation of electricity and magnetism.

It should be noted that, regarding our ability to "see" electricity, nothing has changed. As anyone who has accidentally touched a "live" wire knows, there is nothing to distinguish a wire attached to a source of electricity from a piece of wire "just lying around." Accordingly, some knowledge of electrical phenomenon may have some practical value.

Otto von Guericke (1602-1686), invents first electrostatic generator 1650

Von Guericke was a German scientist[275] who invented the first instrument capable of generating electrostatic energy, a rotating disc with two "brushes" rubbing against it, thereby duplicating the rubbing of amber in a more efficient manner. Electrostatic energy could be extracted from one of the brushes for experimentation[276].

Charles François du Fay (1698-1739) refines the explanation of static electricity

French Chemist du Fay formalized the effects of rubbing amber with fur and a glass rod with silk. The former he termed resinous electricity (amber is a resin) and the latter vitreous electricity (vitreous being the Latin term for glass)[277].

One of Dufay's more important contributions was the summarizing of the electrical knowledge then extant[278]:

1. All bodies can be electrically charged by heating and rubbing, except metals and soft/liquid bodies.
2. All bodies, including metal and liquid, can be charged by influence (induction).
3. The electrical properties of an object unique to color are affected by the dye, not the color itself.
4. Glass is as satisfactory as silk as an insulator.
5. Thread conducts better wet than dry.
6. There are two states of electrification, Vitreous and Resinous.[279].
7. Bodies electrified (charged) with vitreous electricity attract bodies electrified with resinous electricity and repel other bodies electrified with vitreous electricity.

While point 7 is correct, it is not clear how he arrived at this conclusion as an obvious measuring instrument such as the pith ball electroscope was not invented until 1754, (see below), but presumably du Fay arranged some means measuring the effects described in point 7.

An obvious method: suspend two light weight objects from strings with small separation. Then, touch one with a rubbed glass rod and one with rubbed amber which should result in the two objects being attracted as the charges would be unlike. Repeating with either amber or both glass would produce the repellant effect.

Other methods might have been employed; Ben Franklin for example used two parallel line threads as a detector[280].

Pieter van Musschenbroek (1692-1761) invents the a container for electricity-the Leyden jar

One of the most important electricity investigating instruments, the Leyden jar, invented in 1745 was named for van Musschenbroek's residence the city of Leyden in the Netherlands. The compact Leyden jar allowed the storage of large amounts of static electricity in a compact object[281]. Significant experiments, using the stored electricity, were now possible, but detection remained a problem.

John Canton and Abraham Bennet invent instruments that detect electrostatic effects

Since electricity cannot be observed directly, the second element of an electrostatic experiment is a means for detecting the presence of electrical charge. Although du Fay must have devised some detection method, as discussed above, the first formal instrument was the electroscope. Two forms were developed.

In 1754, British weaver's apprentice, John Canton invented the pith-ball electroscope[282]. A pith ball can be any lightweight nonconducting substance. Canton's device employed silk thread hung from an insulated hook. When an object bearing an electric charge, such as previously rubbed amber rod, is brought near the pith ball, the ball will be deflected.

In 1786, a more sensitive instrument, the gold-leaf electroscope, was invented by Abraham Bennet (1750-1799)[283]. The Bennet electroscope employs two gold leaves suspended by a thin nonconductive wire in a glass cylinder. The two leaves are connected to a conductive knob at the top of the jar. When an electrically charged object is brought near the knob, the leaves separate.

While these devices were/are useful for detecting the presence of electrical charge, actually measuring the amount of force generated by an electrical charge requires a more sensitive instrument.

Charles de Coulomb (1736-1806) measures and determines formula for electric force:

Coulomb made two important contributions: he invented the torsional balance, an extremely sensitive force measuring device[284], which enabled him to measure the minute forces exerted by electric charges. Next, he used these measurements to empirically deduce his famous "Coulombs Law," which states that "the force generated between two electrical charges is proportional to the product of the amount of electricity carried by the two charges, Q_1 and Q_2, and inversely proportional to the square of the distance separating them." This can be written in the compact form:

Electrical Force = $Q_1 * Q_2 / r^2$

If Q_1 and Q2 have the same (e.g. negative) charge, the force is repulsive, if they are different, the force is attractive. Coulomb published his results in 1790[285].

Sir William Watson's (1715-1787) discovers current electricity:

Watson, a British physicist and physician, was one of the earliest persons to experiment with discharges from a Leyden jar, being one of the first to observe that a flash of light accompanies a discharge from a Leyden charge. This presumably led him conclude that electric current flows from the static charge in the Leyden jar. Beginning in 1745, he published a series of articles entitled "Experiments on the Nature of Electricity." In assembling his experimental apparatus, Watson coined the term "circuit"[286].

Luigi Galvani (1737-1798) and the famous frog leg twitch experiment:

There is some confusion regarding when and how Italian Physiologist Luigi Galvani observed the twitching of a frog leg connected to a metallic conductor, but Galvani was a physician who performed anatomical studies on frogs (as well as other animals) with a metal scalpel, and was apparently the first person to observe the famous twitch and deduce that electrical action caused muscles to function[287].

In 1780, Galvani carried his frog experiments further by discovering, probably through trial and error with many metals, that when two different metals are connected together and touched to different parts of a frog leg nerve, the leg contracted[288].

Alessandra Volta (1745-1827) Galvani's associate invents the voltaic cell, an improved source of electricity:

Count Alessandro Giuseppe Antonio Anastasio Volta was born in Como, in the Italian province of Lombardy. While Volta made many contributions to the explanation of electricity, his most famous was occasioned by his association with Galvani. Volta deduced that the moist frog tissues could be replaced by water soaked cardboard and that the muscular contraction of the frog's leg, which demonstrated the generation of electrical energy, could be replaced by another detector[289].

Building on Galvani's work with dissimilar metals, Volta created a vertical stack of copper and zinc discs (he had experimentally determined these to be the best materials), separated by cloth or cardboard, soaked in salt water, with all the copper discs and all the zinc discs connected together and terminated in a heavy piece of wire (now called a terminal). This arrangement, known as Voltaic pile and illustrated below, will produce an electrical current when the two terminals are connected by a conductor; thus the pile is a source of electrical energy[290].

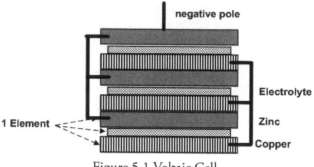

Figure 5-1 Voltaic Cell.

Volta announced his invention to the London Royal Society on March 20, 1800. Volta's invention, now termed a battery, revolutionized electrical investigations since the Voltaic cell provided a continuous source of electricity, not the short duration source available from a Leyden jar.

Ben Franklin's electrical kite

History records that Ben Franklin conducted numerous electricity experiments. In 1750, Franklin published a proposed a method for determining that lightning is the same form of electricity as that produced, through other means, by flying a kite in an electrical storm. Franklin stated that:

> When rain has wet the kite twine so that it can conduct the electric fire freely, you will find it streams out plentifully from the key at the approach of your knuckle, and with this key a phial, or Leiden jar, maybe charged: and from electric fire [Franklin must have thought of lightning as a type of fire] thus obtained spirits may be kindled, and all other electric experiments [may be] performed which are usually done by the help of a rubber glass globe or tube; and therefore the sameness of the electrical matter with that of lightening completely demonstrated[291].

Franklin had a close association with French scientists. In 1752, French scientist, Thomas-François Dalibard (1709-1778)[292] conducted Franklin's experiment (using a 40-foot-tall iron rod instead of a kite) and extracted electrical sparks from a cloud which he stored in a Leyden jar. Dalibard determined that the electricity in the Leyden jar was identical to other forms, just as Franklin had predicted[293].

It's not clear that Franklin actually performed the experiment since he cautioned that the experiment was dangerous. However, some anecdotal evidence suggests that he actually carried out the experiment; nevertheless, the fact that he conceived of and published the method is as important as actually carrying it out.

Franklin is also credited with replacing the terms resinous and vitreous with the more general terms positive and negative which applied to any form of electricity, not just electrostatic. Unfortunately, Franklin deduced that electricity flows from the positive electrode of a source of electricity to the negative electrode. This has caused electrical engineers no small grief since electricity actually flows the other way, but one cannot blame Franklin as no one in Franklin's time knew what the "charges" that carried electricity were.

Another significant Franklin contribution was the invention of the lightning rod. In one of his more astute observations, he noticed that sharp pointed conductors were more effective than rounded pointed conductors. This observation led him to hypothesize that a conductor with a sharp point, placed next to a building with the point a few feet higher than the building and the other end firmly connected to the ground might draw the electrical discharges from a lighting storm and conduct them harmlessly to the ground. His hypothesis was verified by several experiments on his own house. Following these successful demonstrations, the building in Philadelphia that we now know as Independence hall was outfitted with lightning rods in 1752[294].

Michael Faraday (1791 – 1867) and Hans Christian Ørsted (1777-1851) made three fundamental contributions and reveals relationships between E&M

In April 1820, Ørsted serendipitously placed a compass near a current carrying wire and observed that the compass needle was deflected; thus, demonstrating a direct relationship between electricity and magnetism[295].

Faraday continued Ørsted's experiments, this time by placing a wire between two magnets. When a current was passed through the wire, the magnetic field produced by the wire interacted with the magnetic field produced by the magnets, generating a force in the wire. This is the fundamental basis of an electric motor, as shown in this sketch.

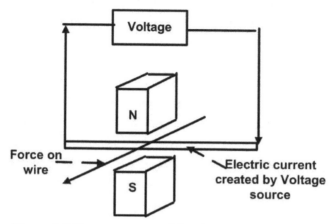

Figure 5-2 Demonstration of the electric motor principle.

Secondly, Faraday demonstrated the inverse effect by passing a wire between two magnets and noting that an electrical current is produced. This illustrates the basis of an electric generator, as shown in this sketch.

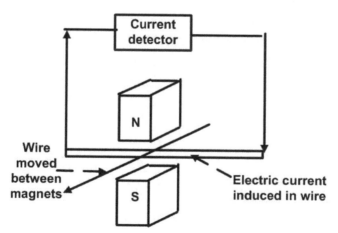

Figure 5-3 Demonstration of the electric generator principle.

Finally, Faraday reasoned that a wire moving through a magnetic field was equivalent to a changing magnetic field in an in adjacent wire. Thus, he concluded that, if two wires are placed parallel to each other, changing the electric current through one by switching the current on and off, would produce a time varying magnetic field that would "induce" a current in the adjacent wire as shown in this diagram.

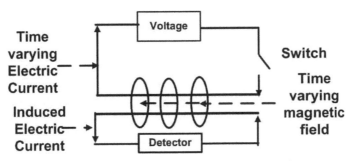

Figure 5-4 Demonstration of electric current induction.

Faraday verified this hypothesis by conducting tests using an apparatus similar to this simple diagram. This phenomenon is termed electromagnetic induction and led to the invention of the induction coil and the discovery of electromagnetic radiation.

By these experiments, Faraday also solved the problem of forces acting at a distance by demonstrating the existence of a "force field" associated with either a flowing current (as shown in the above figure) or a magnet[296].

Faraday's three discoveries were among history's most important technical advances. The generation of force on a wire placed in a magnetic field is the basis of an electric motor. The generation of a current in a wire moving through a magnetic field is the basis of an electric generator, while the induction of a current in wire by a time varying current in an adjacent wire is the basis for radiofrequency transmission which was discovered by Hertz (see discussion below). Thus, Faraday's seemingly simple discoveries became the basis for much of modern life - Michael Faraday is considered to be one of history's foremost electrical experimenters.

William Sturgeon (1783-1850) invents the electromagnet

English Physicist and inventor Sturgeon, presumably learning of Faraday's work, deduced that a current passing through a coil of wire would act like a magnet. Moreover, if a piece of soft iron was placed inside the coil, a much stronger electromagnet would result. Sturgeon demonstrated his new invention in 1825 by lifting nine pounds with the current from a single battery[297].

Nicholas Callan (1799-1864) invents first induction coil in 1836

Reflecting on Sturgeon's electromagnet and Faraday's demonstration of induction between two wires, Irish scientist Callan realized that if he wound a few turns of thick wire around a cylindrical form such as a cardboard tube, then wound many turns of thinner wire on top of the first wire and finally connected a battery to the thicker coil, a voltage would be induced into the second coil when the battery connection was switched on and off; moreover, due to the turns ratio, the voltage in the second coil would be much greater[298].

The induction coil has found many uses such as the "ignition" coil in an automobile.

James Clerk Maxwell (1831-1879) puts it all together

Maxwell was perhaps the nineteenth century's most influential scientist. Through a brilliant set of deductions, rivaling those of Sir Isaac Newton (see chapter 10), Maxwell organized all of the previous experimental data and formulae associated with electricity and magnetism, especially those of Faraday and Coulomb, into an integrated set of equations that bear his name[299]. These equations demonstrated that electricity, magnetism and even light are manifestations of the same phenomenon. Thus, all the "laws of electricity and magnetism" are merely special cases of Maxwell's equations.

Maxwell's equations are a set of *second order differential equations*, a subject beyond the scope of this book except to point out that solutions to equations of this type often represent waves[300]. The characteristics of a typical wave are shown in this sketch:

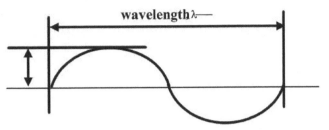

Figure 5-5 Typical E/M wave parameters and shape.

Of particular interest is the relationship between the velocity, **v**, wavelength, **λ**, and frequency, **ν** of a wave:

$$\mathbf{\nu = v/\lambda}$$

In the case of the solutions of Maxwell's equations, the waves are a mixture of electric and magnetic fields; moreover, Maxwell was able to use the solutions to calculate the velocity of Electromagnetic radiation – it was the speed of light[301]. Because of this result, Maxwell commented:

> *The agreement of the results* [solutions of his equations yield a wave traveling at the speed of light] *seems to show that light and magnetism are affections of the same substance, and that light is an electromagnetic disturbance propagated through the field according to electromagnetic laws*

During the middle ages, as mentioned previously, it was believed that we could "see" an object because something was projected from the eye[302], we now understand that we actually see because light is reflected from an object and into our eye, and is the basis of many experiments. Thus, a modicum of understanding of the principals of light is important.

Heinrich Hertz (1857-1894) E/M wave demonstration

Hertz was a German physicist who, building upon Maxwell's equations and Faraday's work on induction, was the first to experimentally demonstrate the existence of Maxwell's predicted electromagnetic (E/M) waves[303]. To generate E/M waves, Hertz employed this apparatus:

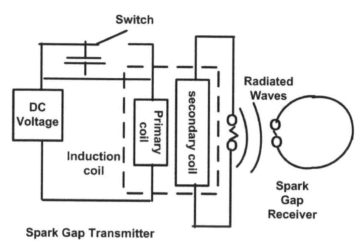

Figure 5-6 Demonstration of E/M wave propagation.

An induction coil configured as a "spark-gap transmitter" and a receiving coil configured as a spark gap receiver. The addition of the capacitor produces an oscillating current when the switch contacts are closed. When the contacts were closed, an oscillating high voltage is induced in the secondary coil which then "radiates" away from the Spark Gap Generator and induces an oscillating current in the receiver which is detected by sparks across the spark gap[304].

Hertz's experiment conclusively demonstrated the existence of the electromagnetic waves predicted by Maxwell. As will be seen below, electromagnetic radiation plays an important part in the establishment of a correct explanation of solid matter. Besides confirming Maxwell's predictions, Hertz's efforts led to the modern radio.

As will be revealed in chapter nineteen, electromagnetic radiation can travel in space and is the first activity from our planet that could potentially be detected on another world.

Otto von Guericke (1602-1686) also invents first vacuum pump in 1650

Von Guericke had many interests; besides inventing the first electrostatic generator, in 1650 Guericke invented a vacuum pump consisting of a piston and an air gun cylinder with two-way flaps designed to pull air out of whatever vessel it was connected to. This became a valuable device since it enabled the fabrication of evacuated glass jars[305]. Guericke's pump or perhaps improvements enabled others, such as Heinrich Geissler, to develop evacuated glass spheres and cylinders which significantly assisted electrical experimentation.

Heinrich Geissler (1814-1879)- uses induction coil to study gases in vacuum tubes

Geissler had two skills that enabled him to invent an important piece of experimental apparatus: the Geissler Tube: the ability to blow glass and a knowledge of physics.

The Geissler tube, fabricated from blown glass has a port which allows withdrawal of air and insertion of gases. The tube also has two electrodes to which an induction coil is connected. The high voltage generated by the induction coil causes gases to glow, a principle used, for example, in neon display tubes[306].

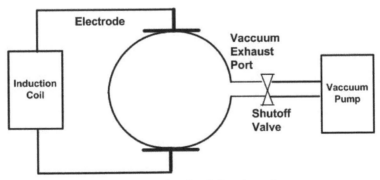

Figure 5-7 Sketch of Geissler tube.

Of particular interest, the light created by the discharge in the tube has a characteristic color, a very important property (discussed below).

Sir William Crookes (1832 – 1919), develops the Crookes tube

Crookes created an evacuated glass cone containing three electrodes as shown in this sketch:

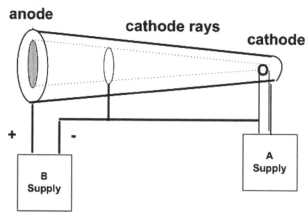

Figure 5-8 Sketch of Crookes tube.

One electrode (the anode) is connected to the wide end, and a second, (the cathode) is connected at the narrow end. The third electrode, a thin piece of sheet metal, Crookes called a shadow mask, is placed in the middle. A low voltage battery, A, is connected to the cathode, while a high voltage battery, B, is connected to the anode[307].

Crookes's principal objective was the investigation of phosphorescent effects that had been observed in Geissler tubes. Phosphorescent material, applied to the anode end of the tube would glow when voltages were applied as shown; however, the middle electrode cast a shadow as shown. Crookes explained this by positing the existence of "rays of particles" emitted by the cathode, which he termed cathode rays that were striking the phosphorescent material and causing the glow.

George Stoney coins the term electron:

In 1891, physicist George Johnstone Stoney (1826-1911) proposed the term electron as the fundamental unit of electric charge[308].

Chapter5 summary: electromagnetic phenomenon investigations prior to 1897

If we include the Greeks, twenty-four investigators of electromagnetic phenomenon labored over a period in excess of two thousand years trying to explain electromagnetic phenomena. By 1897, these efforts had yielded a collection of many facts:

- Electricity comes in two types of "charges": positive and negative. Positively and negatively charged objects repel each other, however, a positively charged object attracts a negatively charged object.
- Electricity can have two forms: static and flowing.
- Electrically "charged" objects generate a force on objects, which "acts at a distance", i.e., the effect of a charged object is observed when the charged object is only bought near another object. The "action at a distance" effect is explained by an electric "field" created by the charged object.
- William Gilbert confirmed that magnetism comes in one type, but each magnet has two so-called "poles" N and S.
- N poles repel each other, S poles repel each other, N and S poles attract each other.
- Magnets generate a force on each other that "acts at a distance", i.e., the effect of a magnet is observed when the magnet is bought near another magnet. As with electricity, the "action at a distance" effect is explained by a magnetic "field" created by the magnet.
- Von Guericke invented first electrostatic generator.
- A container for static electricity, the Leyden jar was invented.
- Canton and Bennet invented devices to detect electrostatic effects.
- Volta invented the Voltaic cell, a continuous source of electricity.
- Ben Franklin invented lightning rod, initially opposed by some religious conservatives.
- Michael Faraday demonstrated that:
- Electricity and magnetism interact.
- A current carrying conductor generates a magnetic field perpendicular to the conductor with N and S poles dependent upon direction of flow.

- A force perpendicular to a current carrying wire is produced when the wire is placed in a magnetic field.
- If two conductors are placed parallel and a current is varying in one conductor, a varying magnetic field is created which induces a current in the other.
- Maxwell developed set of equations which predict E/M waves, and also predicted E/M wave velocity.
- Hertz's experiments confirm E/M wave existence.
- Geissler invented electrostatic discharge globe.
- Crookes extended Geissler globe to a more practical tubular device.

All of this, of course, was extremely useful; however, to this point, no one knew what an electric charge is or how and why it produces the effects it does. Similarly, no one knew what magnetism is or how and why it produces the effect is does.

Looking ahead:

Having followed the path of electricity and magnetism to 1897, we now return to the beginning of "solid" matter investigations.

CHAPTER 6

"SOLID" EARTH INVESTIGATIONS PRIOR TO 1897

Creating the "Solid" Earth illusion:

As mentioned previously, to early observers, and even casual observers today, the earth and all material objects such as animals and plants, rocks, etc. appear to be solid. The "solid" Earth illusion is created by the inability of the human eye to "see" atoms which, on average, are about 10^{-8} inches, or about 0.000000001 inches in diameter[309].

Since atoms are "invisible", it is reasonable to ask "What led anyone to suspect that atoms exist?" The answer to this question has at least two parts:

- Greek curiosity.
- Desire by Alchemists to turn baser metals into Gold.

Earliest Observations of solid matter

An explanation of the underlying structure of matter began with the study of the observable properties of matter, which were undoubtedly known since ancient times. Using their unaided eyes, the earliest observers noted that matter seemed to exist in four basic forms:

- Liquid material, mainly water.
- Gaseous material, mainly the atmosphere.

- Fire, caused by lightning before humans developed methods of creating fire.
- Solid material, mainly the earth.

However, as this table indicates, the ancients must have known these elements

Element	Earliest Use
Copper	Ca. 9000 BCE
Gold	Before 6000 BCE
Lead	7000 BCE
Silver	Before 5000 BCE
Iron	Before 5000 BCE
Carbon	3750 BCE

Table 6-1 Some of the oldest known elements.

Greek explanation of matter

Regarding the existence of atoms, as explained previously, two early Greek philosophers were led to suspect the existence of atoms when they observed the disappearance of water when it evaporated, and asked the obvious question, "Where did the water go?" Also, others observed that water could squeeze through tiny openings.

These and presumably other observations, led the Greek Philosopher Leucippus (fifth century BCE) to formulate the concept that matter is composed of an infinite number of "atoms" (Greek for indivisible)[310].

Very little of Leucippus's writings have survived, so most of our knowledge of his work is found through his student Democritus (460-370 BCE). Both felt that atoms are physically, but not geometrically, indivisible and so small as to be invisible. Between the atoms, they believed was empty space.

On the other hand, other Greek philosophers did not agree with Leucippus and Democritus. However, there was not much agreement regarding which of the four manifestations of matter, water, air, fire and earth, is the most basic. The Greek philosopher Thales (625-546 BCE)

stated that water was the most basic constituent of matter[311]. On the other hand, another Greek philosopher Anaximenes ca (650-528 BCE) argued that air was the primitive element[312], while yet another Greek philosopher Heraclitus (535-475 BCE) preferred fire[313].

Finally, a fourth Greek philosopher Empedocles ca. (492-432 BCE) ended the squabble by agreeing with everyone and proposing that matter was composed of all four classic "elements", water, air, fire and earth[314].

Thus, the Greeks were able to answer the question "of what is matter?" However, they were unable to answer the question "how matter was constructed from these basic 'elements'. Moreover, it is not clear why they did not include some of the elements from Table 1-1 in their list; however, the concept that the basic elements are water, air, fire and earth prevailed. The atomistic view of Democritus posed even more difficulties to explain, especially as atoms were deemed invisible and thus their existence was at the time difficult to prove as it violated *common sense*.

Thus, water, air, fire and earth became the accepted explanation for the constituents of matter for centuries, acquiring considerable authority, until the Arabic alchemists began their search for the magical Philosophers Stone which was a method of converting baser metals such as lead into gold[315]

Alchemists discover the first "new" elements

The origins of Western alchemy are traceable to ancient Egypt and are a part of the Occult Tradition[316]. The term *occult* refers to a number of magical organizations, and the teachings and practices as taught by them[317].

In the eighth-century, an Arab alchemist, whose Latinized name is Geber, analyzed those elements which were classic to the alchemists. These include the four Greek elements, an Indian element aether, plus sulfur, representing the metals, mercury and salt[318]. Geber's studies of the qualities of an element such as its hotness or coldness, led him to believe that one could transmute one element into another by rearranging its basic qualities. These changes would be mediated presumably by the legendary philosopher's stone[319].

Presumably, belief in the existence of the Philosopher's stone developed along with other magical formulas and instruments aided and abetted by the knowledge that lead and gold have similar weights. Hence, there ought to be some way to convert lead into gold. Of course, the philosopher's stone was never shown to exist; but Geber's investigations into various chemical combinations led to the discovery of three new "real" elements: Antimony, Arsenic and Bismuth, ca 800 CE; moreover:

> The practical aspect of alchemy generated the basics of modern inorganic chemistry, namely concerning procedures, equipment and the identification and use of many current substances[320].

Empirical Investigations of solid matter before 1897

The modern study of the behavior of matter is the province of chemistry. Webster defines chemistry as:

> The science dealing with the characteristics of elements or simple substances, the changes that take place when they combine to form other substances and the laws of their combination and behavior under various conditions.

As mentioned above, chemistry was preceded by alchemy, which was initiated by the followers of Islam. While some of the alchemists' goals were outlandish, the early alchemists, such as Geber, did succeed in doing some useful work and their efforts were the main source of knowledge pertaining to matter until about the 1600s. Interestingly, during the 1600s, much of the work now performed by chemists was conducted by physicians seeking new substances to cure their patients.

From Alchemy to Chemistry

One physician in particular, an Irishman, Robert Boyle (1627 – 1691), became one of the important representatives of the transition from alchemy to chemistry[321].

Boyle expanded the efforts of early alchemist/chemist's van Helmont and Paracelsus. Jan Baptist Van Helmont was a Flemish chemist/alchemist, who is considered the "father" of pneumatic chemistry[322]. Van Helmont who originated the term gas, was also a bit of a mystic and a follower of another alchemist/chemist Paracelsus, a.k.a. Philippus Aureolus (1493-1541)[323].

Paracelsus made great contributions to the development of practical medicines and eschewed the barbaric practice of bloodletting; however, his fascinations with mysticism blunted the overall effectiveness of his work.

Building upon these predecessors, Boyle deduced an empirical relationship between the pressure, volume and temperature of a gas which is now known as Boyles Laws of gases[324]: "The product of pressure (P) and volume (V) of a gas at constant temperature is a constant (C)." Stated as a mathematical formula Boyles Law becomes the simple equation:

$$P*V = C$$

Thus, if one decreases the volume of a gas, one also increases the pressure (as anyone who has ever used a bicycle pump knows). Boyle also proposed the first modern definition of an element:

> I now mean by an element, certain primitive and simple if perfectly unmingled bodies, or of one another, immediately compounded, and into which they are ultimately resolved[325].

Boyle summed up his work in the treatise "*The Skeptical Chemist*", published in 1661. Boyle employed the dialogue form (perhaps imitating Plato) and postulated that matter consists of atoms and clusters of atoms in motion.

Boyle's treatise essentially destroyed medieval alchemy[326]. However, there are two important points regarding Boyle's contributions:

1. He had help. He didn't work out the Gas Laws by himself.
2. His formulations were arrived at empirically, through many observations.

Historical discovery of the elements

A delightful article in Wikipedia provides a time line, divided into four intervals for the discovery of the elements[327].

Discovery Interval	Number of Elements Discovered
Known since antiquity	12
1669 to 1787	16
1789 to 1868	**36**
1785 to 2010	**40**

Table 6-2 Four principle discovery periods

Obviously, the preponderance of discoveries occurred in the relatively short time beginning in 1789 to the present; moreover, many recent "discoveries" were manmade beginning with Astatine created by bombarding bismuth with alpha particles.

Here is a list of the years in which many of the elements of interest to this book were identified:

Element	Year identified
Carbon	Antiquity
Phosphorus	1669
Hydrogen	**1766**
Oxygen	**1774**
Nitrogen	1772
Uranium	1789
Potassium	1807
Sodium	1807
Calcium	1808
Radium	1898

Table 6-3 Elements of particular interest to this book.

Those of particular importance such as carbon, hydrogen and oxygen, the basic building blocks of biological matter, are highlighted in bold. Uranium and Radium are listed because they are central to important functions as radioactive dating and nuclear fission.

From a biological viewpoint, carbon is the most important element as it's structure allows extremely complex biological molecules to be constructed. Compounds which are formed with carbon are termed organic, and the importance of carbon is attested by a branch of chemistry, Organic Chemistry, devoted exclusively to carbon compounds. Carbon's unique properties will be discussed below.

Origin of the Elements

This description of the elements provides enough to understand how they were discovered and what they do, but not how they were created. The answer to that question will be presented in Chapter 8.

The Establishment of Chemistry

Antoine Lavoisier (1734-1794): conducted a brilliant series of experiments that conclusively demonstrated that fire is a process whereby an atmospheric gas, which he named Oxygen (Greek for acid former) combines with a gas released by a burning substance. Previous to Lavoisier's experiments, the prevailing view held that combustion was caused by the release of a gas called Phlogiston. Lavoisier demonstrated that a gas was released from a burning object, but the gas was created from the material of the burning object which was not phlogiston[328]. In his publication *Reflexions sur le Phlogistique* (Reflections on Phlogiston) (1783), Lavoisier showed that Phlogiston was an inconsistent explanation for combustion[329].

In this and other experiments Lavoisier represented the transition from alchemy to chemistry, capped by his publication *Traité Élémentaire de Chimie (Elementary Treatise of Chemistry*, 1789)[330] which earned Lavoisier the title of Father of Chemistry[331].

Lavoisier also demonstrated that rust was caused by the combination of oxygen with iron. Thus, Lavoisier was one of the first persons to demonstrate that elementary forms of matter combine to form compounds. Unfortunately, Lavoisier's brilliance did not extend to his political affiliations - he sided with Louis VI and joined him at the Guillotine during the French Revolution. Just as Boyle's "Skeptical Chymist" signaled the end of alchemy, Lavoisier's "Elementary Treatise of Chemistry" created modern Chemical Language. As with Boyle, it should be noted that Lavoisier arrived at his conclusions empirically[332], via many painstaking experiments.

Atomic hypothesis confirmed, Dalton's "Law" of Proportions

While Democritus had proposed the atomic theory for the structure of matter in the fourth century BCE, this hypothesis was controversial until British schoolteacher John Dalton (1766 – 1844)[333], made a number of astute observations that confirmed Democritus. Dalton had access to the discovery of the elements mentioned above, many of which had been revealed by examining compounds formed by the elements. Dalton resolved the issue in favor of Democritus. In his *Foundations of ATOMIC THEORY comprising Papers and Extracts*[334], Dalton states:

> There are three distinctions in the kinds of bodies, or states which have more especially claimed attention of philosophical chemists; namely, those which are marked by the terms elastic fluids [gases], liquids, and solids...
>
> These observations have tacitly led to the conclusion, which seems universally adopted, that all bodies of sensible magnitude, whether liquid of solid are constituted of a vast number of extremely small particles or atoms, of matter bound together according to circumstances, and which as it endeavors to prevent their separation...
>
> Whether the ultimate particles of a body, such as water, are all alike, that is of the same figure, weight, etc., is a question of some importance. ...
>
> Therefore, we may conclude that the ultimate particles of all homogeneous bodies are perfectly alike in weight, figure, etc. In other words, every particle of water is like every other particle of water. ... Chemical analysis and synthesis go no further than to the separation of particles from one another ... we might as well attempt to introduce a new planet into the solar system as to destroy one atom of hydrogen.

(Dalton was, of course, unaware of the fusion process, discovered over a century after his death, in which hydrogen is converted into helium as described below):

> ...
>
> In all chemical investigations, it has justly been considered an important object to ascertain the relative weights of the samples which constitute a compound...Now it is one great object of this work, to show the importance and advantage of ascertaining the relative weights of the ultimate particles, both of simple and compound bodies, the number of simple elementary particles which constitute one compound particle, and the number of less compound particles which enter into the formation of one more compound particles.

The latter is generally known as Daltons "Law of proportions"[335] which essentially states that "atoms combine to form compounds in definite [repeatable] proportions." Thus, water is always a combination of two atoms of hydrogen and one atom of Oxygen, a fact usually written by the formula H_2O.

The exact timing of Dalton's discoveries is a bit uncertain; however, Dalton read a paper in November 1802, in which the law of multiple proportions appears to be anticipated in the words[336]:

> The elements of oxygen may combine with a certain portion of nitrous gas or with twice that portion, but with no intermediate quantity.

As with previous explanation developments, it should be noted that Dalton's Law is an empirical formula, which is deduced from a large number of experimental observations rather than from a more fundamental explanation. Dalton hadn't a clue as to why elements behaved as they do, which as mentioned, is a fundamental problem with empirical explanations, they merely answer the question what, not how or why.

How and why was provided when the atom's structure was discovered.

The elements are related, Mendeleev's Periodic Table.

By 1869, 64 elements had been identified and their properties sufficiently investigated, such that Russian scientist Dimitri Mendeleev (1834 – 1907) was able to observe a "periodic" relationship among the elements and to independently propose the periodic law of the elements which states that: "The properties of an element depend upon the weight of the element."

Of particular significance, they observed that similar properties appeared at regular, periodic intervals in a list of the elements arranged by weight. This led them to an ingenious arrangement of the elements in a periodic "table," published in 1869[337]. An excellent presentation of the periodic is provided in ref [338]. A simple example of the periodicity of the elements is provided in this small portion of the periodic table:

First Column		Next to last Column
Lithium		*Fluorine*
Sodium		Chlorine
Potassium		Bromine
Rubidium		Iodine

Table 6-4 Sample from the periodic table of the elements (showing column relationship)

This portion shows the elements Lithium, Sodium, Potassium and Rubidium which are in the first column of the table. These elements form strong compounds with Fluorine, Chlorine, Bromine and Iodine, which are in the next to last column of the table[339]. Fluorine is italicized as it was not discovered until 1886; but, the existence of Fluorine was predicted by noting that a lighter element with similar properties to the other elements in the next to last column should [340]exist. The remarkable achievement of the periodic table is that it allowed prediction of the properties of missing elements, which greatly assisted in finding them.

Again, it should be emphasized that the periodic table is empirically derived - no one at the time had the foggiest notion why elements behaved in a periodic manner.

Every element has a unique "fingerprint", its spectrum

In addition to the investigations of Boyle, Dalton, Mendeleev, and others of similar inclination, investigation into the nature of matter proceeded along another path in the mid-to-late-1800s - a path initiated by Isaac Newton through his interest in the behavior of light. As will be seen, light and the structure of matter are intimately connected.

Everyone has seen a rainbow or looked at the spread of white light into the colors of the rainbow when it passes through a glass prism. The separation of light by a prism into various colors is termed the spectrum of white light and is due to the fact that light consists of many waves, each color having a unique wavelength.

The wave characteristic of light was conclusively demonstrated in the early 1800s by Thomas Young (1773 –1829) via an ingenious "double-slit" experiment[341]. To appreciate Young's experiment, the ability of waves to interfere, i.e., to either cancel or reinforce each other, must be understood. These two sketches illustrate the situation when light waves cancel and when waves reinforce:

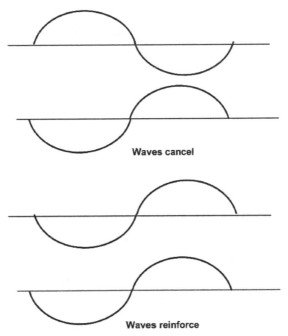

Figure 6-1 Wave cancellation and reinforcement.

In the case of wave cancellation, no light is seen. In the case of reinforcement, light is enhanced.

Young created a deceptively simple piece of apparatus: a cardboard sheet with two narrow slits cut into it, a source of light and a screen. He placed a source of light on one side and a screen on the other. The apparatus and results are shown in this sketch:

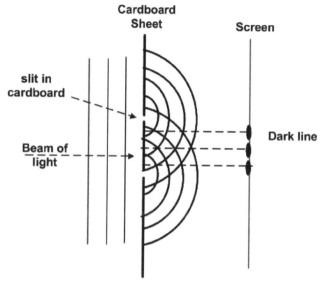

Figure 6-2 Young's Double Slit Experiment.

When a beam of light strikes two slits in the cardboard, Young reasoned that each slit would act as an origin point. If light is a wave, light would exit each slit in curved wave form. The waves from the two slits would overlap and interfere with each other resulting in light (reinforced waves) and dark (canceled waves) bands on the screen. This is exactly what he observed.

Young's crude apparatus was extended by forming hundreds of closely spaced lines on a glass plate; thereby creating a scientific instrument known as a "diffraction grating." These fine lines act as a "super prism" that can spread a beam of light much farther than a glass prism, revealing that light is not continuous as it appears in the spectrum produced by a glass prism, but actually consists of distinct lines.

Generation of an Atom's "finger print"

The property of light spreading by a diffraction grating is particularly useful in the study of gaseous discharges such as those generated in a Geissler tube. As mentioned in the previous section, placing a gas in an evacuated "electric discharge" tube and passing an electric current through it will cause the gas to glow. The glowing light can be studied with a diffraction grating.

For example, if hydrogen gas is placed in a discharge tube and the light from the glowing hydrogen gas is passed through a diffraction grating, this pattern shown in Figure 6-3, part of the hydrogen spectrum that falls in the visible spectrum, 400 nm to700 nm, will be obtained:

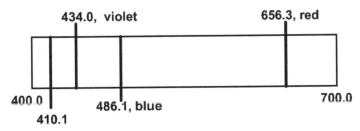

Figure 6-3 Hydrogen Spectrum superimposed on
Visible Spectrum, wavelength in nano-meters.

Since 1 nm = 10^{-9} meters, is a very small number; the wave length of visible light is very small. It should also be noted that spacing between spectral lines diminishes as the wavelength approaches the blue end of the spectrum; the significance of this will be explained below.

As explained in[342], the wavelengths of E/M energy span a much greater range than visible light as shown in this simple pictorial:

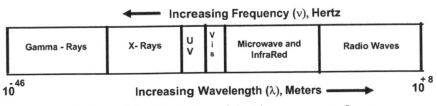

Figure 6-4 Simplified Depiction of the Electromagnetic Spectrum.

This figure demonstrates that increasing frequency, **v**, is opposite to increasing wavelength, **λ**. The relationship between the two can be written in terms of frequency or wavelength:

$$v = c/\lambda$$
$$\lambda = c/v$$

Where, **c** is the velocity of light or actually E/M radiation in general.

Balmer derives the formula for the Hydrogen Spectrum

Noting that the spectrum lines all tended become closer together at shorter wavelengths, **λ,** or increasing frequency **v**, it occurred to some that a formula of the form 1/ **v** might fit the spectral lines since, as **v** increases, 1/ **v** decreases.

A number of investigators attempted to apply this reasoning to the development of a formula for the patterns; however, it was not until 1885 that Johann Jakob Balmer succeeded, demonstrating that the spectrum of hydrogen could be expressed as a simple empirical formula of the form:

$$v = R^*(1/\, n_1{}^2 - 1/\, n_2{}^2)$$

where n_1 and n_2 are constants, **v** is the frequency and **R** is an experimental constant, employed to make values balance named after Johannes Rydberg (1854-1919,[343] who developed the most general series formula in 1896[344].

Please note, it's not important to understand this equation, just remember its form, as it will appear again.

Balmer achieved the best agreement with the experimental lines by allowing n_1 = 2 and letting [345] n_2 = 3,4,5,6,... The experimental value of **R** is:

$$R = 1.097373 \times 10^7$$

Keep this number in mind as well, you will see it again below.

Chapter 6 Summary

As with the E/M investigations, if we include the Greeks, thirteen investigators into the mystery of apparently "solid" matter labored over a period in excess of two thousand years trying to explain matter. By 1897, these efforts had yielded a collection of many facts:

- Democritus's belief in the existence of the atom had been confirmed by the discovery of elements.
- By nineteen hundred most of the elements had been identified.
- The physician Robert Boyle had shown that medieval alchemy's attempts to turn led into gold was impossible.
- Lavoisier had created modern chemistry.
- Dalton had established the "Law of Proportions" which accounted for the configuration of molecules, e.g., a water molecule is formed from two hydrogen atoms and one oxygen atom.
- Mendeleev had shown that elements with similar properties can be arranged in a "periodic" table.
- Thomas Young had demonstrated the phenomenon of light diffraction which led to the diffraction grating, a basic tool for examining atomic spectra.
- Experiments with gases in electrostatic discharge bottles and diffraction gratings had demonstrated the existence of unique patterns in the light emitted from the gas atoms – the atoms spectrum or "finger print."
- Balmer had succeeded in deriving a formula for the spectrum of the simplest atom – hydrogen.

But, as with the E&M investigations, no one knew how or why something like Dalton's Law occurred or how the spectral patterns were generated. And perhaps most importantly of all, no one realized that E&M phenomenon and "solid" matter were related.

Looking ahead:

In a series of ground breaking experiments, investigators finally discovered that E&M and "solid" matter are related.

CHAPTER 7

EMPIRICAL RESOLUTION OF THE "SOLID" EARTH ILLUSION BETWEEN 1897 AND 1911

The preceding two chapters have demonstrated that, by 1897, a large amount of empirical data pertaining to electricity, magnetism and the structure "solid" matter had been accumulated. However, these findings raised as many questions as they answered; moreover, no one realized that these investigative paths were related. The connection between the paths and some clarification of electricity was provided by three definitive experiments in 1897 by Sir J. J. Thompson (1856-1940), using a modified Crookes tube.

This chapter will explain the investigations of "solid" matter, including E&M phenomena between 1897 and 1911. This time period is chosen since most of the investigation between 1897 and 1911 were essentially empirical, which of course doesn't effectively answer the questions how and why.

Thompson's 1897 experiments demonstrated that E&M phenomena are a manifestation of matter

In his first experiment, Thompson examined the effect of a magnetic field on the apparently negatively charged cathode rays produced in Crookes tube.

To conduct this experiment, Thompson constructed a Crookes tube with two "detector" electrodes in the anode end. The two electrodes were in turn connected to an electrometer, an instrument that can measure small quantities of charge. When Thompson connected the voltages to the tube, the electrometer detected electric charge. However, when two magnets were placed against the tube to create a magnetic field, no electric charge was detected proving that cathode rays are deflected by a magnetic field[346].

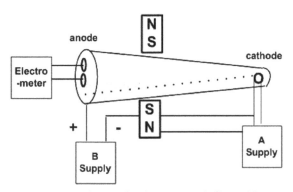

Figure 7-1 Demonstration that cathode rays are deflected by a magnetic field

For his second experiment, Thompson employed a Crookes tube with phosphorescent material on the anode end. When voltage was applied, the cathode rays struck the center of the anode end, but when an electric field was applied using two plates connected to a voltaic cell, the rays were deflected toward the positive plate, conclusively demonstrating that the cathode rays were negatively charged[347]:

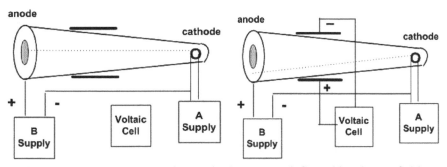

Figure 7-2 Demonstration that cathode rays are deflected by electric field.

In his last experiment, Thompson constructed a tube in which he could measure the ratio between the amount of electric charge carried by a cathode ray and the mass of the cathode ray[348]. This is a simple sketch of the apparatus:

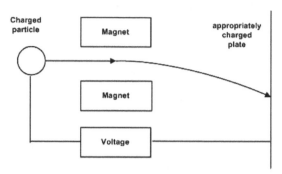

Figure 7-3 Measurement of charge-to-mass ratio of charged particle.

If the voltage and magnets are properly adjusted, deflection will be proportional to the ratio between the amount of charge and the mass of the charged particle, which allows the ratio to be measured.

After many careful measurements, Thompson concluded that the charge-to mass ratio was much greater than the charge-to-mass ratio of the hydrogen ion; therefore, either a cathode ray carries a charge much greater than the hydrogen ion or a cathode ray must be very much lighter.

Summarizing his work, Thompson was forced to invoke Sherlock's theorem and concluded that the cathode rays must not only be coming from the direction of the cathode, but they must be coming from the material of the cathode in the Crookes tube he was experimenting with. Moreover, the deflection experiments and charge-to- mass measurements convinced him that *the cathode rays were the electrons that had previously been predicted* by George Stoney[349]. Sir J. J. Thompson *had discovered the electron*!

Thompson's atom model

The discovery of the negative electron created quite a problem for Thompson. Normal matter is obviously electrically neutral, thus while Thompson couldn't see an atom, he had to conclude that the atom must contain sufficient positive charge to balance the negative electrons. Still believing that atoms are indivisible, Thompson was forced to invoke Sherlock's theorem and postulate a sort of a "raisin muffin" model of the atom, with negatively charged electrons interspersed in the positively charged mass of the atom.

It is important to note that Thompson did not know what this positive mass was, merely that it had to exist in order to balance the negative electron charge; hence, his concept of a raisin muffin in which the positive mass was a contiguous structure was reasonable at the time.

Although a modest advance, Thompson's model was the first revision to atomic structure in 2200 years!

Thompson's discovery explains electricity

The discovery of the electron explained some of electricity and magnetisms "mysteries", in particular that electricity and magnetism are not separate items, they are merely manifestations of effects produced by the electron. From above, these were the basic unanswered questions regarding E&M:

1. What is an electric charge?
2. How is static electricity and electric current produced?
3. What is magnetism?
4. How and why is its effects produced?

Thompson's electron discovery answers the first two questions. There is only one "type" of electric charge, the negative electron; Negative static electricity is produced by a surplus of electrons, while positive static electricity is produced by a deficit of electrons. Electric current is produced by a flow of negative electrons from a negative electrode to a positive electrode. But, Thompson could not answer how and why the effects are produced, this will be explained below.

Magnetism is produced by moving electrons, which explains magnetic effects caused by electric charge flowing through a wire. On the other hand, the existence of the electron could not fully answer the last two questions

Röntgen's Serendipitous discovery of X-rays:

Other persons were experimenting with electric currents in vacuum tubes besides Thompson. In 1895, German physicist Wilhelm Conrad Röntgen (1845-1923)[350], experimenting with various types of electric discharge tubes, performed some experiments with tubes in which the accelerating voltage was very high. Röntgen had intended to place a fluorescent material, barium platinocyanide, inside a tube to examine the effects of electrons on fluorescent material. In order to preclude anything emanating from the discharge tube from producing false data, he covered the tube with cardboard.

However, before he could perform the desired experiment, he observed that a piece cardboard, coated with the fluorescent material in preparation for his next experiment and located a few feet from the discharge tube, was fluorescing. After examining his apparatus, Röntgen was forced by Sherlock's theorem to conclude that something was emanating from the electric discharge tube that could pass through the glass and the cardboard and cause the external fluorescent coated cardboard to fluoresce. Not knowing what the mysterious radiation was, he initially termed them X-rays[351].

Röntgen expanded his experiments and determined that the X–rays would pass through most material except lead. The fluorescent coated cardboard allowed him the take "pictures" of items like his hand – the diagnostic benefits of X-rays had been launched[352].

The determination that X-rays are E/M radiation

The establishment of the proper explanation of X-rays, that they are very high frequency E/M radiation, required many years and a number of experiments. X-rays can ionize gases; hence, X-rays exhibit particle like behavior. This led one of the major X-ray investigators, Sir William Bragg (1862-1942)[353]. to suggest that X-rays are not E/M waves. This is a perfect example of drawing incorrect conclusions due to the lack of a key piece of information. As is discussed below, Einstein's explanation of the photoelectric effect demonstrated that E/M energy can also act as a particle. Perhaps because it was written in German, Bragg was not aware of it. The issue was settled in 1922 by Arthur Compton (1892-1962) who demonstrated the scattering of electrons by light which can only happen if light can behave as a particle[354].

Max von Laue's discovery of X-ray diffraction

German physicist Max von Laue (1879-1960), a, was the 1914 recipient of the Nobel Prize in Physics for his discovery of X-ray diffraction in crystals[355]. Von Laue's discovery has had far reaching consequences, as most of our knowledge about the structure of molecules, in particular the DNA molecule discussed in chapter 12, has been obtained via X- ray diffraction.

Von Laue was aided by a serendipitous chance encounter during Christmas recess walk with crystallographer Paul Peter Ewald, who was exploring the diffraction of light by crystals. Realizing that light waves were too long to have much effect, von Laue wondered if the shorter wavelengths of X-rays would be more effective and devised this apparatus (sketch is very general):

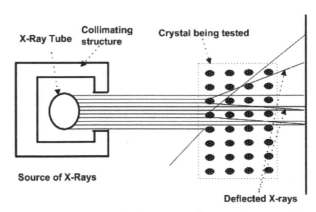

Figure 7-4 Pictorial of X-Ray Diffraction by crystals.

Since X-rays tend to go in all directions, some means of forcing them into a beam, or collimating them must be provided. The regular structure of the crystal acts like a diffraction grating and each atom in the crystal causes the X-rays to be deflected[356]. If the deflected X-rays are captured on a photographic plate, it is possible to "back-track" to find where the X-rays came from and thus deduce the shape of the crystal. Thus, Von Laue's hunch paid off and in 1912, von Laue had discovered X-ray diffraction[357]! X-ray diffraction soon became an indispensable tool for examining the atomic structure of crystals, especially molecules such as DNA, as will be explained in chapter 17.

Henri Becquerel's serendipitous discovery of radioactivy

In 1897, two years after Röntgen's serendipitous discovery of X-rays, Henri Becquerel (1858-1906)[358], discovered the spontaneous emission of "rays" by uranium, a phenomenon Becquerel termed radioactivity[359].

Becquerel's discovery was also serendipitous. To protect photographic plates prior to an experiment, Becquerel, unwittingly wrapped the plates with a paper containing uranium salts. Imagine his surprise, when, before he was able to perform the experiment, Becquerel found that the photographic plates had been fully exposed.

After examining all possible sources of exposure, Becquerel was forced to employ Sherlock's theorem and conclude that something in the uranium containing substance must have somehow exposed the plates. Besides demonstrating that the atom is probably the source of these "rays" and thus not "indivisible" as had been believed for thousands of years, the ability of the rays to penetrate matter suggested that there is indeed space between the atoms which had been believed by Democritus.

Further investigation by Becquerel and others demonstrated that three types of "rays", alpha, beta and gamma, were emitted by uranium as well as other heavy elements such as radium, polonium and thorium[360].

Becquerel, of course, had no idea what these particles and rays were, which is why he named them by the first three letters in the Greek alphabet. As we will see, the particles are associated with the decay of unstable nuclei, the central portion of an atom.

These three rays were identified by the effect upon their motion when they passed between electrically charged plates. The alpha particle is relatively heavy and attracted to a negatively charged plate. Hence, it carries a positive charge. The beta ray or actually beta particle, is relatively light and attracted to a positively charge plate; hence, it is negatively charged. On the other hand, the gamma ray is unaffected by electrically charged plates. Gamma "rays" were eventually determined to be very short wavelength, very high energy E/M radiation.

Rutherford's serendipitous discovery of the atomic nucleus

In 1911 Ernst Rutherford (1871-1937) an associate of Thompson, with the aid of Ernest Masden and Hans Geiger[361], made an exhaustive study of the effects of the particles emitted by radioactive matter; particularly, the effects of the relatively heavy, positively charged Alpha Particle[362]:

> In one of the more important experiments ever conducted, they formed gold into very thin layers of foil; hence, the experiment is sometimes called the "Gold Foil" experiment.

And set up the apparatus, shown in this Figure.

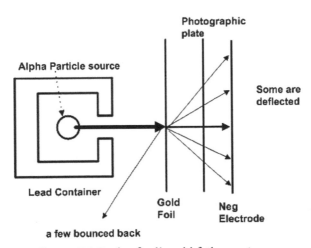

Figure 7-5 Rutherford's gold foil experiment.

This apparatus allowed them observe the interactions of the alpha particles with the gold foil and in particular, the angle into which a particle was deflected after passing through the foil[363].

When Rutherford developed the films, he confirmed that, as expected, most of the alpha particles had passed through the "solid" gold foil; however, he was astonished by the fact that the alpha particles formed a pattern on the photographic film as if some of the alpha particles were deflected by a very heavy object in the foil; moreover, a few bounced back. It was "as if the alpha particle had struck a bowling ball" wrote Rutherford later[364].

Rutherford developed a mathematical formula for the deflection or "scattering" of the alpha particles which related the angular deflection of the alpha particle to the energy of the alpha particle and the displacement of the alpha particle from a line joining the source of alpha particles and the center of the object deflecting the alpha particles.

When Rutherford substituted the observed deflection angles and the energy of the alpha particles into his formula, he obtained a remarkable result: the alpha particles were being deflected by a very small, massive, positively charged object. Thus, Rutherford had discovered that most of the matter in the gold foil was concentrated in small positively charge spheres. What appears to us as solid matter is mostly empty space! Rutherford had resolved *the apparently sold Earth illusion*- it's more like Swiss cheese!

Rutherford's deflection formula allowed him to deduce the approximate size of the central nucleus as .00000000001 inches in diameter (10 zeroes). To appreciate this small size, imagine a one inch circle drawn around an atom. If the diameter of the nucleus is expanded to one inch, the edge of the circle would expand to over fifteen thousand miles away[365]!

Rutherford's atom model, a modification of Thompson's model

Reflecting on his findings, Rutherford was led to conclude that the Thompson's atom model was only partially true. The atom did consist of equal amounts of positive charge and negative electrons, but the positive charge was not dispersed as in a muffin, but concentrated in the center. The concentrated charge in the center Rutherford termed the nucleus. Note that Rutherford, like Thompson, did not know what the positive charge was, merely, that it was concentrated at the center of the atom and thus had no reason to believe that it was not a single positively charged object.

Having established the atom as having a positive nucleus, surrounded by negative electrons, Rutherford was faced with the problem of what to do with the electrons. Lacking any other information, Rutherford borrowed the solar system as a model and postulated that the electrons traveled about the central nucleus in orbits, a postulate that was later shown to be only partly true.

Although not a completely correct picture of the atom, Rutherford's atom confirmed Democritus' hypothesis formulated ca 400 BCE, *2300 years before Rutherford!*

Chapter 7 Summary

- At the close of the nineteenth century, considerable empirical data relative to the atom had accumulated.
- In 1897, Sir J.J. Thompson discovered the electron and deduced that atoms were like raisin pudding: electrons mixed in with positive charges. The first new atomic concept in two thousand years.
- Thompson's discovery also resolves some of the E/M dilemmas:
  - o There is only one type of electric charge.
  - o Static electricity is created by adding or removing electrons.
  - o Electric current is caused by flowing electrons.
- Röntgen discovered X-rays and Bragg demonstrated that X-rays are high energy E/M waves.
- Von Laue discovered X-ray diffraction – the main tool for determining molecular configurations, like DNA.
- Becquerel discovered and identified three types of radioactivity:
  - o "heavy", positively charged alpha particles.
  - o lightweight, negative beta particles.
  - o High energy gamma rays.
- In 1911 Rutherford discovered the tiny, positively charged atomic nucleus and proposed a "solar system" atom, negative electrons revolving around a positive nucleus.
- While these were significant advances, the Rutherford-Thompson atom could not account for Dalton's law (how and why atoms form regular combinations), Mendeleev's table (why atoms have a periodic structure) or why the spectrum emitted by atoms consists

of distinct spectral lines; moreover, there was a gross problem with orbiting electrons.

- In the realm of classical of E/M behavior, an electron traveling in a circle is constantly accelerating; i.e. it is constantly changing its velocity with respect to a tangent to the circle. A classical, accelerating electron radiates and thus should lose energy by radiation and collapse into the nucleus. That it doesn't is obvious, thus the Rutherford-Thompson model was clearly incomplete. Moreover, many questions regarding electricity and magnetism remained, particularly, what is magnetism?

Looking Ahead:

the next two chapters present the final resolution of the "solid" Earth illusion. While these are obviously related, it will become clear that the final development of a proper explanation of the structure of matter actually proceeded in two distinct phases: the initial realization that the rules governing the atom are different than the rules governing the "real" world; and refinement of the "Quantum" concept into a complete picture.

CHAPTER 8

THE "VISIBLE WORLD" RULES DON'T APPLY TO THE MICROSCOPIC WORLD OF THE ATOM

By the early 1900s it was clear that "solid" matter was anything but solid. Rutherford and Thompson had shown that "solid" matter is mostly empty space, populated by atoms containing a tiny nucleus surrounded by electrons. But, the world of the atom is unlike anything we experience in everyday life; one of the reasons why development of a proper explanation of matter was so difficult to attain.

As mentioned above, the final resolution of the solid Earth illusion occurred in two stages. This chapter will address the recognition that the atomic world is governed by new laws, the laws of quantum mechanics.

Max Planck's Quantum leap - the first step towards a correct atomic model -:

The first step toward a true understanding of the microscopic world of the atom was a "quantum leap" taken by German mathematical physicist Max Planck (1858-1947)[366]. Planck, considered to be the founder of the quantum explanation of matter, and one of the most important physicists of the twentieth century, was born in the German city of Kiel, to Johann Julius Wilhelm Planck and his second wife, Emma Patzig. He was the sixth child in the family, though two of his siblings were from his father's first marriage.

Max Planck tackled one of the more perplexing problems of the day, the energy radiated from an object known as a black body[367]. A black body is an object which is a perfect source of radiation and can be closely approximated by employing a hollow ball heated to a desired temperature and having a small hole in it to allow radiation to escape. Of course, if the ball is heated hot enough it won't be "black", but that is the term used.

The problem Planck sought to solve was the creation of a formula the described the radiation from a black body, a task that had frustrated the leading scientists of the day. Planck achieved success because he was apparently among the first persons who suspected that the microscopic world of the atom is not governed by classical physics, i.e. the visible world in which we live. In the visible world, kinetic energy, the energy acquired by a moving object, changes continuously and smoothly as the velocity of the object changes; however, to account for the behavior of things in the microscopic world, Planck hypothesized that energy does not change continuously, but only in discrete amounts of energy termed a quantum.

Thus, in order to express energy of black body radiation, Planck stated the energy must be E/M in nature and must be quantized, i.e., it must exist is small packets of energy, **E,** given by the formula:

$$E = hv.$$

Where **h** is a constant, now known as Planck's constant, and **v** is the radiation frequency. Planck's quantum assumption led him to deduce a formula which fit the black body curve perfectly. Planck published is findings in 1900[368]. This was viewed as a monumental accomplishment, in recognition of which Planck, was awarded the Nobel Prize in Physics in 1918.

Albert Einstein "borrows" Planck's quantum concept and explains the photoelectric effect

If you shine light on certain metals, such as selenium, electrons will be emitted. This phenomenon is called the photoelectric effect and is the process responsible for the ubiquitous photo cell. The photoelectric effect was first observed in 1887 by Heinrich Hertz (1857–1894)[369]. The electrons emitted when light strikes a metal like selenium have certain observable properties:

- The *number* of electrons emitted by the metal depends on the *intensity* of the light beam applied on the metal; more intense the beam, higher the number of electrons emitted. This can be shown by measuring the current produced by a photo cell; however,
- No electron is emitted until the light has reached a *threshold frequency, no matter how intense the light is.*

These observations baffled physicists for many decades, since they cannot be explained if light is thought of only as a wave.

In 1905, Albert Einstein (1879-1955)[370], solved this problem, by asserting another paradox of the microscopic world. As mentioned above, light behaves as a wave. But sometimes light behaves like a particle.

If one assumes that light can sometimes behave as a particle, then, individual particles of light (or *photons*) could penetrate metal and dislodge electrons from atoms. Einstein postulated that the energy of the photon is the same as that deduced by Max Planck, **hv**[371], hence, unless the frequency **v** of the photon was high enough, the photon lacked sufficient energy to dislodge an electron.

In one stroke Einstein showed that light behaves as a stream of particles; hence there was solid evidence for the existence of quanta. His theory could satisfactorily explain all the known properties of the photoelectric effect, and was the first application of the new quantum theory. Einstein's work was entitled (in English) "On a heuristic viewpoint concerning the production and transformation of light[372]."

Einstein is, of course, a household name and is known by many for his theories of relativity; however, ironically, Einstein was awarded the Nobel Prize for developing the explanation for the photoelectric effect, rather than for his more far reaching contributions in relativity.

Depicting objects that cannot be seen

In the electricity and magnetism section, the problem of detecting items that cannot be "seen" was found to be central to the establishment of improved explanations for electricity and magnetism. This problem also encumbered investigations of solid matter. For example, the discoveries of Becquerel and the experiments Rutherford involved indirect observations of the phenomena they were studying. Becquerel never actually "saw" the alpha and beta particles being emitted by the radioactive matter; nor did Rutherford see the alpha particles he was experimenting with. Both observers merely detected the presence of the particles by the particles ability to expose a photographic plate and were able to determine that the particles were charged or uncharged by observing the deflection caused by an electrically charged plate.

The studies of the electron were also indirect – Thompson had to create special electrode detectors and screens in order to detect the presence or absence of cathode rays. Thus, our knowledge of the atom is based fundamentally on a "model" of the atom. Beginning with the Greek model, each improvement in knowledge has involved modifications to the model to align it more closely with observations.

An interesting analogy to the study of the atom was presented in one of my college courses. The professor suggested that determining the structure of the atom was akin to sitting on a hillside outside of an automobile factory and attempting to determine the process of automobile manufacturing by examining what entered and what came out of the factory. Of utmost importance is that knowing what actually happens inside the factory is irrelevant, as long as our model of the factory process accurately accounts for the relationship between what goes into the factory and what comes out.

The same is true of the atom. As long as the model we employ explains all the observations, the model must be deemed correct. Of course, as we have seen, the model is continually refined as more observations are made; however, and this is extremely important, the revised models do not completely displace the old model, merely refine it. Thus, the positive and negative charges of Thompson's model did not disappear when Rutherford proposed a modified model. they were merely rearranged. The next modification of the atom model was supplied by Niels Bohr who applied the developing field of Quantum Mechanics to the atom.

Niels Bohr develops first quantum atom model

In 1911, Danish scientist Niels Bohr (1885-1962)[373], borrowed Max Planck's pioneering quantum concepts and extended the Rutherford-Thompson model of the atom to a model which provided the first successful explanation of the myriad of observations associated with the atom such as Dalton's laws, Mendeleev's Table and the Hydrogen spectrum[374].

Bohr's model was based upon three ad-hoc postulates that apparently apply only in the microscopic world of the atom:

1. The electron moves in a circular orbit about the positively charged nucleus.
2. The energy of the electron, E_e is quantized, given by formula E_e = nh, i.e., it is equal to a multiple, n, of Planck's constant. This postulate implies that the electron cannot be at any arbitrary energy level, but is constrained to only discrete energy levels. The lowest energy is termed the ground level and is the normal level for the electrons in an atom.
3. Light is not emitted from an atom continuously. The frequency of the light emitted by an atom, **v**, is related to the difference between an initial high energy orbit of the electron with energy EH, and final low energy orbit with energy, EL, given by the formula:

$$\mathbf{hv \sim EH - EL}$$

Thus, when an atom is struck by a source of energy, for example a gas atom in a vacuum tube through which an electric current passes, the electrons are "excited" and move into higher energy orbits. When the electrons "fall back" to a lower energy level, light is emitted in quanta of energy.

Applying these postulates to the simplest atom, the hydrogen atom, which has one orbiting electron and one positive unit of charge in the nucleus, Bohr was able to deduce formula for the frequency of light emitted by hydrogen[375]:

$$\mathbf{v = R_*(1/\,n_1^{\,2} - 1/\,n_2^{\,2})}$$

Where:

$$R= 2pm^2e^4/h^2$$

Referring back to Balmer's empirically derived formula, it can be seen that Bohr's equation is the same, with one important difference, Bohr's equation contains the Rydberg constant R, in terms of basic physical properties, where **m** is the electron mass, **e** is the electron charge and **h** is Planck's constant are basic physical constants; and $\mathbf{n}_1$ and $\mathbf{n}_2$ are termed quantum numbers related to the quantized electron energy. Substituting values for **m, e** and **h**, we get

$$R = 1.097373X\backslash x10^7$$

Referring back to Balmer's formula, we see that Bohr's value of the Rydberg constant is the same as Balmer's. Once again, Bohr's equation illustrates the important difference between empirically deduced results and results derived from an understanding of fundamentals.

In a stroke of genius, Niels Bohr had explained why atomic spectra has the patterns it does[376]. One can only imagine Bohr's emotional state when realized that he had deduced the formula for the hydrogen spectrum and the Rydberg constant from an understanding of basic electron behavior (however, as will be seen below, Bohr's understanding was only partially correct).

Bohr's formula was a significant step toward a correct explanation, not only had he explained the origin of spectra, he was able to provide a reasonable explanation of Dalton's "laws" and Mendeleev's table.

Bohr Explains Dalton's law of proportions:

In Bohr's formula for the Hydrogen spectra, two numbers appear: $\mathbf{n}_1$ and $\mathbf{n}_2$. These numbers relate to the quantization of the position of electrons, i.e., electrons can only exist in certain orbits surrounding the nucleus and thus the electron energy is quantized, i.e., the energy can only exist in certain quantities. Finally, $\mathbf{n}_1$ is termed the "principal quantum number."

Bohr's formulation showed that electrons are constrained to "shells" depending upon the value of n_1; hence, the reason for designating n_1 as the principal quantum number. For $n_1 = 1$, the smallest shell, only two electrons are allowed, for $n_1 = 2$, the next largest shell, only 8 electrons are permitted. Thus, as we add electrons to the atom, the first electron yields the element hydrogen, while the second electron yields the element helium. Helium is an inert gas, which is explained by the fact that the electron shell of helium is filled – there can be no more electrons in the inner shell.

To add another electron, we must start with the second shell. Lithium is the element formed when we add the first electron to the second shell. If we continue adding electrons to fill the second shell, we form the elements shown in this table:

Num. of Electrons	Element	Num Extra Electron Spaces Available
1	Lithium	7
2	Beryllium	6
3	Boron	5
4	Carbon	4
5	Nitrogen	3
6	Oxygen	2
7	Fluorine	1
8	Neon	0

Table 8-1 Extract from the periodic table of the elements showing column relationship.

This table illustrates these important atom properties[377]:

- Neon has a filled shell, no room for extra electrons, and is inert as would be predicted.
- Lithium has one electron in the shell. The many unfilled shells imply great activity.
- Fluorine has one space available and is also very active as is observed.
- Oxygen has two spaces available which can be filled by hydrogen to make water.

Chemical compounds are formed when atoms share electrons in such a manner that their outermost shell is filled. The outermost electrons are termed valence electrons and the sharing of electrons establishes a force balance which holds compounds together.

From this table is easy to see that a compound should form between lithium, which has seven empty spaces and fluorine which has one, and lithium fluoride is well known. In like manner a compound should form between beryllium and oxygen, and boron and nitrogen. beryllium oxide and Boron nitride are well known compounds.

Noting that Hydrogen has one electron and one empty location, many compounds should be possible with hydrogen and these are observed, particularly with carbon. Of particular interest is water, which Dalton deduced was formed by two hydrogen atoms and one oxygen atom. Since oxygen has two empty spaces and hydrogen one, two hydrogen atoms fill the two empty oxygen spaces resulting in, H_2O.

Chapter 8 summary: The "visible world" rules don't apply to microscopic world of the atom:

- In 1900, Max Planck deduced that the rules governing the world of the atom are different and postulated that energy can only exist in discreet quantities. This postulate allowed Planck to solve a long-standing problem in Black Body radiation.
- In 1905, Einstein "borrowed" Planck's quantum concept and explained the photo-electric effect.
- Niels Bohr, in 1911, developed the first quantum atom model which explains Dalton's laws, Mendeleev's table and the hydrogen spectrum.
- In addition, Bohr solved the equations of motion for the hydrogen atom which resulted in Balmer's formula, that Balmer had established using measurements of spectral lines.
- Electrons in Bohr's quantum atom exist in layers of quantized energy shells that explained both Dalton's Law and Mendeleev's table.

Looking ahead:

as powerful and useful as Bohr's formulation is, there were still many problems such as the ad hoc assumptions, which while they appeared to "work", were later superseded by a better understanding of atomic fundamentals to be discussed in the next chapter.

CHAPTER 9

THE FINAL RESOLUTION OF THE "SOLID" EARTH ILLUSION

This chapter explains the extension of Bohr's model of the atom to a more appropriate model during the 1920s and 1930s, plus significant observations of atomic behavior by Davisson and Germer, Stern and Gerlach and the inspired explanatory efforts of De Broglie, Schrödinger and Heisenberg, among others, which extended the concepts pioneered by Bohr and completed the establishment of a proper explanation of the structure of matter.

Louis de Broglie's provocative prediction - electrons have a wavelike behavior

Prince Louis de Broglie: (1892-1987)[378] a member of the French aristocracy and a brilliant mathematical physicist. While working on his doctoral thesis in 1924, de Broglie had an astounding epiphany. While comparing the relationship between Einstein's treatment of the photoelectric effect in which Einstein had demonstrated that light can be both wave and a particle with Einstein's development of the special theory of relativity which produced the famous formula $E = mc^2$, deBroglie predicted that the electron, in addition particle behavior, should also have wavelike properties with a wavelength λ[379] of:

$$\lambda = h/mv$$

Where **h** is Planck's constant, **m** and **v** are the electron mass and velocity. De Broglie's insight replaced Bohr's ad-hoc quantized electron orbit assumption and explained why electrons are constrained to certain orbits; an electron orbit must be a multiple of the electron wavelength.

Apparently, this prediction was supposedly met with such derision that it threatened de Broglie's Doctoral Thesis. However, de Broglie was ultimately vindicated by electron experiments performed by Davisson and Germer.

Davisson-Germer (D-G) experiments confirms de Broglie's hypothesis: electrons do have wave properties

Working at the Bell Telephone Laboratories in 1927, Clinton Davisson (1881-1958) and Lester Germer (1896-1971)[380], aware of Bragg's demonstration that X-rays are reflected from a crystalline surface, reasoned that the wavelength of electrons, predicted by deBroglie, was relatively small; hence, if electrons do have wave like behavior, they would also be reflected from a crystalline surface. Accordingly, they prepared an experimental apparatus which allowed them to "fire" slow moving electrons at an angle to the surface of a nickel crystal. In the D-G experiment, electrons were indeed reflected at an angle which agreed with the X-ray diffraction pattern predicted by Bragg X-ray diffraction, if the wavelength predicted for electrons was substituted for the wavelength of x-rays[381].

The D-G experiment clearly confirmed that the electron as well as the photon can behave as either particles or waves depending upon the experimental conditions. *These results form one of the corner stones of modern quantum mechanics.*

Stern–Gerlach (S-G) experiment demonstrates that electrons spin[382].

To the rather bizarre electron behavior disclosed by the D-G experiments, Otto Stern (1888–1969)[383] and Walter Gerlach (1889-1979)[384], demonstrated that electrons also spin or rotate. If an electron rotates, then it is essentially a moving electrical charge, and a moving charge generates a magnetic field as discovered by Michael Faraday.

The S-G experiment involved the passage of electrons through a specially devised magnetic field that would deflect electrons if they had magnetic properties. The experiment was a success, the electrons were deflected as predicted[385].

The consequences of these results were far reaching. The apparatus employed by Stern and Gerlach was later used to demonstrate that some atomic nuclei, such as iron, also spin[386]; thereby, explaining the magnetic properties of iron containing minerals.

Werner Heisenberg (1901 – 1976) and Ernst Schrödinger (1887-1961) develop modern Quantum Mechanics:

In one of the most fundamental physics papers ever published, Heisenberg, in 1927, revealed additional bizarre atomic world behavior by demonstrating that it is not possible to accurately measure velocity and position simultaneously[387]. I.e., the more precisely one the measures the location of an electron, the less one can know about the electron's velocity. This seeming quandary is known as Heisenberg's uncertainty principle and has profound implications, particularly philosophical, regarding the ability to predict the future.

The year before, in 1926, noting that in the atomic world, electrons can behave like waves, Schrödinger further quantified the impossibility of simultaneously knowing the position and velocity of an object like the electron by developing a "wave" equation, another second order differential equation, to describe the behavior of electrons within the atom[388]. This equation, which has become to be known as Schrödinger's Equation, is one of the most basic equations of Quantum Mechanics. A solution to Schrödinger's equation for the hydrogen atom shows why all that can be known about an electron position is where it "probably" is.

Schrödinger's equation didn't "disprove" Bohr's equations

It is *important to note* that Schrödinger's equation *didn't prove* that Bohr's equation *was incorrect*; Schrödinger's equation *merely improved* upon Bohr's work and provided a more accurate picture of the atom. For many applications such as spectroscopy, the Bohr formulation is quite adequate. Thus, when we hear someone say "Why bother paying any attention to (a scientific idea) it will only be refuted in a few years" or, "Scientists are always changing their minds", what is usually occurring is that someone has most likely *generated an improvement that does not normally displace prior knowledge.*

Another consequence of Quantum Mechanics - "Quantum Mechanical Tunneling,"

Yet another bizarre consequence of the Quantum Mechanics probabilistic location property is the ability of a subatomic particle such as the electron or alpha particle to penetrate, or "tunnel" through a "electrical" barrier that is higher than would be possible for a classical sized "electrically charged" particle[389]. While tunneling is a complex phenomenon, it is observed in many electronic items and instruments such as the tunneling electron microscope and various integrated circuits[390]. As will be seen, quantum tunneling is also responsible for the ejection of an alpha particle from an atom.

Structure of the atomic nucleus, identifying the positive charge

Now that we have collected some explanations for the behavior of electrons in an atom, let us examine the structure of the nucleus since it is fundamental to an understanding many atomic phenomena, particularly radioactive decay and Nuclear fusion and fission.

Recall that Rutherford and Thompson had stated that maintenance of electrical neutrality required the electrons in an atom to be balanced by a positive charge, a charge that Rutherford's alpha particle scattering experiments had shown to be a tiny object in the center of the atom. When Rutherford discovered the existence of the nucleus, there was no reason to suspect that the positive nucleus was not a contiguous spherical entity.

World War I interrupted Rutherford's investigations. However, after the war, Rutherford and associates returned to alpha particle experiments. In an attempt to learn as much as possible about the atom, Rutherford apparently fired Alpha particles at everything he could find, examining the resultant effects.

In 1918, he observed that when nitrogen gas was bombarded by alpha particles, his scintillation counter detectors showed evidence of Hydrogen nuclei. After examining all possibilities, Rutherford was forced to apply Sherlock's theorem and conclude that the hydrogen nuclei source was the nitrogen gas. Thus, nitrogen gas must contain hydrogen nuclei. Since the hydrogen nucleus is the smallest possible nucleus, Rutherford concluded that the hydrogen nuclei must be an elementary particle, which Rutherford termed the Proton, from the Greek word for first[391]. David Parker suggests that Rutherford was transmuting Nitrogen into oxygen[392]. However, Rutherford's scintillation detectors probably could not have determined this, since they could only count ionized particles.

Having discovered the proton, Rutherford was led to the logical conclusion that, for an atom to remain neutral, the number of protons in the nucleus must equal the number of electrons[393]. For example, carbon, C, has six electrons which are balanced by six protons.

For convenience, the weight of a proton is given the value one, which then leads to the conclusion that the "atomic weight" of carbon would be 6; however, when measured, it is found to be twelve. Rutherford solved this dilemma by again applying Sherlock's theorem - hypothesizing that the nucleus must contain another, neutral, particle, one comprised of a proton and an electron. This particle would both preserve electrical neutrality and account for the weight of the atom. The neutral particle would have approximately the same weight as the proton since the weight of an electron is much less than a proton. Rutherford dubbed this particle the neutron. Protons and neutrons are termed collectively, nucleons.

Nothing is ever easy - giving the same weight to a proton as a neutron causes problems with detailed measurements. Hence, the Atomic Mass Unit (AMU) is the current standard weight for a nucleon. One AMU is one-twelfth the mass of carbon[394].

Sir James Chadwick discovers the neutron

Through a series of brilliant experiments, for which he was awarded the Nobel Prize in 1932, one of Rutherford's assistants, Sir James Chadwick (1891--1974) confirmed Rutherford's prescient prediction proving the existence of the neutron[395]. Although not quite correct, a neutron can be envisioned as a combined proton and electron; thus, the nucleus consists of two particles, protons and neutrons.

It should be noted that an unattached neutron is unstable and decays into a proton, an electron and a strange item called a neutrino with a "half-life" of approximately fourteen minutes. Recall the definition presented in chapter 1, half-life is defined as the time required for one-half of an collection of unstable particles to decay.

While the neutrino must be mentioned for completeness, it has no particular bearing on this discussion. Also, strictly speaking, the electron emitted during the decay of an unstable neutron is technically a beta particle as the decay of a neutron is termed Beta decay[396].

The Nucleus Spins – origin of natural magnetism:

In 1938, Employing beams of molecules passing through magnetic fields, Galician born Physicist Isidor Rabi (1898–1988)[397] extended the Stern-Gerlach experiment and demonstrated that nuclei with and odd number of either protons or neutrons have an intrinsic spin. The spinning positive nucleus is a moving charge that generates a magnetic field, the source of natural magnetism.

Rabi's experiments were extended by Swiss-American Physicists Felix Bloch (1905–1983)[398] and American Physicist Edward Purcell (1912–1997) with the discovery, in 1948, of nuclear magnetic resonance (NMR)[399] for which they received the Nobel Prize in 1952[400].

NMR is the phenomenon exploited in Magnetic Resonance Imaging (MRI). It is perhaps apocryphal, but the reason MRI is not NMRI, is the apparent concern that the word nuclear would alarm individuals and restrict use of the MRI technique.

Isotopes: the nucleus can have a varying number of neutrons

While the number of protons in a nucleus must equal the number of electrons, neutrons are not so constrained[401]. In the nuclei of the stable lighter elements, the number of neutrons equals the number of protons. For example, carbon has six protons and six neutrons. When an element is classified, the number of protons is termed the Atomic Number and is usually represented by the letter Z, while the weight of element, the combined weights of the protons and neutrons, is termed the Atomic Weight, usually represented by A. Thus, the symbol for an atom can be written:

$$^A\mathbf{X}_Z$$

For example, we would write $^{12}C_6$ for the carbon atom.

But, can we add as many neutrons as we desire, since neutrons are not affected by the positively charged protons? It turns out that the answer is a qualified yes. However, the number of neutrons is limited since the number of neutrons in a nucleus has a dramatic effect upon nuclear stability. For example, if a neutron is added to the hydrogen nucleus, the new structure is termed an isotope of hydrogen, Deuterium[402]. On the other hand, if two neutrons are added, the structure formed is an unstable the isotope of hydrogen, Tritium[403]. Tritium has a "half life" of about 12 years and decays into helium via beta decay. We will encounter other isotopes after a discussion of the "glue" that holds a nucleus together.

What holds the nucleons, especially the protons, in the nucleus?

As we have established above, like electrical charges repel, so the positively charged protons in a nucleus should repel each other. That they don't is obvious otherwise we wouldn't be here discussing the matter; accordingly, there must be another force that holds nucleons in the nucleus, and there is, the (aptly named) nuclear strong force. An exposition of the strong force, other than the elementary observation that the force must operate over relatively short distances, requires a discussion of the arcane subject of Quantum Chromodynamics, which is well beyond the scope of the book. For a beginning discussion see[404]; however, this simple diagram will suffice for this book. Note that the strength of the Strong and E/M forces are exhibited and two protons are held in the nucleus since the Strong Force dominates as protons get close enough.

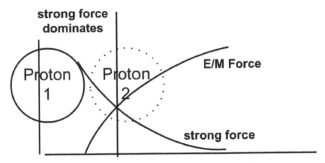

Figure 9-1 Illustration of Strong Force and E/M Force interaction.

To the left of the vertical line, the strong Force exceeds the E/M force and the protons are held in the nucleus. To the right of the line, protons are repelled as the E/M force exceeds the strong force. As will be seen below, another term for the relationship between the strong and E/M forces is the binding energy of the nucleus - the amount of energy required either to pull a nucleon from a nucleus or push one onto a nucleus.

In view of the fact that the E/M force acts further from a nucleon than the strong force, the question then arises; how is a nucleus with two or more protons formed in the first place? Before addressing that question, we must examine two basic nuclear processes.

Nuclear Fusion and Nuclear Fission

Nuclear Fusion and Nuclear Fission release more energy than any other energy source on earth and play a critical part in the story of matter.

Nuclear fusion, as the phrase implies, is the joining or fusing of two or more nuclei. Nuclear Fusion was first demonstrated by Sir Mark Oliphant (1901 – 2000)[405] in 1932 while working in the Cavendish Labs in Great Britain[406].

Nuclear fission on the other hand is the splitting of a nucleus into two "daughter nuclei" usually of approximately the same weight[407]. Fission was first demonstrated in 1934 by Enrico Fermi (1901-1954), when he bombarded uranium with neutrons. Since neutrons are "neutral" and not repelled by the positive charge of the nucleus, they can strike a nucleus. However full confirmation of uranium fission was not obtained until experiments in 1938 by German chemists Otto Hahn (1879 –1968) and

Fritz Strassmann (1902 –1980) demonstrated the detection of barium after bombardment of uranium with neutrons. Barium is about half the weight of uranium which was expected for a true splitting of uranium. Hahn's results were confirmed by Otto Frisch (1904 –1979) in 1939, Hahn received the Nobel Prize in Chemistry for his discovery[408].

Although complex in the details, the essential elements of Fusion and Fission are captured in this diagram which shows the energy that binds a nucleus together, termed, obviously, the binding energy, displayed for all the elements as a function number of nucleons in a nucleus, i.e., the AMU of the element[409].

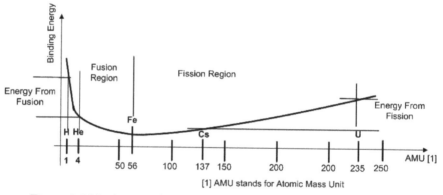

Figure 9-2 Nuclear Binding Energy and Fusion-Fission Relationships.

Beginning with the lightest element hydrogen (H), the Binding Energy per nucleon decreases until Iron (Fe), the most stable element, is reached; thereafter binding energy per nucleon increases. As noted in the diagram, the left side bounded by iron is termed the Fusion Region, while the other is termed the Fission Region. As described below, these two regions hold the key to the life and death of stars which are central to the formation of the earth and life on it.

In the Fusion Region, atoms with higher AMU are formed from the lighter elements by the fusion of their nuclei. Of particular interest: the helium (He) nucleus consists of two protons and two neutrons and is created by the fusion of four hydrogen atoms two of the hydrogen electrons join two of the protons to become neutrons; hence it has an atomic weight of four.

Due to the electrostatic proton repulsion, a great deal of force must be exerted to cause protons to penetrate the electrostatic repulsion barrier and reach the point where the strong force overcomes the electrostatic repulsion. In the Sun and other stars, the necessary enormous forces are created by gravity which is sufficient to cause the lighter elements like hydrogen to overcome the repulsive barrier and combine to form helium.

Since the Binding Energy per nucleon of helium is less than that of hydrogen. When hydrogen nuclei fuse to form helium, there is excess binding energy per nucleon – this excess energy is released as radiant energy. It is important to note the source of this energy is the conversion of mass into energy, as predicted by Einstein's famous equation e = mc2 illustrated by this table which compares the weight of four hydrogen atoms with the weight of one helium atom:

Element	Atomic weight, AMU
Hydrogen	1.07825
Helium	4.002602
4 times Hydrogen	4.3176
Difference, converted to energy	0.314998

Table 9-1 Illustration of energy generated by fusing hydrogen into helium.

The mass difference, 0.314998, converted to energy is the source of the sun's energy, although not unlimited, it is sufficient to last for about 5 billion years, far beyond the wildest imaginings of nineteenth century scientists.

On the other end of the binding energy curve, binding energy per nucleon increases; however, as the number of neutrons in a nucleus increases, the nucleus becomes increasingly unstable, until the heaviest elements, e.g., uranium, become inherently unstable and will fission via neutron bombardment, or will spontaneously expel a particle via nuclear decay. Since the binding energy per nucleon is less in the fission particles than fusion, less energy is released in fission.

Radioactivity is caused by Nuclear Decay

As explained in Chapter 1, it is now understood that the phenomenon Becquerel termed radioactivity, is actually the decay of an unstable nucleus in which one of the three objects, an alpha particle, a beta particle, or a gamma ray, is spontaneously emitted. Due to their importance in the controversy regarding radiometric dating, emphasized in web sites such as *Answers in Genesis*[410] or *The Radiometric Dating Deception*[411], a short discussion of the first two is in order.

Alpha Particle Emission is caused by tunneling:

In 1928, Russian mathematical physicist George Gamow (1904-1968), who emigrated to the U.S., deduced, from the principals of quantum mechanics, that nuclear decay is caused by the emission of an Alpha particle due to tunneling[412]. The alpha particle has been demonstrated to be the nucleus of a helium atom which consists of 2 protons and 2 neutrons, and is positively charged because it lacks the two electrons of the helium atom (which renders the helium atom neutral). Accordingly, when an Alpha particle is emitted, the nucleus loses 2 protons and 2 neutrons and becomes a new element. Gamow was able to explain the wide variation of half-life by differences in the element's electrostatic repulsion barrier heights that the alpha particle had to tunnel through.

Beta Particle Emission by Beta Decay

Nuclear decay via the emission of a beta particle is caused by the phenomenon of beta decay, introduced above. Beta decay is more complex than alpha particle emission, being first explained in relatively simple terms by Enrico Fermi in 1931[413] and later in more correct, albeit considerably more complex terms, the electro-weak force[414], by Abdus Salam (1926 -1996), Sheldon Glashow (1932-) and Steven Weinberg (1933-) in 1976, for which they received the Nobel Prize[415]. As mentioned above, for the purposes of this book, the beta particle can be considered an electron.

Gamow, Fermi, Salam, Glashow and Weinberg are some of the most brilliant physicists that have ever lived, each having won many awards including the Nobel Prize. The radioactive decay processes explained by these gentlemen have been studied and employed in radiometric dating under a wide variety of conditions. Claims by pseudo-scientists representing creationism that radiometric dating is unreliable is an insult to these Noble Prize winning scientists, and just not supported by the facts as will be seen in the ensuing chapters.

Illustrations of the effects of nuclear decay

Since, the material provided in this chapter is background for the ensuing chapters, some examples of the effects of alpha and beta particle decay is provided below for reference:

This table illustrates the changes to a nucleus when an Alpha particle is emitted beginning with p protons and n neutrons (recall: the AMU = number of protons plus neutrons)

Element	Protons	Neutrons	AMU
Original nucleus	p	n	p + n
Alpha particle	2	2	4
New nucleus	p - 2	n - 2	p + n - 4

Table 9-2 Effect of Alpha Particle decay on a nucleus.

The table shows the original nucleus, the constituents of the alpha particle and the new nucleus which results from the alpha particle emission.

A typical example of nuclear decay via alpha particle emission is the decay of uranium 238, $^{238}U_{92}$ into Thorium 234, $^{234}Th_{90}$ as exhibited in this table:

Element	Protons	Neutrons	AMU
Original nucleus	p	n	p + n
Alpha particle	2	2	4
New nucleus	p - 2	n - 2	p + n - 4

Table 9-3 Conversion of $^{238}U_{92}$ into $^{234}Th_{90}$ by alpha particle decay.

This table illustrates the changes to a nucleus when a beta particle is emitted:

Element	Protons	Neutrons	AMU
Original nucleus	p	n	p + n
Alpha particle	2	2	4
New nucleus	p - 2	n- 2	p + n - 4

Table 9-4 Effect of beta decay on a nucleus.

Since a beta particle is essentially an electron, in beta decay, a nucleus loses a neutron and gains a proton and a companion electron when a beta particle is emitted.

A typical example of beta decay is the decay of Thorium 234 into Protactinium 234:

Element	Protons	Neutrons	AMU
Original nucleus	p	n	p + n
Alpha particle	2	2	4
New nucleus	p - 2	n- 2	p + n - 4

Table 9-5 Conversion of $^{234}Th_{90}$ into $^{234}Pro_{91}$ by Beta decay.

Note that the atomic weight does not change, but the atomic number increases due to the addition of a proton.

Another important example of beta decay is the decay of carbon 14, $^{14}C_6$ to nitrogen 14, $^{14}N_7$:

Element	Protons	Neutrons	AMU
$^{14}C_6$	6	8	14
$^{14}N_7$	6+ 1 = 7	8 − 1 = 7	14

Table 9-6 Conversion of $^{14}C_6$ into $^{14}N_7$ by Beta decay.

Some typical nuclear half-lives

The half-lives of all of the elements that undergo either Alpha particle emission or beta particle emission have been exhaustively measured and verified many times as will be discussed in detail below. Here are a few of the more important half lives:

Element	Protons	Neutrons	AMU
$^{14}C_6$	6	8	14
$^{14}N_7$	6+ 1 = 7	8 – 1 = 7	14

Table 9-7 Some typical nuclear decay half-lives.

The Standard Model – The Finishing Touch

The last two chapters have resolved the solid earth illusion by revealing the basic atomic structure of matter, which is mostly empty space and consists of a nucleus surrounded by negatively charged electrons. The nucleus in turn consists of positively charge protons and neutral neutrons. Furthermore, the number of electrons equals the number of protons.

Electrons are held in their orbits by the electrostatic force, while protons and neutrons are held together by the strong force.

While this seems to satisfy the need to explain the solid earth illusion, there are a number of unanswered questions such as: "How do the electrostatic and strong forces exert their influences?" Questions like this and many others have led to an improved description of matter known as the Standard Model. Unfortunately, as with some other explanations in this book, an in-depth explanation of the Standard Model is rather involved and well beyond this book's scope; but I would be remiss in not providing enough material to understand why billions of dollars were invested in something called a Hadron accelerator in Switzerland and what was all the celebration about when the accelerator accomplished its objective by finding something called the Higgs Boson.

The Standard Model – the step in the resolution of the Solid Earth Illusion

The Standard model, developed in the last half of the twentieth century, provides the final step in the solid earth illusion resolution by demonstrating that electrons, protons and neutrons consist of even smaller -subatomic particles[416] of which there two kinds: elementary particles and composite particles. In addition, the Standard Model describes three interactions between particles: the electromagnetic, weak and strong nuclear interactions.

Fundamental to the Standard Model is the concept of a particle.

From the viewpoint of this text, one of the more important particles is the hadron[417] which is divided into two families: baryons and mesons. Protons and neutrons are baryons. Since protons and neutrons comprise most of the matter in the universe, they are obviously of interest.

Baryons are in turn made of bizarre elementary particles known quarks. Quarks were introduced independently by physicists Murray Gel-Mann (1929-)[418] and George Zweig (1937-)[419] to account for the outcome of some esoteric particle experiments, however, initially there was little evidence for their physical existence.

In addition to quarks, there is another entry in the "particle zoo" known as a lepton[420]. Leptons and quarks are the building blocks from which all matter is built. That is, they are seen as the "elementary" particles[421]

Gel-Mann supposedly purloined the term quark from James Joyce's classic tale *Finnegan's Wake*, in which the phrase "Three quarks for Muster Mark" appears[422].

Subsequent experiments demonstrating the existence of quarks were performed in particle accelerators such as the Large Hadron Collider (LHC) the world's largest and most powerful accelerator[423].

As implied above, one the inspirations for the LHC was the proposed existence of the Higgs boson by British Physicist Peter Higgs (1929-)[424] who proposed the Higgs boson as the particle that created a "field" which imparted mass to particles. Obviously, particles have mass, but "the central problem in particle physics[425]" was the source of mass. Since the Higgs boson had an extremely large mass, an immense accelerator was needed to cause it to appear.

The Higgs boson discovery was announced in July 2012 in the classic understated manner of science:

> On 4 July 2012, the ATLAS and CMS experiments at CERN's Large Hadron Collider announced they had each observed a new particle in the mass region around 126 GeV (billion electron volts). This particle is consistent with the Higgs boson predicted by the Standard Model[426].

[427]ATLAS is a convoluted acronym describing the LHC equipment (*A Toroidal LHC ApparatuS*) implying that the LHC has a donut or torroidal shape.

There is of course much more to the Standard Model and if you are interested, there is a fairly accessible introduction on this Wikipedia web site[428].

Chapter 9 summary: The "final" resolution of the "solid" earth illusion.

During the twentieth century, the fundamental explanations of matter were "finalized," and the solid earth illusion resolved, *a stunning accomplishment!*

- In 1918, Rutherford discovered the proton and proposed that nucleus consists of protons and another elementary particle, the neutron; thereby finalizing the basic explanation of atomic structure. The number of protons equals the number of electrons; while the number of neutrons is determined by number of neutral items need to satisfy atomic weight.
- In 1924, De Broglie predicted electron waves which explains why Bohr's electron orbits can only have certain radii, the orbit circumferences are multiples of an electrons wave length.
- In 1927, Davisson and Germer confirmed de Broglie's hypothesis.
- In 1922 Stern and Gerlach demonstrated that electrons spin which explains some magnetic effects.
- In 1928, Heisenberg and Schrödinger developed modern Quantum Mechanics which explains that the location of an electron is probabilistic and why the electron location cannot be known exactly.
- Quantum Mechanical tunneling is shown to be consequence of an electrons probabilistic location.
- In 1938, Rabi extended the Stern–Gerlach experiment to show that certain nuclei spin; thereby, explaining natural magnetism.
- Continued experiments disclosed that a nucleus can have differing numbers of neutrons, these nuclei are known as isotopes.
- The strong force, the force that holds the nucleus together is confirmed, explaining why protons are not ejected from the nucleus.

- In 1932 Oliphant demonstrated nuclear fusion.
- In 1934 Fermi demonstrated nuclear fission.
- Curve of binding energy was developed and explains that the fusion of four hydrogen atoms to create one helium with the release of an enormous amount of energy which explains how the sun's energy is generated.
- Nuclear decay by either alpha particle emission proved to be due to tunneling or beta particle emission, proved to be due the complex phenomenon of beta decay, explained radioactivity. This is on of the key methods for dating objects.
- The standard model, developed in late 1900s, explains matter in the *best detail to date*. E.g., The LHC finds the Higgs boson the source of mass. The word "finalized" is in quote as there may be more developments

Some salient points regarding the development of a correct explanation of matter: The development of a proper explanation of "solid" matter was achieved by many investigators, working in many locations over thousands of years. Their efforts resemble a group working on a giant puzzle with each investigator adding a piece as he found it:

- Many discoveries were serendipitous such as Becquerel's and Roentgen's discoveries of radioactivity and X-rays.
- There were many inspired conclusions, some invoking Sherlock's theorem, such as Thompson's and Rutherford's conclusions regarding the Atom's structure.
- There were many other inspired explanations which resemble Alexander's approach to the Gordian Knot[429] such as Planck's quantum hypothesis or Einstein's hypothesis that light can also be a particle.
- Some achievements were more important than others; however, all were necessary to achieve the explanatory goal.
- While there were blind alleys and mistakes, in general, the development of explanations proceeded in a rather continuous, logical flow.

- Surprisingly, relatively few people, mainly those with a college education, knew of these developments until public education became more wide spread.
- A principal problem encountered in the attempt to understand/ explain matter was the fact that the rules governing the world of the atom do not obey classical physics a new quantum physics had to be invented.

But! Where did the elements originate?? The Earth is approximately 5 billion years old, the universe formed 11 Gya – where did the elements come from? This question will be answered in chapter 19 when we examine the life cycle of the universe

Looking ahead:

To the resolution of the three "Astronomical" Illusions. Having solved the "solid" Earth illusion with the establishment of a correct explanation for the structure of matter, we next address three related, astronomical illusions, astronomical as they involve objects not on the earth and thus typically observed with astronomical instruments such as the telescope:

- The apparent motion of the Sun and Planets around the Earth illusion – determining the solar system's shape.
- Solving the apparent same Moon and Sun size and distance illusions – determining the solar system's size.
- The apparent close stars around Earth illusion determining the size of the universe.

The resolution of these three illusions will be explained in three chapters:

- Chapter 11 will address the resolution of the first illusion and will establish the correct explanation for the shape of the solar system.
- Chapter 12 will address the resolution of the second illusion and establish the correct explanation for the size of the solar system

which enables astronomers to measure distances to the stars which ultimately leads to the size and age of the Universe.

- Chapter 13 will address the resolution of the third illusion and will establish the correct explanation for the size and age of the universe plus the formation of the stars (includes the sun), the formation of planets (includes the Earth) and the creation of the elements (within certain stars).

At the conclusion of these three chapters, we will have located the correct place for the Earth, how it and the sun were created and have established the irrefutable fact that the Universe is 13.7 billion years old which makes a six-thousand-year-old Earth impossible.

CHAPTER 10

RESOLVING THE SUN, MOON AND STARS AROUND EARTH ILLUSION – THE CORRECT EARTH ORBITAL SHAPE

The three astronomical illusions

As discussed in the Introduction, the illusions associated with objects above the Earth's surface have been divided into three groups. This chapter addresses the Sun and planets, the essential elements of the Solar System.

Creating the illusion

- You are visiting Hawaii and currently standing on the porch of your west facing beachfront hotel. It is early evening and the sun is nearing the horizon, painting the low hanging clouds brilliant shades of red and orange, a faint hint of Hyacinth fills the air – another gorgeous sunset. As you gaze upon this scene, the sun slowly sinks toward the water and finally disappears from view. The sun appears so close, you almost expect to see steam.
- The night is warm, so you linger. Soon it becomes dark enough to see the first stars. If you are able to return to this location and watch the sun set each night and observe the stars after the sun has set, you may notice that as many as five "stars" appear to move relative to the rest of the stars. Also, some of these "stars" seem

much brighter than others, particularly, an extremely bright star that often appears in the western sky.

- If you are able to view the stars over enough nights, you will note that certain star patterns termed constellations (CON) appear to slowly move to the west as shown in Figure 10-1. In the summer, constellation, for example Orion, will be visible. In the Fall a different constellation will appear. If you are able to observe for a full year, you will note that in the summer, the constellation Orion returns.

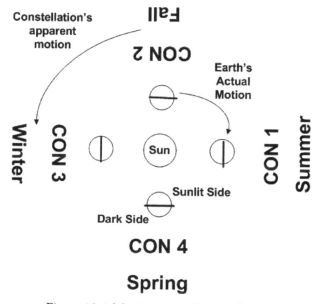

Figure 10-1 Moving constellation Illusion

But the apparent star motions are just two illusions: As you contemplate the gorgeous sunset, the deep purple of the night sky and the myriad stars, you find it difficult to remember that everything you have witnessed is one of the universe's grand illusions. The only thing that has been moving is your viewing platform - the Earth:

- The sun and planets around earth illusion is created by the earth's axial rotation.

- The "stars" that appear to move against the background of all the stars, are not stars, but planets, like the earth, that revolve around the sun.
- The apparent motion of the constellations is also an illusion caused by the earth's revolution about the sun – one of the better proofs of the sun centered solar system

However, not too many years ago, no one realized that what you have just witnessed are illusions, very powerful illusions. As mentioned previously, 2,500 years ago, some far sighted Greek philosophers were apparently the first to deduce that the sun around Earth is an illusion, but they were "outvoted" by those who couldn't abandon the illusion and the comforting belief that we are at the center of the universe.

One thousand years later, a far sighted Polish Monk "rediscovered" the fact that it is an illusion, but his discovery was suppressed by religious authorities and others. The truth finally emerged, but today there are still those who cling to the illusion as is easily demonstrated by entering the phrase "The Earth Does Not Move" into a search engine like Google where you will find many web pages devoted to this nonsensical idea[430].

Here are some astronomical observations that were available to early humans, which anyone can make today:

- The full moon rises at the same time the sun sets.
- The sun and moon occasionally change shape from full to a portion of full over a relatively short time - a phenomenon called an eclipse.
- The sun does not rise and set at the same point on the horizon every day. Careful observation shows that the rising and setting points of the sun cycle move north and south over the period of one year.
- Upon several occasions when the moon is new, the entire face of the moon is dimly lit, a phenomenon now termed "earth shine" – the reflection of the sunlit side of the earth onto the moon.
- Five of the "stars" which are more visible move in strange patterns. The Greeks termed these "stars" planets from the Greek word for

wanderer. Venus, the brightest planet never rises more than about 40 degrees from the horizon; hence, it never really "goes around the Earth." Neither does the less easily visible planet mercury. Other planets appear to move in the Earth's direction sometimes and sometimes opposite to the Earth's direction.

- Observation over considerable time shows that the planets occasionally appear at the same time as the moon and their appearance will always "move" along a line which comes close to the Moon.

- Examination over time of the constellations depicted in Figure 10-1 definitely reveals the apparent constellation motion and is one of the best ways to demonstrate that the earth revolves around the sun.

Earliest Observations/Explanations of the Sun and Planets around Earth Illusion

As with the solid Earth Illusion, as discussed in chapter 4, the Bible provides little insight into the astronomical illusions or observations listed above. Recall the hypothesis advanced earlier that the illusions were shown to have led the writers of Genesis to the creation story which mirrors the illusions.

Greek Philosophers Anaxagoras, Heraclides and Aristarchus solve the illusion

It began with the Greeks – again. Anaxagoras, Heraclides and Aristarchus, knowing about the above observations of the sun and planets and perhaps some others, realized the sun around Earth is an illusion, which they resolved by showing that the best explanation of these observations was a heliocentric solar system (Helios was the God of the sun) with the planets revolving about the sun, as opposed an Earth centered, or geocentric explanation. However, they were, unfortunately, too far ahead of their time.

Anaxagoras (500? –428 BCE)[431] was the first to make a real contribution to the resolution of this illusion. Born in Ionia ca. 500 BCE, Anaxagoras first explained that the moon shined by reflected light and gave the first correct explanations for eclipses: the earth, moon and sun are essentially in the same plane. As the moon revolves about the earth it is occasionally between the earth and sun causing a solar eclipse[432]. Also, the shape of the earth's shadow in lunar eclipses showed that the earth was spherical.

Heraclides of Pontus[433]," deduced" that Venus and Mercury revolve about the sun, probably because he observed that Venus and Mercury rise only a finite distance above the horizon, after which they sink back to the horizon. This motion is difficult to explain if one argues that the planets revolve about the earth. However, as we shall see, some ingenious solutions were created which actually allow Venus and Mercury to revolve about the Earth. Heraclides also adopted the view that the earth rotates on its axis every twenty-four hours.

But, Aristarchus of Samos[434] was the star of the show, and deduced that the best explanation for all the observations was a heliocentric solar system with all planets, including the earth, revolving in circles about the sun.

Aristarchus then realized if the Earth revolved about the sun, the Earth-sun distance must be greater than earth-moon distance since the moon revolved about the earth, and actually attempted to measure the earth-sun distance. This task is made more difficult than measuring distances on the earth, since the measurement of the distance to an object that cannot be reached, must be measured by a technique termed triangulation.

For example, to measure the width of a river, one might use this approach

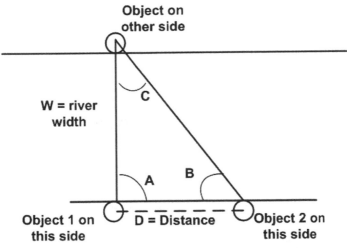

Figure 10-2 Distance measurement using triangulation.

We create a triangle by locating two objects, A and B on our side of the river and another on the other side. We arrange the objects so that a right triangle, angle A, is formed and then measure the distance, D, and angle B. We can then determine the width of the river by this trigonometric formula[435]:

$$W = D*TanB$$

Where **TanB** represents the tangent of angle **B** and is defined as the ratio **W/D**. Those who have studied some trigonometry may recognize this formula; however, if not, all that is necessary to know is this formula is accurate. In addition, tables of values of the tangent of an angle can easily be found on the Web. Aristarchus tried, with limited success, to employ triangulation to determine the earth-sun distance. First, he needed a baseline and chose the earth-moon distance as the baseline. He estimated the earth-moon distance by observing how earth's shadow moved across the moon during a lunar eclipse[436]. Next he tried to establish a triangle, similar that above, with the sun as the object across the river and the earth and moon as the objects on this side of the river. Unfortunately, Aristarchus had rather crude angle measuring equipment and since angle C is very small due to the great earth-sun distance, Aristarchus's estimate of nineteen times the earth-moon distance was highly inaccurate; the actual value is approximately four hundred.

Heliocentric view rejected

Ultimately proven correct, the three Greek Philosopher's heliocentric view conflicted with the geocentric view[437] supported by Greek mythology and eventually by the Christian religion. In addition, it was just too revolutionary to be accepted by Aristarchus' contemporaries and conflicted with the natural desire of humans to be at the center of things as well as the powerful Aristotle's concept that all objects fall to the center of the Earth, thus the heavy earth must occupy the lowest and central point in the cosmos.

Aristotle (384–322) BCE)[438] was one of the foremost Greek philosophers, a student of Plato and teacher of Alexander the Great[439]. He wrote on many subjects. However, as in the case of sun and stars around the earth Illusion, Aristotle often got it wrong. As the noted Philosopher Bertram Russell comments regarding Aristotle's influence[440]:

> Ever since the beginning of the seventeenth century, almost every serious intellectual advance, has had to begin with an attack on some Aristotelian doctrine in logic.

Aristotle also believed that the stars were attached to a spherical shell (also known as the celestial sphere[441] and similar to the dome mentioned in *Genesis*), the outermost or first heaven, which enclosed the universe. This shell revolves about the earth, carrying the stars with it. This view was reasonable due to the illusion that the stars are relatively close and appear to be the same distance away.

Inside this heavenly shell, the five visible planets, sun and moon moved in their orbits around the central earth. The movements of planets were not as simple to explain as the stars, especially Venus and Mercury as mentioned above. However, the clever Aristotle is reported to have used the computations of an older astronomer, Eudoxus of Cnidos (ca. 390– ca. 337 BCE), to fabricate an elaborate scheme of fifty-five major and minor orbits known as epicycles and cycles to explain the planetary motions[442].

Ptolemy casts geocentric view in concrete:

Besides Aristotle, the ancient astronomer who exerted the greatest ultimate influence on western beliefs about the solar system was Claudius Ptolemy (83-161)[443]. Ptolemy conducted his observations in Alexandria Egypt about 150 CE, and published his findings and explanations of the universe in a thirteen-volume treatise he entitled Mathematical Composition[444].

Ptolemy adopted the views of Aristotle, also rejecting the idea that the earth moves. He pointed out that the earth is round and that gravity is directed toward the center of the earth. He placed the motionless earth at the center of the universe, around which the sun, moon and stars revolved at various speeds. Ptolemy believed that the stars were brilliant spots of light in a concave hemisphere that arched over everything. Ptolemy traced the motion of the planets against the "fixed stars," and expanded Aristotle's epicycles and cycles to further improve this method of explaining the motion of the planets.

Ptolemy's work, which eventually became known as the Almagest (Greek-Arabic for "The Greatest"), was the revered and accepted view of the universe for twelve centuries[445]. Furthermore, it became incorporated into the doctrine of the Catholic Church giving it religious authority.

Regarding religious authority, Bertram Russell suggests that Aristotle's authority was equally as great[446]:

> ...and after his death it was two thousand years before the world produced any philosopher who could be regarded as approximately his equal. Towards the end of this long period his authority had become almost as unquestioned as that of the Church.

Empirical Development of a proper explanation of The Sun and Stars around Earth Illusion, Copernicus resurrects Aristarchus:

As mentioned previously, the Polish monk Nicolas Copernicus was the first person in two thousand years who dared question the geocentric view by perhaps reviving the heliocentric view proposed by Aristarchus et al in ancient Greece.

It is not clear if Copernicus was aware of Aristarchus, some such as Russell argue not; however, it seems reasonable to suggest, that since the monks preserved much of Greek and Roman culture, and Copernicus, being a monk, may have been aware of Aristarchus. However, whether Copernicus was aware is of no import. Important findings are sometimes lost and rediscovered as will be discussed in chapter twelve regarding the case of Gregor Mendel.

For completeness, a brief review of Copernicus's great treatise, *"De Revolutionibus Orbium Coelestium"* as introduced in the Preface will be provided.

Copernicus's treatise was dedicated to Pope Paul III and is organized in five parts[447]:

- The first part contains a general vision of the heliocentric theory, and a summarized exposition of his idea on the World.

- The second part is mainly theoretical and describes the principles of spherical astronomy and a list of stars (as a basis for the arguments developed in the subsequent books).
- The third part is mainly dedicated to the apparent movements of the sun and to related phenomena.
- The fourth part contains a similar description of the Moon and its orbital movements.
- The fifth and the sixth parts contain the concrete exposition of the new system.

It is important to note, that, although the Copernican explanation was perhaps no more accurate than the Ptolemaic, the Copernican view had one significant advantage; it was much less complex. Instead of the cycles and epicycles required by Ptolemy, Copernicus could explain the visible phenomenon by simply having planets go around the sun. As will become apparent, reduction in explanation complexity is often a significant aspect of improved explanations.

Copernicus also realized that the planets moved in the same plane and in the same direction around the sun. However, why they do was not determined until the formation of stars and planets became understood, as explained in Chapter thirteen.

Development of the telescope, one o the first steps toward the beginning of Science-determining the true shape of the solar system:

As mentioned earlier, the almost simultaneous discoveries of the telescope and microscope in the early 1600s, made possible by the discovery of glass and the glass lens[448], greatly extending the human eye's observation ability is logically the starting point for the development of modern science often called the Scientific Revolution[449].

Although not certain, invention of the telescope is generally credited to Dutch eyeglass maker Hans Lippershey (1570 –1619) [450]. In 1608, Lippershey tried to lay claim on a device with three-times magnification. Lippershey exhibited his telescope in October 1608, in the Netherlands, the country that produced the first useful microscope.

Galileo makes the telescope famous[451]. As mentioned previously,

Galileo, using his improved telescope, "rubbed salt into the wounds" inflicted by Copernicus's heliocentric concept, when he discovered something that was not mentioned by the "revealed truth" of *Genesis*, the four moons of Jupiter. Revealed truth held that celestial objects were perfect and the four moons of Jupiter upset this celestial perfection. Galileo published his findings in *Sidereus Nuncius* in March 1610[452].

Reaction of the Church:

As introduced in the Preface, Copernicus's and Galileo's findings profoundly upset what had been the accepted dogma for thousands of years. But, the genie was out of the bottle and more liberal countries such as Protestant Denmark supported continued astronomical investigation.

Tycho Brahe's observatory, finally some accurate astronomical observations

While Copernicus had to labor with the relatively poor astronomical observation equipment available to him - his eyes, Tyge Ottesen Brahe (Latinized to Tycho Brahe) (1546 – 1601[453], born in what is now modern-day Sweden, was granted an estate on the Danish island of Haven by Protestant King Fredrick II of Denmark, no friend of the Catholic church. King Frederick also provided Brahe funding to build an astronomical/astrological observatory (Uraniborg in Swedish), which he equipped with large astronomical instruments and became famous for making accurate astronomical observations, especially of the planets. In keeping with the transitional nature of the times, Brahe was also well known as an astrologer and alchemist.

From 1576 when the observatory was constructed, until the death of his patron in 1586, Brahe and his assistants amassed a vast amount of planetary position data, far more accurate than any previously recorded.

Brahe, however, was not able to use the observations to provide an improved explanation of planetary motion. It remained for Brahe's most brilliant assistant, Johannes Kepler, to analyze the data and extract the mathematical formulas which accurately describe planetary motion.

Kepler determines correct shape of planetary orbits

Johannes Kepler (1571-1630)[454] born at Wurtemberg in 1571 studied astrology, mathematics and astronomy. He became obsessed with the idea of finding the mathematical harmonies in the mind of the Creator, and the data collected by Tycho Brahe was ideal for this endeavor since the planetary orbits must surely demonstrate these harmonies. Kepler struggled with the mass of data Tycho Brahe had so laboriously collected for a number of years but his interest in astrology and other mysticisms prevented him from fitting the correctly shaped figure to the data as he was trying to fit Brahe's data to the celestially perfect circle[455].

Finally, after nearly twenty years of frustration, he had to abandon this quest and bowing to Sherlock's theorem, Kepler accepted the inescapable conclusion that the equation of a planetary orbit is not a circle, but an ellipse. An ellipse is a "flattened" circle with one "radius" longer than the other as shown in this sketch:

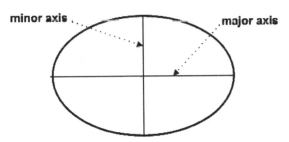

Figure 10-3 Sketch of an Ellipse.

whereas, the radii of a circle are all the same length. Kepler's struggle was compounded by the fact that the deviation of a planetary orbit from a circle is rather small. The deviation of an ellipse from a circle is termed the "eccentricity" of an ellipse. The eccentricity of the earth's orbit is only 0.0167[456]; hence, Kepler's desire to fit the planetary equation to a circle is understandable.

Kepler set forth his three "laws" of planetary motion in "*De Harmoice Mundi*", which was published in 1619. The first "law" is the most important[457]: "The orbit of a planet is elliptical, and the sun, the source of the motion, is in one of the foci."

Kepler's explanation of the planetary orbits completed the second phase of the determination of the shape of the solar system; the orbits of all the planets are ellipses.

It is important to note that, due to his religious leanings, Kepler incorporated religious arguments and reasoning into his work, motivated by the conviction that God had created the world according to an intelligible plan that is accessible through the natural light of reason[458].

Newton develops the proper explanation for planetary motion from Fundamental Principles:

A few years after Kepler published his classic analysis of planetary orbits, solar system investigations moved on to next phase with the amazing contributions of Sir Isaac Newton (1642 – 1727)[459], the derivation of planetary motion from fundamental principles.

Newton was born at Woolsthorpe, Lincolnshire, and entered Cambridge University in 1661 at age nineteen. His amazing intellect surfaced early since his progress at Cambridge was rapid, being elected a Fellow of Trinity College in 1667 and Lucasian Professor of Mathematics in 1669, just eight years after entering Cambridge.

Newton's most productive years were 1665-1666, which he spent largely in Lincolnshire because of plague in Cambridge[460].

Newton's interest in the problem of planetary motion was aroused by correspondence with British scientist Robert Hooke introduced in chapter 1, who played an important role in the scientific revolution, making contributions in many areas[461], through both experimental and theoretical work. Hooke's experiments led him to deduce that gravity obeys an inverse square law which Newton expanded upon during his eighteen months in Lincolnshire. Newton combined two fundamental concepts related to planetary motion to calculate the equation of a planetary orbit from basic principles.

First, he finalized Hooke's experimental deductions into a formula for gravitational attraction between two bodies such as the earth and the sun as:

The gravitational force, **Fg** between two bodies is proportional to the product of the two bodies masses and inversely proportional to the square of the distance separating them[462],

Which can be written as:

$$Fg = M1*M2/r^2,$$

Where **M1** and **M2** are the two masses and **r** is the separation distance.

Second, Newton completed Galileo's investigation of accelerating bodies. Galileo, used the clever approach of rolling cannon balls down an inclined plane so that they accelerated slowly; thereby, enabling him to time the canon ball motion using his pulse as crude, but effective timing device, which revealed that acceleration was caused by a force acting upon an object. In the case of the cannon balls, it was the force of gravity. Prior to Galileo's discovery, it was (incorrectly) thought that velocity was related directly to force.

Building on Galileo's observations, Newton deduced the formula, introduced in chapter 1, for the motion of an object subject to a force:

> ...a force **F** acting on a body of mass **m**, produces an acceleration **a** proportional to the force and inversely proportional to the mass[463],

Which can be written as:

$$a = F/m$$

Newton combined the formulae for gravitational force with his formula for the motion of an object to create an equation for a planet orbiting the sun. Unfortunately, the equation is a second order differential equation, probably the first one ever devised.

This led Newton to his third and perhaps most important contribution, the invention of the calculus, which he used to solve the differential equation[464].

Of particular importance, Newton's solution of his equation was *identical to Kepler's*! Newton had arrived at the formula, upon which Kepler labored almost twenty years, in a matter of weeks and, more importantly, from fundamentals. Newton understood that the inverse square law of gravitational force acting on the planets was why the planetary orbits are elliptical.

It should be noted that the relationship between Kepler's empirical result and Newton's mathematically derived result is similar to Balmer's empirical formula for the hydrogen spectrum and Bohr's mathematically derived spectrum. In both cases *the mathematical solution* provided greater information because it *answered the basic question*: why?

Newton's accomplishment ranks as one of the turning points in astronomy and science in general. One report of his success states that

> …he determined it to be an ellipse, so informing Edmond Halley in August 1684. Halley's interest led Newton to demonstrate the relationship afresh, to compose a brief tract on mechanics, and finally to write the Principia…[465]

The full name of the Principia is *Mathematical Principles of Natural Philosophy*[466]), was published in 1687 and became revered as one of greatest written scientific documents. (I presume Newton also informed Hooke of his findings).

la Place puts the icing on the "Newtonian" cake

A successor to Newton, the celebrated French mathematician and astronomer Pierre-Simon Marquis de la Place (1749-1827)[467], was central to the development of mathematical explanation of astronomy. La Place extended Newton's work and published a three-volume treatise *"Celestial Mechanics"* which placed celestial mechanics on a firm footing[468].

Emperor Napoleon III, ruler of France at the time had heard about la Place's treatise and that it contained no mention of the creator. When la Place implored Napoleon to accept a copy of his work, Napoleon is reported to have teasingly asked[469]:

> M. Laplace, ils me dit que vous avez écrit une grand livre sur le systeme du univers, sans mention du Creator ["M.

Laplace, they tell me you have written this large book on the system of the universe, and have never even mentioned its Creator."]

La Place, always sure of himself, answered bluntly: "Je n'avais pas besoin de cette hypothèse-là. [I did not have need for that hypothesis]"

I have read that some believe the religion- science conflict began with this exchange. Sources for this exchange make no mention of this and there are many origin places for the religion- science conflict, in particular, the reaction to Copernicus, which I believe is the true beginning of the conflict, as Copernicus had the "unmitigated gall" to displace man from his cherished position at the center of the universe.

Einstein demonstrates that "it's all relative"

Albert Einstein one of the world's most famous scientists, early in the twentieth century, published two extraordinary papers introducing the concepts of Special and General Relativity. While relativity is a complex subject, a little knowledge of the basic ideas is essential to the understanding of the earth and the universe. Einstein's fundamental paper on special relativity was published in 1905[470], while the equally fundamental paper on general relativity was published in 1917[471].

The term "relative" in Special Relativity, refers to two observers riding on two separate platforms that are moving at constant velocity relative to each other. Einstein, refined and extended previous efforts (no one does it alone) to develop equations that showed what a observer on one platform would see on the other platform. Central to Einstein's' formulation is the fact that light has a constant velocity, independent of the motion of an observer (see chapter 12 for a discussion of the discovery that light has a finite velocity) hence there would be a time-lag in receiving information from the moving platform, especially if the platform was moving at a velocity close to that of light (relativity really only applies in cases like this).

In order to accommodate the time delay, Einstein showed that a proper description of the physical universe required the inclusion of time as a fourth dimension to properly locate an object. Einstein termed this "space-time," see also Stephen Hawking's celebrated book, *"A Brief History of Time*[472]*."*

The Special Theory of Relativity:

One of the most significant results of special relativity was the demonstration that mass and energy are equivalent and interchangeable as embodied in an equation everyone knows:

$$E = m_0 c2$$

Where m_0 represents the mass of an object at rest, i.e., not moving, and **c** is the speed of light.

This equation is normally written without the qualification of mass at rest. However, the energy of a moving object increases with increasing velocity, since the effective mass increases with increasing velocity, becoming infinite when the velocity reaches **c** as disclosed by this equation:

$$m_{meas} = \sqrt{1 - \frac{v^2}{c^2}}^{m_0}$$

where **v** is the velocity of the mass object m_0. Clearly when **v = c** the denominator becomes 1 - 1 which is zero and 1/0 approaches infinity. This increase in mass as velocity approaches the speed of light, renders such phrases as "Ahead warp fact 4 (speed = 4 x c) Scotty," famously intoned by Captain Kirk, impossible and has been amply demonstrated in particle accelerators where large increases in energy are required to gain relatively small increases in velocity as the velocity approaches that of light.

A material object cannot exceed the speed of light. However, even if it were possible to exceed the speed of light, at "Warp factor 10 (10 times light speed)" travel to the nearest star would require about 1 month, a bit longer than depicted in one of my favorite TV space operas.

The special theory makes many predictions that are counter to common sense such as the slowing of time or the shrinking of objects traveling near the speed of light and was initially rejected by many; however, all legitimate attempts to disprove the theory have failed.

The General Theory of Relativity:

The general theory addresses accelerating objects. As shown above, Sir Isaac Newton deduced an equation which established the relationship between the motion of an object when acted upon by a force, i.e., the object accelerates. Einstein extended Newton's formulation to show that there is no experiment that can be performed that would distinguish between a person in a closed box on the earth and a person in a closed box being accelerated with a force equal to that of gravity.

Einstein derived a set of complex equations which showed that gravity is a consequence of the curvature of 'spacetime' especially observable if one is near a massive body such as the sun. In the presence of the sun, spacetime is curved like net with a basketball in the center. Just as a small ball would be drawn to the basketball, the earth would be drawn to the sun except for the centrifugal outward force created by the earth's motion.

Illustrating the source of our gravity.

Einstein's general theory solved a problem that must have bothered Newton, Laplace and others since neither Newton nor Laplace could explain what gravity was and the fact that it acted at a distance was particularly troublesome.

Einstein's general theory solved a couple of apparently minor issues, e.g. a slight difference in the orbital period of Mercury when Kepler's "Laws" are applied; moreover, no experiment to date has disproved the theory.

The crowning achievement of the general theory has been in the field of cosmology, the field which investigates the universe and will be discussed in Chapter 18.

But "Houston" there is a problem!!

Most of the Universe is missing! The motion of the stars and galaxies allow astronomers to weigh it [the universe], and when they do, they see a major discrepancy in cosmological accounting. For every gram of ordinary matter that emits and absorbs light, the Universe contains around five grams of matter that responds to gravity, but is invisible to light. Physicists call this stuff dark matter, and as the search to identify it is now in its fourth decade, things are starting to get a little desperate[473].

Clearly, the issue of dark matter is rather complex. Some very bright individuals have been chasing this problem for many years and I introduce the subject for completeness – you may read about it and the *Nature* article referenced supplies considerable information.

Chapter 10 Summary: Resolving the Sun, Moon around Earth Illusion, and the correct Earth orbital shape.

Many observations that did not agree with sun around the earth concept, led early Greeks, especially Aristarchus, to deduce the truth; a heliocentric (sun centered) solar system in which the earth and planets revolve around the sun. However, this view was in conflict with the more established geocentric or sun around earth view, championed by such philosophical giants as Aristotle, so it was abandoned.

- Aristotle, and later Ptolemy, solved the varying planetary motion problem with a series of ad hoc orbits that properly predicted the planet motion, even Venus and Mercury, to within the measurement accuracy available. This explanation remained unchallenged for almost 1,500 years.
- In 1543, Polish Monk Nicolas Copernicus reopened the issue with new observations and calculations and reproposed the heliocentric explanation.
- In 1608, Galileo perfected the telescope such that he found the four largest moons of Jupiter causing another outburst from the Church.
- Despite determined opposition by the Church, the Copernican explanation eventually prevailed.
- Danish King Fredrick II facilitated the construction of a large observatory where Tycho Brahe labored for twenty years, observing planetary motion.

- His associate Kepler, spent the next twenty years laboriously analyzing Tycho's measurements, finally and reluctantly, deducing that planets revolve about the sun in elliptical orbits.

- Between 1635 and 1636, Sir Isaac Newton deduced the equation for gravitational attraction, finished Galileo's work on accelerating bodies and deduced the equation that describes an object moving under the influence of a force. Newton combined these equations into the world's first differential equation, the equation for the motion of a planet revolving around the sun, invented the calculus to solve it and arrived at Kepler's empirically derived equation.

- Albert Einstein extended Newton's work by postulating that the proper frame of reference of motion in the presence of a large mass is four dimensions. From this, Einstein developed the Special Theory of Relativity whose equations also yielded elliptical orbits, but were more accurate, as they resolved some small discrepancies in the orbit of Mercury due its closeness to the Sun.

- Einstein's General Theory explained the phenomenon of gravity.

A footnote regarding the religious controversy originally engendered by Copernicus and Galileo. It is interesting to note that Pope John Paul finally pardoned Galileo, hundreds of years after Galileo's heresy[474].

Looking ahead:

Having solved the sun around earth illusion by establishing the proper explanation of the basic structure of the solar system, we next address the size of the solar system as this is a critical stepping stone to the size of the universe, which will also reveal the age of the universe and by implication, the age of the Earth.

CHAPTER 11

RESOLVING THE APPARENT SUN AND MOON CLOSENESS - THE CORRECT EARTH ORBIT SIZE

Creating the Illusion

Size and distance illusions are created by the manner in which we estimate distances with the unaided eye. Our eyes can only present a truly three dimensional image for objects within about twenty feet. Beyond that, we determine distance by comparing the perceived size of a familiar object. Given two automobiles, one will appear to be more distant if it appears to be smaller. As shown in this figure of two same size objects, possibly automobiles, the further object appears smaller, since the "subtended angle," the angle the object makes with the eye, is smaller thus creating the illusion that the further object is smaller and thus more distant.

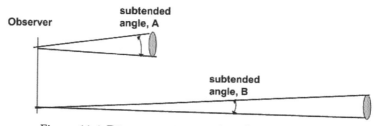

Figure 11-1 Distance estimation by relative object size.

Of critical importance is our ability to recognize the two objects. If we have confidence that the two objects are the same, such as cars, horses, etc, then we can conclude that B is further away than A. Our ability to determine distance fails when we try to judge distance to unfamiliar objects such as the box and oval shown in this example:

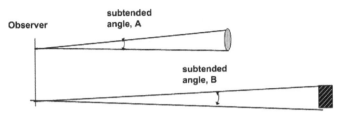

Figure 11-2 Incorrect Distance estimation due to similar subtended angles.

The box is larger than the oval and further away, however, it subtends the same angle; therefore, it will appear to be the same distance from the observer. Illusionists often use this device.

A distance-size problem occurs when we lose relationships between objects. An interesting example of this problem occurs under foggy conditions, objects that are close and small appear large as we perceive them to be farther away.

If we consider an estimate of the size and distance to the moon and sun, we cannot really judge size and distance because we have no size representative to judge distances by. For example, the sun and moon appear to be the same size, due to the fact that they subtend the same angle as shown in the box-oval illusion above.

Shape is not necessarily related to size:

It is important to note that knowing the shape of an object provides no particular information regarding its size, just as knowing the size of an object may not convey any information regarding its distance from the observer as discussed above. This is particularly true of the solar system. Hence, we must examine both the size and distance of the various visual objects in the solar system, i.e., the planets and the sun, to gain a complete picture of the solar system.

Measuring distance to the planets and sun:

As discussed in the previous chapter, the first person to attempt a measurement of the Earth-sun distance was Aristarchus who attempted to use triangulation. However, due to the limited mathematical knowledge available to Aristarchus (decimals had not even been invented) he was unable to make more than a crude distance estimate.

The first practical measurements of distances to objects beyond the Earth also employed triangulation, but of a different type. The basic technique, involves not the right triangle employed by Aristarchus, but an isosceles triangle depicted below:

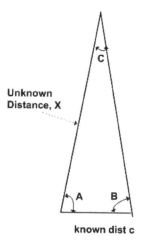

Figure 11-3 Distance measurement via triangulation with an Isosceles Triangle.

Isosceles means equal angels, i.e., angles A and B are equal. Given a measurable, known distance **c**, and the ability to measure angles A and B, we can find the magnitude of the unknown distance **x**, by using a trigonometric identity known as the law of sines (trigonometry was also not available to Aristarchus). Details are provided in the Trigonometry reference listed in a previous chapter. However, the desired formula yielding the value of **x**, which I provide for those who have either had trigonometry or are just curious, is:

$$x = c*SinA/SinC$$

Of course, the accuracy of the determination of the unknown distance **x**, depends upon the accuracy of measuring angles A and B as well as the known distance **c**. In astronomy, angles A and B are known as parallax angles. The first application of this technique was the measurement of the distances to the planets and sun, but first an accurate measurement of the circumference of the Earth had to be made, since portions of the circumference provide the baseline, **c**.

Eratosthenes measures the circumference of earth

The first person to make a reasonable attempt at measuring the circumference of the Earth was Eratosthenes of Cyrene (275-194 B.C.), a Greek scholar who lived and worked in Cyrene and Alexandria[475]. Eratosthenes noted that on certain days the sun shone to the bottom of wells in Cyrene indicating that the Sun was directly over head. Over the course of a few years, he found that the sun was overhead on the same day each year. Having traveled back and forth from Alexandria to Cyrene on many occasions, he knew the distance from Alexandria to Cyrene. Armed with this knowledge, Eratosthenes devised a clever, but simple method for measuring the Earth's circumference as shown in this diagram:

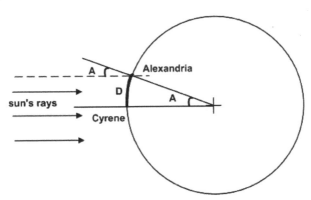

Figure 11-4 Eratosthenes's measurement of Earth's circumference.

On the day the sun was overhead in Cyrene, Eratosthenes stationed an associate in Alexandria with instructions to measure the angular deviation of the sun from vertical, the angle A in the figure. Knowing that there were

360 degrees in a circle, Eratosthenes used this simple formula to determine the circumference:

$$Circumference = D*360/A$$

Eratosthenes measurement of 25,000 miles was remarkably close to the correct value of 24,900 miles.

Giovanni Domenico Cassini (1625-1712) makes first scientific measurement of the Earth-Sun distance:

Italian mathematician, astronomer, engineer and astrologer Giovanni Cassini was born in what was at that time the Republic of Genoa and made the first reasonably correct Earth-Sun distance measurement in 1672[476] via triangulation. As with any triangulation measurement, Cassini first had to establish a base line. Since the orbit of Mars is outside that of Earth, Cassini knew that at some time, Mars would be in a position to provide a proper baseline; accordingly, Cassini decided to measure the Earth-Mars distance to use as his baseline.

To accomplish this, Cassini sent a fellow astronomer, Jean Richer to Cayenne, French Guiana in South America -- a long distance from Genoa and thus providing a long baseline. They observed Mars at the same time, carefully measuring its position in the sky relative to background stars. Since the two astronomers were located at different point on the Earth, they saw Mars in slightly different positions and thus slightly different angles.

So, knowing the distance between the two observing points, and the angles, they were able to calculate the actual distance to Mars in miles. They were also able use it to determine the distance from the Earth to the sun. While the determination of the earth-sun distance using the earth-mars distance was of great import, it is rather involved; hence, I will merely provide some references for those who would like some details a fairly readable description is found in this reference[477].

It should also be noted that the measurement Cassini and Richer made was very difficult, and their number wasn't terribly accurate. However, it was the first big step, and the number was later refined. Now we know it to an accuracy of meters!

Determining the size of the solar system

Once the distance from the earth to the sun and mars had been determined, it was relatively easy to employ the same triangulation techniques to determine the size of the orbits of the other planets.

In addition, the earth-sun distance provides a means for measuring distances to the nearer stars as will be discussed in the next Chapter.

Resolving the apparently infinite velocity of light illusion:

One planet in particular, Jupiter, provided a Danish astronomer an opportunity to make a startling discovery. Once the earth-sun distance had been determined, a number of interesting developments followed, in particular, the serendipitous discovery by Giovanni Cassini and Olaf Roëmer (1644-1710)[478] of another, illusion, which had not been detected due to its great velocity which produces "instantaneous" images, the apparent infinite velocity of light.

Cassini had been observing Jupiter's moons for two years beginning in 1666 and had noticed some measurement discrepancies. In 1672, Danish astronomer Roëmer joined Cassini as his assistant and continued the Jupiter moon investigations.

Over time, Roëmer noticed that the time for the appearance of Jupiter's moons varied by about one thousand seconds depending upon the relative position of the Earth and Jupiter with respect to the Sun. By carefully examining the positions of the Earth and Jupiter in their orbits, Roëmer found that a one thousand second delay occurred when Jupiter and the Earth were on opposite sides of the sun, but there was no delay when Jupiter and the Earth were on the same side[479].

After some deliberation, Roëmer was forced by Sherlock's theorem to conclude that the delay existed because the velocity of light was not infinite, as had been believed, but was actually finite. Since the diameter of the earth's orbit is 186 million miles, Roëmer estimated the velocity of light at 186,000 miles per second which is quite close to the currently accepted value.

This relatively simple discovery was to have far reaching consequences as we shall see in the next chapter where we employ the position of the

Earth, at times six months apart, to begin the measurement of the size of the Universe, which then allows the determination of the age of the Universe.

Michelson–Morley (M-M) demonstrate velocity of light is constant and independent of measurement direction[480]

In 1887, via an ingenious experiment Albert Michelson (1856-1931)[481] and Edward Morley (1938-1923)[482] proved that the velocity of light is a constant independent of measurement direction.

Prior to the M-M experiment, the existence of a "Luminous Aether" was invoked to explain the ability of the apparently wave-based light to propagate through empty space, something that waves should not be able to do[483]."

Michelson and Morley constructed a platform floating in mercury supporting an interferometer, a devise that accurately measures the velocity of light[484]. M-M measured the velocity of light and the rotated their interferometer ninety degrees so that measurements were made perpendicular to the first. No difference was detected, ergo no Aether.

Over the years, "Michelson–Morley type experiments have been repeated many times with steadily increasing sensitivity." but no Aether has been detected because light is E/M radiation and does not require a medium for transmission.

Chapter 11 Summary: Resolving the apparent Sun and Moon closeness - the correct Earth orbital size

- The illusion is created by lack of proper distance reference.
- Measuring distance to objects above the Earth's surface, e.g., the planets, requires triangulation. The obvious baseline is Earth, so first the size of the Earth had to be measured.
- In approximately 200 BCE, Greek scholar Eratosthenes measured the Earth as twenty-five thousand miles in circumference – close to the presently accepted value.

- In 1672, Cassini, using triangulation from two locations on Earth, made the first reasonably accurate measurement of the Earth-Mars distance.
- Cassini then used this measurement to deduce the Earth-Sun distance, also known as an Astronomical Unit (AU).
- The Earth-Sun distance and observations of Jupiter's moons by Danish Astronomer Olaf Roëmer, which showed that the appearance time of Jupiter's moons differed by approximately one thousand seconds, led Roëmer, in 1672, to realize that light had a finite velocity of approximately 186,000 miles per second.
- Michelson–Morley (M-M) demonstrated that the velocity of light is constant and independent of measurement direction.

Looking ahead:

Having solved the sun and planets around Earth illusion which led to a proper explanation of the solar system shape – elliptical planetary orbits; and the apparently same moon and sun size illusion which led to a proper explanation of the size of the solar system, especially the 186 million mile major axis size of the Earth's orbit, the stage was set for the resolution of the apparent closeness and motion of the stars around Earth illusion which led to a determination of the size and hence age of the universe.

CHAPTER 12

RESOLVING THE STARS' APPARENT CLOSENESS PLUS THE SIZE AND AGE OF THE UNIVERSE

Creating the apparently close stars' illusion:

It's a clear night, you are gazing up at the stars that seem so close, "You can almost touch them" I believe someone once wrote. As you stand there, you are arriving at the same conclusion regarding the distance to the stars as the ancients who believed that the stars appear to be close, a fixed distance from the earth and attached to a celestial or crystal sphere.

As introduced previously, if you continue to observe the stars for a while, you will notice that they seem to "drift" toward the west. Closer observation will disclose that the stars appear to be rotating about a star in the Northern sky, a star now termed the pole star.

The star closeness illusion is not caused by the same reference problem that causes the apparently same size and closeness of the sun and moon illusion. We can actually "see" the sun and moon, but we cannot "see" any of the stars in the conventional sense. Because of the extreme distance to the stars, the human eye and even the most powerful telescope lacks the power to resolve a star. We can "see" a star since it is a source of light, but we cannot see any details of stars, what we "see" is an optical phenomenon, known as an Airy disk named for its discover, British mathematician and astronomer Sir George Biddell Airy (1801–1892)[485].

The Airy disk is a series of concentric rings of varying intensity that only show where a star is but cannot be used to determine a star's characteristics. Accordingly, we cannot determine the actual distance to a star: all stars appear to be the same distance from us and lacking a reference, appear to be relatively close for reasons discussed above.

A word about Cosmology:

The solution of the apparent close stars' illusion involves the arcane subject of Cosmology which is defined as "The study of the contents, structure, and evolution of the universe from the beginning of time to the future[486]." This is, perforce, quite a broad subject and I intend to only extract those parts that will:

- Development of a proper explanation of the "close" stars illusion
- Explain, in general terms, how and why we know the size and age of the universe.
- Explain how and why the elements were created.
- Explain how and why the sun and earth were formed.
- Explain why all planets revolve around the sun in essentially the same plane and in same direction.
- Provide additional alternate and independent methods for determining age of earth.

Development of a proper explanation of the apparently close stars Illusion:

Resolving the close stars' illusion ultimately revealed that the universe is extremely large and very old. However, as with resolving other illusions, the resolution required contributions from many persons, beginning with the measurement of the distance to the nearest stars which builds upon our knowledge of the size of the solar system.

Distance to the nearer star using parallax

Knowing the earth-sun distance, we can, in principal, measure the distance to any star using the triangulation method illustrated in this diagram:

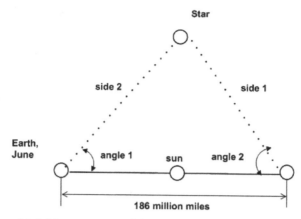

Figure 12-1 Measurement of distance to a star via triangulation.

We merely measure angles 1 and 2 in a triangle formed by the earth-sun-earth line and the star. The difference between the two angles is very small, imperceptible to the human eye; hence the length of either side 1 or side 2 will also be the distance to the star. The difference between the two angles is known as the parallax of a star[487]. The same Trigonometric formula, which was discussed previously, will yield the distance, Side 1:

Side 1 = EOD x Sin Angle 1/Sin Angle 2

Where, EOD represents the Earth Orbit Distance, 186 million miles. This table, extracted from this illustrative 3-D web site presents the eight nearest stars as measured by parallax:

Star	Distance from Earth, Light years,
Proxima Centauri Alpha Centauri C	4.3
Rigil Kentaurus Alpha Centauri A	4.3
Alpha Centauri B	4.3
Barnard's Star	5.9
Wolf 359	7.6
Lalande 21185	8.1
Sirius A	8.6
Sirius B	8.6

Table 12-1 Eight of Earth's nearest stars.

Due to extreme the distance to even the closest star, distance to the stars is measured in light years. A light year is the distance light travels in one year. which is 365 days/year x 24 hours/day x 60 minutes/hour x 60 seconds/minute x 186,000.000 miles/second or 5,878,499, 810,000,000 miles/second. Thus, our nearest star, Proxima Centauri, is 25,277,000,000,000 miles away. Clearly, astronomical distances are almost impossible to comprehend. Note also that Sirius, the brightest star, is not the closest.

Limits to parallax measurements:

As the distance to a star increases; there is a limit to the ability of triangulation due to lose of parallax angle measurement accuracy. This limit occurs at a distance of about 65 light years[488]. However, serendipity solved this distance measurement limitation via the discovery of an unusual star.

John Goodricke's unusual star:

In 1784, John Goodricke (1764 – 1786) an eminent and profoundly deaf amateur astronomer[489] discovered an unusual star whose brightness varied with a fixed period. The variable star was termed Delta Cephi as it was found in the constellation Cephus (the King); hence, stars of this type are termed Cepheid variables[490]. The use of a Cepheid variable as an astronomical yardstick was developed by Henrietta Lovett.

Henrietta Leavitt (1868-1921) develops a "yard stick" for very distant stars:

Henrietta Swan Leavitt graduated from Radcliffe College in 1893 and obtained a position at the Harvard College Observatory in the unchallenging capacity of "computer," assigned to measure and count the brightness of star images on photographic plates. Leavitt's study of star images, in particular the Cepheid variables discovered by Goodricke, led her to develop a ground breaking concept that became the basis for the extension of astronomical distance measuring beyond parallax.

As Leavitt cataloged thousands of variable stars in images taken of a group of stars known as the Magellanic cloud stars, she was the first to realize the importance of Goodricke's discovery. Leavitt noted that a few of the variables showed a pattern: brighter ones appeared to have longer periods. Leavitt published her results in the 1908[491]. By 1912 she had confirmed that the variable stars of greater intrinsic brightness were actually Cepheid variables that did indeed have longer periods. The relationship of brightness to period was quite close and predictable, which permitted Leavitt to produce a precise mathematical formula for this relationship. Leavitt published her formula in a 1912 paper[492], confirming that a Cepheid variable can be used as a standard to determine the distance to the stars beyond the capability of parallax.

The reason that Cepheid variables can be used as standards relates to this simple fact: as an object of known, or intrinsic, brightness moves into the distance, the "apparent" brightness decreases as the square of the distance[493]. An objects intrinsic brightness is the amount of visible energy emitted from the object per unit time and is a fixed quantity known as an object's luminosity[494].

The relationship between period-luminosity and distance can be calibrated with great precision using the nearest Cepheid stars which can be measured by parallax. Therefore, greater distances can be determined as demonstrated with great success by Edwin Hubble, explained below.

Vesto Melvin Slipher (1875-1969) discovers the "red shift"

Slipher, an American astronomer, spent his entire career at the Lowell observatory in Flagstaff Arizona[495], founded in 1894 by businessman, author, mathematician, and astronomer Percival Lowell (1855-1916). Slipher became observatory director in 1926.

Slipher's specialty was the use of spectroscopy to investigate astronomical phenomenon. In 1912 while examining the hydrogen spectrum of various galaxies, he made a startling discovery: the spectrum of hydrogen for galaxies at great distances from the earth was shifted toward the red end of the spectrum as shown in in this figure:

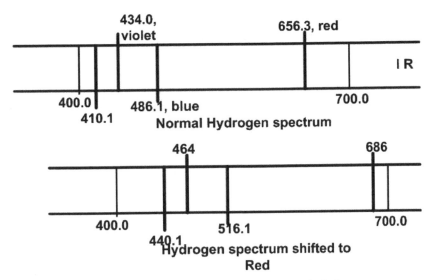

Figure 12-2 Depiction of Hydrogen Red Shift.

Slipher had made a momentous astronomical discovery, the galactic redshift[496]. As with Leavitt's discovery of Cepheid variables, the red-shift discovery was another important piece of the astronomical puzzle.

Alexander Friedman predicts an expanding universe:

In 1922, Russian cosmologist and mathematician Alexander Friedman (1988 –1925)[497] made an astonishing discovery; a solution to the equations of Albert Einstein's general theory of relativity which demonstrated the possibility of an expanding universe. This was something entirely foreign to any existing explanation of the universe, as it contradicted the prevailing view that all the stars were contained in the Milky Way galaxy[498]. Friedman's calculations were one more piece of the puzzle and set the stage for one of the foremost astronomers who ever lived --Edwin Powell Hubble.

Edwin Hubble (1889 – 1953) assembles the pieces: --the universe is expanding!

By properly assembling the pieces of the astronomical puzzle, Edwin Hubble, profoundly changed our understanding of the universe[499]. To place his contributions in context, on the 100th anniversary of Hubble's birth, another celebrated astrophysicist, Alan Sandage paid Hubble this tribute[500].:

> From 1922 to 1936 Hubble solved four of the central problems in cosmology, any one of which would have guaranteed him a position of the first rank in history.

We will discuss three of them:

- The Extreme size of universe.
- The Expanding universe.
- The Big bang.

In 1919, Hubble accepted a position at the Mount Wilson, California observatory, arriving just after the completion of the one hundred-inch Hooker Telescope, the world's largest telescope then in existence. When Hubble arrived at Mount Wilson, astronomers believed that all stars were contained in the collection of stars known as the Milky Way galaxy. Astronomy had progressed beyond the initial concept of a very small universe due to the illusions discussed above, but not nearly as much as it would during Hubble's tenure.

Discovery of the Andromeda Galaxy -the Milky Way is not unique:

Hubble was aware of Harriet Leavitt's work on Cepheid variables and using the power of the 100-inch telescope, soon discovered a Cepheid variable in the star cluster Andromeda. When Hubble applied Leavitt's distance formula to this Cepheid variable, Hubble arrived at the almost unimaginable distance of one million light years! All of the stars were not in the Milky Way; Andromeda was a separate galaxy[501,] the most distant object you can see with the unaided eye. Since then, more precise measurements have been made with the present value of the distance is 2.5 million light years[502]. It should be emphasized that the discovery of Andromeda had the same "Oh-My-Gosh" effect as the discovery of Neandertal.

Hubble soon examined other galaxies, finding Cepheid variables in others. As he assembled the distances, he realized the universe was vastly larger than anyone had imagined!

Discovery of the expanding universe:

Next, Hubble and his assistant, Milton L. Humason, compared the distances they were measuring with the red shift data, originally provided by Slipher, but also being collected at Mount Wilson, and found that a galaxy's distance was approximately proportional to its red shift. Applying Sherlock's theorem, Hubble realized that the galaxies are moving away from us and the farther away the galaxies are, the faster they are moving away *the universe is expanding*!

In 1929 Hubble and Humason were able to formulate the empirical Redshift Distance Law of galaxies, nowadays termed simply Hubble's law, which states that the greater the distance between any two galaxies, the greater their relative speed of separation.

Hubble's observations of the expanding universe corroborated Friedman's solution to general relativity. However, Friedman's solutions supported two possibilities, a steady state universe in which matter is created in sufficient quantity to support the expansion and a universe that began in one place with a "Big Bang." As will be discussed below, further observations support the Big Bang.

Discovery of the Big Bang:

In retrospect, an expanding universe seems quite logical. The force of gravity, acting on two objects will, absent any constraints, tend to pull them together. The reason the earth is not pulled into the sun is because the centripetal force created by the earth's motion, balances the force of gravity. But what prevents the galaxies from being pulled together? The answer lies in the fact that they must be moving away from each other. This is exactly what one would expect if the universe began with an unimaginably large explosion which hurled matter apart. Accordingly, Hubble's discovery leads to the conclusion that the universe began with a bang. However, one would expect that the action of gravity should slow down the galaxies and eventually cause them to stop and begin to fall together ending with a big pile up. That this does not appear to be happening is one of the weirder aspects of the universe, but that's not relevant to our discussion.

The determination of the size and organization of the Universe is one of the *more important philosophical accomplishments in all of history.* As mentioned by Sandage[503]:

> From this work, by him and by others of his generation, it is widely believed that some glimpse of a "creation event of the universe" became available to science by an objective method, <u>not, as in other times</u>, by metaphysics or speculation.

Hubble's determination firmly established the fact of the great size and thus the great age of the universe; however, the Big Bang was still a speculation, until the discovery of radiation left over from the Big Bang.

George Gamow predicts the type of radiation to be expected from a big bang:

Besides explaining alpha particle emission, in another seminal paper, George Gamow suggested that the observed abundance of hydrogen and helium in the universe could be explained if the universe began with a big bang[504]. Moreover, in a paper published in the 1948 Physical Review[505], Gamow predicted that the extremely hot radiation, which would be the radiation from black body produced in the big bang, would, over the billions of years that the universe has existed, cool to a temperature close to 5 degrees above absolute zero, where the radiation would be in the form of microwaves. Unfortunately, microwave receivers capable of testing this hypothesis were not available at the time.

Serendipity strikes again, accidental detection of Gamow's predicted radiation:

As we have seen several times in this book, serendipity is one of the most valuable scientific assistants; such was the case with Gamow's predicted radiation.

In 1965, two young radio astronomers, Arno Penzias (1933-) [506]and Robert Wilson, accidentally discovered Gamow's predicted radiation. They were developing an exceptionally sensitive microwave receiver to study radio emissions from the Milky Way. Soon after turning on the receiver, they detected a strange radiation that was soon determined to be diffuse, emanating uniformly from all directions in the sky, and had a temperature of approximately 2.7 degrees above absolute zero. Initially, they could find no satisfactory explanation for their observations, and considered the possibility that their signal may have been due to some undetermined systematic noise within the receiver. They even considered the possibility that it was due to "a white dielectric substance" (i.e., pigeon droppings) in their horn[507]!

Robert Dicke and Jim Peebles solve the noise problem:

Penzias and Wilson discussed the problem with others, including physicists Robert Dicke and Jim Peebles of Princeton University, who realized that Penzias and Wilson had detected the background radiation that had been predicted in 1948 by George Gamow. This background of microwaves, now termed the Cosmic Microwave Background (CMB) was, in fact, the cooled remnant of the primeval fireball - an echo of the Big Bang. The CMB is perhaps the most conclusive (and certainly among the most carefully examined) piece of evidence for the Big Bang, as noted on this web site[508].

> When the intellectual history of the 20th century is written, a few achievements will tower over all. Einstein's theory of general relativity will be one; the laws of Quantum Mechanics will be another. The so-called Big Bang Theory of the origin of the universe will be a third.

Wilkinson Microwave Anisotropy Map satellite examines details of the CMB

At first the CMB was believed to be isotropic, a fancy word meaning that intensity of the CMB radiation was the same regardless of arrival direction; however, it was argued that, since the universe has structure, there should be a small, but measurable variations, technically known as anisotropic variations in the CMB.

In 2003, NASA launched the Wilkinson Microwave Anisotropy Map (WMAP) satellite[509] to search for the predicted variations in the CMB[510]. The WMAP has been spectacularly successful. There is not room for a full discussion of the WMAP findings; these are discussed in several articles e.g. [511]. For our purposes, these are the significant, and irrefutable, WMAP findings[512]:

- The age of the universe is 13.7 billion years +/- 200,000 years.
- The width of the universe is at least 78 billion light years.
- The universe is composed of 4 percent ordinary mater, 23 percent of an unknown type of dark matter and 73 percent of a mysterious dark energy.
- Current theories applied to the WMAP data and studies of supernovae; indicate that the Universe will expand forever (see note re new information re universe's expansion below).

Formation of the universe - stars, planets and galaxies:

The renowned American physicist and Nobel laureate Steven Weinberg summarized the amazing WMAP findings regarding the beginning of the Universe[513] starting at 0.02 seconds after the Big Bang:

Time	Event
0.02 seconds	Universe basically E/M radiation (light)
0.11 seconds	Excess of protons over neutrons appear
1.09 seconds	Light cannot escape primordial fireball
3 min 42 seconds	Deuterium stable, Helium 26 % universe's mass
400 kyrs	Hydrogen coalesced from electron-proton cloud
700 kyrs	Universe cool enough: H_2 and He stable atoms
400 Myrs	Stars emerge and form stable galaxies

Table 12-2 The initial Universe events after the Big Bang.

Star Formation[514]

Star formation begins with thin swirling clouds consisting mainly of the most abundant element in the universe: hydrogen. The swirling motions cause atoms to occasionally come close enough to form small pockets of gas where each atom exerts a small gravitational attraction on its neighbor, which counters the tendency of the atoms to disperse due to electrostatic repulsion. If the number of atoms in a gas pocket becomes large enough, the accumulation of all these separate forces will hold it together indefinitely, forming an independent cloud of gas[515].

With the passage of time, gravity's constant influence causes the gas cloud to contract toward the gravitational center of the cloud. The contracting gas begins to rotate, just as a skater begins to rotate as the arms are brought in.

Two things happen to the rotating gas:

- Some of the material begins to form a disk, termed the circum solar disk.
- The remainder of the material, the majority of it, approaches the center, the atoms' velocity increases, which heats the gas to ever higher temperatures[516].

This shrinking, continuously self-heating ball of gas is an embryonic star. The temperature of the shrinking cloud steadily increases until it reaches the critical temperature of 20 million degrees Fahrenheit, where the hydrogen atoms in the gas have sufficient velocity to penetrate the nuclear repulsive force and fuse into helium with a concomitant release of the energy of fusion as described in chapter 9.

This release of energy marks the birth of the star. At this point in the life of the star, the diameter of the ball has shrunk to about one million miles, which is the size of our sun and other typical stars.

During the hydrogen burning phase of a star's life, the energy generated by fusion passes to the surface and is radiated away in the form of light, by which we see the star in the sky. The energy release generates an outward pressure that halts further contraction of the star, which lives out the rest of its life in a balance between the outward pressures generated by the release of nuclear energy at its center and the inward pressures created by the force of gravity.

Galaxy Formation:

As soon as a few stars had formed, they began to form groups which we term galaxies. The first galaxies appeared at approximately the same time as the first stars, about 400 million years after the big bang[517].

Today, there are billions of galaxies in the universe; our galaxy the Milky Way, is one. Our solar system is located in one of the "arms" of the Milky Way, approximately twenty-six thousand light years from the Galactic Center[518].

The end of a star's life:

Just as stars are born, when their fuel has been consumed, they must die completing the star's life cycle. The end of a star's life depends completely upon its size. The fusion of hydrogen to form helium continues until all of the hydrogen has been converted to helium; typically, this is about 99 percent of a star's lifetime.

After a star's hydrogen is exhausted, fusion of helium becomes the star's energy source as three nuclei of helium combine to form the nucleus of the carbon atom. The fusion of helium requires higher temperatures and generates more radiation pressure; therefore the star expands greatly and becomes a red giant[519]. An example of a red giant is Betelgeuse, easily seen in the Orion Galaxy.

In the case of our sun which is cataloged as a small star, the red giant stage will not be reached until about five billion years in the future, at which time the sun will have expanded sufficiently to engulf the Earth. Obviously, all life will be obliterated. Our descendants; if there are any, will need a new home. Once the helium is consumed, what happens next depends upon the size of the star.

The death of stars, small stars

If the star is relatively small, like our sun, the star, having stopped producing energy, slowly cools, continuing to shrink, which generates enough heat and light so that it remains visible, becoming a white dwarf. But the star continues to cool eventually becoming just a black ball[520].

The death of stars, massive stars and the creation of the elements:

If a star is sufficiently massive, the temperature produced by the stars continuing collapse will reach another critical level, six hundred million degrees, at which time the carbon nuclei at the center of the star fuse, forming still heavier elements than carbon such as oxygen[521]. Eventually the carbon is consumed and the next heavier nuclei fuse.

This process continues "down the binding energy curve" until the massive star successively manufactures all elements up to iron. As shown in the binding energy curve, the next element has less binding energy than iron, so iron cannot continue the fusion process and the star's nuclear furnace shuts down, rather suddenly. With no radiation pressure to support it the star collapses under the force of its own weight with a cataclysmic explosion. The heat generated by this explosion creates temperatures so high, up to 100 billion degrees, that fusion forces, great enough to create of all the elements heavier than iron, are possible[522].

After the cataclysmic collapse, an equally cataclysmic rebound which disperses the contents of the star at extremely high velocity. The exploding star is termed a Supernova, one of the most violent events in the universe, and, the source of the "extra bright stars" observed by ancient astronomers.

Thus, without supernovae, the elements that comprise the earth would not exist and we would not be here to appreciate them.

It is interesting to note that the life cycle of stars mimics the cycle of life on earth. If we didn't die, evolution could not have occurred and you wouldn't be reading this.

This chapter answers this question by combing appropriate material from the previous chapters with the latest research in an ever-changing search for our origins. We begin with Earth's formation.

We interrupt this discussion for an important update!

In 2012, the Hubble telescope revealed that not only is the universe expanding, the rate of expansion is increasing. In other words, *the universe expansion is accelerating*[523]! The acceleration was detected by the study of a unique stellar explosion known as a type I supernova[524] occurring when the gravitational attraction between two stars causes them to orbit each. One star pulls matter from the other until it explodes in a gigantic thermonuclear explosion the makes a hydrogen bomb seem like a fire cracker.

Formation of the planets

As recently as one or two generations ago, scientists were very uncertain regarding how planets formed. As Robert Jastrow points out in *Red Giants and White Dwarfs*[525],

> When I was in High School (approximately 1900), a popular explanation of planet formation involved a close encounter with another star which ripped material from the sun which then formed the planets.

However, as Jastrow further observes, this explanation can be eliminated via simple statistics. The stars are separated by vast distances; hence, the probability of a stellar collision is extremely remote, in fact perhaps only one or two have occurred in the entire lifetime of the Galaxy.

On the other hand, astronomers have found another planet circling a star; something long predicted, but when the first planet was discovered[526], it was another OMG event--"We may not be alone!" It should come as no surprise that astronomers continue to find more and more extra solar planets, as noted in this article from July 2008's *Science News*[527],

> ...an orb, dubbed MOA-2007-BLG-192-Lb and weighing only 3.3 times Earth is found... the 300th extra solar planet found to date.

A much more reasonable explanation for planet formation, now being verified by computer simulation and observation of extra solar planets is found in the formation of stars from clouds of dust and gas explained above.

As the gas cloud that would give birth to the sun contracted, it began to rotate (just as a skater spins as the skater's arms are drawn in). This rotation produced a disk of matter surrounding the sun, termed a circum-stellar disk. Eddies in the circum-stellar disk gave rise to small islands due to the accretion of matter sufficiently concentrated into very small islands of material in the disc surrounding the developing sun to develop into the planets.

The formation of planets in a disc rotating about its star is the reason why all of the planets revolving about the sun move in approximately the same plane and in the same direction.

An excellent explanation of planet formation[528], which describes a computer simulation program written by the Planetary Science Institute (PSI) with sufficient capability to chart a course from a cloud of dust to a solid planet. While planetary formation cannot be solved exactly, it would require the ability to follow all the particles and observe their behavior, computer power has reached the point where a computer program, such as the PSI program, can "follow" enough particles to determine how the terrestrial planets (and others) were formed.

The PSI program models the motions of particles at different distances from the sun, and tracks the results of collisions based on actual physical and mechanical properties. The model shows that adjacent particles undergo collisions at relatively low speed, in the same way that high-speed racecars moving around a circular track might nudge into each other. The slowly colliding particles "stick together," providing strong evidence that dust particles tend to aggregate.

When the PSI program is executed with different starting conditions, the aggregation of innumerable small particles into smaller numbers of small "building bodies" called planetesimals can be observed. Once the aggregation starts, the larger planetesimals tend to sweep up the smaller ones. As this process continues, the gravity of the biggest planetesimal, now resembling a planetary body tends to dominate the aggregation, and the larger planetary body sweep up most of the other bodies, producing a system with a few planet-sized worlds. Eventually the planetesimals continue aggregating until a system of a few planets is formed and few small planetesimals remain.

Additional simulations of planetary formation have refined our understanding of planetary formation, but the basic process has not changed.

It is tempting to state that, in view of this chapter and the previous chapter, the age of the Earth issue is resolved. However, completing the picture, by demonstrating how the resolution of the unchanging Earth illusion developed before the advent of cosmological explanations, which will be provided in the next chapters (sort of a bottom up approach), should conclude the debate regarding the Earth's age. Twelve independent methods for the determination of the Earth's age will be provided.

Formation of the Earth:

We live on a rocky sphere, eight thousand miles in diameter, covered by a thin veneer of soil and water shrouded in a protective atmosphere; encircling a minor star at a distance where life can thrive; revolving in a small spiral galaxy lost in the depths of an expanding universe 11.7 billion years old. From a distance, our planet is a beautiful blue circle. How did this amazing place originate?

> No known rocks have survived from the first five hundred Myrs (million years) of Earth history, but studies of single zircons (ancient minerals exceptionally resistant to chemical changes, and the oldest known materials on Earth) suggest that some continental crust formed as early as 4.4 Ga, 160 Myrs after accretion of the Earth [from the primordial solar disk], and that surface temperatures were low enough for liquid water[529].

The immense energy imparted by impacts of asteroids striking the Earth at high velocity plus the heating caused by accretion created a molten rocky ball.

The first person to propose a molten earth was Lord Kelvin, a thermodynamics expert, who believed the earth was cooling down from a molten state. Presumably Kelvin got his insight from the fact that Volcanoes emit molten rock. However, we now know, but Kelvin couldn't have known that the Earth's internal heat is generated by nuclear decay; hence the cooling rate Kelvin used was much too fast, yielding an earth age much too young.

A new analysis of ancient minerals called zircons, exceptionally resistant to chemical changes, and the oldest known materials on Earth [530] offer a window in time as far as back as 4.4 ba, when the planet was a mere 150 million years old. Because of these properties, zircon crystals have become the gold standard for determining the age of ancient rocks, says University of Wisconsin-Madison geologist John Valley[531] used these tiny minerals to show that rocky continents and liquid water formed on the Earth much earlier than previously thought, about 4.2 billion years ago[532].

As motioned above, an excellent, simulation based explanation of planet formation, including the Earth is found in Science[533]. Additional simulations of planetary formation have refined our understanding of planetary formation, but the basic process has not changed.

Formation of the Earth's crust

The earth's crust is surprisingly thin, like the skin of an apple, and consists of two layers, basalt and granite. Granite is the principal constituent of continents. However, granite was not among the first rocks that formed; these were mainly Basalt. Basalt is formed when molten magma flows from the earth's interior onto the Earth's surface as lava. It is usually gray to black and fine-grained due to rapid cooling of the lava on the Earth's surface. Unweathered basalt is black or gray[534].

Granite is usually formed under the Earth's surface from molten magma and cools into a rock with no particular structure and a medium to coarse grained texture. Granites occasionally display relatively large crystals and can be pink to dark gray or even black, depending on their chemistry and mineralogy[535].

The density ratio between granite and basalt explains why granite "floats" on basalt. The specific gravity of granite is approximately 2.7[536] while the density of basalt is 3.0[537]; hence, the ratio between granite and basalt is 0.9 which is the same ratio as ice and water. Just as ice floats on water, granite "floats" on basalt.

Due to the constant changes that occur on Earth due to erosion and plate tectonics, most of the earliest granites have long disappeared. However, as pointed out *by* Dr. Lorence G. Collins, Department of Geological Sciences, California State University Northridge:

> Granites in the bottom of the Grand Canyon give Precambrian ages of 1.58 and 1.65 billion years, younger than the 1.7-1.85 billion-year-old Vishnu schist[538].

Dr. Collins's paper is also another interesting answer to Creationist arguments regarding the age of the Earth's rocks.

So exactly when enough Granite was formed to create the continents is difficult ascertain with great detail; however, granite was definitely formed before the Grand Canyon rocks in order for the rock layers to exist.

Creation of earth's Oxygen

Regarding the creation of earth's free Oxygen, there are two points of agreement:

1. There was no free oxygen when the earth formed; although there was oxygen locked in minerals such as silicates (SiO_2).
2. The current atmosphere contains approximately 20 percent Oxygen.

Other than these rather obvious facts, there are many explanations for the formation of Oxygen.

One of the more prominent involves cyanobacteria photosynthesis in stromatolites as the source of the Earths O_2. The stromatolite O_2 generation also played a prominent role in the formation of the iron ore deposits found throughout the earth[539].

During the formation of earth's oceans, iron compounds, probably sulfates dissolved in the oceans. When stromatolites began generating O_2, the O_2 was initially dissolved in the oceans where it "rusted" the dissolved iron, forming layers of iron oxides now termed the banded iron layers[540].

These iron oxide layers are one of the main sources of commercial iron ore including the Mesabi Range in Minnesota.

Once all the iron in the oceans had been "rusted," the O_2 began to accumulate in the atmosphere changing the atmosphere from one dominated by CO_2 to one dominated by O_2[541] As a result of the Oxygen generation, the oceans and sky turned blue. It is estimated that as much as 20 times more oxygen is sequestered in the banded iron oxides than in the atmosphere[542].

Creation of Earth's atmosphere

Some scientists describe three stages in the evolution of Earth's atmosphere as it is today[543]:

1. The original atmosphere was probably just hydrogen and helium, because these were the main gases in the circumsolar disk
2. The atmosphere came from Earth itself – steam (H_2O), carbon dioxide (CO_2) and ammonia (NH_3).
3. CO_2 dissolved in the earliest Earth's atmosphere is believed to have contained extremely high levels of carbon dioxide - maybe ten thousand times as much as today. At [those levels], you would have had vicious acid rain and intense greenhouse [effects]. That is a condition that will dissolve rocks[544].

Beginning with conditions like this, there is the fundamental question, "How did this barren rock become the blue planet, we know and love?" The answer is an intertwined combination of actions both biological and physical that performed the transformation over a period of 4.5 billion years.

This is obviously a complicated story and there is only room to sketch the bare essentials. However, we will see how the resolution of the unchanging earth illusion, which led to the correct explanation of the Earth's biological and physical processes, allows us to explain how the Earth was really created. This will further confirm the findings of the previous two chapters, especially evolution.

Creation of Earth's water:

Regarding creation of earth's water, there are two questions:

1. Where did Earth's water come from?
2. When did it first appear?

Regarding the second part of the question, there is also accumulating evidence that water existed in the solar system as early as 4.4 billion years ago[545] [546]. Pillow lavas, introduced in chapter 1, agree with this evidence as they provide possibly the earliest date for the appearance of water since pillow lava is formed when molten magma is excreted into water, usually fairly deep water[547]. Thus, the presence of pillow lava is proof that water existed at the time the pillow lava was formed.

Some of the oldest pillow lava formations are found in South Africa and have been dated to over 3.4 ba[548]. Thus, water has been on Earth at least since the time the pillow lava formed and probably much longer since time was required for water to accumulate.

Regarding the first part of the question, "Where did the water come from?" To get water, Earth had to have help from somewhere else[549] [550]. However, until recently there was no agreement on the origin of water on Earth and Mars. A number of sources have been proposed - here are some candidates which have been considered:

- The initial molten Earth cooled sufficiently such that volatile components being outgassed, which initially escaped, were held to the Earth when the atmosphere acquired sufficient pressure for the stabilization and retention of water[551].
- Meteorites known as Carbonaceous chondrites[552], which it is generally agreed formed in the outer reaches of the asteroid belt, have a water content of sometimes more than 10 percent of their weight; moreover, the Deuterium/Hydrogen ratio in these chondrites is similar to Deuterium/Hydrogen ratio in ocean water[553].
- One researcher, A. Morbidelli proposes that the largest part of today's water comes from these objects when they plunged toward the Earth[554].

- There is also the possibility of comets or asteroids as the delivery system, which appears to hold the best explanation.

For decades, researchers have debated whether comets or asteroids delivered Earth's water. At first glance, comets seemed a likely source. Originating beyond the orbit of Neptune, comets are the coldest part of the solar system. Ice in these chunks of rock has been sequestered within their interiors since the formation of the solar system.

Some comets are occasionally thrown inward after a close encounter with a planet or passing star; hence it makes sense that, during the chaos of the early solar system the bombardment by asteroids a few million years after the start of the solar system could have easily delivered enough ice, locked inside the rocks, safe from the sun's heat, to account for Earth's oceans, computer simulations indicate[555]. Water makes up to about 20 percent of the mass of some of these asteroids. On Earth, despite having more than 70 percent of its surface blanketed in blue water, water accounts for only 0.023 percent of the planet's mass. Compared with some asteroids, Earth is positively parched.

More will be provided concerning the earth in Chapter 18.

Chapter 12 Summary: Resolving the stars' apparent closeness – the size and age of the Universe.

- The illusion is created by the same problem with the sun and moon size, lack of proper distance reference.
- Stars are too distant to "actually" see them, what we "see" is an optical phenomenon, known as an Airy disk.
- Resolution of the illusion began with attempts to measure the distance to a star – Triangulation is required with the earth's orbit as base line.
- Use of triangulation is limited to about sixty-five light years.
- The distance limitation was solved when unusual stars whose brightness varied with a fixed period, known as Cepheid variables were discovered.
- An unusual star whose brightness varied with a fixed period. The variable star was termed Delta Cephi as it was found in the

constellation Cephus (the King); hence, stars of this type are termed Cepheid variables.

- Vesto Melvin Slipher examining the spectrum of hydrogen for galaxies at great distance from the Earth found that spectrum was shifted toward the red end of the spectrum – Slipher had discovered the red shift.
- Alexander Friedman found a solution to the general relativity equation which predicts an expanding universe.
- Edwin Hubble, combining Slipher's measurements with Friedman's prediction, cam to the conclusion that the universe was expanding.
- George Gamow suggested that the observed abundance of hydrogen and helium in the universe could be explained if the universe began with a big bang; moreover, Gamow predicted the radiation would be in the form of microwaves.
- In 1965, two young radio astronomers, Arno Penzias and Robert Wilson, accidentally discovered the predicted radiation, eventually termed the Cosmic Microwave Background (CMB) radiation.
- Wilkinson Microwave Anisotropy Map (WMAP) satellite examined the details of the CMB and revealed three irrefutable, WMAP findings:
  o The age of the universe is 13.7 billion years +/- 200 thousand years.
  o The width of the universe is at least 78 billion light years.
  o The universe is composed of 4percent ordinary mater, 23percent of an unknown type of dark matter and 73percent of a mysterious dark energy.
- The WMAP findings explain the beginnings of the universe.
- Star formation is described.
- Galaxy formation is described.
- The death of stars, massive stars, Supernovae and the creation of the elements is described.
- The formation of the planets, including earth is described.
- Finally, the formation of the Earth, ready for the arrival of life is described:
  o Formation of the Earth's crust.

o   Creation of Earth's oxygen.

o   Creation of Earth's atmosphere.

o   Creation of Earth's water.

Looking ahead: resolving the unchanging earth illusion

The next chapter introduces the transition from the belief that the earth does not change to the realization that the earth does change - continually. In the next five chapters 14 through 18, we examine how the apparently unchanging features of the earth illusion was resolved leading to a true understanding of the Earth's creation; thereby, completing the explanation of Earth's formation begun in this chapter.

However, as explained in the Introduction and General Overview in order to place the explanation of the apparently unchanging earth illusion in proper perspective, it is necessary to recognize that there are actually two, separate but related, parts to this illusion:

1.   Apparently unchanging physical features of the earth, essentially the field of geology.
2.   Apparently unchanging biological features of the earth – the field of biology.

While geology and biology are generally considered separate subjects, from an historical perspective, the development of a proper explanation of the apparently unchanging nature of the earth, these two subjects are intertwined, for example, in the interrelationship of fossils (biology) and rocks (geology); hence, we will follow both paths of discovery in five related chapters:

•   Chapter 14 will introduce the similarity in the initial recognition and explanation of both the physical and biological illusions.
•   Chapters 15 and 16 will be devoted to the final resolution of the unchanging Physical features illusion.
•   Chapters 17 and 18 will be devoted to the Biological features illusion.

Explanation of the Physical features illusion resolution is divided into two chapters since, as will be seen, there was a significant difference in the development of understanding during these two periods.

In a similar manner, the resolution of the apparently unchanging biological features will be divided into the period that ends with Charles Darwin's publication of "The Origin of Species..." which will be addressed by chapter 17 and the period after Charles Darwin in which the full explanation of the Evolution phenomenon was developed which will occupy chapter 18.

Finally, a fifth chapter 19 will employ the material presented in chapters 9 through 12 to explain the true creation of the Earth, beginning as a molten ball of rock, the result of the accretion of material described in this chapter, and then proceed through the many changes, some violent, that ultimately culminated in the brilliant blue planet we enjoy today.

CHAPTER 13

RESOLVING THE APPARENTLY UNCHANGING EARTH ILLUSION

Creating the Illusion:

Section 1 introduced a profound concept: throughout thousands of years of human history people lived on an apparently "unchanging world." An illusion, actually two related illusions: unchanging physical and biological features, created by objects that change and are plainly visible but change on a timescale vastly greater than human life spans and are therefore undetectable unless one knows how to look.

In addition, as discussed in the section: *The Writing of Genesis*, there is nothing in *Genesis* to suggest the Earth is not Young. Moreover, as distinguished author Simon Winchester (1944-)[556], whose excellent biography of geologist William Smith, *The Map That Changed the World*[557] will be encountered below, "The people living in the English Town of Churchill where Smith was born in 1769, held implacable beliefs that William was born 5772 years, four months and 16 days after the creation[558]."

On the other hand, by the mid-1800s, an army of geologists had demonstrated that the earth was indeed changing, albeit imperceptibly slowly. Moreover, the Earth was vastly older than biblical reckoning predicted. However, only a relatively few educated individuals who shared their investigations and conclusions in scholarly journals participated in the revolution. The average person was generally unaware of the revolution. Hence, the revolution took a long time to seep down to "the man on the street." In fact, when it did, many viewed the new explanation of the Earth as Blasphemy: this reaction will be discussed below as it is still extant.

Just as the resolution of the solid Earth and sun around Earth illusions required drastic revisions in our understanding of the world in which we live, produced by a large number of investigators, resolution of the apparently unchanging and therefore relatively young Earth illusions also required drastic revisions. Thus, the efforts of many were required to gain an understanding of the unchanging and apparently young Earth illusion.

Examining the history of discoveries related to the unchanging earth illusion discloses that the first person who had an interest in the possible changing of the earth's features was a person you would probably never expect--it was a person who had a profound interest in fossils which was fortuitous since fossils provided the first clue which was "hiding in plain sight."

Fossils: the first clues pertaining to the unchanging earth illusion

As described in the Natural Treasures website [559]:

- Fossils are the remains or traces of animals or plants which have been preserved by preservation processes in the earth's crust. Fossils are windows which serve as insights into the earth's past.
- Fossils have been known to people for many centuries. Fossil shells used for the purpose of adornment have been discovered at Paleolithic sites.

As usual, the Greeks, for example Herodotus and Xenophanes[560] were among the first to identify fossils as the remains of long dead animals.

Aristotle[561] got it wrong - again

Unfortunately, the powerful Aristotle disagreed with this interpretation of fossils, mistakenly believing in spontaneous generation of life; the belief that complex, living organisms are spontaneously generated by decaying organic substances. According to Aristotle, it was a readily observable truth that aphids arise from the dew which falls on plants, fleas from putrid matter, mice from dirty hay, crocodiles from rotting logs at the bottom of bodies of water, and so forth even brilliant individuals from the right side get things wrong[562].

Amazingly, Aristotle's ideas persisted until the Middle Ages when, as will be discussed below, enlightened minds began to identify fossils for what some of the other Greeks had known, but had been over ruled by Aristotle, the remains of extinct animals[563].

In general, lacking a proper framework, such as an understanding of the earth's true age, early explanations of fossils were rather bizarre. In one of his excellent PBS travel shows, Rick Steves displays a painting of a giant ten to twelve-foot man on a covered board walk at Lake Lucerne in Switzerland, a painting based upon Mammoth bone fossils that the locals mistakenly believed were the remains of a giant man[564].

In her informative discussion of *"The Fist Fossil hunters: Paleontology in Greek and Roman Times*[565]," Adrian Mayer also suggests that early explanations of fossils ascribed them to prehistoric monsters. In her book, Mayer:

> ...explores likely made connections between the rich fossil beds around the Mediterranean and tales of griffins and giants originating in the classical world. Striking similarities exist between the *Protoceratops* skeletons of the Gobi Desert and the legends of the gold-hoarding griffin told by nomadic people of the region, and the fossilized remains of giant Miocene mammals could be taken for the heroes and monsters of earlier times.... Building a vivid picture of how the ancient Greeks, Egyptians and Romans might encounter these strange artifacts and attempt to make sense of them.

Thus, while fossils were known to exist, and some of the first investigators apparently realized they were probably the remains of extinct animals, with no understanding Earth's true age, they were incapable of arriving at a correct explanation of their origin.

Clearly, the age of the Earth was an important component to many investigations. As discussed in chapters 1-4 the recognition that the Earth had not been constant, but had changed over vast quantities of time, developed in the eighteenth and nineteenth centuries relative to our origins; moreover, with one exception, the unraveling of the Earth's unchanging physical properties proceeded independently of the biological investigations.

Leonardo initiates a proper investigation of fossils that provides evidence that the earth changes:

Another famous polymath, Leonardo di Vinci (1452-1519)[566] renowned for his paintings, e.g., "The Mona Lisa," plus his intriguing inventions[567], was an ultimate member of the "right-side" club, having a brilliant, inquisitive mind.

Leonardo was the illegitimate son of Messer Piero Fruosino di Antonio da Vinci, a Florentine notary and a peasant girl Caterina, in the Tuscan hill town of Vinci in the lower valley of the Arno River near Florence on the edge of the Apennine Mountains[568].

While Leonardo was born more than one hundred years before James Usher; Leonardo's secretive way of writing, mirror image Italian, resulted in his work being little known until eighteenth century with the appearance of the Codex Leicester[569].

Leonardo apparently abhorred absurd ideas such as the Biblical Flood; hence, he was one of the first to resolve the mystery of fossils, if only to disprove the Biblical Flood with a reasoned, systematic study of fossils.

Leonardo represents one of the transitions from the religious centered explanation of the earth to an explanation based upon verifiable observations. As has been seen in other areas, this transition occurred toward the end of the 15th century with the development of improved observational and explanatory techniques. However, Leonardo appears to have arrived at his conclusions independently a few years earlier.

In his delightful and insightful book *Leonardo's Mountain of Clams and the Diet of Worms*[570], Stephen Jay Gould (1941-2002)[571] discusses the codex which, among other things, describes Leonardo's conclusions derived from his observations of fossils in the nearby Apennines; moreover, as Gould points out:

Leonardo did not observe fossils for pure unbridled curiosity, with no aim in mind and no questions to test. He recorded all his information for a stated and definite purpose-to confute the two major interpretations of fossils current in his day.

Leonardo's fossil observations absolutely refute the Biblical flood: he summarized his findings with these observations[572]:

- Fossils are found in separate rock layers, thereby demonstrating that the fossils could not have been deposited by a single flood.
- Worm tracks are found which would have been washed away by a giant flood.
- Clam shells, still in their connected position, are found which would have been torn apart by a flood.

Leonardo effectively refutes the idea that a single cataclysmic flood could have produced his observations. As Gould points out, Leonardo had harsh words for those who believed in spontaneous generation as a reason for the existence of fossil shells in rocks above sea level[573].

And if you should say that these shells have been and still constantly are being created in such places as these by the nature of the locality and through the potency of the heavens in those spots, such an opinion cannot exist in brains possessed of any extensive powers of reasoning because the years of their growth are numbered upon the outer coverings of their shells and both small and large ones may be seen, and these would not have grown without feeding or feed without movement, and here [that is, in solid rock] they would not be able to move. ..Ignoramuses maintain that nature or the heavens have created [fossils] in these places through celestial influences.

Of interest, Leonardo made many important discoveries, but he could not really explain them. For example – fossils; Leonardo had no idea how they got there: it just wasn't the flood. However, his reasoning, based upon his limited knowledge base was exemplary and a good example.

It's not clear whether Leonardo pondered the earth's age, but he must have known it was rather old. Of course, Leonardo hadn't met the Bishop of Usher who was born 60 years after Leonardo died.

As noted, due to Leonardo's secretive style, his findings were lost for many years; thus, his findings re fossils, strata and erosion disappeared. However, they were picked up later when modern Geology began to develop.

Floods, the nemesis of humanity

Besides a story of the creation of the Earth, Genesis also contains a fairly detailed description of an immense flood, the Biblical Flood, which continues to have great impact on the origins debate; often being employed to explain the formation of the earth, canyons, rocks in strange places, etc. E.g., The Answers in *Genesis* Web Site contains this statement regarding the Flood (italics in original statement)[574]:

> ...the "geologic column," which is cited [by geologists] as *physical evidence* of evolution occurring in the past, is *better explained* as the result of a *devastating global flood* which happened about 5000 years ago, as described in the Bible.

Accordingly, a brief exploration of the biblical flood and a description of a real "mega flood" will provide balance.

Reflecting on the *Answers in Genesis* statement, it is ironic that ancient fossils easily found in exposed rocks that obviously had been under water is far superior evidence of life's change over far greater periods of time than the five thousand years described in the Bible when the rocks are properly dated.

Simon Winchester, in his delightful book *The Map That Changed the World* introduced above, offers an interesting observation regarding the penetration of the Flood story into common lore by recounting the reaction to strange "pound stones." These round, slightly flattened stones about four inches in diameter and weighing approximately a pound, hence the name, British local farmers had been digging up for hundreds of years:

> People began to wonder if these stones might actually be the relics of living things, and placed where they were found by no less an agency than what they liked to call the Noachian Deluge-Noah's flood.
>
> Perhaps somehow the flood could be implicated in shifting these objects, even to where they now existed in the rocks of high mountain ranges and on the Oxford shire meadows. Perhaps somehow this same flood could also be implicated in the process that created the objects in the first place. Perhaps the rocks and all that lay inside them-the Chedworth Buns, the pundibs, the oyster shells, the fern leaves, and the crystal corals, fish skulls, and lizard bones-had all somehow been precipitated or had crystallized themselves from the fluid of a universal, flood-created sea. Perhaps, if such things were demonstrably true, then maybe, just maybe, the matter of intense puzzlement that had already confused untold generations of naturalists-"what were fossils and why were they found where they were"?-might be solved. The flood, in short, was to be the eighteenth-century answer to everything[575].

The account of the biblical Flood in *Genesis* does not say anything regarding geological occurrences as a result of the flood, such as the placement of fossils in mountains. However, in order to employ the Biblical flood to support creationism, a number of theories, based upon inventive interpretations of *Genesis*, have been advanced to "prove" the existence of the Flood, and are well documented in the *Answers in Genesis* web site[576] which contains this statement:

> The fossils, and the sedimentary deposits they were entombed within, have simply been *misinterpreted* by the scientific community. The fossil record is instead a recording of a devastating global scale flood.

This is an interesting statement, but totally unsupported by any evidence. Moreover, it is interesting to wonder why the *Genesis* authors failed to mention fossils if fossils are a "recording of a devastating global scale flood."

As with other aspects of "Answers in *Genesis*," there are few "facts," much supposition and several appeals, e.g., to "a number of [unspecified] scientists." However, it is not true that "there is no scientific evidence that the biblical account of Noah's ark is a myth or fable."

One of the more interesting stories of an individual's struggle with the *Genesis* creation story previously recounted[577] is Dr. Stephen Godfrey's biography where he laments, "My strict young-earth creationist position began to seriously unravel" when he joined a fossil hunting group. The fossil record completely refutes creationism but it took awhile for Godfrey to accept this. As I have mentioned previously, crossing the bridge from the religious explanations to the scientific explanations is a mind-wrenching experience.

The Greek Flood

I find it intriguing that the Greeks also had a flood myth that loosely parallels the biblical flood[578]. It is perhaps reasonable to believe that super flood stories appear in many civilizations, but in the Greek flood, there is the question of God's/Zeus's desire to destroy human kind: the origin of this is probably lost. If God/Zeus was powerful enough to create the universe, it would seem that he could have maintained discipline among his creations.

A real mega flood - The Lake Missoula Flood

The Lake Missoula Flood may have been the greatest flood ever and provides the evidence that should be observable if a mega flood had really has occurred[579].

I have personally visited the area in eastern Washington State that was devastated by this flood and it is difficult to exaggerate its impact; moreover, the story of the three men who first recognized that a flood had occurred and then solved the mystery of what caused the flood is a fascinating scientific detective story. Furthermore, if a Biblical Flood actually happened, there would be evidence everywhere of the type found in eastern Washington and none has ever been found – obviously, the biblical flood never occurred.

As with many of the discoveries related to the apparently unchanging earth illusion to be recounted in this book, the Missoula Flood escaped detection until a determined geologist, J Harlan Bretz (1882-1981) decided to investigate the strange geological features of eastern Washington. Bretz was then aided by two other geologists to fully explain his findings: *Bretz's Flood, The Remarkable Story of a Rebel Geologist and the World's Greatest Flood*[580].

Across sixteen thousand square miles of Washington, approx 200 mi east of Seattle, the landscape changes from undulating farmland to a wild landscape known as the Channeled Scablands which has abrupt rips and scars, tall canyons, immense dry waterfalls higher than Niagara Falls, gigantic potholes and a gorge, the Columbia River Gorge, thousands of feet deep.

The answer to the mystery of the Channeled Scablands was an audacious theory, that defied all scientific convention (in keeping with many other theories until proven correct), formulated during the 1920s by Harlen Bretz. Bretz had studied the Scablands for years, patiently examining the rocks and other Scabland features and became convinced that in true Sherlock's theorem form, only a huge volume of water could explain his observations. The Scablands had been formed by a gigantic flood!

On the January 12, 1927, Bretz presented his completely unconventional and controversial theory to a specially convened meeting of fellow scientists in Washington, D.C.[581]. Unsurprisingly, his fellow geologists dismissed this "biblical flood" as totally preposterous with the basic question: "where did the water come from?" A reasonable question until all the details were worked out.

The Missoula flood water source

Sitting in the audience, was another geologist, Montana Joseph Thomas Pardee (1871-1960)[582], who would ultimately supply the answer to the Missoula water source[583]. Pardee, studying markings on the walls of a valley near Missoula Montana, realized that the watermarks represented an enormous lake, which led to the next obvious question, how had the lake formed?

The answer was found in scratches on the bedrock of the valley. Apparently a large glacier had moved into the valley.

Pardee and others realized that a glacier had come from Canada during the last Ice Age. The ice had moved down the valley, filling the entire valley until it encountered a mountain at the valley's end blocking the river valley.

The river began to back up against this wall of ice, eventually trapping a lake containing an astounding 520 cubic miles of water that became known to geologists as Glacial Lake Missoula. Here was Bretz's water – a huge body of water able to travel at a fantastic speed!

But how/why did the Missoula water ice dam collapse so rapidly?

The answer to this remaining piece of the puzzle was provided by glaciologist Matthew Roberts[584] who was studying the collapse of glacier caused ice dams in Iceland. After years of analysis, Roberts eventually worked out the process that causes an ice dam to fail[585].

Normally, water freezes at zero degrees centigrade, but the pressure deep at the base of an ice dam lowers the freezing point of water resulting in what is known as "super-cooled" water. The highly pressurized, super-cooled water begins to force its way into tiny cracks which always form in ice. Once super-cooled water has begun to trickle through these cracks, the flowing water alone is enough to trigger a very peculiar process. This moving water creates tiny amounts of friction; which releases energy in the form of heat. Thus; as the water moves through the glacier, it melts the ice. Soon, the minute cracks become giant ones, several feet across. A tunnel under the dam is formed which enlarges rapidly and suddenly, the ice dam is destabilized and collapses almost instantaneously; this was the cause of Bretz's flood!

Summarizing the Missoula Flood Story:

Eventually, a variety of geologists working on the problem established the details of the great Missoula flood. Recent work by Richard B. Waitt has identified up to one hundred floods, with the earliest and largest separated by fifty to one hundred years and the last and smallest were separated by only a few years.

Regarding the Missoula flood, Steven Dutch has created an excellent overview web site with many photos of the Scablands area that vividly illustrate the immense forces that have operated in the area as Dutch summarizes[586]:

> ...it is difficult to imagine excavating something like Grand Coulee with one or a few large floods, however huge, but several dozen make the task more manageable."

So ends the flood controversy.

Chapter 13 Summary: Resolving the Apparently Unchanging Earth Illusion.

- Just as the resolution of the solid Earth and sun around Earth illusions required drastic revisions in our understanding of the world in which we live, resolution of the apparently unchanging and therefore relatively young Earth physical and biological features illusions also required drastic revisions.
- Fossils, the first clues regarding the unchanging earth illusion were introduced.
- The Greeks, especially Herodotus and Xenophanes were among the first investigators to identify fossils as the remains of long dead animals.
- The lack of an understanding of the earth's true age impeded the discovery of change.
- Leonardo da Vinci, seeking to prove the biblical Flood never happened, initiated a proper investigation of fossil clams which he found on mountain walls, an impossible placement for a flood and proof that the earth changes – raising the clams from their watery birthplace to a place high above the water.
- Floods, the nemesis of humanity, are discussed to counter arguments that the Biblical flood explains the earth's form.

- Another mythical flood, the Greek Flood is explained.
- Then a real Mega Flood that occurred in eastern Washington is explained to illustrate what one should find if a large flood had occurred - none of which is recorded with the biblical Flood.

Looking ahead:

The next four chapters present the resolution of the apparent unchanging physical and biological features of the earth. As discussed in this chapter, the realization that the earth changes/has changed was difficult for some, especially those who adhered strongly to the Christian Church:

- Chapters 14 and 15 will present some basic elements of geology and the development of the understanding the glacially slow forces that cause the physical features of the earth change.
- Chapters 16 and 17 will present some basic elements of biology and the development of the understanding the glacially slow force that causes the biological features of the earth change.

CHAPTER 14

RESOLVING THE EARTH'S APPARENTLY UNCHANGING PHYSICAL FEATURES ILLUSION: BETWEEN 1750 AND 1850

With the exception of Leonardo, whose work was unfortunately lost, nothing of interest regarding the explanation of earth's unchanging physical features illusion occurred until approximately 1750. Then between 1750 and 1850, a significant portion of the unchanging physical features illusion was resolved in what can best be described as an understanding revolution introduced in my Author's Note.

The period between 1750 and 1850 can be viewed as the equivalence of the "Pick and Shovel" phase of Archeology when much needed "spade work" was done laying the foundation for the dramatic demonstrations of a changing earth in the twentieth century. By the mid-1800s, an army of geologists had demonstrated that the earth was indeed changing, albeit imperceptibly slowly over vast time intervals.

A little basic geology:

The surface of the Earth is mainly rocks or decomposed rocks sand and soil. There are three main rock types: igneous, sedimentary and metamorphic.

Igneous rock[587] is formed through the cooling and solidification of magma or lava, which is formed within the earth by the heat from nuclear decay. Igneous rock may be produced with or without crystals, either below the earth's surface where they are termed intrusive (plutonic) rocks or on the surface where they are termed extrusive (volcanic) rocks. Magma can be derived from partially melted existing rocks in either a planet's crust or mantle.

Typical igneous rocks are granite and basalt: granite is composed of "glassy" quartz and varied colored alkali "feldspar." Granite is normally formed below the earth's surface and termed an intrusive rock, cooling slowly to form large crystals. Basalt is a dark-colored, fine-grained, normally black igneous rock. It most commonly forms as an extrusive rock, such as a lava flow, where it cools rapidly forming small crystals but it can also form in small intrusive bodies

Sedimentary rock[588], as the name suggests is consists of sediments often created either from sand or silt formed by erosion in which case the rock is termed sandstone or from the shells of small animals living in the ocean which settles to the floor which is termed limestone. Sedimentary rock is the most common rock observable.

Metamorphic rocks[589] arise from the transformation of existing rock types by the application of heat and pressure, a process called metamorphosis. Metamorphic rock can be created from either sedimentary or igneous rock.

Five important Geologic investigators and their theories:

Among the many initial geologic investigators, these five are perhaps the most important. I have listed them in alphabetic order to avoid the illusion of favoritism; however, they were assisted by many others whom I will weave in as appropriate:

- Jean Louis Agassiz (1807-1873).
- James Hutton (1726 -1797).
- Charles Lyell (1797-1875).
- William Smith (1769 - 1839).
- Abraham Werner (1749-1817).

The magnitude of the effort and number of people involved in the resolution of the apparently unchanging Earth illusion precludes an in-depth discussion. My objective will be, as in previous chapters, to provide sufficient information to unequivocally establish the validity of the explanations that developed between 1750 and 1850.

The efforts of all investigators were per force intertwined and it is not clear who was aware of whom at the time; although communication between investigators was greatly facilitated by the formation of the Geological Society of London in 1807[590]. Due to the intertwined aspect of their investigations, I will present them in the order that seems most reasonable

Three early explanations, Neptunism, Plutonism and Catastrophism:

Unsurprisingly, the early investigators' initial explanations, although, reasonable when first formulated, were eventually shown to be incorrect and discarded. But they illustrate the difficulty early investigators had grappling with the new revelation that the earth changed even though the change was hard to detect.

Abraham Werner (1749-1817) suggests Neptunism:

Werner, a German geologist who became famous as a gifted teacher and hence was very influential in the early development of geology[591], became interested in the problem of explaining the existence of rock layers and somehow determined that the Earth had been initially covered with an all-encompassing ocean. When it gradually receded to its present boundaries it precipitated all of the rocks and minerals of the earth. Werner termed the phenomenon, Neptunism, in honor of the Roman god of the sea.

While Neptunism gained adherents, it foundered on its inability to explain one of the most common rocks, basalt, since basalt is known to be extruded in lava flows, some which cover vast areas such as the 1,500,000 square-kilometer Siberian Traps[592].

James Hutton (1726-1797 suggests Plutonism:

Neptunism was ultimately supplanted by a rival theory, Plutonism[593] in honor of the Roman god of the underworld, which accorded much geologic activity and source of rocks to volcanism.

Georges Cuvier (1789-1832) favors Catastrophism

Cuvier, a well regarded French investigator attempting to explain the patterns of extinction that he and others were observing in the fossil record became a leading proponent of Catastrophism which hypothesizes that the Earth has been affected by sudden, short-lived, violent events that were sometimes worldwide in scope[594]. Catastrophism was the dominant belief regarding the development of the earth's physical features until the development of another "ism," Uniformitarianism by Hutton and Charles Lyell.

The biblical flood is a prime example of catastrophism; moreover, catastrophism was basically the only way early geologists could rationalize their observations with the (*Genesis*-based) young Earth belief prevalent before the eighteenth and nineteenth centuries (as mentioned previously, *Genesis* muddled investigations).

Of course, real catastrophes have been well been documented, but they are spread out over Earth's history. When they occur, they have had significant impact on the Earth such as an asteroid impact[595] which ended the age of the dinosaurs. More on this in chapter 18 which will discuss two extinctions that were "hum-dingers": one almost ended life on Earth.

William Smith's amazing Stratigraphic map of England

As discussed above, Simon Winchester has produced an excellent biography of geologist William Smith (1769 –1839); hence, I will merely provide some highlights from Winchester's book[596]. Winchester describes William Smith's map and the effort required as:

> ...a work of genius, and at the same time a lonely and potentially soul destroying project. It was the work of one man, with one idea, bent on the all-encompassing mission of making a geological map of England and Wales. It was unimaginably difficult, physically as well as intellectually. It required tens of thousands of miles of solitary travel, the close study of more than fifty thousand square miles of territory that extended from the tip of Devon to the

borders of Scotland, from the Welsh Marches to the coast of Kent.

The task required patience, stoicism, the hide of an elephant, the strength of a thousand, and the stamina of an ox. It required a certain kind of vision, an uncanny ability to imagine a world possessed of an additional fourth dimension, a dimension that lurked beneath the purely visible surface phenomena of the length, breadth, and height of the countryside, and, because it had never been seen, was ignored by all customary cartography.

The development of Smith's map began when Smith was sent to perform a survey that included a mine called the Mearns Pit. The Mearns Pit, as Winchester points out "has the standing in geology that the Galapagos Islands have in evolutionary theory[597] When Smith first entered the mine, it had been worked for many years and was nine thousand feet deep in places. During his survey, Smith made extensive notes of the mine layers from which he drew a layer map that allowed him to examine the succession of rock layers and fossil types. Fossil types were particularly important since they were less ambiguous regarding a determination whether rock strata were connected than plain rock. The same fossil found in rock layers at different locations meant the layers must have been connected. Hence Smith became an avid fossil collector.

Examining other mines, Smith began to realize that the same formations appeared in other mines. Thus, he knew the layers (the strata of rocks) must be connected. Smith also began to realize that all rocks, not just coal were connected. Eventually, Smith was able to trace the various rock layers, in particular coal seams over wide areas.

As Smith continued to accumulate data, he made a fortuitous encounter in the influential Bath Society. Two farmers, Benjamin Richardson and Thomas Davis had drawn a map of the area surrounding Bath which showed the geographical extent of soils and vegetation. Of particular interest to Smith was the use by Richardson and Davis of color to better delineate the different items on the map.

Almost immediately Smith realized that this technique could be applied to a geological map where the colors would indicate the various layers under the ground.

Smith eventually needed the aid of a person capable of printing large maps in color. Through another fortuitous encounter, he met John Carr, Britain's eminent cartographer, probably at a London meeting in 1794. Smith and Carr's collaboration lasted many years and eventually led to publication in 1815 of the first geological map of Great Britain, where the various geological types were indicated by different colors.

Even though the maps were hand colored, the maps are remarkably similar to modern geological maps of England, which firmly marks William Smith as the "father" of Stratigraphy"; Smith's map provided, for the first time, a detailed picture of the subsurface rock layers.

Since each layer represented a different time, the map was a key to England's geologic history, extending back millions of years. Also, of particular importance, the map clearly demonstrates that England had changed considerably over time.

On the other hand, during Smith's lifetime, while many investigators believed the world was much older than biblical reckoning, attempts to determine the earth's age were inconclusive until Arthur Holmes developed dating based upon nuclear decay and finally determined the earth's true age.

James Hutton (1726-1797, prosperous farm supports Hutton's geologic pursuits

I am unaware of a James Hutton biography as eloquent as Simon Winchester's William Smith biography, but James Hutton has his own web site and much deserved cheering section[598]. Hutton is a favorite son of Scotland whose website states that:

> James Hutton (1726-1797, was truly a man of the Earth.
> Founder of modern geology and farmer in the Scottish
> Borders, he was a hero of the Scottish Enlightenment.

A bit hyperbolic, but the Scots can be forgiven as Hutton did indeed make important contributions. However, "Founder" is a bit of a stretch.

Hutton had the good fortune, as with many successful investigators, to be born into an affluent Scottish family, inheriting his father's Berwickshire farms of Slighhouse[599] a lowland farm that had been in the family since 1713, and the hill farm of *Nether Monynut*[600]. These resources freed him from the obligation to work for a living. Instead, he could spend his time improving his mind[601]. In the early 1750s he made improvements in his farm and introduced farming practices from other parts of Britain[602].

His farm work developed an interest in geology; clearing and draining his farm provided ample opportunities to examine the Earth, and his theoretical ideas began to come together. In 1764 he went on a geological tour of the north of Scotland with George Maxwell-Clerk, ancestor of the famous James Clerk-Maxwell we encountered previously[603].

Economic improvement boosts Intellectual productivity:

The fact that individuals such as Hutton were privileged to being born into affluence is a consequence of dramatic economic developments beginning in the late 1700s and accelerating in the 1800s is superbly explained in Dr. William Bernstein's survey of economic developments chronicled in *The Birth of Plenty*[604], *How the Prosperity of the Modern World was Created*. Hutton was no more intelligent than people one hundred years earlier, he just had the opportunity to exploit this intelligence. As will be seen, to a considerable degree the spread of affluence may have been as important to scientific development as the microscope.

Hutton's Theory of rock formations

Hutton had a number of ideas to explain the rock formations he observed around him, but according to John Playfair (1748–1819), a Scottish mathematician, physicist, and geologist, who presented Hutton's methods and principles in his *Illustrations of the Huttonian Theory of the Earth* (1802)[605]. Hutton:

> ...was in no haste to publish his theory; for he was one of those who are much more delighted with the contemplation of truth, than with the praise of having discovered it.

After some twenty-five years of work, Hutton's *Theory of the Earth; or an Investigation of the Laws observable in the Composition, Dissolution, and Restoration of Land upon the Globe*[606] was read to meetings of the Royal Society of Edinburgh on April 4, 1785. In it, he explained that "the solid parts of the present land appear in general, to have been composed of the productions of the sea, and of other materials similar to those now found upon the shores." Hence, we [Hutton] find reason to conclude[607]:

> 1st, That the land on which we rest is not simple and original, but that it is a composition, and had been formed by the operation of second causes [of course, at the time Hutton had no idea what they, but at least he was aware - a major step].

> 2nd, That before the present land was made, there had subsisted a world composed of sea and land, in which were tides and currents, with such operations at the bottom of the sea as now take place. And,

> Lastly, that while the present land was forming at the bottom of the ocean, the former land maintained plants and animals; at least the sea was than inhabited by animals, in a similar manner as it is at present.

Hutton concluded that the greater part of our land, if not the whole had been produced by operations "natural" to this globe; but in order to make this land a permanent body, resisting the operations of the waters, two things had been required:

1. The consolidation of masses formed by collections of loose or incoherent materials.
2. The elevation of those consolidated masses from the bottom of the sea, the place where they were collected, to the stations in which they now remain above the level of the ocean.

In 1787 Hutton observed what is now known as the Hutton Unconformity, one of the more striking of the many formations that Hutton studied, at Jedburgh, a small town that lies on a tributary of the Teviot River, only ten miles from the border with Great Britain, reference[608] notes that:

> Whilst visiting Allar's Mill on the Jed Water, Hutton was delighted to see horizontal bands of red sandstone lying 'unconformably' on top of near vertical and folded bands of rock.

In 1788, He found a similar formation at Siccar Point, a rocky promontory in the county of Berwickshire which is famous in geologic circles. Just mentioning it at a scientific meeting usually yields a knowing nod and an interesting conversation. I experienced the effect at the AAASPD meeting where I presented my "Last of the Hominidae" paper. One of the attendees to whom I mentioned Siccar Point announced his upcoming trip to the point in three weeks, whereupon I asked the time worn question "Do you need someone to carry your bags?"

Studying Siccar Point, Hutton reasoned that the formations had been created in three steps illustrated below:

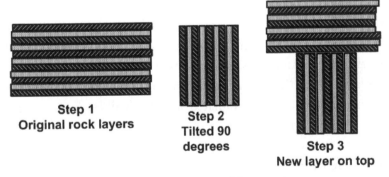

Step 1
Original rock layers

Step 2
Tilted 90 degrees

Step 3
New layer on top

Figure 14-1 Formation of Siccar point.

In the first step, many layers of sediment had been deposited on the ocean floor and over time (an enormous time) hardened into rock. In the second step, Hutton reasoned that this sedimentary rock must have "somehow" been uplifted and tilted. After the rock was tilted, it was worn down by erosion. Finally, new layers of sediment formed on top of the eroded rock leaving the formations he observed at Jedburgh and Siccar Point.

Later in 1788, Hutton reported on his investigations in a paper that he presented at the Royal Society of Edinburgh[609] where he reported that as:

> The result, therefore, of this physical inquiry, is that we find no vestige of a beginning, no prospect of an end.

While it is doubtful that Hutton had any notion regarding the source of the forces that "somehow" created the Jedburgh and Siccar Point formations, he reasoned, correctly, that these formations were unequivocal evidence that the Earth was much older than currently believed, millions of years were his apparent estimates; however, he had no basis with which to guess the true age of the Earth. Moreover, Hutton's investigations clearly demonstrated that the earth's physical features change.

These conclusions, which Hutton termed gradualism, are some the essential elements of "Uniformitarianism." As will be discussed below, Charles Lyell adopted and expanded Hutton's explanations making Uniformitarianism into a formal explanation of the creation of the Earth.

The discovery of the ice ages

Snow typically falls in the winter months in the northern hemisphere and melts in the summer. When more snow falls than melts, snow accumulates. If enough snow accumulates, the snow will compact into ice. If snow/ice accumulation is sufficient and occurs in mountainous terrain (the usual place), the weight of the accumulated snow/ice will begin to move down the mountain creating a glacier.

Glaciers are not mentioned in *Genesis* since they don't occur in the regions where the four *Genesis* authors lived, further eroding *Genesis* as a reliable explanation source. However, glaciers are numerous in Switzerland.

Glaciers belong to an interesting category between the apparently unchanging physical features of the Earth, those things that cannot typically be observed to change in one or more human lifetimes, and those things that can be observed within a human lifetime; however, glaciers move so slowly that careful observations are required to observe their motion.

On the other hand, valleys that have been traversed by glaciers are very different from valleys cut by rivers. River valleys are V shaped, while Glaciated valleys are U shaped due to the carving action of glaciers. Thus, even though a glacier may no longer be present in a valley, a distinct U shape is irrefutable evidence of past glaciation. Besides U shaped valleys, glaciers leave another easily visible clue for those who know how to interpret them – moraines. As a glacier moves down a mountainside, it pushes a large amount of material ahead of it. If the glacier eventually retreats, the material, termed a moraine, remains behind as a mound. Lakes are often impounded behind the moraines.

Besides glaciers in Switzerland, there are other objects, quite visible, such as large rocks and boulders, some weighing several tons, that are "strewn around the landscape," which defied explanation for a long time. Of particular interest, the rocks were often very different than the rocks they were lying on; e.g., granite boulders lying on sandstone layers.

Early humans apparently ascribed these rocks and boulders to the work of supernatural beings such as fairies or giants. One proposal for placement of these objects as mentioned above was the Biblical Flood (as Winchester remarked, "the Flood was the answer to everything"). However, investigators in Europe were unaware of the Missoula flood which could move large boulders, and most dismissed the Biblical Flood as a myth for reasons discussed above.

Astute observers had begun to realize that the random positioning of large rocks and boulders indicated that some extremely large force had been active in the Swiss Alps. Three investigators in particular pursued the origin of the force: Jean de Charpentier, Karl Friedrich Schimper and Louis Agassiz finally made the connection between glaciers and strangely placed rocks. Charpentier and Schimper made the first observations and proposed tentative explanations. Agassiz built upon them and created the modern explanation of ice ages.

Jean de Charpentier (1786-1855)[610] - geologic causation by vanished glaciers

Charpentier's father was a mining engineer which was a good profession in Switzerland; hence, Charpentier also pursued a career as a mining engineer. He excelled in his field while working in the copper mines in the Pyrénées and salt mines in western Switzerland. However, in 1818 a lake created by a glacier ice dam, created a massive flood when the ice dam suddenly collapsed, causing many deaths, a similar situation that had occurred in Lake Missoula, which had a lasting impact on Charpentier.

After the disaster, he made extensive field studies in the Alps attempting to learn more about glaciers. Using evidence of erratic boulders, the difference between river carved and glacier carved valleys, and the moraines left when a glacier melts and retreats, he hypothesized that Swiss glaciers had once been much more extensive. These boulders, characteristic of glaciers, were strewn as if brought there by glaciers that no longer existed.

Charpentier's concept of geologic causation by vanished glaciers contrasted significantly with the previous idea that ancient flooding (the biblical Flood again) caused this deposition. However, he wasn't sure how glaciers formed, moved, or how they disappeared; hence, he had only part of the answer; however, his ideas aided Agassiz who expanded upon them.

Karl Friedrich Schimper (1803-1867) initiates some modern geologic theories

Schimper was a German naturalist and poet. Born in Mannheim, he studied theology at the University of Heidelberg. His beginning research expanded the field of plant morphology[611]. He is perhaps best known as the originator of the theory of prehistoric hot and cold eras, and was one of the initiators of the modern theories of ice ages and climatic cycles.

Bill Bryson[612] states in his celebrated book, *A Short History of Nearly Everything*[613], that Karl Schimper, presumably making the same observations as Charpentier, extended Charpentier's concept. In addition to the idea of glaciation, Schimper proposed the *radical idea* that ice sheets had once covered much of Europe, Asia, and North America. Unfortunately, Schimper was reluctant to write and never published his ideas. He did, however, discuss them with Agassiz, who went on to appropriate them as his own and, much to Schimper's dismay, undeservedly received much of the credit for the origination of the ice age concept.

Jean Louis Agassiz (1897-1873)[614]- discovery of the ice age

Louis Agassiz was born in Môtier in the canton (similar to a U.S. state) of Frobourg in western Switzerland, the French speaking area; hence, Agassiz natal language was most likely French. However, as with almost everyone else in Switzerland, he spoke German and probably Italian plus a passable amount of English.

Adopting medicine as his profession, he studied at universities in Zurich, Heidelberg and Munich. During his medical studies, Agassiz developed an interest in natural history; thus, he received a PhD in 1829 and an MD in 1830: a true polymath. After graduation, he moved to Paris and met George Cuvier who initiated Agassiz's interest in both geology and zoology[615].

Initially Agassiz devoted his energies to zoological interests, in particular fish. His researches culminated in the 1830 issuance of a report pertaining to fish[616]. His appointment as professor of natural history at the University of Neuchatel in 1832 brought Agassiz to Monte Boloca, an area rich with fossil fish. The existence of the fossils was well known, but little studied. Displaying his customary zeal, Agassiz made an exhaustive study of fish fossils which resulted in a five-volume treatise entitled *Recherches sur les poissons fossiles* ("Research on Fossilized Fishes") produced over between 1833 and 1843.

During his fossil fish research, Agassiz became aware of Charpentier's and Schimper's research and conclusion that the rocks scattered over the slopes and summits of the Jura Mountains were the result of glacial action. Agassiz discussed their findings and perhaps, as Bill Bryson surmised, Agassiz may have appropriated their ideas without due credit.

Whether this is true or not, Agassiz attacked the problem with considerably more energy and in considerably great depth than either man, going so far as to construct a hut on one of the glaciers of the Aar river, a tributary of the Rhine river, in order to study the glacier "up close and personal." Agassiz made the hut his home for enough time to thoroughly investigate glacial structure and motion which resulted in a two-volume work entitled *Etudes sur les glaciers* ("Study on Glaciers")[617] in which:

...he discussed the movements of the glaciers, their moraines, their influence in grooving and rounding the rocks over which they travelled, and in producing the striations and *roches moutonnees* seen in Alpine-style landscapes. He not only accepted Charpentier's and Schimper's idea that some of the alpine glaciers had extended across the wide plains and valleys drained by the Aar and the Rhone rivers, but he went still farther. He concluded that, in the relatively recent past, Switzerland had been another Greenland; that instead of a few glaciers stretching across the areas referred to, one vast sheet of ice, originating in the higher Alps, had extended over the entire valley of northwestern Switzerland until it reached the southern slopes of the Jura.

Agassiz extends concept of ice age to the entire European continent

In 1840, Agassiz, accompanied by The Very Rev. Dr William Buckland (1784-1856) a British geologist, paleontologist and Dean of Westminster[618], who wrote the first full account of a fossil dinosaur, but was essentially a creationist, attempting to reconcile *Genesis* by postulating that "In the beginning":

> ...meant an undefined period between the origin of the earth and the creation of its current inhabitants, during which a long series of extinctions and successive creations of new kinds of plants and animals had occurred.

Definitely an interesting companion. As I demonstrate in my Creationism paper, Creationism is very persistent.

The two visited the mountainous districts of Scotland, England and Wales where they found extensive evidence of glaciations, after which Agassiz concluded that all these countries had been covered with great sheets of ice, which combined with his European investigations, convinced Agassiz that a large portion of Northern Europe had been covered by a massive sheet of ice – an ice age had occurred.

It is doubtful whether Agassiz was able to date the ice age with any accuracy – like everyone else, he lacked a good dating tool; however, discovering it was a significant achievement.

Sir Roderick Impey Murchison (1792-1871) initiates an organized Geologic Time Scale:

Murchison was born at Ross and Cromarty, in the highlands of northern Scotland[619]. He attended Durham military college, serving eight years in the Scottish Military. Leaving the military, Murchison married Charlotte Hugonin, and after two years in Europe, settled in Barnard Castle, County Durham, England. In 1818 he made the acquaintance of Sir Humphry Davy, noted British chemist, who urged Murchison to turn his energy to science.

Murchison became fascinated by the young science of geology and joined the Geological Society of London, soon becoming one of its most active members. Among his colleagues were Charles Lyell, Charles Darwin and noted geologist Adam Sedgwick[620], who devised a classification system for the Cambrian rocks and with Murchison, worked out the order of the Carboniferous and underlying Devonian strata[621].

In 1831 Murchison explored the border of Britain and Wales, attempting to determine whether the greywacke rocks underlying the Old Red Sandstone could be organized into a definite succession order. Murchison's efforts established the Silurian geologic "organization" system, named for a Welsh Celtic tribe, the Sillures. Murchison's system grouped, for the first time, a remarkable series of formations, each replete with distinctive organic remains other than, and very different from those of the other rocks of England. This research, together with descriptions of the coalfields and overlying formations in south Wales plus the English border counties, were embodied in *The Silurian System* (1839)[622].

Geologic Time Scale – Geologists realize that rock formations could be organized

Murchison's pioneering Silurian System was a significant contribution, as Geologists soon realized that most, if not all, of the various rock formations could be organized into unique systems, in a similar manner, by employing their distinctive characteristics. This greatly simplified the organization of the Earth's time scale and led to the modern organization of the The Geologic Time Scale of the Earth, presented in Appendix B where the Silurian System is illustrated[623]. The geologic time scale shown in the appendix has the correct ages of the various systems, which of course were unknown in the early 1800s (the Earth's age issue will be addressed at the end of this chapter).

Except for unusual places like the Grand Canyon, the rock layers representing the entire geologic time scale are not visible either above or below ground at any one location, and even the Grand Canyon has gaps. Sections of rock layers representing the geologic time scale at a particular location are called Stratigraphic columns[624].

Charles Lyell (1797 - 1875) Establishes Uniformitarianism as the best explanation for Earth's physical features:

Charles Lyell was born in Forfarshire (now Angus) in eastern Scotland, into a wealthy, well educated family similar to others such as Hutton's and Agassiz's, allowed him the luxury of study[625]. Lyell attended Exeter College, Oxford, later moving to London where he planned to become a lawyer. However, his poor eyesight made this profession impossible and so Lyell turned to his real interest science

Geology soon became his forte and as member of the Geological Society, he took part in the lively debates in the 1820s about how to reconcile the biblical account of the Flood with geological findings (the debates unfortunately continue).

Lyell rebelled against the prevailing theories of geology of the time, as he thought the theories were biased and based on interpretations of the book of *Genesis*. He thought it would be more practical to exclude sudden geological catastrophes to vouch for fossil remains of extinct species and believed it was necessary to create a vast time scale for Earth's history. This concept was called Uniformitarianism, a concept first identified by Hutton as gradualism. A concept that Lyell and others slowly came to realize was a superior explanation for their geologic observations.

Uniformitarianism - a fundamental and axiomatic geologic principle

Uniformitarianism avers that "the same processes that shape the universe occurred in the past as they do now, and that the same laws of physics apply in all parts of the knowable universe[626]." Lyell ultimately became the leading proponent of Uniformitarianism arguing that geological processes observable today, have not changed throughout Earth's history. E.g., mountain building and mountain eroding forces operate at the same rate today just as they did in the past. While Lyell made many contributions, he is best known today for championing the Uniformitarianism principle.

To demonstrate that gradual processes could be responsible for great changes, Lyell used an engraving of the Temple at Serapis[627] as his frontispiece. The Temple was one of the more magnificent Roman structures produced. Later Roman Empire author Ammianus Marcellinus[628] commented that:

> Its splendour [of the Temple] is such that mere words can only do it an injustice but its great halls of columns and its wealth of lifelike statues and other works of art make it, next to the Capitol, which is the symbol of the eternity of immemorial Rome, the most magnificent building in the whole world. It contained two priceless libraries.

The Temple had, during the course of human history, been above sea level, then for a long period partially submerged, and again was above sea level as attested by the dark bands of damage caused by waterborne life across the columns; thereby proving Lyell's hypothesis[629].

As the evidence for Uniformitarianism continued to accumulate, Lyell's associates such as Roderick Murchison and George Poulett Scrope, realizing the superiority of this concept became outspoken opponents of the diluvial (biblical flood) position. To date, no informed observations have refuted the general concept of Uniformitarianism. However, as noted, a number of catastrophic events have occurred in the past; hence, uniformitarianism must be leavened with a pinch of catastrophism.

Lyell's wide ranging geological interests included volcanoes, stratigraphy, paleontology, and glaciology. His best known single contribution to geology, however, is his role in popularizing the doctrine of uniformitarianism.

Lyell's greatest contribution, The Principles of Geology

Lyell's greatest overall contribution was his great geological opus: *The Principles of Geology*[630], subtitled, *"An attempt to explain the former changes of the Earth's surface by reference to causes now in operation." Principles* was initially published in three volumes from 1830-1833. In various revised editions (twelve in all, through 1872), *Principles* was the most influential geological work in the middle of the nineteenth century, and did much to establish modern geology.

The second edition of *Principles* introduced new ideas regarding metamorphic rocks, describing them as one form of **rock** that has changed to another form under the influence of heat, pressure, or some other agent without passing through a liquid phase. Examples are marble, which can be formed from limestone, and slate, which is formed from shale[631].

. His third volume dealt with paleontology and stratigraphy. Lyell stressed that the antiquity of human species was far beyond the accepted theories of that time.

An important contributions Lyell made in *Principles* was the explanation of the cause of earthquakes, by focusing on recent earthquakes (less than 150 years ago), evidenced by surface irregularities such as faults, fissures, stratigraphic displacements and depressions, which are readily observable[632].

Lyell's work on volcanoes focused largely on Vesuvius and Etna, both of which he had studied previously. His conclusions supported gradual building of volcanoes, "backed up-building[633]," as opposed to the upheaval argument supported by other geologists.

Lyell's extended the field of Stratigraphy, pioneered by William Smith. From May 1828, until February 1829, Lyell traveled to the Auvergne volcanic district in southern France and to Italy. Observations in these areas led him to conclude that the recent strata (rock layers) could be categorized according to the number and proportion of marine shells encased within. Based on this he proposed dividing the Tertiary period (see Appendix B) into three parts: the Pliocene from the Greek words (*pleion*, "more") and (*kainos*, "new") meaning roughly "continuation of the recent," referring to essentially modern marine animals, the Miocene, meaning "less recent" and finally the Eocene which refers to the "dawn" of modern ("new") mammalian animals that appeared during the epoch.

Reportedly, Lyell rejected Lamarck's view of evolution; however Principles is notable for being one of the first to use the term "evolution" in the context of biological speciation[634] but as he was a devout Christian, Lyell had great difficulty accepting Darwin's view of evolution, especially Natural Selection. Lyell was supposed to have remarked, "If evolution is true, then religion is a joke[635]." (Ironically, as explained in chapter 15, Lyell's rejection of Natural Selection was correct but for the wrong reason.)

Summary for Chapter 14: Resolving the earth's apparently unchanging physical features between 1750 and 1850

- Leonardo da Vinci initiated the proper investigation of fossils and used his observations to refute the biblical Flood, at least in his eyes. His observations demonstrated that the biblical Flood was absurd.
- Neptunism, Plutonism and Catastrophism were proposed as explanations of the development of the Earth and had been proven incorrect; however, more recently (see chapter 18), a different form of catastrophism has been documented that has had significant effect on the Earth such as the asteroid impact which may have ended the age of the dinosaurs.
- William Smith produced the first stratigraphic map of England, laying the groundwork for the important geological field of stratigraphy.
- James Hutton made a number of important observations, including the interesting but difficult to explain sedimentary rock formation at Siccar Point, a rocky promontory in the county of Berwickshire. Hutton reasoned that the formation had been produced gradually over a vast amount of time which he estimated to be thousands, perhaps millions of years. Hutton termed his conclusion gradualism.

- Jean de Charpentier, Karl Friedrich Schimper and Louis Agassiz exhaustively studied the glaciers of Switzerland. Agassiz extended their studies to the rest of Europe and showed that the only rational explanation for all of the observations was an ice sheet that had covered most of northern Europe. The ice age had been discovered! In 1840 Agassiz et al showed that glacial action rather than a biblical Flood accounted for boulders strewn around the surface of Switzerland.

- Sir Roderick Impey Murchison demonstrated that rock formations along the border of Britain and Wales could be organized into a system he termed the Silurian System (named for a Welsh Celtic tribe, the Sillures). This pioneering organizational approach was adapted by other Geologists who organized the various rock formations into unique systems leading to the modern synthesis of the geologic time scale of the earth.

- Sir Charles Lyell became one of the foremost geologists of the period with wide ranging geological interests including volcanoes, stratigraphy, paleontology, and glaciology. His best-known contribution to geology was his role in adapting and expanding Hutton's concept of gradualism to the more general concept of uniformitarianism, and then popularizing the doctrine.

- Lyell's greatest overall contribution was his great geological opus: *The Principles of Geology* subtitled, "An attempt to explain the former changes of the Earth's surface by reference to causes now in operation." Principles was initially published in 3 vols. from 1830-1833. In various revised editions (twelve in all, through 1872), *Principles of Geology* was the most influential geological work in the middle of the 19th century, and did much to establish modern geology.

Looking ahead:

By 1850, Geologists had made great progress in resolving the apparently unchanging physical features of the Earth illusion and had gathered sufficient evidence to demonstrate that the Earth was much older than the

6,000 years calculated by the good Bishop. However, for all this progress, there were still some items regarding the Earth that could not be properly explained such as:

- What is the source of the sun's energy and age of the sun? The sun had to be at least as old as the Earth, but no one could explain the sun's energy source. As discussed in chapter 6 nuclear fusion provides the sun's energy, but this did not become known for another 100 years.
- What was the source of the forces that raised the sedimentary rocks at Siccar Point to a vertical position and that created the Alps and other mountain ranges? Geologists were completely stumped. Again, as discussed in chapters 8 and 9, the forces that raised the rocks were generated by the heat created by nuclear decay, something not determined until the 20th Century.

The next chapter proceeds to the "high tech phase" of geology borrowing from other fields such as nuclear physics and will explain how these quandaries were resolved.

CHAPTER 15

THE FORCES THAT CAUSE EARTH'S PHYSICAL FEATURES TO CHANGE

The field of geology has seen much progress since the 1850s as the field moved into the "High Tech" Phase. Geology is clearly an involved subject; hence, we will only cover those developments of interest to this book: Earth's interior, Plate Tectonics, Erosion, Seismology and Earth dating methods:

- Nuclear decay within the earth's interior creates enormous heat energy which cause the interior rocks to melt and become molten lava. Circulating convection currents form in molten lava providing forces that move the earth's crust.
- Plate Tectonics explains the source of the forces that raised Siccar Rock, and shape the Earth in general, which had eluded nineteenth century geologists, providing one of the better indicators of the Earth's age and the fact that physical features change.
- Erosion is the process that wears down rock in opposition to the Plate Tectonics process which lifts rocks.
- Seismology is the study of "earthquake" waves, created by plate motion, especially violent motion along boundaries where plates contact. These waves travel through the earth and reveal the details of the Earth's interior structure.
- Earth dating methods will expand upon the discussion in Chapter1; at least 12 independent methods for dating the Earth will be explained.

We begin with the formation of the Earth's solid outer layer, usually termed the crust.

The Formation of the Earth's crust:

As mentioned previously, the earth's crust consists of two layers, basalt and granite. Granite is the principal constituent of continents. However, granite was not among the first rocks that formed; the first rocks were mainly basalt. Basalt is formed when molten magma flows from the earth's interior onto the Earth's surface as lava. It is usually gray to black and fine-grained due to rapid cooling of the lava on the Earth's surface[636].

Granite is usually formed under the Earth's surface from molten magma and cools into a rock with no particular structure and has medium to coarse grained in texture. Granites occasionally display some relatively large crystals and can be pink to dark gray or even black, depending on their chemistry and mineralogy[637].

Also, mentioned previously, the density ratio between Granite and Basalt is 0.9 which explains why Granite "floats" on Basalt.

Due to the constant changes that occur on Earth due to erosion and plate tectonics, most of the earliest granites have long disappeared. However, *Dr. Lorence G. Collins, Department of Geological Sciences, California State University Northridge* pointed out that:

> "Granites in the bottom of the Grand Canyon give Precambrian ages of 1.58 and 1.65 billion years, younger than the 1.7-1.85 billion-year-old Vishnu schist [metamorphic rock that the granitic rocks covered until the Colorado river cut down through the granite to the schist][638]."

Dr. Collins's paper has another interesting answer to Creationist arguments regarding the Age of the Earth's rocks, they are at least 1.85 billion years old.

So exactly when enough Granite was formed to create the continents is difficult ascertain with great detail. However, Granite was definitely formed before the Grand Canyon rocks in order for the rock layers to exist.

The Earth is hot inside

As discussed in chapter 9, nuclear decay is a source of significant heat energy. Atoms with unstable nuclei within earth are a major source of the earth's internal heat. Four radioactive isotopes are responsible for the majority of radiogenic heat, uranium-238, uranium-235, thorium-232 and potassium-40[639]. Temperatures within the earth reach ten thousand degrees Fahrenheit, hot enough to melt the most stable element - iron; hence, all rocks within the earth are molten, often termed magma.

Plate Tectonics, the Earth's surface moves

Convection currents form in the magma which provides forces that move the earth's crust. The discovery that the Earth's surface moves, another "Oh-My Gosh" moment, began with the inauguration of the great age of European exploration outside of local European waters, which can probably be dated to the discovery of the Azores islands by Portuguese navigators[640] [641]. The islands are 950 miles west of Lisbon, Portugal, obviously, a significant distance west of Europe. The existence of the islands was known in the fourteenth century, with parts of them recorded in the Atlas Catalan (Catalan is now part of Spain), Published in 1375, the most important Catalan map of the medieval period[642].

Columbus'1492 discovery of North America set off a flurry of exploration of North America. In 1497-1498 Vasco de Ga rounded Cape of Good Hope en route to India[643].

Hence, by the early 1500s, the essential coastal outlines of Eastern North America, Western Europe and Africa were well known and documented on a large number of maps. When people began to examine them, they noticed an odd thing, if you moved the eastern edge of North America over to the western edge of Europe and Africa, the fit was pretty good; too good, actually, to be a coincidence.

Alfred Wegner (1880-1930) discovers plate motion[644]

Briefly introduced earlier, Wegner was the first person to apply Sherlock's theorem to the apparent connection between the eastern and western

Atlantic coasts. Wegner was a brilliant interdisciplinary scientist, who, after extensive exploration, advanced a preposterous idea that North America and Europe-Africa had, at one time, been joined in a huge continent he termed Pangaea, Greek for "All the Earth[645]" Wegener's inventive understanding of science summarizes one of this book's objectives well; to emphasize that:

> Scientists still do not appear to understand sufficiently that all earth sciences must contribute evidence toward unveiling the state of our planet in earlier times, and that the truth of the matter can only be reached by combing all this evidence. It is only by combing the information furnished by all the earth sciences that we can hope to determine 'truth' here, that is to say, to find the picture that sets out all the known facts in the best arrangement and that therefore has the highest degree of probability. Further, we have to be prepared always for the possibility that each new discovery, no matter what science furnishes it, may modify the conclusions we draw[646].

Wegner's proposal was, of course, met with derision since Wegner had no mechanism to account for the movement of continents three thousand miles. This should remind you of Harlan Bretz's problem - finding a source of water for his flood - or Charles Darwin's dilemma-- what caused evolution to occur?

Wegner did however, gain some assistance from paleobiology (once more, an "unrelated area of science" came to the rescue). In 1911, he discovered a scientific paper that listed fossils of identical plants and animals found on opposite sides of the Atlantic[647]. One of the most extensively studied fossils were trilobites, extinct arthropods (spider like creatures)[648]. Trilobites are particularly important because they were extremely diverse in type, were distributed all over the globe, and were relatively short lived. Hence, if a species is found in two places, there is certainty that they lived at the same time. The characteristics of animals such as Trilobites cause them to be used as "index fossils."

Of interest to Wegner's theory, the same species of trilobite lived in Oklahoma and Morocco at the same time. Land bridges between North America and Africa were the first explanations, but were quickly discarded as prosperous when the depth of the Atlantic became known. Wegner's theory offered a plausible explanation. However, one still had to explain how continents move.

Arthur Holmes proposes a continent mover mechanism

The first realistic proposal for a mechanism that would move continents was made by Arthur Holmes introduced in Chapter 1 - the person who developed the first practical dating mechanism, hypothesized (correctly) that convection currents in the Earth's mantle could provide the forces which could move continents if a heat energy source could be found[649]. By this time radioactive decay was well known as a potential heat source; hence, mantle convection currents powered by radioactively generated heat was the essential idea embodied in plate tectonics, where the dictionary defines tectonic as[650]:

> ...designating, of, or pertaining to changes in the structure of the earth's crust, the forces responsible for such deformation, or the external forms produced.

The word derives from the Latin tectonicus which in turn derives from the Greek tektonikos meaning builder.

Continents "float"

Having found a mechanism which could move continents, there was this little question, "how could solid granite continents move?" In a previous section, the fact that granite floats on basalt was demonstrated. Obviously, there is a vast difference between the viscosity of continents on basalt versus ice on water: it is much easier to move ice!

However, if mantle convection currents are strong enough, the continents will move and they do! Regarding the plates, the outer shell of the earth consists of an interlocking pattern of fifty-two granite plates.

Among these plates, two groups can be distinguished: a group of seven large plates of similar area covering up to ninety percent of the planet's surface and a group of smaller plates whose areas follow a distribution that can be defined mathematically[651].

It can also be shown that the plate layout has a property that characterizes a dynamic feedback between mantle convection and solid crust strength that creates plate motion[652].

Plate tectonics explains the widening of the Atlantic Ocean:

One of the significant explanations provided by plate tectonics is the widening of the Atlantic Ocean due to sea floor spreading, a concept first proposed in the early 1960s by the American geologist and naval officer, Harry H. Hess[653].

Development of highly sophisticated seismic recorders and precision depth recorders in the 1950s led to the discovery, in the early 1960s, of the Mid-Atlantic Ridge[654], a vast, undersea mountain chain in the middle of the Atlantic Ocean. Ultimately, it was found that the Mid Atlantic Ridge was a small segment of a globe-girdling forty-thousand-mile-long undersea mountain system.

In many locations, this mid-ocean ridge was found to contain a gigantic gap, or rift, twenty to thirty miles wide and about 1 mile deep. At the ridge, the Atlantic Ocean floor is split into two sections. Lava, upwelling through the rift fills the gap formed as the plates move apart under the enormous convection current forces.

In 1975, scientists of Project FAMOUS (French-American Mid-Ocean Undersea Study) - any good project name must devolve into an easily pronounced acronym - used the undersea robot *Alvin,* to dive on the Mid-Atlantic Ridge for the first direct observation of seafloor spreading[655].

Subduction

One of the major features of plate tectonics is subduction which occurs when one plate collides with another, sliding (or subducting) under it as shown in this simple diagram:

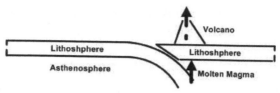

Figure 15-1 Simple Subduction Zone diagram.

Figure 15-1 provides a simple diagram illustrating a subduction zone. In this case, the boundary between the Pacific (Pac) Plate (west) and North American (NA) plate (east) is illustrated.

The plate motion on the west coast of NA is directly influenced by a huge geological formation in the mid Atlantic known as the mod-ocean ridge. It is one of the longest mountain ranges on earth and separates the NA plate and the Eurasian plate. Lava upwelling at the mid-Atlantic ridge is forcing the NA plate and Eurasian plate apart. So the Atlantic Ocean is growing and the Pacific Ocean is shrinking about 2.5 centimeters per year (it will be awhile before you live in Hawaii).

Another feature of subduction is the creation of volcanoes. As shown in Figure 15-1, the West Lithosphere is forced down into the molten lava where it melts and is then forced up through the east lithosphere creating a volcano. There is a north-south range of volcanoes along the west coast of North America resulting from this process.

In addition to the creation of volcanoes, the friction caused by the two plates passing by each other creates earthquakes. Actually, the entire Pacific Ocean boundary the Pacific Rim is subject to earth quakes and known as the "Ring of Fire." Plate tectonics is an important subject for those who live near a plate boundary which includes most of earth's inhabitants.

Deep Sea Drilling Project provides further verification of Plate Tectonics

A number of explorations have contributed to the establishment of plate tectonics as the proper explanation of the Earth's surface. One of the more important was the Deep Sea Drilling project, funded by the National Science Foundation, and directed by the Joint Oceanographic Institution for Deep Earth Sampling (JOIDES), a consortium of leading U.S. oceanographic institutions[656]. The primary drilling vessel was the

Glomar Challenger, displacing 10,500 tons and capable of drilling a core in 2,500 feet of sediment in 20,000 feet of water, the first ship of its type. The Deep-Sea Drilling Project drilled about six hundred holes into the ocean floors over the world.

The project was remarkably successful, verifying that the present ocean basins are relatively young and confirmed plate tectonics. It also discovered thick bedded salt layers from cores taken out of the Mediterranean Sea, indicating that the Mediterranean had completely dried up between five and twelve million years ago; that Antarctica has been covered with ice for the last twenty million years; and that the northern polar ice cap was much more extensive five million years ago[657].

Direct observation of plate movement:

It is possible to visit certain sites on Earth and directly observe the effects of plate tectonics: one of the best is the Point Reyes peninsula on the California coast. The dividing line between two continental plates is termed a fault. There are many types of faults, a principal one being the place where two plates slide by each other. Such a fault is the San Andreas Fault, one of the most famous geological features on Earth[658]. To the west of the San Andreas Fault lies the Pacific Plate[659], while to the east is the North American (NA) Plate[660].

Measurements have shown that the Pacific Plate moves northwest relative to the NA Plate at the rate of about two inches per year; however, the Pacific Plate also "subducts" under the NA plate[661]. As a consequence, the subducting NA plate melts and then forces its way up through cracks in the crust forming volcanoes (as shown in Fig. 16-1). There is a line of volcanoes along the western United States; among the most famous are Mount Saint Helens which erupted in 1980 and Mount Rainier, the tallest mountain in the West.

Of particular interest, there are places on the Point Reyes peninsula where the boundary between the two plates is exposed. At one place, the west side of the fault is made of granite, while the east side a rock termed chert, easily distinguished from granite. Approximately three hundred fifty miles south along the fault, near the City of Los Angeles, on the east side of the Fault, one finds granite that exactly matches the granite found on the west side at Point Reyes. At two inches per year, approximately eleven million years has elapsed since the granite left Los Angeles! No wonder our ancient ancestors did not realize the earth changed!

Plate tectonics solved many other mysteries:

Uplifts of large amounts of rock such as Siccar Point or the creation of mountain ranges are easily explained by Plate Tectonics. As continents spread from a starting point, they eventually collide. Hutton's Unconformity identifies geological sites where the junction between the collision of two types of rock formations can be seen[662]. One of the most famous is Siccar Point

As discussed above, when continents collide, enormous forces are created and one continent subducts under another causing the other to fold up, just as a carpet does when it is pushed against a wall. This process is termed *orogeny* or mountain building[663]. The uplift Hutton observed was caused by collisions between plates. This is also how the Alps are being created today.

Western United States has many examples of subduction zones besides Point Reyes. E.g., the Pacific Plate subducting under the NA Plate resulted in the formation of the Sierra Nevada. Approximately 250 million years ago, the pressure and friction that resulted from the grinding of the plates as the Pacific Plate subducted, causing the crust of the Pacific plate to melt, forming plumes of liquid rock termed "plutons" that eventually rose toward the surface.

These plutons combined into the single, massive deeply buried rock: the Sierra Nevada. Further pressure from the collision of the two plates caused the deeply buried Sierra rock to rise, pushing up the sedimentary rock that was part of the NA Plate above it. Beginning about 80 Ma, the uplifted sedimentary rock began to erode, exposing the unique Sierra Nevadan granite[664].

There is much more to the story of plate tectonics, but this should suffice for now, and we turn our attention the related subject of seismology.

Seismology, the scientific study of earthquakes[665]

Earthquakes are a consequence of Plate Tectonics generally produced by the "scraping" motion of the various plates which comprise the Earth's as they move past each other. This scraping motion produces elastic "waves" in the rock that propagate through the Earth[666] and provide much information about the Earth's interior.

John Winthrop (1714–1779) made first earthquake studies

Winthrop was one of the first to make scientific studies of earthquakes. Born in Boston, Winthrop was one of the first American intellectuals to be taken seriously in Europe, and was noted for his attempt to explain the 1755 earthquake in Lisbon as the result of known physical forces as opposed to a religious phenomenon[667] (recall that supernatural causation was often advanced to explain difficult or unusual phenomenon).

By analyzing seismic data from a 1909 earthquake near Zagreb (now in Croatia), the Austro-Hungarian meteorologist Andrija Mohorovicic discovered a boundary between the crust and an interior section of the Earth, known as the mantle and now called the Mohorovicic discontinuity or Moho[668].

Charles F. Richter (1900-1995) invents the Richter scale

Seismologist Charles F. Richter, born on a farm near Hamilton, Ohio, north of Cincinnati, made a number of contributions to Seismological studies. One of the more significant contributions was the development, in collaboration with Bento Gutenberg (1889-1960)[669], of the seismic magnitude scale which bears his name. The Richter earthquake scale describes earth quake magnitude as measured by a device known as a seismograph. Due to the wide amplitude ranges of seismic waves generated in an earthquake, Richter's scale is necessarily logarithmic which many find confusing. The logarithmic scale Richter employed is based on 10; hence each point on the Richter scale represents a ten-fold increase in amplitude of a wave launched by an earth quake[670]. Thus, a magnitude 6.0

earthquake is ten times stronger that a magnitude 5.0, while a magnitude 7.0 is one hundred times stronger than a magnitude 5.0.

Despite the obvious value of seismology to earth quake prediction, our interest in seismology is its ability to determine the Earth's interior structure which is accomplished by carefully observing the two principal earthquake waves: Primary or P-waves and Secondary or S-wave[671]. Both waves travel through the earth. P-waves arrive first followed by S-waves. Both waves also arrive before surface waves

Like any wave, the direction of seismic waves is changed or refracted. Careful measurement of the waves reveals the earth's inner structure. This is a simplified diagram of the Earth's Interior[672] that has been deduced by evaluating earthquake waves.

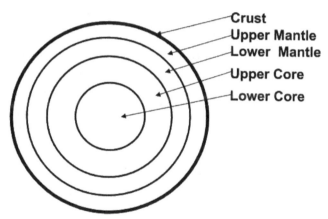

Crust
Upper Mantle
Lower Mantle
Upper Core
Lower Core

Figure 15-2 Earth's Interior Structure, not to scale.

Tomography is the integration of several observations of an object taken from different observation points to obtain a three-dimensional view[673]. Computed tomography (CAT) has a well known application in medicine. The application of computed tomography to earthquake waves has facilitated the creation of a complete "map" of the Earth's interior to a resolution of several hundred miles. This resolution allows geologists to detect and identify large scale features such as mantle plumes which are principal sources of volcanoes.

Based upon analysis of seismic waves, the upper core has been deduced to be liquid (due presumably to radioactive element decay) because it does not transmit S-waves and because the velocity of compressional P- waves that pass through it is sharply reduced. The inner core has been deduced to be solid because the behavior of P-waves and S-waves passing through it are different than the upper core[674].

The search for reliable and verifiable earth and universe dating methods:

Much of the material that has been presented in this book either directly or indirectly supports the fact of an Earth much older than six thousand years.

The essence of a reliable technique for measuring ancient objects was introduced in chapter 1. The physics underlying reliable dating was presented in Chapter 9 under the heading of "Radioactivity is caused by Nuclear Decay" where the two types of nuclear decay, alpha particle emission and beta decay which modifies atoms and can therefore be measured.

Unfortunately, radiometric dating continues to be challenged by websites such as Answers in Genesis[675]. Rather than debate the subject, the next section will summarize twelve independent methods that can be used to reliably and verifiably determine the age of the earth and universe. However, the development of reliable dating methods has not been an easy task.

Determining the sun's age:

As pointed previously, despite the obvious advantage of the data that had been collected by many geologists, Lyell et al had to contend with the enigma of the sun's age which was important since obviously, the Earth couldn't be older than the Sun. Consequently, all Earth age estimates made during the 1800s were much too low and the true Earth's age would not be determined until the twentieth century.

The source of the sun's energy was discussed above in Chapter 9: Sir Mark Oliphant demonstrated nuclear fusion of hydrogen is the energy source in 1932. It has been estimated that the sun has enough hydrogen for another 5 billion years. As mentioned occasionally, one discipline aids another

Another issue, related to the dating problem was the source of the Earth's inner heat. As mentioned above, we now understand that Earth's interior heat is generated by nuclear decay, not discovered until 1897 and not fully understood until the early 20th century.

A Summary of reliable and verifiable earth and universe dating methods:

This section will summarize several of the reliable, verifiable and independent dating methods, beginning with one of most useful methods, radiometric dating.

Method 1: Radiometric dating:

As described in chapter 1, radiometric dating employs the well known phenomenon of nuclear decay, the spontaneous emission of particles from a nucleus.21-1 lists four useful dating elements. Here are some more useful radioactive elements for dating[676].

Parent	Daughter	Half-life, Billions of Yrs	Materials that can be dated
^{235}U	^{207}Pb	0.704	Zircon, uraninite, pitchblende
^{40}K	^{40}Ar	1.251	Muscovite, biotite, hornblende, volcanic rock, glauconite, K-feldspar
^{238}U	^{206}Pb	4.468	Zircon, uraninite, pitchblende
^{87}Rb	^{87}Sr	48.8	K-micas, K-feldspars, biotite, metamorphic rock, glauconite

Table 15-1 Some of the more useful radiometric dating materials.

The first person to make practical use of nuclear decay dating was Arthur Holmes (1890-1965), mentioned previously, an exceptionally accomplished geologist who was instrumental in creating the nuclear decay method. Holmes published his first findings from his study of the decay of uranium (U) into lead (Pb) in which he determined that the Earth was about 1.6 billion years old. This was much greater than other estimates and was met with some skepticism. Measuring the products of nuclear decay is a tedious task and Holmes devoted the majority of his life to the task. By 1946 he felt he had enough evidence to state that the Earth was at least 3 billion years old and probably older.

Method 2: Isotope ratios

An informative web article by Chris Stassen points out that ratios of isotopes, such as isotopes of lead, (known as isochron dating), will yield more accurate results than simple use of the nuclear decay equation[677].

As pointed out by Stassen, the most direct means for calculating the Earth's age is a Pb/Pb isochron age, derived from samples of the Earth and meteorites. This involves measurement of three isotopes of lead (^{206}Pb, ^{207}Pb, and either ^{208}Pb or ^{204}Pb). A plot is constructed of the ratio of ^{206}Pb to ^{204}Pb versus ^{207}Pb to ^{204}Pb.

Since most of Earth's earliest material has been destroyed by plate tectonics, complete measurements of the earth's age must rely on extra terrestrial objects such as meteorites[678].

If the solar system formed from a common pool of matter, which was uniformly distributed in terms of Pb isotope ratios, then the initial plots for all objects from that pool of matter would fall on a single point.

Over time, the amounts of ^{206}Pb and ^{207}Pb will change in some samples, as these isotopes are decay end-products of uranium decay (^{238}U decays to ^{206}Pb, and ^{235}U decays to ^{207}Pb) giving an accurate age of the rock being dated[679].

Method 3: Universe dating techniques:

Chapter 13 discussed Edwin Hubble's discovery that unique stars termed Cepheid variables could be used as a yard stick for measuring distances to the distant galaxies and determined that the closest galaxy, Andromeda, is 2.5 million light years from Earth. Since light travels one light year per year, the Andromeda galaxy is at least 2.5. million years old. Using this new distance measuring technique, Hubble demonstrated that the universe is expanding, which led to the hypothesis that the expansion began with a "Big Bang." As mentioned Chapter 13, The Big Bang hypothesis was shown to be correct when radiation from the Big Bang, was discovered. Exhaustive study of this radiation by the Wilkinson Microwave Anisotropy Probe confirmed that the universe is 13.7 billion years old +/- 200 thousand years.

An excellent article by Ian Plimar[680], lists six independent means for dating the Earth and objects on it. Since radiometric dating, has already been mentioned, we will only include methods 4 – 8 from Plimar's list.

- Method 4: Measure the electrons captured in minerals as a result of long periods of solar and cosmic radiation bombardment, the number of electrons is an indication of the minerals age[681].

- Method 5: The direction of the Earth's magnetic field reverses and can be used to determine when magnetic minerals formed and thus date the host material[682].

- Method 6: Biological material such as amino acids undergo decay at known rates; therefore, measurement of chemicals in old biological material enables an estimate the decay time of the material[683].

- Method 7: As bones age, nitrogen is lost and fluorine is gained from ground water at known rates. Measurement methods 1 and 6, along with bone chemistry change provide three independent bone age estimates[684].

- Method 8: Employs the simple fact of tidal or seasonal cycles. E.g., more sediment from erosion occurs in summer than winter.

- Method 9: The age of the chemical elements:[685] The age of the chemical elements can be estimated using radioactive decay to determine how old a given mixture of atoms is. The most definite ages that can be determined this way are ages since the solidification of rock samples. When a rock solidifies, the chemical elements often get separated into different crystalline grains in the rocks.

- Method 10: The age of the oldest star clusters:[686] When stars are burning hydrogen which produces helium in their cores, they fall on a single curve in the luminosity-temperature plot known as the Hertzsprung - Russell diagram after its inventors, Hertzsprung and Russell. This track is known as the main sequence, since most stars are found there. Since the luminosity of a star varies, the lifetime of a star on the main sequence varies by a constant. Thus, if you measure the luminosity of the most luminous star on the main sequence, you get an upper limit for the age of the cluster.

- Method 11: The age of the oldest white dwarf stars:[687] As explained above, a white dwarf star is an object that is about as heavy as the Sun but has only the radius of the Earth. The average density of a white dwarf is a million times denser than water. White dwarf stars form in the centers of red giant stars, but are not visible until the envelope of the red giant is ejected into space. When this happens the ultraviolet radiation from the very hot stellar core ionizes the gas and produces a planetary nebula. The envelope of the star continues to move away from the central core, and eventually the planetary nebula fades to invisibility, leaving just the very hot core which is now a white dwarf. White dwarf stars glow just from residual heat. The oldest white dwarfs will be the coldest and thus the faintest. By searching for faint white dwarfs, one can estimate the length of time the oldest white dwarfs have been cooling.

- Method 12: Accelerator mass spectrometry (AMS):[688] This technique is unique relative to other types of mass spectrometry in that it accelerates ions to extremely high energies which gives it the ability to separate a rare isotope, e.g., ^{14}C from an abundant neighboring mass e.g., ^{12}C. The technique is particularly useful in dating delicate materials. E.g., AMS was used to date the Shroud of Turin[689] which is so delicate, that only a few fibers could be examined and has been used to identify aspects of our ancient ancestor as discussed in Section 1.

Thus, there are twelve independent methods from several independent sources of credible information regarding the determination of the both the age of the Earth and the Universe. These range from the use of various forms of nuclear decay to exotic techniques such as the age of White Dwarf Stars and the Wilkinson Microwave Anisotropy Probe. In order to retain the belief that the Earth is only 6000 years old, every one of these must be proven false, an impossible undertaking, especially as those who have attempted this feat have been uniformly unsuccessful.

Accordingly, there is no credible evidence that disputes the fact that the Earth is 4.5 billion years old and that the universe began with a bang, 13.7 billion years ago. Thus, statements like

There is no reason not to believe that God created our universe, earth, plants, animals, and people just as described in the book of Genesis!

are patently ridiculous!

Chapter 15 Summary: The forces which cause of earth's physical features to change.

For this book's purpose, establishing the proof that the earth changes; there were three key developments after 1850: the discovery of Plate Tectonics, the establishment of Seismology, and refinement of Earth and Universe dating techniques (the process of erosion is self-evident and I mentioned it above for completeness).

Above the mantle lies a relatively thin crust of solid rock, of which there are two kinds: Basalt and granite. granite has a slightly lower specific gravity than basalt; hence, granite "floats" on the basalt. Although the coefficient of friction between granite and basalt is rather large, there is sufficient strength in the mantle convection forces to slowly move the granite plates, a phenomenon termed Plate Tectonics. Plate Tectonics explains many mysteries: the shape of the Atlantic Ocean, the building of mountain ranges and the configuration of Sicar Point. The extremely slow pace of Plate tectonics is one of the many indications that the Earth must be very old.

Seismology, the study of the passage of Earthquake waves through the Earth revealed Earth's internal structure in considerable detail, revealing that the Earth consists of a series of concentric spheres beginning with a solid iron inner core and a liquid iron outer core. Above these cores, lies an upper and lower mantle. The Earth's interior has been measured in sufficient detail to preclude the possibility of large pockets of water that could have produced "The Fountains of the Deep."

The decay of radioactive elements provides the Earth's inner heat, especially the heat energy sufficient to cause convection currents in the upper mantle.

Age of the Earth: In addition to the conclusive proof that the Universe is 13.7 billion years old, 11 independent methods of determining Earth's age, besides the controversial radioactive dating which has never been convincingly proven to be incorrect, such as fluctuation in the Earth's magnetic field and the decay of biological material. Moreover, a paper by Dalrymple which debunks Creationist objections and dubious dating methods was briefly discussed.

The bottom line: Chapters 14 and 15 have explained the resolution of the apparently unchanging physical features of the Earth illusion in enough detail to establish beyond any reasonable doubt that the Earth has been changing ever since it was created from the primordial disk that surrounded the birth of the sun some 4.5 ba

These chapters compare the Religious explanation of the creation of Earth's physical features, essentially found in one book, the *Book of Genesis*, with the scientific creation explanation found in a library full of books. We have seen how the Religious explanation can answer the question of who created the physical features, but is unable to explain how or why the features were created; whereas, Science cannot answer who created the features, since there was no creator, but can, in great detail, explain how and why the features were created.

Looking ahead:

Having explained the resolution of the apparently unchanging physical features illusion, we next move to the resolution of the apparently unchanging biological features illusion in the next two Chapters.

CHAPTER 16

RESOLVING THE EARTH'S APPARENTLY UNCHANGING BIOLOGICAL FEATURES ILLUSION

The growing recognition that life might have evolved is probably one of the more controversial aspects of the realization that the earth changes. Copernicus had eliminated man's place at the center of the universe, evolution would separate man from his maker--these findings had a devastating effect! Not only were we not alone (chapter 2), *we were not very special.*

Fossils - the starting point for the detection of biological change:

As pointed out in chapter 14, the starting point for a reasoned explanation of life on earth is the many clues such as fossils, first employed by Leonardo to prove the fallaciousness of the biblical Flood story and demonstrate that the earth changes (unfortunately, Leonardo's discoveries were hidden).

Other investigators continued accumulating evidence which gradually led to the recognition that the apparently unchanging biological features of the Earth was an illusion. Evolution had occurred: animals had developed over a vast interval of time.

Six scientists played important roles in the investigation of these new ideas:

- Georges de Buffon (1707-1788).
- Jean-Baptiste de Lamarck (1744 - 1829.

- Étienne Geoffroy St. Hilaire (1772-1844).
- Georges Cuvier (1769-1832).
- Louis Agassiz (1807-1873).
- Ernst Haeckel (1834-1919).

Four were from France, one from Germany and one from Great Britain, all with very different personalities, educations and views. They were particularly interested in answering two key questions: has Evolution occurred? And if so, how does it work? In considering these investigators, keep in mind that none of them understood very much about the engine of evolution: reproduction, a full understanding of which has only been achieved recently. We begin with:

Georges-Louis Leclerc, Comte de Buffon (1707-1788)

Buffon, a member of the French scientific elite, was a naturalist, mathematician, biologist and cosmologist, truly one of the great polymaths[690]. Buffon's views influenced the next two generations of naturalists, including Lamarck and Darwin (see below) Darwin himself stated that, "The first author who in modern times has treated [evolution] in a scientific spirit was Buffon[691]."

Buffon first made his mark in the field of mathematics and in *Sur le jeu de franc-carreau* (On the game of chance) introduced differential and integral calculus into probability theory.

Buffon's most famous work was *Histoire naturelle, générale et particulière* (Natural history, general and particular) prepared between 1749 to 1778, and published posthumously.

Buffon observed that different regions have distinct plants and animals despite having similar environments. These observations led him to the *radical conclusion* that species must have "improved," i.e., evolved after dispersing away from a center of creation, following in the footsteps of such iconoclasts as Aristarchus and Copernicus, who defied convention regarding the shape of solar system and Thompson and Rutherford who defied convention regarding the shape of the atom, Buffon's observations also led him to assert that climate change must have facilitated the worldwide spread of species.

Buffon, in his prescient book, *Les époques de la nature* (The epochs of nature) published in 1778, discussed the origins of the solar system, speculating that the planets had been created by comet collisions with the sun[692]. This was almost two hundred years before the collision theory was discredited by improved explanations (chapter 11.)

Buffon continued his iconoclastic ways by making a calculation of the cooling rate of iron to estimate that the age of the earth was seventy-five thousand years, which he published in his seminal "Les Époques de la Nature" (The epochs of Nature). This obviously implied that the earth originated much earlier than Archbishop Ussher's 4004 BCE date, which made him perhaps the first person to challenge the existing position of the Catholic Church. Unsurprisingly, this *provoked a clash with the Church* condemning him and burning his books[693].

Apparently unaware of Leonardo's efforts, Buffon "poured salt on the wound" by also denying that the Biblical Flood ever occurred and observed that some animals retain parts that are vestigial and no longer useful, suggesting that they have evolved rather than having been spontaneously generated; moreover, he anticipated Hutton and Lyell's "uniformitarianism."

Finally, his examination of the similarities between primates and humans suggested a common ancestor which apparently led him to believe in organic change, but he could not specify how it worked[694]. Buffon was a hard act to follow.

Jean-Baptiste Pierre Antoine de Monet, Chevalier de Lamarck - acquired features are passed on via inheritance

Jean-Baptiste Lamarck, another member of the "French Naturalists," was influenced by Buffon to embrace the concept that evolution is a process governed by natural laws [695]. However, Lamarck developed the rather controversial concept that evolution occurred when animals improved by acquiring more useful capabilities, which they passed on to their offspring, a concept known as "The inheritance of acquired characteristics."

Although the concept of passing on acquired characteristics will be shown below to be impossible, Lamarck constructed what may be the first comprehensive theoretical framework of organic evolution: S. J. Gould argues that Lamarck was the "primary evolutionary theorist[696]."(This is a surprising conclusion since neither Lamarck or any of the six had the foggiest notion how evolution occurs).

Lamarck was one of the first persons to employ the term Biology[697] and was also one of the main contributors to Cell Theory.

Lamarck was a transitional scientist, part modern, part medieval, in that he opposed Lavoisier's modern chemistry in favor of alchemy and preferred the classical view of earth wind, fire and water as Earth's principal elements.

Étienne Geoffroy St. Hilaire (1772-1844) - form is conserved.

Another French naturalist, who, in his two volume 1818 work, *Philosophie anatomique,* argued that form is conserved[698]. Geoffroy asserted that vertebrate animal organization reflected one uniform type since he saw all vertebrates as modifications of a single archetype, a single form. Currently unneeded organs, such as the appendix, might serve no functional purpose, but the fact that they still existed demonstrated that animals are derived from an archetype.

Georges Cuvier (1769-1832): form follows function

Another prominent French scientist, Georges Cuvier, considered to have been one of the greatest scientists of his time[699], disagreed with Geoffroy. Based upon careful observations, Cuvier argued that form does follow function. In a famous 1830 debate with Geoffroy, Cuvier convincingly demonstrated how many apparent examples of structural unity proposed by Geoffroy to support the conservation of form concept were in fact contrived and superficial, which thus supported that form follows function[700].

Regarding evolution, in his 1813 Essay *on the theory of the Earth,* Cuvier proposed that new species were created after periodic catastrophic floods[701] (eliminating many species); hence, he would naturally be opposed to anyone, such a Lamarck, who proposed some type of evolution.

Among his many other accomplishments, Cuvier is credited with the foundation of vertebrate paleontology. Cuvier also convinced his contemporaries that the controversial subject of extinction was a fact. However, as shown above, that was settled fairly well by Leonardo; unfortunately, Leonardo's findings were buried under indecipherable text.

Cuvier's study of the Paris basin with Alexander Brongniart established the basic principles of biostratiography[702].

Louis Agassiz (1807-1873) - opposed to evolution

Interestingly, Agassiz's biology was not as good as his geology; he resisted Darwin's theories on evolution. Agassiz denied that species originated in single pairs, whether at a single location or at many. He argued instead that multiple individuals in each species were created at the same time and then distributed throughout the continents where God meant for them to dwell. This is essentially creationism and was consistent with the generally accepted views of the time. His lectures on polygenism (the theory that different races have different origins)[703] were popular among the slaveholders in the South, for many, this opinion legitimized the belief in a lower standard for the African American[704].

Ernst Haeckel (1834-1919)

German biologist, naturalist, philosopher and physician, Ernst Haeckel shared Darwin's belief in evolution, but did not share Darwin's enthusiasm for natural selection as the main mechanism for generating the diversity of the biological world. Haeckel instead believed that the environment acted directly on organisms, producing new races (a version of Lamarckism). Haeckel did argue that the survival of the races depended on their interaction with the environment[705]. As will be seen Haeckel was on the right track..

Has evolution occurred? And if so how does it work? Here is a summary of the six explanations discussed above:

Investigator	Evolution occurred?	How does it work?	Dates
Buffon	Y	Didn't know	1707-1780
Lamarck	Y	Inheritance of acquired characteristics	1744-1829
Geoffrey	Y	Not clear he had a concept	1772-1844
Cuvier	N	Improvements by extinctions and restarts	1769-1832
Agassiz	N	Believed in creationism	1807-1873
Haeckel	Y?	Variation on Lamarckism	1834-1919

Table 16-1 Summary of six investigator's views regarding Evolution.

So, if these votes decided the issue, evolution has occurred. However, the mechanism for evolution was hardly clear except for Lamarckism which was ultimately proven wrong. On the other hand, considering the limited state of biological understanding at this time, these findings represent remarkable prescience; moreover, the stage was set for Darwin.

Charles Robert Darwin (1809 – 1882) - almost in the right place at the right time

Darwin was one of those persons fortunate to be almost in the right place at the right time[706]. But, he was born too soon to have the necessary genetic knowledge to prepare a correct explanation of evolution. While, as mentioned above, Darwin did not specifically discover the phenomenon of evolution, he made three key contributions that established the fact of evolution and biological change.

1. He was the first to collect and organize enough fossils to allow him to conclusively demonstrate the existence of the evolutionary phenomenon.
2. In view of the unfriendly religious climate, Darwin had the courage to publish his results.
3. Darwin provided the first attempt at an explanation of the Evolution Phenomenon.

Most importantly, Darwin was one of the first persons to conclusively demonstrate that life changed; thereby resolving the unchanging biological illusion.

Born in 1809, into a well educated and prosperous family. The son of wealthy society doctor and financier, Robert Darwin and the grandson of Erasmus Darwin, an English physician, natural philosopher, physiologist, inventor and poet. Erasmus Darwin was one of the founding members of the Lunar Society[707], a discussion group of pioneering industrialists and natural philosophers.

Darwin was also born at a time of great intellectual ferment, particularly in the controversial issue of biblical literacy.

While Darwin was growing to manhood, he met Charles Lyell who was to become an influential mentor.

Darwin received a sound, fairly general education, studying first medicine at Edinburgh University and then theology at Cambridge. These studies instilled in Darwin a keen interest in natural history; hence, this was the field he ultimately followed.

The fateful voyage of the Beagle

Darwin's interest in science was greatly enhanced when he had the good fortune to be selected as a "a gentleman companion" by Robert Fitzroy, captain of the British survey ship *Beagle*[708]. The *Beagle's* journey was to be long and Fitzroy dreaded such a voyage without suitable companionship, as the previous captain had committed suicide. It is noteworthy that Darwin carried a copy of Volume one of Lyell's treatise on geology – but, as mentioned previously, Lyell argued against evolution. Lyell rejected Lamarck's idea of organic evolution, proposing instead "Centers of Creation" to explain diversity and territory of species. However, many of his letters demonstrated that he was fairly open to the idea of evolution.

Originally scheduled for two years, the *Beagle's* voyage was extended to five years (1831-1836) circumnavigating the Earth, stopping at many interesting places, especially the Galapagos Islands. For Darwin, the Galapagos were one of the most ideal locations on Earth to study the development of Life:

> The islands lie in the Pacific Ocean about 1,000 km (approximately 600 miles) from the South American coast and straddle the Equator. There are 13 large islands, 6 smaller ones and 107 islets and rocks, with a total land area of about 8,000 square kilometers (approximately 300 square miles). The islands are volcanic in origin and several volcanoes in the west of the archipelago are still very active[709].

Of particular importance, the islands are sufficiently separated to allow independent evolution, but close enough to be readily accessible. While exploring the islands, Darwin became especially interested in small birds on the islands. Darwin noted that the bird's taxonomy (physical features) varied from island to island and that beaks were particularly well adapted for the different types of seeds found on different islands. Since Darwin was actually more of a geologist than ornithologist; in examining the birds, he concluded they were a mixture of blackbirds, grosbeaks and finches. When he arrived back in England, Darwin's collection included several samples of each to exhibit.

In addition to collecting many samples of wildlife, Darwin had made many important geological discoveries, which he sent back to England on those occasions when the Beagle stopped at a British controlled location. These discoveries were well received such that when he returned to England he was celebrated as a rising naturalist of great capability

Evolution is for the Birds:

Upon his return, Darwin wrote his first paper, demonstrating that the South American landmass was slowly rising[710]. This was met with great enthusiasm, especially by Lyell as it supported Lyell's contention that very slow geological forces shaped the landscape. (Even though he had no idea what the forces were).

With Lyell's enthusiastic backing Darwin read his paper to the Geological Society of London in January 4, 1837.

Later the same day, with Lyell's assistance, Darwin presented his mammal and bird specimens collected during his second *Beagle* voyage to the Society. Fortuitously, the bird specimens were given to the resident ornithologist for identification.

John Gould (1804-1881)- another at the right place at the right time but to no avail[11].

Gould a poorly educated gardener's son, was born in Dorset, England. Gould adopted the gardening vocation which gave him the opportunity to examine the birds that flocked around the garden and led to an interest in taxidermy. Gould became an expert taxidermist as well as an expert in bird identification through a bird's structure, and soon established a taxidermy business in London. His skill enabled him to become the first curator and preserver at the museum of the London Zoological Society. This position brought him into contact with the leading naturalists, which often allowed him to examine new bird collections. This placed him in the fateful position of being the first ornithologists to view Darwin's bird specimens[712].

Gould set aside his paying work to examine Darwin's bird collection, and at the next Society meeting, on January 10, reported that the birds Darwin had brought from the Galapagos Islands, which Darwin had identified as blackbirds, "gross-bills" and finches, had been misidentified by Darwin. This was not really a surprise since Darwin was more interested in geology. The birds were in fact: "a series of ground Finches which are so peculiar" as to form "an entirely new group, containing 12 species[713]." Darwin's Galapagos wren "was another species of finch and the mockingbirds he had labeled by island were separate species rather than just varieties, with relatives on the South American mainland[714]."

Not realizing the importance of his bird collection, Darwin had not bothered to label his finches by island, but other expedition members had taken more care. He now sought specimen locations collected by captain Fitzroy and crewmen which allowed Darwin to establish that each species was unique to an island.

When he found that the birds' beaks matched the seeds they ate, Darwin must have been stunned, for the implications were clear: the finches and mockingbirds must have had a common ancestor that had somehow been carried to the islands and due to the separation between the islands, had evolved over unknown thousands of years into separate species adapting their beaks to the food available on the island. Darwin's efforts provided proof that *Evolution has occurred! Life changes.*

Why isn't evolution John Gould's Theory?

John Gould apparently did not arrive at the same conclusion as Darwin. Why not? Gould had the information first, he could have "scooped" Darwin and announced his (Gould's) proof that evolution occurs? The answer is actually rather simple. As a *News Scan Daily* article, dated, 28 May 1999 points out[715]:

> The information was there, but he [Gould] didn't quite know what to make of it. He assumed that since God

made one set of birds when he created the world, the specimens from different locations would be identical. Gould was a biblical literalist and couldn't understand why God would make 12 finch species. Gould thought the way he had been taught to think, like an expert taxonomist, and didn't see, in the finches, the textbook example of evolution unfolding right before him.

Thus, John Gould fell into the same trap as Stephen Godfrey (and many Americans) - Gould was just incapable of "crossing the Beckoning Bridge" to arrive at the correct solution.

For Darwin, having established evolution as a fact, there remained two nagging questions:

1. What caused evolution to occur?
2. Since enormous amounts of time were necessary, where did the time come from?

Thomas Malthus and "the survival of the fittest":

A partial answer to the first question was provided by Thomas Malthus. Malthus's studies of population had convinced him that, all things being equal, population tends to grow geometrically while resources grow linearly. Thus, ultimately, population growth should overwhelm resources. This led Malthus to conclude that in such a situation, only the most fit would survive[716]. This idea had a "decisive influence" on Darwin and his explanation of evolution.

Darwin saw the struggle for existence of all creatures as the catalyst by which the process which causes evolution to occur would produce the most fit. When he ultimately published his book, he gave tribute to Malthus by stating that his [Darwin's] theory was an application of Malthus' doctrines.

Darwin, a life-long admirer of Malthus, referred to Malthus as *"that great philosopher"* (Letter to J.D. Hooker 5th June, 1860) and wrote in his notebook that *"Malthus on Man should be studied."*

While Malthus's investigations had led to the correct deduction regarding population growth, there was a flaw in his reasoning.

Unless perturbed by external forces such as disease or predation, population does not grow geometrically, but grows exponentially, since the rate of population growth is proportional to the size of the population. This sentence can be converted into a simple linear differential equation of this form:

$$P(t) = Cx\ dP(t)/dt$$

The population at a time **t**, **P(t)** is proportional to the rate of change with time for the population. The larger the population, the greater will be the rate of change. The solution to this equation is:

$$P(t) = P(0) + e^{C \cdot t}$$

Where **P(t)** is the population at any given time, **P(0)** is the initial population (usually zero) and C is a constant. Of import, exponential growth which is presently occurring is more serious than geometrical growth.

Developing the correct explanation of the phenomenon of evolution:

As mentioned above, having made a momentous discovery, Darwin attempted to determine what caused evolution to occur. However, as the scientific community was just beginning to digest the realization that life changed but had not discovered important information such as cell division and genetics, it would have been impossible for Darwin to have determined evolution's causes. It has to involve the creation of new genes. However, he needed an ending for his book's title.

From Malthus, he realized that evolution must have a selective cause; moreover, artificial selection would be totally incorrect so he changed artificial to natural which gave him the title ending he needed – Natural Selection. However, as explained in Chapter 18, Natural Selection does not explain the phenomenon of evolution; on the other hand, Natural Selection does provide a superficial explanation.

Lyell's Geology did answer the second nagging question. As discussed above, Lyell and associates had deduced that the earth was much older than had been generally believed. While Lyell's geological information and age estimates were too short by modern terms, they were sufficient for Darwin. However as mentioned above, Lyell was equivocal regarding evolution.

Lyell's book., *Geological Evidences of the Antiquity of Man*[717], brought together Lyell's views on three key themes from the geology of the most recent Geologic Period in Earth's history, the 1.6-million-year Quaternary Period: glaciers, evolution, and the age of the human race.

First published in 1863, the book was widely regarded as a disappointment because of Lyell's equivocal treatment of evolution. Lyell, being a devout Christian, had great difficulty reconciling his beliefs with evolution which essentially precluded the need for a creator. (another standing in the middle of the beckoning bridge)

As will become clear in the remainder of this chapter, when all of the details of evolution are explained, the lack of a need for a creator will be further emphasized.

Publish or perish: Besides the dilemma of a complete explanation of "Natural Selection," Darwin's next dilemma was publication of his confirmation that evolution occurs and his explanation of the cause. As mentioned above, the religious climate in the mid 1800s was not particularly receptive to ideas that challenged accepted dogmas:

> Darwin was well aware of the implication his demonstration that Evolution had occurred for the origin of humanity and the real danger to his career and reputation as an eminent geologist of being convicted of blasphemy. He worked in secret to consider all objections and prepare overwhelming evidence supporting his proof that evolution had occurred[718].

Hence, Darwin agonized about publishing his obviously controversial findings, as He was perhaps mindful of the reaction to the publication 300 years earlier of Nicolas Copernicus's groundbreaking opus, "On the Revolutions of the Celestial Spheres."

Enter stage left, Alfred Russell Wallace (1823-1913):

In view of Darwin's presumed familiarity with the reaction to Copernicus's publication, Darwin's caution and desire to be as correct as possible is quite understandable. However, Darwin wasn't the only person working on the problem of evolution. British naturalist, explorer, geographer, anthropologist and biologist, Alfred Wallace had also stumbled on evidence that evolution had probably occurred[719].

Like Darwin, Wallace traveled extensively particularly in South East Asia, investigating the straits between the islands of Borneo, Java and Sumatra, termed SUNDA and Australia plus some islands off the coast of NW Australia termed SAHUL. In 1859, Wallace observed significant biological differences across the narrow "line" separating SUNDA and SAHUL formed by species distribution. Australian species reside west of the line while a mixture of species of Asian and Australian reside east of the line which became known as the Wallace Line[720].

Wallace's studies led him to arrive at the same conclusion as Darwin: Natural Selection i.e., evolution could explain what he had been observing[721]. Interestingly, Wallace was also greatly influenced by Thomas Malthus. After finding about Darwin's work, Wallace is reputed to have:

> Called Malthus's ...*the most important book I read...* and considered it *the most interesting coincidence* that both he and Darwin were independently led to the theory of evolution through reading Malthus[722].

Knowing about Wallace, Darwin's friends and associates constantly urged him to publish lest he be scooped by Wallace. Finally, while Darwin was writing up his explanation of his investigations in 1858, Wallace sent him an essay which described a similar idea, prompting immediate joint publication of both of their essays in 1859. Darwin entitled his book[723]:

> *On the Origin of Species by Means of Natural Selection, or the Preservation of Favoured Races in the Struggle for Life.*

When Wallace read Darwin's book, Wallace realized that Darwin's was much superior and offered to withdraw his paper. Darwin, being a magnanimous person insisted that both papers be published, and they were.

Strange career twists and modern resurgence of Alfred Wallace:

Unfortunately, Wallace's career took a strange twist and he became a spiritualist. Later Wallace maintained that Natural Selection cannot account for many human characteristics such as mathematical, artistic, or musical genius; moreover, something in "the unseen universe of Spirit" had interceded at least three times in history[724]:

1. The creation of life from inorganic matter.
2. The introduction of consciousness in the higher animals.
3. The generation of the above-mentioned faculties in mankind.

Wallace was obviously a partial believer in the concept of Intelligent Design (ID); (the theory that life, or the universe, cannot have arisen by chance and was designed and created by some intelligent entity.[725])

These new views greatly disturbed Darwin, who argued that spiritual appeals were not necessary and that sexual selection (correct, but for the wrong reason) could easily explain such apparently non-adaptive phenomena as musical genius.

Notwithstanding Wallace's strange views, a resurgence in interest in Wallace has begun. An article in the December 20, 2008 Wall Street Journal trumpets, "Alfred Russell Wallace's Fans Gear Up for a Darwinian Struggle – Anniversary of 'Origin of Species' Nears; Rival is Touted, Charges of Plagiarism Fly. David Hallmark, a British Lawyer having researched Wallace, including retracing Wallace's travels, wants to prove that Mr. Darwin was a cheat[726]."

These folks don't seem to realize that neither Wallace nor Darwin had an important key to the puzzle; what is the cause of the phenomenon of evolution. Moreover, if Darwin or Wallace hadn't discovered evolution, someone else would have.

Darwin's last comments pertaining to Evolution:

In the conclusion to "On the Origins" Darwin revealed that he apparently did realize that reproduction was a key and that variation was associated with inheritance as he wrote on the last page:

> It is interesting to contemplate a tangled bank, clothed with many plants of many kinds, with birds singing on the bushes, with various insects flitting about, and with worms crawling through the damp earth, and to reflect that these elaborately constructed forms, so different from each other, and dependent on each other in so complex a manner, have all been produced by laws acting around us. These laws, taken in the largest sense, being Growth with Reproduction; Inheritance which is almost implied by reproduction; Variability from the indirect and direct action of the conditions of life, and from use and disuse; a Ratio of Increase so high as to lead to a Struggle for Life, and as a consequence to Natural Selection, entailing Divergence of Character and the Extinction of less-improved forms. Thus, from the war of nature, from famine and death, the most exalted object which we are capable of conceiving, namely, the production of the higher animals, directly follows. There is grandeur in this view of life, with its several powers, having been originally breathed by the Creator [not sure Darwin believed in a Creator, but he had to pay homage] into a few forms or into one; and that, whilst this planet has gone cycling on according to the fixed law of gravity, from so simple a beginning endless forms most beautiful and most wonderful have been, and are being, evolved[727].

The key phrases in this conclusion are:

- Growth with Reproduction.
- Inheritance which is almost implied by reproduction.

- Variability from the indirect and direct action of the conditions of life, and from use and disuse.
- A Ratio of Increase so high as to lead to a Struggle for Life, and as a consequence to Natural Selection.
- Entailing Divergence of Character and the Extinction of less-improved forms.

His statement "Inheritance which is almost implied by reproduction" was agonizingly close, but he didn't know how reproduction works and produces inheritance. In the next section, we will see how inheritance works and why a person can inherit their father's eyes, but their mother's nose.

Science and Religion diverge in response to Evolution:

Reactions to Darwin's publication of On Origin of Species were very different in the scientific and religious communities. Some scientists, especially those like Lyell who held strong religious beliefs, had their doubts and concerns about evolution and its consequences. (Recall that Lyell had said, "If evolution is true, religion is a joke.") On the other hand, progress in gaining an understanding of underlying biological processes continued, not necessarily with the objective of proving or disproving evolution-- many of the discoveries such as those which led to an understanding of reproduction, contribute to the explanation of the evolutionary phenomenon.

The reaction of many in the religious community, especially in the United States, was vehement denunciation of and opposition to evolution. While the Copernican heliocentric concept was bad enough and logically the action which initiated the religion-science conflict, Darwin's concept of evolution, which displaced humans from their cherished position as a special creation of God, was "the last straw," inflaming the conflict between religion and science, a conflict, as mentioned in the Introduction and General Overview that continues today.

Chapter 16 Summary: Resolving the earth's apparently unchanging biological features Illusion.

- Early humans did not realize that the unchanging biological nature of the Earth was an illusion. They observed the natural life cycle of birth and death of plants and animals, but that didn't suggest change.

- The origin of life as described in the *Book of Genesis* is merely a listing of the facts of existence – what can be found on the Earth and who made them. However, there is no mention of how or why life exists as it does; hence, *Genesis* does not provide much of an explanation.

- Gradually, beginning in the 17th century, observations began to accumulate that suggested that biological processes did change and that life had actually evolved over a long-time period. Four French scientists, one German scientist and on British scientist were in the forefront of this accumulation and realization that life changed. Their conclusions are tabularized in table 11-1.

- While none of these explanations were correct, most at least acknowledged that evolution had occurred. The stage was thus set for Charles Darwin.

- Darwin was able to fortuitously tour the world collecting geological samples and animal samples, particularly birds that he presented to a meeting of the scientific society.

- Ornithologist John Gould attended this meeting, and correctly identified Darwin's collection as multiple finch species, providing the key that allowed Darwin to conclude that they had evolved from a common ancestor; thereby, enabling him to be the first person to conclusively demonstrate that evolution had occurred.

- In view of the unfriendly religious climate, Darwin also had the courage to publish his results.

- Darwin's findings vaulted him into the inner circle of British science and he was allowed to present his bird collection at a meeting of the Royal Society.

- Darwin spent several years refining his findings, With the help of Thomas Malthus who had conceived the concept of "Survival of the Fittest" and Darwin's mentor Charles Lyle, who supplied the time needed for evolution, wrote his ground-breaking book "*On the Origin of Species by Means of Natural Selection.*"
- However, as introduced in chapter 1, Natural Selection does not explain the phenomenon of evolution – Darwin lacked the detailed biological understanding to develop an explanation.

It has been suggested that religion and science diverged in response to evolution; however, as demonstrated in chapter 4, science diverged from religion when improved observation equipment and techniques demonstrated religion's inability to satisfactorily explain ourselves and our surroundings.

Looking ahead:

we come now to the *Pièce de résistance*, an explanation of the genetic basis of reproduction which completes the explanation of Evolution.

Of course, it took almost 150 years after Darwin's publication to put all the pieces together. The next chapter explains how it was done.

CHAPTER 17

THE PROCESS THAT CAUSES EARTH'S BIOLOGICAL FEATURES TO CHANGE

Chapter 1 presented sufficient elements of biology to comprehend the material in the first four chapters. Chapter 16 introduced Charles Darwin and his triumph of demonstrating that Evolution had occurred - that life changes; thereby resolving the apparently unchanging biological illusion. However, there was one problem, as mentioned previously, Darwin's "Theory" of Natural Selection did not explain what caused evolution to occur.

This Chapter will explain the details of the development of our understanding how life developed and the force that causes life to change – the phenomenon of Evolution.

In the beginning was the gene

In 1865, a reclusive monk Gregor Mendel, (1822-1884) published the results of his experiments with the lowly pea plant. Mendel[728] painstakingly traced the characteristics of successive generations of peas and published his work in 1865, first in German and then in English as "Experiments in Plant Hybridization" in which he reported the results of pea plant experiments whose results he could only explain by postulating the existence of something either in the stamen or pistle or both that determined pea plant inheritance. Mendel termed the mysterious item a gene (from Greek *genea* "generation, race)[729]. While Mendel had no idea what exactly a gene is, using his gene concept, Mendel could predict the inheritance outcomes of generations of peas[730].

Extending Mendel's work with peas to human children, Mendel, or someone who came after him, realized that the something he termed the gene, controls the results of the reproduction process and influences the children that result from this process. These children are subject to evolution's adaptability bell curve introduced in Figure 1-9 which determines the most fit to survive.

The task leading to an understanding of what a gene is and how it effects heredity is then straightforward: locate and identify the genes and determine the mechanism whereby, they control heredity and perhaps you will find the key to evolution. This task was, of course, not simple. As mentioned in Chapter 2 it took almost 150years.

Unfortunately, Mendel's work was lost only to be rediscovered in 1900 by three scientists, Carl Correns[731], Erich von Tschermak[732] and Hugo de Vries[733].

Reproduction begins with a single cell:

The elements of reproduction provided in chapter 1 were introduced to establish the fact that the only biological entity that can reproduce directly, i.e., make a copy of itself, is a single cell. I can be accused of placing the cart before the horse (the discovery of the cell had not been explained), but I reasoned that this would facilitate understanding of much of the early material. Just as Sir J. J. Thompson's discovery of the negative electron and Rutherford's discovery of the positive Nucleus largely resolved the "solid" matter illusion by explaining that "solid" matter consisted of unseen atoms as had been speculated by the ancient Greeks, the discovery of the cell ushered in a revolution in our understanding of life. Whereas, the atom was determined to be the fundamental building block of matter, the cell was ultimately determined to be the fundamental building block of life.

Invention of a practical microscope and discovery of the cell

As discussed in the previous chapter, the fossil record provided some of the first clues that unchanging life is an illusion. However, a more important clue was provided by the discovery of the basic building block of life, the cell, the detection of which had escaped detection until the development of that extension of the human eye – the microscope which was made possible by the invention of the optical lens.

Also, introduced in chapter 1, Robert Hooke is credited with the cell's discovery and naming when he examined cells of wood whose shape reminded him of a Monk's cell which became the name of a biological cell[734]. Unfortunately, Hooke's crude microscope did not allow the observation of much detail.

The person generally credited with the invention of the first practical microscope was Dutch fabric merchant Anton van Leeuwenhoek (1632-1723)[735]. Van Leeuwenhoek, a perfectionist, was not satisfied with existing crude lenses to examine his fine cloth, and he learned to grind his own, much improved lenses. This led to his first of many microscopes which he continued to improve.

Perhaps "on a lark" using one of his handcrafted microscopes Van Leeuwenhoek placed a dish of pond water under the microscope. What he saw must rank as another OMG discovery! Imagine Van Leeuwenhoek's surprise when he found *living objects in the water*! Van Leeuwenhoek was the first individual to observe and describe single celled organisms, referring to these tiny organisms as *animalcules*, which we now refer to as microorganisms.

Van Leeuwenhoek's contributions toward the establishment of microbiology earned him the title "The Father of Microbiology." He was also the first to record microscopic observations of muscle fibers, bacteria, blood cells and sperm cells.

Twenty years after he began his investigations, van Leeuwenhoek presented his findings to the Royal Society of London. His widely-circulated research, revealed to the scientific community a vast array of "invisible" microscopic life never before observed. The importance of Van Leeuwenhoek's discoveries of the microscopic biological world parallels the discovery of the microscopic world of the atom – both were invisible until *proper observational tools were develop*ed!

Lacking formal scientific training, the astounding and detailed nature of van Leeuwenhoek's discoveries resulted in his induction as a full member of the Royal Society in 1680, where he joined the ranks of many other scientific luminaries of his day.

Establishment of basic cell concepts

Encouraged by van Leeuwenhoek's findings, other investigators, employing ever improving microscopes were discovering that cells are the building blocks of all tissue.

By 1839, enough cellular evidence had accumulated for German biologists Theodor Schwann (1810-1882)[736] and Jakob Schleiden (1804-1881)[737] to enunciate a fundamental cell concept. Schwann had been examining the cells of animals[738], while Schleiden had been pursuing plant cells[739]...as the story goes[740]:

> In 1838, Schwann and Schleiden were discussing their cell studies while enjoying after-dinner coffee. When Schleiden described his studies of plant cells with nuclei to Schwann, Schwann noted a similarity of Schleiden's plant cells to cells he had observed in animal tissues. The two scientists went immediately to Schwann's lab to examine his slides and quickly confirmed that both plant and animal cells had the same basic structure implying that all life was composed of cells.

In 1839, they articulated their cell theory or cell doctrine, which states that all organisms are composed of similar units of organization, called cells. Schleiden & Schwann's concept has remained one of the foundations of modern biology and is equivalent to the concept that all matter is composed of atoms.

Schwann published a book describing animal and plant cells in 1839 which unfortunately, contained no acknowledgments of anyone else's contribution, including that of Schleiden.

Interestingly, their idea predates other great biological concepts including Darwin's concept of evolution (1859) and Mendel's laws of inheritance (1865). However, the mere awareness of cells wasn't sufficient to explain evolution.

Schleiden made other contributions by recognizing the significance of the cell nucleus which had been discovered, previously, in 1831 by the superb investigator Robert Brown who also discovered Brownian motion. Schleiden sensed the connection of the nucleus with cell division and was one of the first German biologists to accept Darwin's concept of evolutionary.

"All cells come from other cells."

Finally, in 1855, studies by the famous German polymath physician, anthropologist, public health activist, pathologist, prehistorian, biologist and politician, Rudolf Ludwig Karl Virchow (1821-1902), allowed him to state a basic axiom: "All cells come from other cells[741]." Virchow also founded the field of Social Medicine and is honored as the "Father of Pathology."

Thus, nearly two hundred years after the 1680 discovery of cells by van Leuwenhoek, the observations of Virchow, Schleiden, and Schwann established the classic, basic understanding of cells[742]:

- All organisms are made up of one or more cells.
- Cells are the fundamental functional and structural unit of life.
- All cells come from pre-existing cells.
- The cell is the unit of structure, physiology, and organization in living things.
- The cell retains a dual existence as a distinct entity and a building block in the construction of organisms.

It is not clear if Virchow, Schleiden, and Schwann realized that their "All cells come from pre-existing cells" axiom in principal should be traceable to the first 3.5 billion years old primordial cell.

Two kinds of cells exist: To this list of basic cell features we need to add another important piece of information, all cells contain chromosomes[743], which were probably discovered around 1848, and delineate two types of cells:

- Somatic cells which comprise most of the body's cells contain two sets of chromosomes and are termed diploid,
- Sex cells, also called gametes, contain only one set of chromosomes and are termed haploid.

The significance of these two different cell types will become clear in the next two sections, where we introduce one of the most important cell processes, cell division, of which there are two kinds Mitosis and Meiosis.

Flemming Discovers mitosis - maintainer of life's continuity:

Walther Flemming (1843 – 1905) development of special dyes to better observe cell features probably allowed him to be the first person to actually observe a chromosome:

> ... [Flemming] used dyes to study the structure of cells. He found a structure which strongly absorbed dye, and named it Chromatin. He observed that, during cell division, the chromatin separated into stringy objects, which became known as Chromosomes. Flemming named the division of somatic cells, Mitosis from a Greek work for thread[744].

As demonstrated in chapter 1, the only living entity that can replicate itself directly is a single cell, and single celled eukaryotes reproduce via mitosis. Hence, mitosis ensures life's continuity. It should be emphasized that Mitotic cell division only applies to somatic cells.

Flemming published his work in 1882, just fifteen years after Darwin published "The Origin" and three years after Darwin's death. Although Flemming did not know the purpose of chromosomes, he did observe that a complete set of two each (twenty-three pairs in humans) was inherited by each of the two "daughter" cells that result from mitosis.

Hertwig Discovers Meiosis - maintainer of life's variability:

Meiosis is a special type of cell division which produces a cell with only twenty-three unique chromosomes rather than the pairs of chromosomes found in a somatic cell. The result of meiosis is termed a haploid cell, the only kind that can join to produce a zygote as explained in chapter 1.

German biologist *Oscar Hertwig (1849-1922)* discovered meiosis for the first time in sea urchin eggs (no surprise, eggs and sperm are the only cells that undergo meiosis), and published his results in 1886 [745] (I am reasonably sure that Hertwig had no idea that his was the first step along the tortuous path which led to the understanding of the evolution phenomenon).

While meiosis begins with mitosis, meiosis differs from mitosis in a very significant way; Meiosis adds a second cell division. As described above, most cells are diploid having two sets of chromosomes. In Meiosis, after Mitosis produces two new diploid cells, each of the two new, diploid cells undergo an additional cell division. In this second cell division, the new pair of daughter cells receives only one chromosome from each pair of chromosomes, selected randomly from the diploid cell.

When a haploid egg and a haploid sperm fuse, the resultant zygote receives a set of chromosomes from male and a set from the female, thereby, reestablishing the diploid state in which a cell has two sets of chromosomes. However, the zygote is genetically unique, and considerable variation can occur: this is one of the drivers of evolution. But, as with others before him, Hertwig did not fully understand the significance of his discovery, although there is some indication that he suspected it was important in reproduction[746].

Belgian embryologist Van Beneden revisits meiosis

Edouard Van Beneden (1846-1910) studies of a horse parasite also demonstrated that Chromosomes were involved in Meiosis[747].

Morgan determines meiosis's role in reproduction.

In 1911, American geneticist, *Thomas Hunt Morgan (1866-1945)* working with the fly Drosophila melanogaster, established the first true understanding of the role of meiosis in reproduction. More on Morgan's contributions when we revisit mitosis and meiosis after we've gathered additional background material.

Miescher discovers nuclein:

Another clue in the mystery of reproduction was provided by *Johan Friedrich Miescher (1844 – 1895)* while working on pus cells at a hospital in Tübingen[748].

Miescher noted the presence, in pus, of something that "cannot belong among any of the protein substances known hitherto." A fact he was able to demonstrate by showing that itis unaffected by the protein-digesting enzyme pepsin. He also showed that the new substance was derived from the nucleus of the cell alone and consequently named it "nuclein". Miescher was soon able to show that nuclein could be obtained from many other cells and was unusual in containing phosphorus in addition to the usual ingredients of organic molecules - carbon, oxygen, nitrogen and hydrogen[749].

Miescher published his results in 1871. It is important to note that Miescher employed tests for organic elements in nuclein developed by those who had initially isolated them to demonstrate that these molecules were indeed present.

Zacharias discovers that chromatin and nuclein are the same:

In 1881, botanist Eduard Zacharias, employing a series of comparison experiments, was able to demonstrate that nuclein and chromatin are the same entity[750].

Fischer identifies pyrimidines and purines:

In1889, organic chemist *Herman Emil Fischer (1852-1919,* identified two important organic molecules: pyrimidines and purines, termed bases, due their chemical reactions[751]. As important as these early discoveries ultimately became, like many other clues being discovered during the late 1800s Fischer did not appreciate their significance.

Richard Altmann (1852-1900) discovers that nuclein is nucleic acid:

Zacharias's discovery that nuclein and chromosomes were the same entity, spurred investigation of nuclein since it was obviously involved in reproduction, being a major constituent of eggs and sperm. At the end of the nineteenth century, experiments with nuclein in which extraneous material was removed, demonstrated that nuclein was an acid. In 1890, German pathologist *Richard Altmann (1852-1900)* published his findings and is credited for the discovery and naming of "nucleic acid[752]".

Kossel demonstrates pyrimidines and purines presence in nuclein:

Albrecht Kossel (1853-1927) advanced the understanding of nuclein, by demonstrating that nuclein contained both protein and non-protein (nucleic acid) parts. He further demonstrated that nucleic acid, when broken down, produced nitrogen-bearing compounds: two pyrimidines, (cytosine and thymine), and two purines, (adenine and guanine). These four molecules are usually identified by C, T, A, and G. Kossel also found that carbohydrates (i.e., sugars) were also present.

The pyrimidines, C and T, and the purines A and G have unique, complimentary shapes as shown in diagram below: A -C and T–G always go together, In the diagrams, H stands for hydrogen which forms a rather weak bond holding either A and T or G and C together. The A-H-T or G-H-C pairs so formed are termed a Base Pair[753].

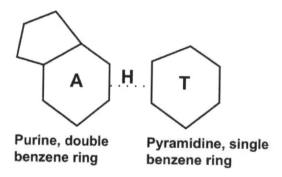

Purine, double benzene ring   **Pyramidine, single benzene ring**

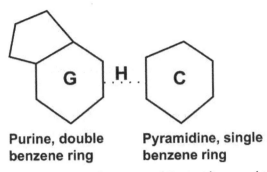

Purine, double benzene ring   **Pyramidine, single benzene ring**

Figure 17-1 Diagrams of Purine and Pyrimidine combinations.

In 1910, Kossel was awarded the Nobel Prize for Physiology or Medicine for demonstrating that two pyrimidines (Cytosine and Thymine) and two purines (Adenine and Guanine) are present in nucleic acids[754].

Levene discovers basic chemicals in nucleic acid

In 1909, Russian-American biochemist, *Phoebus Levene (1869-194)* discovers the sugar, Ribose and in 1929, he discovered a similar sugar but with one less oxygen atom, (Deoxyribose[755].)

Levene's main interest was the structure and function of nucleic acids. He characterized two different forms of nucleic acid, DNA (deoxyribonucleic acid) and RNA (ribonucleic acid).

Levene extended Kossel's work by demonstrating that not only are the two pyrimidines (cytosine and thymine) and two purines (adenine and guanine) present in nucleic acids, but that they are the principal constituents of DNA along with deoxyribose and a phosphate group. He further demonstrated that the DNA components were linked in the order: phosphate – sugar- base pair, to form a unit he termed a *nucleotide*.

RNA, on the other hand also contains the two purines (adenine and guanine) and ribose, but the pyrimidine Uracil replaces the pyrimidine Thymine[756], which is why Uracil is involved in codon creation, described below.

Currently it's highly accepted that RNA was the first nucleic acid to exist and that DNA evolved from it; accordingly, the changes in the sugar and one of the nitrogenous bases (thymine for uracil) must have some advantage. The evolutionary substitution of thymine for uracil may have increased DNA stability and improved the efficiency of DNA replication[757].

Feulgen develops special DNA staining solution

In 1914, German chemist *Robert Feulgen (1884-1955)* developed the fuchsin staining technique, which demonstrated that chromosomes contain DNA[758].

Griffith demonstrated that DNA may carry inheritance information:

In 1928, British medical officer and geneticist, *Fredrick Griffith (1879-1941)* demonstrated that the traits of one form of the bacteria *Pneumococcus* could be transferred to another form of the same bacteria by mixing an entity common to both that Griffith termed a *transforming principle*[759].

Astbury experimentally demonstrates regular structure of DNA

In 1937, British physicist and molecular biologist *William Astbury (1898 – 1961)* produced the first X-ray diffraction patters of DNA showing that DNA had a regular structure; however, Astbury was unable to produce a complete picture of the DNA structure[760].

Avery demonstrates Griffith's transforming principle is DNA

In 1944, physician, medical researcher and pioneer molecular biologist, *Oswald Avery (1877-1955)* along with coworkers Colin Macleod and Maclyn McCarty demonstrated that Griffith's transforming principle is DNA. Avery was also a pioneer in a branch of science known as immunochemistry, the field of chemistry concerned with chemical processes in immunology, but he is best known for his 1944 discovery, with his co-worker Maclyn McCarty, that Griffith's transforming principal is actually DNA, the material where genes reside, and the carrier of inheritance[761].

Hershey and Chase experimentally confirm gene's location is DNA

In 1952, bacteriologist and geneticists Alfred Hershey (1908-199) and *Martha Chase (1927-2003)* confirmed Avery's result by conducting a series of experiments, now known as the Hershey-Chase experiments, with a tiny virus like entity that infects bacteria, termed the T2 bacteriophage. These experiments confirmed that the T2 bacteriophage DNA contains the material of T2 bacteriophage inheritance, and therefore, is the location of the genes[762]. As noted above, in 1859, Miescher had discovered nuclein, which ultimately was shown to be DNA. Prior to the Avery- Hershey Chase experiments, it was assumed by most molecular biologists that proteins carried the information for inheritance.

Crick, Franklin and Watson Determine DNA's shape:

Knowing that DNA is the location of genes does not provide an explanation of what a gene is. However, researchers were getting closer; at least they knew where the genes are.

Once it became certain that genes are located on the DNA, the race was on to discover the DNA shape and then perhaps the exact identity of a gene.

The first attempt at a solution was made by California Technology chemist, Linus Pauling (1901-1994), who proposed a single strand helix, later shown to be incorrect[763].

Ultimately, the race was won in 1953, when British biophysicist and X-ray crystallographer, Rosland Franklin (1920 – 1958) produced DNA X-ray diffraction images of sufficient quality to permit British molecular biologist, physicist and neuroscientist Francis Crick (1916-2004) and American molecular biologist, mathematician, James Watson (1928-) to analyze Franklin's X-Ray patterns and deduce the structure of DNA[764] as a double helix. Considering the size of the DNA molecule and its complex double helix structure, this was *an amazing accomplishment.*

When we discuss the cell division by mitosis from a genetic viewpoint, we will see that the double helix structure of DNA should have been obvious. Below is the basic structure of a short piece of one strand of the double helix DNA – note the A and T or C and G always exist in pairs, which follows from their structure exhibited in Figure 17-1:

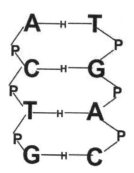

Figure 17-2 The structure of a short section of one DNA strand.

The purine-pyrimidine links of A and T or C and G, held together by relatively weak hydrogen bonds, are connected into a ladder-like structure by a Phosphate deoxyribose backbone, P. The "ladders" are then entwined in a double helical structure. As mentioned above, Phoebus Levene termed the combination of base pairs (A and T or C and G) plus one phosphate molecule, and a deoxyribose sugar molecule, a nucleotide, a term you will see often.

The elucidation of the DNA structure was *one of the monumental achievements of science*. Regarding DNA's discovery, there are, of course, many excellent publications on the subject including Watson's book[765]. There is also a very readable online guide to Watson's book[766].

What is a gene and what is its relation to DNA?

Regarding genes and DNA, thus far, we have established these facts:

- Genes are located in/on the DNA.
- DNA is a "ladder-like" structure composed of four molecules: two purines, thymine and cytosine, and two the pyrimidines, adenine and guanine, usually represented by the letters T, C, A or G. connected in pairs, termed base-pairs which form the "rungs" of the ladder shown in Figure 17-2.
- There are a huge number, approximately three billion, base-pairs[767].

Intensive study of DNA has shown that a gene is a sequence of A, C, G, or T on <u>one side</u> of the DNA ladder. Thus, the positioning of the two purines, T and C, and two the pyrimidines A and G along the side of a DNA, termed a "strand," form a set of "DNA codes", which identify the amino acid specified by a particular gene. However, the "DNA codes" cannot select the amino acid for addition to the protein being built – this is accomplished by RNA codes known as codons. But first – How are the RNA codes created?"

Gamow's conjecture – three "letters" identify an amino acid:

Presumably it was George Gamow (him again) who first realized that three of the four "letters" would be sufficient to encode twenty amino acids. This is demonstrated by noting that the arrangement of base-pairs is arbitrary, all possible arrangements of the four "letters" A, C, G, or T, from AAAA to TTTT are possible.

These arrangements are known mathematically as permutations and the formula for the number of permutations of **N** items taken **r** at a time when repeats are permitted is:

$$N^r$$

In the case of DNA, **N** = 4 and **r** can range from 1 to 4. Regarding the number of letters needed to specify twenty amino acids we then have these possibilities:

$$4^1 = 4, 4^2 = 16 \text{ and } 4^3 = 64$$

Clearly, four and sixteen are insufficient, but sixty-four is more than enough, but a minimum of three bases is required to construct the codon for an amino acid; accordingly, sixty-four combinations must be allowed.

Putting it all together – DNA to RNA to codon to Amino Acid

Figure 17-3 depicts the relationship between DNA, RNA, and the codon which selects the Amino Acid Serine

First, the "DNA code" is transcribed to the RNA molecule which, unlike DNA is a single strand. The correlation between DNA "letters" and the RNA "letters" is:

DNA -- RNA
A – U
C – G
G – C
T – A

Note that thymine is replaced by another pyrimidine, uracil. As mentioned previously, adenine and uracil form a pair similar to adenine and thymine. (as an aside, I have used an ointment, fluorinated uracil to treat sunburn which is caused by damage to the thymine base in skin cells)

Once the DNA code is transferred to RNA, three letters termed a codon are added to a messenger RNA (mRNA) which facilitates the amino acid selection. As an example, the codon shown in Figure 17-3 is one of four possible that can select the Serine amino acid as illustrated by the codon cube, Figure 17-4

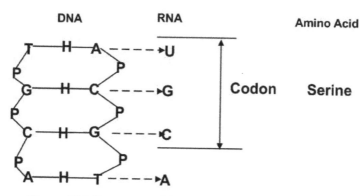

Figure 17-3 Depiction of the relationship between DNA, RNA, a codon and the Amino Acid Serine

It should be emphasized that the excessive number of codons: sixty-four codons- twenty amino acids = forty-four excess codons; implies that the genetic code is "degenerative"-- more than one codon can be formed to select an amino acid. Codon degeneracy is illustrated by this portion of a "codon cube[768]."

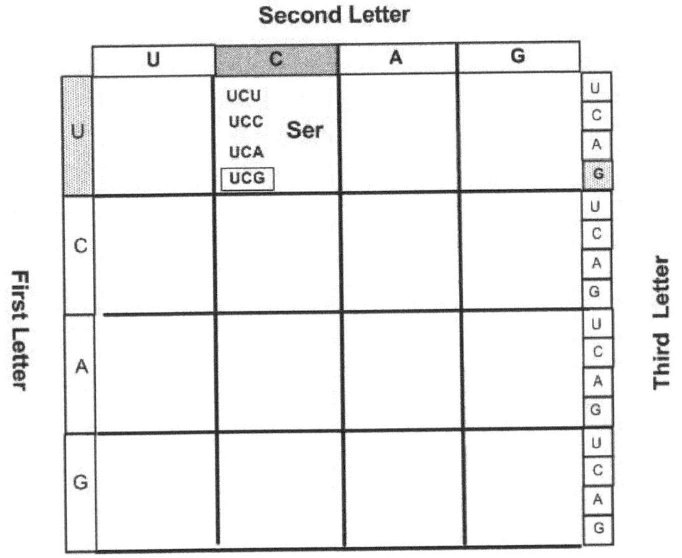

Second Letter

	U	C	A	G	
U		UCU UCC **Ser** UCA UCG			U C A G
C					U C A G
A					U C A G
G					U C A G

First Letter (left axis) · Third Letter (right axis)

Figure 17-4 Codon Cube.

The cube illustrates the correlation of three of the four nucleotides U, C, A and G that code for a particular amino acid. Strictly speaking the cube has three sides, but the above configuration illustrates the 3-D form by repeating the four nucleotides in all rows on the right side. The amino acid highlighted is serine, shown Figure 17-3 which only depicts one of the codon combinations that provide a code for serine. As shown in Figure 17-4, four combinations of nucleotides provide a code for serine: UCU, UCC, UCA and UCG - the one highlighted. The complete cube can be found on-line.

Of note, some codons are used as start and stop codons which specify where on the DNA sequence to begin using the codons to specify amino acids and when to stop as will be explained below.

Crick and Brenner experimentally confirm Gamow's conjecture:

In 1961, Francis Crick and South African biologist and 2002 Nobel Laureate in Physiology or Medicine, Sydney Brenner (1927 -) experimentally demonstrated that three base-pairs of DNA code for one amino acid[769], thus confirming Gamow's conjecture.

Connecting genes to protein manufacture:

Protein manufacture was briefly described in chapter 1, beginning with Table 1-2 through Figure 1-7 and will not be repeated here except the basic elements to maintain continuity; and with this significant difference, the location and structure of a gene has been identified – a significant improvement in understanding!

The basic split-gene structure jointly discovered by Sharp and Roberts, an OMG event disclosed in chapter 1 is repeated in Figure 17-5 for convenience:

Exon	Intron	Exon	Intron	Exon	Intron	Exon

Figure 17-5 A gene is divided into exons and introns.

Extraction of the codon for an Amino Acid can be accomplished by either of two splicing processes: Normal and Alternative. Alternative splicing will be repeated for continuity and because of it importance as a source of new genes.

To make protein fabrication seemingly more complex reproduction "invented" a second splicing technique alternative splicing. Good thing, since it is one of the sources of new genes, without which we wouldn't be here:

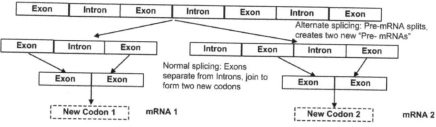

Figure 17-6 Alternative gene splicing.

The evolutionary advantage of alternative slicing described in chapter 1 with respect to embryogenesis is illustrated more generally in Figure 17-6:

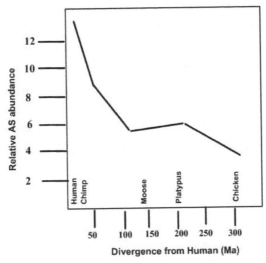

Figure 17-7 Effect of alternative gene splicing over time.

The improvement in life with increasing number of alternative splicings is illustrated 17-7. Also in the Science article[770] from which Figure 17-7 was created, author Nuno L. Barbosa et al stated:

> Over the past decade, it has been shown that alternative splicing (AS) is a major mechanism for the enhancement of transcriptome and proteome diversity, particularly in mammals.

Viewed from the vantage point of 2016 and the CRISPR study reported in August 2016, Barbosa et al had made only a tiny step, but at the time it was ground breaking!

What exactly does a gene do?

Actually, not very much, except life would not exist without them. As mentioned previously, a gene provides the codon which selects the proper Amino Acid for a protein; hence without genes, there would be no proteins -- no life. However, it is the protein that performs useful functions such as tissue building.

Another process Epigenetics can modify the functioning of a gene, without modifying the gene, to produce a protein variation sometimes beneficial, sometimes not. There are many ways this can happen; one possible method, known as methylation, involves the attachment of a methyl ion CH_3 to either the cytosine or adenine nucleotide[771]. Methylation usually disables a gene, For more detail see [772]. For the purpose of this book, protein production is not simply transferring the amino acid manufactured from a genes code to a Ribosome for protein manufacture, the process can be modulated by epigenetic factors. The importance of this will become clear below.

Identifying specific genes – The Human Genome Project

Once the basic genetic structure had been identified and the basic gene function determined, the next step was the location of all the genes in the human genome, a mammoth undertaking considering that there are approximately three billion base-pairs in human DNA.

The project was initiated in 1990 by the U.S. National Institutes of Health (NIH). James Watson, co-discoverer of the DNA structure was the initial head, but he was forced to resign over disagreements with the head of NIH, Bernadine Healy and was replaced by Francis Collins (1950-). Collins's appointment may seem odd -- he is a controversial individual who apparently believes that DNA was invented by a supernatural being. Collins set forth his ideas in *The Language of God*[773].

A parallel project undertaken by Celera Genomics Inc. headed by Craig Venter(1946-) was aided by DNA sequencers developed by Applied Biosystems Inc.

The story of establishing the first copy of the human genome is an exciting one, but beyond the scope of this book. Ventner's group at Celera published the first copy in the Feb 16, 2001 issue of *Science*[774]. Celera's genome contained 20,000 – 25,000 genes.

Back to mitosis and meiosis:

Now that we have acquired some useful knowledge of DNA and genetics, let us return to the discussion of mitosis and meiosis.

The Mitotic process: As it is less involved, we begin with mitosis. As noted above, mitosis was discovered by Flemming who published his findings in 1882 in which "He observed that, during cell division, the chromatin separated into (stringy objects,) which became known as chromosomes."

We now know that the 'stringy objects' are DNA molecules. When a cell divides, as shown in Figure 17-8, chromosomes must separate -- becoming physically distinct – step B.

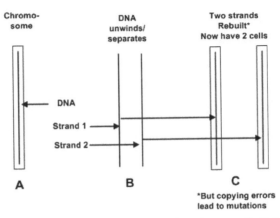

Figure 17-8 Separating DNA strands to begin cell division.

Research reported in the July 2016 issue of Nature, revealed that a newly discovered protein, Ki-67 assists the separation of chromosomes by reducing their "stickiness" enabling them to move independently of each other for segregation of precisely one copy of the genome to each of the nascent daughter cells[775] step C (cell division remains an active area of investigation).

After chromosome separation, enzymes cause the DNA molecule to separate from the chromatin. Both chromatin and DNA are shown - step A. Enzymes next separate the DNA molecule into two strands - step B. One strand goes to each new daughter cell- step C; this is, of course, why DNA is a double helix. Enzymes in the new cell rebuild the DNA molecule, adding the appropriate bases necessary for the second strand; thereby, recovering the double helix form.

However, during the rebuilding, despite elaborate error correcting functions, occasionally, the wrong base is added to a gene, resulting in a mutation. Sometime these are benign, but other times; the mutated gene will not produce its proper protein. Many medical problems result from these mutations. Also, mutations in bacteria DNA can lead to anti-biotic resistant bacteria.

The Meiosis process: Most cells have two sets of chromosomes and are termed diploid. Meiosis provides an essential ingredient for reproduction – a haploid cell, one with only one set of chromosomes. Then a male haploid cell (M1), the sperm and a female haploid cell (F1), the egg can fuse, creating a diploid Zygote which then divides beginning embryogenesis.

Meiosis, diagrammed in the next two figures, begins with each pair of homologous (identical) chromosomes aligned as shown in Figure 17-9. Note that while lined up, genetic recombination can occur.

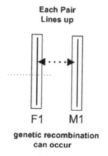

Figure 17-9 Homologous (identical) chromosomes line up.

Then one chromosome from each pair is selected, randomly, to create two haploid cells, haploid cell 1, and haploid cell 2 as shown in Figure 17-9.

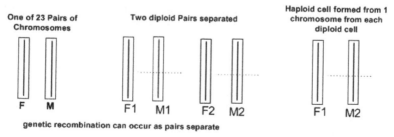

Figure 17-10 Cell divisions leading to two haploid cells.

The Reproduction Process

We now have enough information to explain the phenomenon of evolution - but first, a review of reproduction now that the genetic basis has been established.

The basic elements of the reproduction process are exhibited in Figure 17-11, an expanded version of Figure 1-5:

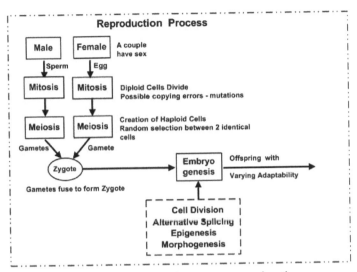

Figure 17-11 Reproductive process details.

Reproduction begins with mate selection and sexual activity between the two mates. This activity leads to Zygote creation – the fusion of two haploid cells. Once formed, embryogenesis commences with the Zygote beginning a frenzy of cell division. Many cells are required to "build a baby" in nine months. The essential embryogenesis steps are:

1. Extensive cell division.
2. Protein fabrication occurs, since we need protein to survive This provides the opportunity for alternate splicing: a source of new genes; a significant player in speciation.
3. Epigenesis can occur with the addition of a molecule or molecules to a gene which generally disables it.
4. Finally, there is morphogenesis.

The output of reproduction is a bell curve:

The previous section demonstrated that reproduction is a random process, a process governed by the mathematical field of probability and statistics. A giant in this field, Karl Friedrich Gauss (1777–1855 introduced what is now known as a Gaussian distribution, the Gaussian function and the Gaussian error curve. He showed how probability could be represented by a bell-shaped or "normal" curve, which peaks around the mean or expected value and quickly falls off toward plus/minus infinity, which is basic to descriptions of statistically distributed data[776].

In view of Gauss' mathematics, the output of reproduction will conform to a bell curve implying that all human characteristics fit a bell curve as illustrated in Figure 17-11 which shows the general distribution of below average and above average characteristics, illustrating how any genetically determined characteristic, such as height, hair color and intelligence for example. will be distributed. Fitness, of interest to evolution will also be distributed in a similar manner.

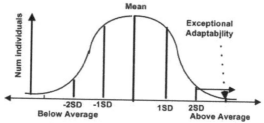

Figure 17-12 Typical Human Characteristic Distribution.

The vertical lines denote variation from the average or mean termed or standard deviation (SD): each line represents one standard deviation.

Unfortunately, Inequality is "built-in" to reproduction!

This section addresses one of the foremost and controversial issues confronting society today -- inequality. As a person who is fortunate to reside on the right side, I add this short section to perhaps assist you in coming to grips with a vexing problem for which little of practical value can be done.

Figure 17-12 illustrates a particularly important aspect of the human condition – a consequence of the bell curve output of reproduction; *there are very few exceptional individuals something everyone knows, but has difficulty addressing.*

The *Sage of Omaha*, Warren Buffet placed the situation in context in a trenchant article quoted previously in Chapter 2, partially repeated here for continuity and to add the line in italics:

> "… economic rewards flowing to people with specialized talents [greater cognitive ability] have grown dramatically faster than those going to equally decent men and women possessing more commonplace skills [median cognitive ability]" *There is nothing good intentions can do to alleviate this.*

An informative and provocative "companion" article related to the inequality issue describes Professor Julian Stanley's study of highly intelligent individuals published on the September issue of Nature *How to raise a genius*[777].

> Professor Stanley's article begins with the chronicle of a bored twelve-year old boy named Bates. Stanley met him in a Johns Hopkins computer course his parents had arranged for him. Having *leapfrogged* ahead of the adults in the class, the child kept himself busy by teaching the FORTRAN programming language to *graduate students*[778].

Of particular interest to the *inequality problem*, Stanley and others set up a center at Johns Hopkins to study those who scored in the top 1 percent on university entrance exams. This group includes such well known individuals as Facebook's Mark Zuckerberg, Google co-founder Sergey Brin and musician Stefani Germanotta (Lady Gaga).

"Whether we like it or not, these people really do control our society," says Jonathan Wai, a psychologist at the Duke University Talent Identification Program in Durham, North Carolina, which collaborates with the Hopkins center… "The kids who test in the top 1% tend to become our eminent scientists and academics, our Fortune 500 CEOs and federal judges, senators and billionaires."

A study published in 2016 by Makel et al[779] compared the outcomes of students in the top 1% of childhood intellectual ability with those in the top 0.01%. Whereas the first group gained advanced degrees at about 25 times the rate of the general population, the more elite students earn PhDs at about *50 times the base rate*!

Reproduction-- the process that causes evolution to occur

We can now easily demonstrate how evolution occurs, beginning with the adaptability bell curve introduced in Chapter 1, copied here to assist continuity as Figure 17-13:

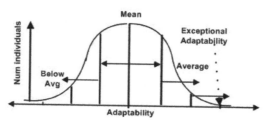

Figure 17-13 Adaptability distribution

It is axiomatic that those fortunate to have above average fitness/adaptability are the ones most likely to survive and will create the inevitable improvements that accompanies evolution. We merely combine the reproduction diagram with the adaptive bell curve and voila – the phenomenon of evolution is displayed as shown in Figure 1-4. The better adapted individuals contribute to evolution, the average adapted individuals contribute to species maintenance, while the less adapted are consigned to extinction. It is sobering to note: 99 percent of all species that have appeared on earth are now extinct[780] - extinction happens!

Summary for Chapter 17: The process which causes earth's biological features to change.

- In 1865, an obscure monk, Gregor Mendel, after thousands of experiments with peas, announced the existence of something he termed a "gene" which held the key to heredity. It was not until the late twentieth century that Mendel's genes were isolated, identified and the mechanism whereby they control heredity explained.

- Perhaps it's self evident, but the simple fact that reproduction is required for species survival is rarely articulated; moreover, reproduction is the driver of evolution.

- Since the only animal that can reproduce itself directly is a single celled animal, multi-celled reproduction must begin with a single cell, which of course is what we observe.

- An understanding of cells began with the invention of the microscope in the late 1600s; however, it required almost two hundred years to establish the basic cell properties which are:
   o All organisms are made up of one or more cells.
   o Cells are the fundamental functional and structural unit of life.
   o All cells come from pre-existing cells.
   o The cell is the unit of structure, physiology, and organization in living things.
   o The cell retains a dual existence as a distinct entity and a building block in the construction of organisms.

- In approximately 1848, cell structure had been refined sufficiently to understand that all cells contain a nucleus and that each nucleus contains filament like entities termed chromosomes. Most cells contain two sets of chromosomes and are termed diploid, while some cells, the sex cells, contain only one set of chromosomes and are termed haploid.

- In order for reproduction and growth to occur, cells must divide. There are two kinds of cell division: mitosis, discovered in 1882, just fifteen years after Charles Darwin's death, the division associated with most cells in which the two new "daughter" cells contain a complete set of chromosomes and meiosis, discovered four years later, the division of sex cells, in which the two new "daughter" cells contain only one set of chromosomes.

- Following the discovery of cell division, especially meiosis, a series of discoveries followed that solved the puzzle of reproduction, evolution's mechanism:

o   1871: Miescher discovered a non-protein molecule in the nucleus, which he named nuclein.

o   1881: Zacharis discovered that nuclein is the same as the material of chromosomes, chromatin.

o   1889: Fisher discovered two molecules which would prove fundamental to familiar objects: pyrimidine and purine.

o   1890: Altman discovered that nuclein is an acid and names it nucleic acid.

o   1910: Kossel demonstrated that pyrimidine and purine are present in nucleic acid.

o   1909-1929: Levene determined that there are two different forms of nucleic acid, DNA and RNA., that there are two pyrimidines (cytosine and thymine) and two purines (adenine and guanine) present in nucleic acids, that they are the principal constituents of DNA along with deoxyribose and a phosphate group, and that the DNA components were linked in the order: phosphate – sugar- base-pair, to form a unit he termed a nucleotide.

o   1928: Griffith demonstrated that DNA carried the inheritance information.

o   1952: Hershey and Chase demonstrated that genes are located in DNA.

o   1953: Crick, Franklin and Watson used X-ray diffraction to determine DNA's shape, which revealed some important details of cell division:

•   At the beginning of cell division, the DNA helix unwinds and is split into two strands by enzymes.

•   One strand goes to each of the new daughter cells. The creation of a strand for each daughter cell is the reason for the double helix.

•   Enzymes then add the appropriate bases to the single strand; thereby, recovering the double helix form.

•   Mutations occur when the wrong bases, termed copying errors, are added to the single strand.

- 1955: Gamow showed that any three of the four bases, C, T, A, or G should be sufficient to code for an amino acid and is termed a codon.
- 1961: Crick and Brenner experimentally confirmed Gamow's hypothesis.
- 1993: Sharp and Roberts shared the Nobel Prize for the discovery of the "split-gene" structure: Intron – Exon – Intron, with Introns being non-coding and Exons carrying the code for an amino acid.
- 2001: Venter et al published first sequence of human genome.
- Since 2001: the basic function of genes has been determined:
  - o A codon is extracted from a gene located on DNA via a process termed splicing.
  - o Messenger RNA (mRNA) carries the codon which is copied onto Transfer RNA (tRNA),
  - o tRNA selects the amino acid using the codon and carries the amino acid to a ribosome "protein factory"
  - o The ribosome assembles the amino acids into a protein.
- Finally, the reproductive process was presented which then leads to the bell curve distribution of all human characteristics, especially adaptation. Combining reproduction with adaptation yields the evolution phenomenon.

At the end of this sequence of discovery, it was clear that reproduction is the process that Darwin sought that causes evolution but he was unfortunately born 150 years too soon.

Looking ahead:

We have now resolved the apparently unchanging physical and biological aspects of the Earth by explaining how the physical and biological processes actually function, in particular how Evolution works. In the next chapter, we pick up from Chapter 1 and explain how these processes created the Earth and all the life on it.

CHAPTER 18

BIOPHYSICAL DEVELOPMENT OF THE EARTH

Preparation of the Earth for Life's appearance: Chapters 12 through 17 described creation of an environment suitable for the development of life on earth and the forces that change the planet possibly thwarting life's development:

- Chapter 12 addressed the resolution of the close stars' illusion by explaining the creation of the universe which included the creation of our solar system and the related items pertaining to the Earth - formation, creation of an oxygen atmosphere, and water
- Chapter 13 explained the resolution the apparently unchanging earth illusion - the fact that the earth does change.
- Chapters 14 and 15 explained resolution of the apparent unchanging physical features illusion and the determination of the forces causing the earth's physical features to change.
- Chapters 17 and 18 explained resolution of the apparent unchanging biological features illusion and the determination of the processes causing the earth's the biological features to change – reproduction and adaptation which results in evolution

The stage is now set for an improved explanation of life's evolution, and the geological changes that have occurred over the last 3.7 billion years resulting in the lovely place we call home.

The appearance of Life:

The appearance of life as a primordial cell was explained in chapter 1. For many years, the oldest known single celled life was the Stromatolites located in Sharks Bay Australia dated at 3.6 Ga. Recently, discoveries made in Canada have pushed the appearance of life back to 3.7 Ga.

Plate tectonics activity: tectonic activity began early in Earth's history. A report summarized in the Jan 3, 2009 issue of *Science News*[781], states:

> Rocks in the Jack Hills of Western Australia hosted zircon crystals that contain tiny mineral inclusions.... The zircons and inclusions are more than 4 billion years old and contain evidence suggesting an early start for tectonic activity on Earth.
>
> The chemical composition of ancient crystals now found in Australian rocks bolsters the notion that tectonic plates may have jostled across Earth's surface more than 4 billion years ago. Scientists call the first 600 million years of Earth's history the "Hadean eon" because of the presumably hellish temperatures on the freshly coalesced and largely molten planet. Also, radioactive isotopes, which generate heat inside Earth as they decay, were much more common than they are now, says Mark Harrison, a geologist at the University of California, Los Angeles.

Formation and ultimate separation of super-continents Rodinia and Pangaea—prelude to complex life:

Two of the more spectacular consequences of plate motion that have had significant impact upon the Earth's creation has been the occasional uniting of most, if not all, of the earth's crust into a single "super continent" two of them are called Rodinia (from the Russian word for mother land or home land) and Pangaea[782].

The existence of super continents such as Rodinia and Pangaea have been disclosed by the observational technique known as paleomagnetism; an examination of the variation of the Earth's magnetic field over long periods of time preserved in various magnetic materials[783] such as nickel, iron and cobalt[784]. The study of paleomagnetism has demonstrated that, over time, the Earth's magnetic field has varied substantially in both orientation and intensity[785]. Unfortunately, the record of the Earth's magnetic field only provides latitude information. To obtain longitude information, strata must be compared. However, if the magnetic orientation, strata and age of two crustal pieces match, then, even if they are presently miles apart, they must have been connected at some time in the past.

Rodinia began forming about 1.3 billion years ago from three or four pre-existing continents, one of which is termed the Grenville Province, a rock structure running from Labrador to Texas, consolidated perhaps 1,100 to 1,000 Ma.[786].

Rodinia formed during a period that geologists term the Neoproterozoic Era, which extends from the time 1000 Ma. to 542 Ma., see Appendix B. Rodinia caused severe climate change, significantly cooling the earth leading to the Cryogenian period[787].

Cryogenian period

The Cryogenian period began approximately 850 Ma. and ended approximately 635 Ma. This period was marked by large scale glaciation which may have covered the entire planet, the so-called "snowball" Earth. However, while glaciation did occur, it's uncertain whether the entire planet was covered or the glaciations were local. Regardless, it was a time when the Earth was very cold. Also, during the Cryogenian period, the supercontinent Rodinia began to break up.

Ediacaran bacteria, the next stage in life's development:

The last period of the epic known as the Neoproterozoic was the the Ediacaran (named for the Ediacara Hills in South Australia), where some the first Ediacaran fossils were discovered as described in chapter 1. The Ediacaran period lasted from about 650 to 540 Ma[788].

Evidence of extensive lava flows and volcanic eruptions during the Ediacaran period, such as those that covered an area of about 350,000 square kilometers in eastern Europe[789], suggest that Rodinia began to rift apart no later than 750 Ma[790], and probably sooner as noted above.

As mentioned in chapter 1 multicelled organisms appeared in the Ediacaran period. These organisms appeared soon after the Cryogenic period thawed. Although extremely old, Ediacaran fossils can be found in a few localities around the world[791].

The Cambrian Explosion: multifaceted life begins - captured in shale:

Shale, the most common sedimentary rock, consists of very fine particles that collect in very slow moving water such as off shore of sandy beaches. The slow accumulation of fine particles accompanying the formation of shale is an ideal environment for the preservation of small animals and soft body parts.

About 530 million years ago, shale forming in various places on earth preserved an astonishing increase in the number and complexity of life forms. This rapid increase is usually termed the Cambrian Explosion. Cambria, the Roman name for modern Wales, is one of the first places that this fossil record was found[792]. Actually, it wasn't exactly an explosion; the process took over ten million years. However, most known animal phyla appeared in the fossil record as marine species during this time[793]. Moreover, ten million years is relatively short when compared to the 3.5-billion-year overall development of life.

The seemingly rapid appearance of fossils in this "Primordial Strata" was noted as early as the mid nineteenth century and generated extensive scientific debate, even a reference to divine participation[794]. Charles Darwin feared it could be used as an objection to his concept of evolution by Natural Selection[795]. However, his fears were misplaced since Natural Selection does not explain the evolutionary phenomenon. On the other hand, we now know that ample time has been available for evolution.

Regarding the cause of life's "rapid" development during the Cambrian, it is worth recalling Ian Tattersall's comments about the evolution of the brain:

> ...it is becoming increasingly clear that the acquisition of [symbolic thinking] was an abrupt and recent event."

But, as Tattersall explains, the genetic explanation of the "abrupt and recent event" …does not fit into the <u>Modern Genetic Synthesis</u> (MGS) [one more nail in the Natural Selection coffin]

Tattersall's comment could also apply to the Cambrian; however, the explanation of evolution provided in this book addresses his concern and demonstrates that reproduction, the biological "force" causing evolution could have easily caused the rapid development of phyla. As discussed in chapter 1, a rapid increase in oxygen was also probably a major contributor[796].

As would be expected, many forms seen in the fossil record of the Cambrian disappeared without trace as explained by the adaptive bell curve. Once the body plans that evolution had found most successful had evolved they came to dominate the biosphere.

Evolution of body plans:

The arrival of new phyla in the Cambrian led to considerable improvement in the development of body plans over the five hundred million years since the Cambrian, which is an important aspect of evolution; therefor, a few words regarding this important topic are in order. An extract of the survival requirements table will aid this discussion (recall that, while reproduction is not necessary for individual survival, it is a must for species survival).

Requirement for Survival	Individual Survival
Oxygen	Y
Water	Y
Food	Y
Metabolism of food	
Suitable Environment	Y
Proper temperature	
Dry	
Safe	
Reproduction	N

Table 18-1 Basic survival needs of an individual.

Thus, the cells in a multi-celled animal must be arranged to provide the items indicated in the above table to assure survival. Accordingly, means must be provided for:

- Ingestion of O_2 and transfer to all cells – implies the need for a respiratory system.
- Ingestion of Water and transfer to all cells implies the need for a digestive system.
- Access to food which in most cases implies some form ability to locate and move to food.
- Ingestion of and metabolism of Food to extract the useful nutrients and transfer them to all cells also implies a digestive system.
- Transferring O_2, water, and nutrients to all the cells implies some form of a circulation system.
- Suitable environment, which in most cases also implies some ability to locate and move to a suitable environment, e.g., "get out of the rain."
- Combining sex cells to assure reproduction occurs.

In addition to these items, which are directly related to the table, additional capability will be needed:

- Locating water, food and a suitable environment implies the need to sense the environment. There are five items in the environment that can be sensed: light, sound, odors, taste and objects (sense of touch); hence, organs able to sense these would logically evolve.
- Accessing water, food and a suitable environment implies the need for some form of locomotion.
- As the multi-celled animal becomes more complex, some form of control system was needed.

As we review the development of various animals, we will examine how each species has met these survival needs, and how the ability to meet these needs improved over time. We will treat the first large animal, the fish, in more detail than the others to establish the basic pattern which is followed with improved capability throughout the evolution of the all animals. Figure 1-6 presents what I term *"the ladder of life"* and reproduce it here as Figure 18-1 for convenience:

Mya						
4.5	Fish	Amphibian	Reptile	Mammal	Primate	Homo
30	Fish	Amphibian	Reptile	Mammal	Primate	
100	Fish	Amphibian	Reptile	Mammal		
300	Fish	Amphibian	Reptile			
400	Fish	Amphibian				
500	Fish					

Figure 18-1 The Ladder of Life: Evolution from Fish to Homo.

Origin of Fish in the Cambrian

One of the animal species common today that originated in the Cambrian is the fish; but the original fish barely resemble any alive today. Fish are members of the vertebrates, animals with backbones and the first fish were jawless, toothless, soft-bodied fishlike creatures that wriggled through the water, sucking up microscopic food particles[797].

Modern fish with skeletons appeared in the late Silurian period 443 Ma to 416 Ma or the early Devonian period (named for Devon Great Britain where some of the early Devonian formations were found), approximately 395 Ma[798]. Fish became the dominant animal on Earth during the Devonian; the Devonian is sometimes called the Age of fish[799].

The fish body plan is well known, but it is worth a few words reviewing how a fish meets the needs discussed above:

- Ingestion of O_2 is performed by gills and a circulation system transfers O_2 to all cells.
- Ingestion of Water, i.e., do fish drink water? Fresh water fish absorb water thru their skin cells, while salt water fish drink water with the gills removing the salt[800].
- Food is ingested by mouth and metabolized in a digestive system that extracts the useful nutrients and transfer it to cells via a circulation system. The waste products of metabolism are passed

to the circulation system and excreted through an anal pore at the lower rear of the fish.

- Food is generally found in the water through which a fish swims. Fish have eyes the front of their heads to locate the food, olfactory sensors to assess food and fins to provide locomotive power to propel them through water to the food (fins also allow fish to evade predators).

- In general, the water in which a fish lives provides a suitable environment.

- Female fish lay eggs which fuse with sperm released by the male fish. Typically, the female deposits many eggs to improve the probability that enough will survive to reproduce.

- The fish has a rudimentary brain, primarily devoted to the eye, nose and balance maintenance.

The basic fish body plan has bi-lateral symmetry. The vertebrate fish spine occupies the center of the fish and provides structural stability.

The salient features of a fish are summarized in tabular form in Appendix D. Other species will be added to this table which will illustrate the improvements provided by the evolution phenomenon over time.

Origin of the Amphibians

The generation of O_2 eventually led to the development of an ozone layer that provides protection from the sun's lethal UV rays; allowing life to move from the sea to land.

While fish dominated the Devonian, some adventurous fish (perhaps to escape overcrowding or were stranded) began to venture onto land. One of the first fish to make the critical step was the Tiktaalik, which appears in the fossil record 382 Ma. Tiktaalik had many of the features of tetrapods (animals with four legs)[801]. Tiktaalik is an example from several lines of ancient fish with lobed fins that eventually evolved into legs as an adaptation to the oxygen-poor shallow-water habitats of its time[802].

The Tiktaalik lobbed front fins featured arm-like skeletal structures that resembled a crocodile including shoulder, elbow and wrist. The rear fins and tail have not yet been found. A significant difference between

Tiktaalik and a fish was its ability to move its neck independently of its body, something a fish cannot do; moreover, its neck and ribs are similar to those of tetrapods. The ribs supported its body and aided in breathing via lungs, something else fish don't do, but is a sine qua non for a land animal[803]. Tiktaalik is truly a transition animal. Its mixture of fish and tetrapod characteristics led one of its discoverers, American paleontologist and evolutionary biologist Neil Shubin, to characterize *Tiktaalik* as a "fishapod"[804]. Shubin gained considerable fame for his discovery of Tiktaalik[805].

Lobbed finned "fishapods" such as Tiktaalik led to the evolution of amphibians. Well-preserved Tiktaalik fossils were found in 2004 on Ellesmere Island in Canada[806].

Amphibians obviously represent the transition between life in the sea and life on land since amphibians lay eggs in water which are fertilized in water, like fish. When the amphibian eggs hatch, the resultant "tadpoles" spend their first few days in water slowly metamorphosing into a frog. Anyone who has lived near a pond has witnessed this amazing transformation.

While in the water, the tadpole satisfies its needs basically as a fish does. Once the transformation to Amphibian is complete, the Amphibian has lost its gills, which means it must breath air which is accomplished by breathing in through the mouth to lungs which then transfer the oxygen to a circulatory system. An amphibian has four legs which provide it mobility to search for food and a mate.

Although able to live on dry land, amphibians usually live more in water than on dry land[807]. Amphibian characteristics are summarized in Appendix D, where the ability to live partially on land can be seen as an improvement

The Carboniferous period and the Origin of Amniotes:

The geologic period following the Devonian was the Carboniferous which began 359 Ma and ended 299 Ma Carboniferous means "coal-bearing," since many beds of coal were laid down all over the world during this period[808].

One of the greatest evolutionary innovations of the Carboniferous was the Amniotic membrane [protection for an embryo]. The survival advantage provided by the Amniotic membrane is so important; those animals whose embryos are protected by an amniotic membrane are termed Amniotes[809].

All new animals begin as a zygote (fusion of egg and sperm) which becomes an embryo that grows and eventually becomes a mature animal ready to repeat the reproductive cycle. All embryos require a fluid "bath" in which to develop. In the case of fish which are constrained to live their lives entirely in water and amphibians which must begin their lives in water and remain near water most of their lives, the fluid bath provided for the eggs is the body of water where the eggs are laid. This places the eggs in considerable danger; hence, the large number of eggs laid.

With the advent of the amniotic sac, zygotes did not have to contend with open water. Moreover, animals could live their entire lives on land, which opened up significant possibilities; access to new territories, more diverse living conditions, and ultimately the exploitation of the Earth's surface resources.

There are actually two groups of Amniotes:

Sauropsida that includes reptiles, dinosaurs and birds[810].
Synapsida that include mammals and mammal-like reptiles[811].

The terms "Sauropsida" ("Lizard Faces") and "Theropsida" or Synapsida ("Beast Faces") were coined in 1916 by British zoologist Edwin S. Goodrich (1868 – 1946)[812] to distinguish between lizards, birds, and their relatives on one hand (Sauropsida) and mammals (Synapsida) on the other[813].

The oldest known synapsid is Archaeothyris, found in Nova Scotia, which lived in the mid-carboniferous period about 320 Ma. Archaeothyris is the precursor of all synapsids including mammals[814]; hence, the Archaeothyris is one of our most distant ancestors.

Reptiles, primary member of the Sauropsida.

Reptiles first appeared about 320 Ma. during what is known as the Pennsylvanian portion of the Carboniferous period, so named because the first fossils were found in Pennsylvania.

Reptiles are bilaterally symmetric with a head at the front of the body which contains eyes, ears, a mouth, an excretory anal pore at the back followed by a tail. The circulation system of most reptiles is driven by a three-chamber heart consisting of two atria and one ventricle[815]. Reptiles are air-breathing; hence they have lungs which transfer oxygen to the circulatory system. Reptiles have a digestive system whereby food is ingested through the mouth and digested in a series of organs spread along the body with waste excreted at the back. The products of digestion are passed to the circulatory system.

The reptile's body is supported by a skeletal system. Reptiles are cold blooded; hence they have only rudimentary thermal control and become lethargic in the cold. They have scaly skin and four legs attached to the skeletal system for locomotion.

Reptiles also reproduce via eggs as do fish and amphibians, with one important improvement, eggs and sperm fuse within the protective female environment (in the fallopian tube that transports the egg). The resultant embryo is enclosed in the all important protective amniotic membrane within a hard shell that provides structural strength and, when mature enough, is deposited in a protected place for further maturation until the egg "hatches." While most reptiles lay eggs, some are capable of giving live birth and some have a placenta similar to mammals, indicating another transitional variation[816].

Reptiles have a rudimentary nervous system, including a spinal cord that is terminated with an enlarged mass of tissue in the head --the first indication of a brain, and obviously termed the reptilian brain[817]. Various clumps of cells in the reptilian brain determine the brain's general level of alertness and control basic life functions such as the autonomic nervous system, breathing, heart rate and the fight or flight mechanism. Lacking language, its impulses are instinctual and ritualistic. The reptile is concerned with fundamental needs such as survival, physical maintenance, hoarding, dominance, preening and mating[818].

While reptiles no longer dominate to the extent they did earlier, a few such as crocodiles, alligators, turtles and snakes have survived the various extinctions and are a part of life on earth today.

However, reptile species have begun to decline on a global scale. Six significant threats to reptile populations are: habitat loss and degradation, introduced invasive species, environmental pollution, disease, unsustainable use, and global climate change. [819] Amphibian populations are also declining.

The essential reptilian features are summarized in Appendix D. One important member of the reptilian family, the dinosaur, will be discussed below, but first a few words about an event that almost ended life's experiment.

The Permian period began 299 Ma, ended with a bang 251 Ma[820].

The Permian named by Sir Roderick Murchison after the Russian kingdom of Permia[821], followed the Carboniferous period. During the Permian, the super continent Pangaea, discussed above, completed its formation, and due to its large size caused the sea levels to remain generally low. Permian terrestrial life included diverse plants, fungi, arthropods and a variety of tetrapods, dominated by amphibians. Toward the end of the Permian, reptiles grew to dominance among vertebrates, because their special adaptations enabled them to flourish in the drier climate[822].

Of particular interest, near the end of the Permian, the first archosaurs (Greek for "running lizards) appeared. Archosaurs are a reptilian group from which dinosaurs evolved and which are represented by modern birds[823].

During the prolific Permian, the first cynodonts appeared. Cynodonts belonged to the Synapsid class, possessing nearly all the characteristics of mammals; they were probably warm blooded and had hair. Theses characteristics allowed them to survive an event that ended the Permian, the catastrophic P-T Extinction and continue their evolution into mammals[824].

Major Catastrophic Extinction Events:

Before a continuation up the ladder of life, it is important to discuss events which significantly affected the climb.

As mentioned in chapter 14, one of the early explanations for both the physical and biological features of the earth was the theory of catastrophism. While the catastrophism theory has been shown to be incorrect, since the events included in catastrophism occurred too recently, catastrophes have definitely occurred in Earth's history with significant effect – mass extinctions. Thus, they are an important aspect of geology if viewed properly.

These are the five main catastrophic extinction events observable in the fossil record:

Extinction Event	Time Ma.	Percent Extinction
Ordovician – Silurian	450	40
Late Devonian	375	40
Permian-Triassic	250	95
Triassic- Jurassic	200	30
Cretaceous- Ternary	65	35

Table 18-2 Summary of the five most severe extinction events.

Clearly, the Permian-Triassic (P-T) Extinction, discussed below, was the most severe; the candle of life was almost blown out. To place the P-T extinction in perspective, we begin with a brief description of the Permian period.

The Permian period began 299 Ma and ended with a bang 251 Ma[825]. Sir Roderick Murchison, introduced in chapter 1 as a person interested in the Silurian system, named the Permian period after the Russian kingdom of Permia[826].

During the Permian, the super continent Pangaea, discussed above, completed its formation, and due to its large size caused the sea levels to remain generally low. Permian tterrestrial life included diverse plants, fungi, arthropods and a variety of tetrapods, dominated by amphibians. Toward the end of the Permian, reptiles grew to dominance among vertebrates, because their special adaptations enabled them to flourish in the drier climate[827].

Of particular interest, near the end of the Permian, the first archosaurs (Greek for "running lizards) appeared. Archosaurs are a reptilian group from which dinosaurs evolved and which are represented by modern birds[828].

During the prolific Permian, the first cynodonts appeared. Cynodonts belonged to the Synapsid class and had nearly all the characteristics of mammals; they were probably warm blooded and had hair. Also, they survived the P-T Extinction and continued their evolution into mammals[829].

P-T Extinction details: The (P–T) extinction event, informally known as the Great Dying occurred 251 Ma thus forming the boundary between the Permian and Triassic periods[830].

The extent of the devastation is summarized in this table[831] [832]:

Extinction Event	Time Ma.	Percent Extinction
Ordovician – Silurian	450	40
Late Devonian	375	40
Permian-Triassic	250	95
Triassic- Jurassic	200	30
Cretaceous- Ternary	65	35

Table 18-3 Summary percent extinction during P-T extinction event.

This event has been described as the "mother of all mass extinctions." Due the extreme loss of life forms, the recovery of life on earth was much slower than after other extinction events. A detailed listing and discussion of the P-T Extinction can be found online[833], and is recommended for those who wonder how close to the edge we came.

Two possible causes of this extinction have been suggested:

1. Collision with a Near Earth Object (NEO)[834] such as a comet or asteroid.
2. Volcanic eruption.

The fairly conclusive evidence that a NEO caused the end of the Cretaceous period as well as the dinosaurs, suggests that a NEO might have caused the P-T Extinction. Although most of any P-T extinction evidence has been swept into the Earth by the plate tectonic subduction conveyer belt, enough evidence does not exist to eliminate either proposal.

Regarding volcanic eruption, the obvious candidate is a vast outpouring of lava that occurred in Siberia between about 250 Ma and 251 Ma; exactly coincident with the P-T event. This Lava flow is termed the Siberian Traps;

the word "traps" is derived from a Swedish word for stairs -- the Siberian lava flows have a step-like appearance.

The volume of lava was immense. Today the area covered is about 800,000 square miles and estimates of the original coverage are as high as 2.8 million square miles. The original volume of lava is estimated to range from 250,000 to 1,000,000 cubic miles. The volcanism continued for about a million years[835].

Regarding the effect of this amount of lava flow, Dr. Norman Macleod, of the Natural History Museum in London discussing another large lava flow, the Deccan Traps, points out:

> We're talking about catastrophic effects in terms of changes in habitat, changes in rainfall patterns, changes in climate, all of the things you can think of that are going on in the modern world magnified many many times, many many orders of magnitude indeed[836].

To date, questions surround each of these possible causes and it may have been a combination, but the effects are still being felt today.

The Triassic period – the world had changed!

The Triassic period opens on a rather different world and extends from the end of the P-T Extinction to another extinction, 199 Ma the Triassic-Jurassic extinction.

In 1834, German geologist Dr. Friedrich von Alberti (1795-1878) published the results of his investigation of three, apparently distinct sedimentary rock deposits, found all over Germany and Northern Europe. Red sandstone, overlain by chalk (calcium carbonate rock) covered by black shale. The fossils found in the three layers were the same; hence, von Alberti realized that the three layers were actually part of the same formation, which he then termed "Trias" (from the Latin for triad). The time period occupied by these rocks, von Alberti termed the Triassic.

The Triassic landscape was dominated by the supercontinent Pangaea, which remained intact until the next geologic period, the Jurassic, when Pangaea began to break up.

Terrestrial animals of interest in the Triassic period are reptiles, some of them had survived the P-T Extinctions, plus the archosaurs and cryodonts which had also survived the P-T extinction. Toward the end of the Triassic, the archosaurs[837] evolved into dinosaurs (see next section). Cryodonts "laid low" avoiding the dominant dinosaurs, awaiting their turn as the first mammals during the Jurassic.

The unforgettable Dinosaurs

Few extinct animals have captured the public's interest more than that most famous of reptiles, star of stage, screen and a gazillion books, the Dinosaur. As mentioned above, dinosaurs diverged from a group of reptiles known as Archosaurs[838] approximately 230 Ma during the Triassic period.

As with other discoveries, evidence of dinosaurs first surfaced as fossils. People have been finding dinosaur fossils for hundreds of years, probably even thousands of years[839]. Of course, the belief in a young earth prevented the early "fossil hunters" from properly understand their discoveries

The Greeks and Romans may have found [dinosaur] fossils, giving rise to their many ogre and griffin legends.

Gideon A. Mantell (1790-1852) another early British fossil hunter and physician, described and named the Iguanodon a duck-billed plant-eater in 1825 based upon teeth and a few bones were found in Sussex in 1822, probably by his wife Mary[840].

As more and more bones were found and the name was changed to dinosaur. The term "dinosauria" was first coined in 1842 by British biologist and paleontologist Sir Richard Owen[841] (1894-1892) and derives from Greek deinos meaning "terrible," "powerful," and "saura," meaning "lizard." Dinosaurs dominated the Earth for more than 160 million years beginning in the Triassic period about 230 Ma and ending with the blinding flash of an asteroid that caused the Cretaceous-Tertiary extinction event 65 Ma.

Considerable confusion exists regarding what is and isn't a true dinosaur. E.g., many older books include the flying pterosaurs and swimming ichthyosaurs as dinosaurs; however, they are now considered to belong to their own classes. Dinosaurs were an extremely varied group of animals. According to a 2006 study, more than five hundred dinosaur genera have been identified with certainty so far, and the total number of genera preserved in the fossil record has been estimated at around 1,850; hence it is estimated that nearly 75percent remain to be discovered[842].

Research beginning in the 1970s has demonstrated dinosaurs are the most likely ancestors of birds - most paleontologists regard birds as the only surviving dinosaurs[843].

K-T Extinction[844]

Sixty-Five Ma another of the five major extinctions occurred. Because this ended the rein of the dinosaurs, more interest has been expressed in the K-T extinction than any other.

The extinction effects varied, and almost 35 percent of the extant life forms perished. However, some of the fish survived, perhaps due to the protection of the oceans. Besides the demise of the dinosaurs, the K-T extinction marked the rise of mammals which slowly came to dominate the Earth.

As with other extinctions, the cause of the K-T is still contentious, and, similar to the P-T extinction, there are two possible explanations: collision with a large NEO, perhaps an asteroid, or a large volcanic eruption.

The asteroid impact cause explanation was originated by Nobel Laureate Luis Alvarez, who made a strong case for the Asteroid impact[845]. The Alvarez explanation rests upon two observations:

1. A layer of the metal iridium at the K-T rock layer boundary. This layer is found all over the Earth. Iridium is extremely rare on Earth but is commonly found in meteorites; hence, the concept of an asteroid impact.

2. In 1990, based on the work of Glen Penfield in 1978, an impact crater was identified, the Chicxulub Crater buried under the coast of Yucatan, Mexico. This crater is oval, with an average diameter of about 112 miles, approximately the size calculated by the Alvarez team. Also, material expelled when the crater was formed was dated to 65 Ma[846].

The alternate explanation is a volcanic eruption known as the Deccan Traps, a large layer of flood basalt located in west central India. While not as extensive as the Siberian Traps, a contender for the P-T extinction, the Deccan Traps cover an area of two hundred thousand square miles and are more than 6,000 feet thick[847]. Dr. Macleod's comments on the effect of the Deccan Traps were quoted above.

As with the P-T extinction, experts can debate the causes, but for our purposes, the events occurred and altered the course of Earth's creation, especially the Earth's biological creation.

The rise of the Mammals- primary member of the synapsids

The main event of interest following the K-T extinction which eliminated many of the top predators was the rise of the Mammals. They became the supreme, dominate species on Earth.

Mammals are bilaterally symmetric vertebrates with a head at the front of the body which contains eyes, ears, a mouth, and an excretory anal pore at the back followed by a tail. Mammals differ from reptiles by having sweat glands including some sweat glands, termed mammary glands (hence the name Mammal) modified for milk production[848].

The circulation system of mammals employs a four -chamber heart consisting of two atria and two ventricles[849]. Mammals are air-breathing; hence they have lungs which transfer oxygen to the circulatory system. Moreover, Mammals have a digestive system whereby food is ingested through the mouth, digested in a series of organs spread along the body with waste excreted at the back. The products of digestion are passed to the circulatory system for transfer to the body's cells.

The Mammalian body is supported by a skeletal system. Mammals are warm blooded; hence, they have a more sophisticated thermal control than reptiles; since warm bloodedness eliminates the lethargy that hampers reptiles when it gets cold. As with reptiles, mammals have four legs attached to the skeletal system for locomotion. With the exception of the primate branch, all mammals walk on four legs.

Mammalian eggs and sperm fuse within the protective female environment (similar to reptiles) the resultant embryo is enclosed in the all important protective amniotic membrane. However, mammals possess a significant improvement over reptiles in that the mammals have an extended amniotic enclosure termed the placenta in which an embryo develops until a mammal can give birth to live offspring. This obvious survival advantage is augmented by the mammary glands which allow female mammals to feed their young. The continuing reproductive cycle improvement increased the odds of species survival.

The mammalian brain adds a new structure to the reptilian brain, the limbic system, which overlays the reptilian portion. The term "limbic" comes from Latin *limbus*, meaning cap[850]. The limbic system also operates by influencing the endocrine system and is highly interconnected with the brain's pleasure center which plays a role in sexual arousal and the "high" derived from certain recreational drugs. The limbic system is also tightly connected to the prefrontal cortex, the forward part of the brain[851]. We will encounter the limbic again when we discuss human behavior.

The essential mammalian characteristics are included in Appendix D.

As mentioned above, Mammals made their initial appearance in the Triassic, evolving from advanced cryodonts, developing alongside dinosaurs, but of course avoiding them. However, more modern mammals appeared in a geological time interval termed the Eocene, or Dawn epoch, first identified by Lyell, began 56 Ma and ended with another small extinction, the Grand Coupure, 34 Ma[852].

Eocene extinction - the Grande Coupre

The Eocene extinction was termed the Grande Coupre in 1910 by Swiss paleontologist Hans Stehlin who observed a dramatic turnover of European mammals[853].

The Post Grande Coupre mammals included pigs, hippos, cattle, goats, sheep and horses. This turnover gave European humans a significant advantage over humans in other parts of the world which was eloquently demonstrated by Jared Diamond in "Gun, Germs and Steel"; discussed in Chapter 3.

Primates, the ultimate mammal:

Primitive Primates may have first appeared before the K-T extinction; however, "real" primates, a category which includes humans, appeared several million years after the K-T extinction[854].

Recent findings in overall human evolution:

It must be noted that human evolution did not begin a few million years ago with the divergence the chimpanzee and human lineages[855]. Perspective on the enormous evolutionary activity that has led to us is obtained by tracing the evolution of the order primates of which we are the dominant member. There is, of course, much detail in the following two diagrams and certainly not sufficient room to describe each of these steps in our evolution. I present them to illustrate the amount of detail modern archaeology has discovered and to provide some feeling for our overall evolution.

Technically, we are discussing the evolution of the portion of the Primate order we occupy, the anthropoids. By definition, Anthropoids include all species, living and fossil, descended from the last common ancestor currently extant. The last common ancestor is the suborder Haplorhini exhibited in Figure 18-2 - prosaically named the "dry-nosed" primates[856], to distinguish from the Strepsirrhini or "wet-nosed primates"[857]. It should be noted that the Anthropoids are also known as the Simians or Simiformes, the next level under the Haplorhini in Figure 18-2.

Developmental changes can be observed in the earlier branches of the primate family tree, such as changes in sensory ability, increases in brain size, and reorganization of the brain's components setting the stage for language's development and for many of our other exceptional cognitive abilities requiring millions of years to evolve.

This diagram illustrates the order of descent from the order primates beginning with the suborder Haplorhini - note that the approximate time when each group divided in the tree is shown:

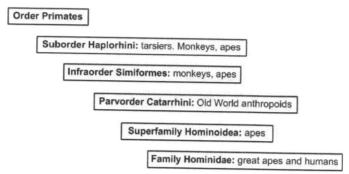

Figure 18-2 Order of descent in the Primate
Order to the Family Hominidae.

The Family Hominidae[858] can be further divided (as shown this Figure 18-3) which leads to H. sapiens, us:

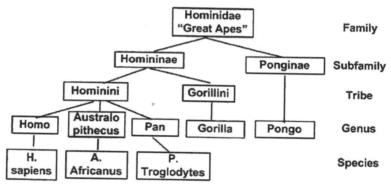

Figure 18-3 Order of descent in the Primate
Order from Hominidae to Homo.

Our diverging journey from the main Primate group began about sixty-five Ma. If we assume that the average number of years to reach sexual maturity is about ten years (e.g., monkeys reach maturity in a few years) then almost seven million iterations of the reproductive cycle have occurred.

Considering the many variations possible in the reproductive process, it is not difficult to image how we arrived at our dominant position. However; it is clear that over the last sixty-three million ye250ars considerable adjustments have been made courtesy of reproduction. The final divergence, the human-chimpanzee (Pan) split from our closest "relative," occurred between five and seven Ma.

The divergence between human and pan brings us full circle to our arrival in Europe as described in Chapter 3.

Chapter 18 Summary: The Biophysical Development of Earth

- Preparation of the Earth for Life's appearance and the earliest phases of life: chapters 12 through 17 described creation of an environment on Earth suitable for the development of life.
- Life's appearance beginning with the primordial cell was introduced in chapter 1 along with the appearance of multi-cellular life. Next the Ediacaran Period was explained which led to a brief discussion of the ladder of life. Finally, chapter 1 also introduced the phenomenon of evolution responsible for the ladder of life.
- Chapter 18 picked up the discussion of life's development with the tectonic formation and ultimate separation of super-continents Rodinia and Pangaea the prelude to complex life.
- Chapter 18 discussed the Cryogenian period and reviewed the Ediacaran where fossils discovered in the Ediacaran Hills of South Africa demonstrate the existence of simple multicelled life spanning a period of 650 – 540 Ma. The existence of multicelled life during the Ediacaran period, demonstrates that meiosis, the requirement for sexual reproduction had evolved. This development set the stage for the "Cambrian Explosion" between 540 and 500 Ma.
- During the Cambrian explosion, most of the known phyla formed and began a sequence of steadily improving life forms.
- Primitive fish originated during the Cambrian. However, modern fish did not appear until the late Silurian and Devonian periods, 443 Ma to 395 Ma. Fish are constrained to water. Female lays large number of eggs which the male "fertilizes" by releasing a mass of sperm greatly increasing the odds of zygote creation.
- The transition from oceans to land began about 382 Ma with the evolution of Tiktaalik, a lobe finned fish, that was capable of living on land. Tiktaalik is a transition to the next higher life form, the

Amphibian whose fossil record is poor, but is found at the end of the Devonian, 360 Ma. Amphibians begin life in the water; the female lays large number of eggs which the male fertilizes. If fertilized, the zygote ultimately matures into an animal that can live on land.

- Amniotic membrane evolved during this period which added to an animal species' survival ability as the membrane protected the developing embryo. This capability was first employed by reptiles.
- Reptiles, the first animal capable of existing exclusively on land appears about 320 Ma. Reptile eggs are fertilized in the female's body and the growing embryo is protected by the amniotic membrane. Upon maturity, a hard-shell form around the embryo. The female lays eggs containing the developing embryos in a shell, which provides more protection than loose eggs in water.
- Five extinctions occurred over the time interval 450 Ma to 34 Ma. One of greatest extinctions occurred between the Permian and Triassic periods about 251 Ma in which about ninety-five percent of all species became extinct.
- After the Earth recovered from the P-T extinction, some reptiles survived and the precursor to mammals, the cryodont appears. Also, the famous dinosaur arrives.
- The next most severe extinction, the Cretaceous – Ternary (K-T), probably caused by a large asteroid, occurred 65 Ma, ended the age of dinosaurs and ushered in the age of mammals. Mammals have the survival advantage of larger brains, warm bloodedness and live birth.
- About 34 Ma a small extinction, the Grand Coupure, caused a dramatic change in the European animals with the appearance of pigs, cattle, goats, sheep and horses. These animals provided improved diets and furs which enabled Europeans to thrive and ultimately dominate the Earth.
- This chain of ever improving life produced by improved reproduction and adaptability was an important demonstration of evolution.

- The detailed evolution of humans beginning within the order primates was illustrated to provide a simple overview of the details of our evolution
- The divergence between human and pan (Chimpanzee) between five and seven Ma brings us full circle to our arrival in Europe as described in chapter 3

Looking ahead:

We come now a logical conclusion for this discussion- The life cycle of our universe, from its fiery beginning to its frozen end with a short review of our Brief Shining Moment eight billon years after the Big Bang.

CHAPTER 19

THE LIFE CYCLE OF OUR UNIVERSE, FROM ITS FIERY BEGINNING TO ITS FROZEN END

Even a universe has a life cycle. Previous chapters have presented sections of our universe's life cycle. This chapter will organize these pieces and add additional material as necessary to properly present the life cycle of our universe from its beginning to its inevitable end including a few words about our "Brief Shining Moment"

Initial understanding of the universe

Although we can probably never know for certain, evidence available at archeological sites such as Pinnacle Point, suggest that our first understanding of the universe began thousands of years ago, when our emerging cognition, hobbled by our limited innate observational ability, established the first explanation of the universe and our position in it:

> We live at the center of a relatively small, young, unhanging universe that revolves about us – a universe created by an all-powerful, undetectable being called God in the English-speaking parts of the world.

This explanation, and its variations, underpin most religions and remained relatively unchanged for thousands of years until Copernicus made the startling discovery that the Earth is not the center of the universe. Copernicus's observations placed the sun at the center.

A few years later in the early 1600s, observational capability took a "giant leap forward" with the almost simultaneous invention of the microscope and telescope. With respect to the universe, the telescope and its ever improving descendents provided an increasingly detailed view of the universe such as its unimaginable size.

The first theoretical advance regarding our understanding of the universe was supplied by Albert Einstein, who in a flash of amazing intellect formulated two sets of equations: one that that described the observations of two observers moving at two constant velocities relative to each other followed by a second set of equations that described the observations of two observers accelerating relative to each other -particularly observers in a gravitational field which accelerates objects.

The first set formed the basis of the Special Relativity while the second formed the basis of the General Theory of Relativity – two of the most ground breaking achievements of the human mind in history.

The General Theory published in 1919 is essentially a mathematical description of the universe[859]. For example, it explains that what we perceive as the force of gravity arises from the curvature of spacetime.

1922 Russian cosmologist and mathematician Alexander Friedman (1988 –1925)[860] made an astonishing discovery-- a solution to the equations of Albert Einstein's General Theory of Relativity demonstrating the possibility of an expanding universe.

Friedman's predictions were soon corroborated in 1929 by Edwin Hubble and his assistant, Milton L. Humason, who compared the spectrum of hydrogen from stars at varying distances from earth and found that as the distance to a star increased, the hydrogen spectrum was shifted to the left or red end of the spectrum – a redshift. Applying Sherlock's theorem, Hubble realized that the galaxies are moving away from us and the farther away the galaxies are, the faster their distance from us in increasing. *The universe is expanding!*

Discovery of the Big Bang:

In retrospect, an expanding universe seems quite logical. The force of gravity, acting on two objects will, absent any constraints, tend to pull them together. The reason the earth is not pulled into the sun is the centripetal force created by the earth's motion, balances the force of gravity. But what prevents the galaxies from being pulled together? The answer lies in the fact that they must be moving away from each other due to an initial explosion of unimaginable violence – a Big Bang!

George Gamow predicts the type of radiation to be expected from a big bang:

In another seminal paper, George Gamow suggested that the observed abundance of hydrogen and helium in the universe could be explained if the universe had begun with a Big Bang[861]. Imagine Gamow's surprise, when in 1965, two young radio astronomers, Arno Penzias (1933-) [862]and Robert Wilson, accidentally discovered the predicted radiation. The radiation appeared to be coming uniformly from all directions. Accordingly, it was named the Cosmic Background Radiation (CMB).

At first the CMB was believed to be isotropic, a fancy word meaning that intensity of the CMB radiation was the same regardless of arrival direction. However, it was argued that, since the universe has structure, there should be small, but measurable variations, technically known as anisotropic (non-isotropic) variations in the CMB.

The Wilkinson Microwave Anisotropy mapping satellite confirms the variation and reveals the universes 'beginnings

In 2003, NASA launched the Wilkinson Microwave Anisotropy Map (WMAP) satellite[863] to search for the predicted variations in the CMB[864]. The WMAP satellite has been spectacularly successful. There is not room for a full discussion of the WMAP findings; these are discussed in several articles[865].

Chapter 12 explained how the WMAP was shown to have described the beginning of the universe -- this chapter will also reveal that the end of the universe is dictated by the laws of nuclear physics. Between the beginning and the end lies the brief shining moment of mankind.

Regarding our universe's beginning, data from the WMAP satellite conclusively demonstrates that the universe began approximately 13.7 billion years ago with an explosion of unimaginable violence: The Big Bang (BB). In a relatively short time vast quantities of matter, basically hydrogen was launched into empty space. Today you are ensconced upon a ball created by the ancestors of this original matter.

Chapter 12 also recounts Nobel laureate Steven Weinberg's tabulation of the events occurring in the first four hundred million years of our universe's life as determined by the WMAP satellite. Weinberg's table is repeated here for convenience:

Time	Event
0.02 seconds	Universe basically E/M radiation (light)
0.11 seconds	Excess of protons over neutrons appear
1.09 seconds	Light cannot escape primordial fireball
3 min 42 seconds	Deuterium stable, Helium 26 % universe's mass
400 kyrs	Hydrogen coalesced from electron-proton cloud
700 kyrs	Universe cool enough: H_2 and He stable atoms
400 Myrs	Stars emerge and form stable galaxies

Table 19-1 The initial Universe events after the Big Bang from table 12-2

Of interest for this discussion approximately four hundred Myrs after the BB, stars emerge- a pivotal event since star formation is central to element creation and the origin of life in our solar system and undoubtedly any others similar to ours where life could have begun.

As described previously, star formation begins with the great volumes of hydrogen gas created in the BB. Huge pockets of hydrogen gas eventually accumulate and gravitational attraction between hydrogen molecules, minuscule as it is, will cause the gas to begin to contract. Eventually the gas will contract sufficiently to allow the gravitational forces generated by the large amount of hydrogen to cause hydrogen molecules to fuse into helium. The process of nuclear fusion had begun releasing enormous amounts of energy and a star is born.

Creation of the elements

At this stage in the universe's development only two of the ninety-two elements (H and He) existed. The creation of all elements up to iron was produced by the tremendous energy released by nuclear fusion in the stars that began forming four hundred Myrs after the BB.

The production of elements up to iron is illustrated in the modified binding energy curve below:

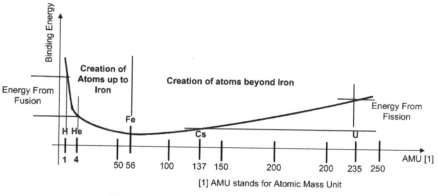

Figure 19–1 Creation of the elements 2

Beyond iron, more than the "ordinary" fusion force produced by normal stars is required to create elements. Elements beyond iron up to uranium are produced in unique massive stars known as super novae. In all stars, while nuclear fusion continues, sufficient radiation is produced to maintain a star's size. Eventually all of the material that could be fused is consumed and the star stops radiating energy. Without the outward pressure of radiation, the star suddenly collapses with an enormous explosion so violent that a hydrogen bomb resembles a fire cracker. The immense force of the explosion creates the heavy elements beyond iron while they are being ejected into space.

Star formation continued repeatedly until all of the atoms up to Uranium had been formed.

Our brief Shining Moment

About eight billion years after the Big Bang, a very special cloud of gas began to condense into a star we call the sun. As this star formed it began to rotate causing a circumstellar disk of material to be formed around the sun. Eventually matter within the disk began to form proto-planets under the gravitational forces of the particles in the disk. Accretion of material onto the proto-planets continued until the final formation of planets.

The first four planets formed are called the terrestrial planets. The first, Mercury, is much too hot to sustain life. The next planet from the sun, Venus is also is too hot to sustain life. Finally, we come to a planet far enough away from the sun to be in a temperature range where life can form. The fourth planet is too far from the sun and is too cold to support life. Beyond that planet, the planets were huge balls of gas.

The third planet of course is the planet we call home – Earth. Earth was initially very hot, but it eventually cooled sufficiently to allow water carried by asteroids raining down upon the surface to collect in hollows in the rocky surface forming the oceans. Radiometric dating of rocks that were formed early indicates that the oceans formed about 4.3 billion years ago.

Eventually the concentration of atoms in the ocean - oxygen, carbon, hydrogen, nitrogen and other elements necessary for life became sufficient to form the first biological entity that could be considered to be alive. This primitive entity is known to have been alive because it could perform two tasks essential for life. First, it could reproduce itself, which we know is true because all living objects descendent from the primordial first living entity have finite lives and thus must reproduce themselves or their species becomes extinct. Second it could metabolize energy from the sun to provide the energy to support itself. This initial living entity was cyanobacteria which was first found in Shark's Bay Australia and has been dated to 3.7 Ga.

In 1653, the noted investigator Thomas Hooke examining the descendent of the first biological entities which formed the structure of wood, named them cells because they reminded him of a monk's cell.

After about 1.5 billion years ago, primitive single cell organisms that we now call Prokaryotes formed more complex cells - cells with nuclei termed Eukaryotic cells. These improved cells began to combine into groups of multicelled animals. This grouping conveyed considerable advantages which came at a price. Multicelled animals had to invent a reproduction technique that began with a single cell, since only a single cell can reproduce itself (recall that all living entities on the Earth begin life as a single cell).

Manufacture of protein began about this time with the development of DNA- essential for protein manufacture.

Multi-celled animal development continued slowly until about five hundred million years ago an extraordinary event occurred, the expansion of multicelled life known as the Cambrian explosion. The progression of life following the Cambrian was presented previously in chapter 1

The "ladder of life" illustrates the "rungs" of life beginning with fish and progressing to amphibians, reptiles, mammals and primates culminating with our species Homo sapiens.

An important characteristic of each new species on the ladder is the continued improvement in reproductive capability and adaptability. The phenomenon associated with continued reproduction and adaptability improvement is generally known as evolution.

As discussed in chapter 2, our species appears in the fossil record in Africa about Two hundred thousand years ago. A 195,000-year-old fossil from the Omo 1 site in Ethiopia, exhibited previously in Figure 2-2, shows the beginnings of the skull changes that we associate with modern humans, especially the vertical front of the skull case and possibly a projecting chin, as opposed to the sloped Neandertal skull (larger than H. sapiens, but no room for frontal lobes,

One of the more important features of our species development in Africa was the ability to speak. Data found at the Pinnacle Peak archaeological site in Africa (introduced above) related to the manufacture of specialized tools and weapons suggests that only individuals who can communicate via language made these tools. Physiologically the ability to speak was enabled by our unique skull shape which allowed the development of the frontal lobes essential for symbolic thinking and speech.

Sometime during our development in Africa, we also invented the thrown spear and the bow and arrow. The thrown spear is the most important weaponry development in all history – it permitted the infliction of injury or death from a distance. Hand to hand combat or killing of animals for food by direct contact was no longer required.

As the study of fossils progressed, DNA was added to the investigative tools available – a relatively recent addition which was a game changer. DNA analysis allowed accurate dating of fossils provided sufficient, actually not very much, tissue remained.

Regarding the contribution of DNA analysis to human migration DNA analysis data presented in chapter 3, Figure 3-2, demonstrated that Europe was populated by three migrations. The first began forty thousand years ago when the initial group of our species arrived in Europe directly from Africa, quickly vanquishing the Neanderthal and developing four Hunter gatherer cultures. One other group of our species migrated to the east where they learned farming. A third group migrated east and north where they became cattlemen and learned to ride horses.

About seven thousand years ago those who migrated east and learned farming began to experience overpopulation, unfortunately associated with farming, and migrated to Europe where they displaced the hunter gatherers.

Four thousand years ago the group who had migrated east and north returned as cattlemen riding horses, herding cattle and using wagons displaced both farmers and hunter gatherers. The latest arrivals known as Yamnaya were violent individuals and brought war to Europe.

DNA analysis contributed significantly to the controversial issue of human migration out of Africa. Three international collaborations reporting in the October 2016 issue of *Nature* describe 787 high-quality genomes from individuals from geographically diverse populations and settled the issue[866].

Our species continued to develop in various parts of the world however Europe has dominated for a variety of reasons described in the first four chapters. For example, most scientific developments occurred in Europe; moreover, Europeans enjoyed superior resources. Europeans eventually fanned out across the globe, colonizing vast areas such as the entire Western Hemisphere.

Regarding the colonization of the Western Hemisphere, dating information resembles a Kaleidoscope. Until recently, "the earliest settlement date of North America, had been estimated at 14,000 years Before Present (BP)[867]" however "new archeological finds in the Bering Straits were reported to have been radiocarbon-dated at 19,650 years, which is equivalent to between 23,000 and 24,000 cal BP (calibrated years Before Present), 10,000 years earlier[868]. No sooner had this information been digested, an "archeological site in S. California was dated at 130 ka.[869]

Regarding the future:

Three developments associated with our species success on the planet offer clues to our future:

1. Population growth,
2. Climate change – global warming
3. Resource exhaustion.

To a large extent, the last two have been exacerbated by population growth.ma

Population growth:

As introduced in chapter 1, population growth is caused by our insatiable need for sex to assure species survival plus the extreme enjoyment derived from sexual activity. Initially a central element of human survival however population growth has now become excessive. The explosive population growth over the last two hundred years is illustrated in this figure, adapted from a presentation I made at the annual American Association for the Advancement of Science in June 2010:

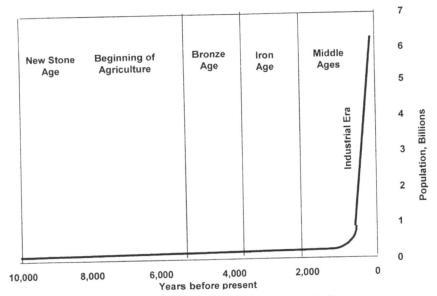

Figure 19-2 Population growth over past 10 kyrs

Inspiration for this paper was an MIT study of potential limits on human population growth sponsored by The Club of Rome[870]. The "knee" of the curve is approximately 1800. The MIT study group created a feedback "World Model" that incorporated variables such as population growth, availability of raw materials and food production. It provided the ability to examine the effects of such important items as available land and produced a population prediction – which usually showed a steep population decline in the 21st Century.

A partial explanation for Figure 19-2 is provided by William Bernstein's excellent economic history of industrialization, *The Birth of Plenty-How the Prosperity of the Modern World was Created.*[871] Bernstein pointed out that prosperity is generally not about physical objects or natural resources. Rather it is concerns how human beings interact and carry on business.

Bernstein states that four developments stand out as prerequisites for economic growth[872]:

- Secure property rights not only for physical property but also for intellectual property and one's own person – civil liberties.

- A systematic procedure for examining and interpreting the world --the scientific method.
- A widely available and open source of funding for the development and production of new inventions-- the modern capital marketplace.
- The ability to rapidly communicate vital information and transport people and goods.

In addition to the uplifting effects of prosperity, the vanquishing of childhood diseases such as Cholera, Malaria, Diphtheria and Typhoid Fever plus the cancellation of many of the medieval medical practices on children in the nineteenth century had a dramatic effect on childhood deaths[873], which had a multiplying effect on population since children grow up to be parents. The average mother at the time had between five and eight children[874]. Thus, it is little wonder that population expanded rapidly

It should be noted that Figure 19-2 was created about fifteen years ago. Our population has now expanded until there are now over 7.5 billion of us. In addition, consider the following population related items:

- In a September 28, 2016 Nature article entitled *where to put the next billion people*[875], Richard Foreman states that by 2030, 1.1 billion more people will live on Earth -- bringing the total to about 8.5 billion. Most of them will arrive in dense Asian and African cities, exacerbating pollution and resource exhaustion.
- A book entitled *"feeding the Ten billion*[876]"suggests that our population may grow to as many as ten billion.
- An article in the October 13 issue of Nature stated:" More urban area will be built in the next thirty years than ever before[877]."

Climate change

The second significant problem is the controversial contribution of man-made carbon dioxide largely caused by a growing population that consumes fossil fuel which generates the greenhouse gas carbon. The effect of human contribution to global warming must be balanced by changes to earth's orbit due to the influence of other astronomical residents of the solar system such as the large planets. Serbian polymath Milutin Milankovitch [878]was the first astronomer to calculate the effects of which there are three:

- Change in the eccentricity of the earth's orbit about 5 percent about every 100 kyrs
- Chane in the axial tilt from 21.5 degrees to 24.5 degrees about every 41 kyrs
- Change in precession – location of the northern hemisphere relative to the sun about every 23 kyrs

A crude sketch showing the Milankovitch effect on carbon dioxide vs man made effects is provided in Figure 19.5 Of interest, the carbon dioxide level has not exceeded 300 ppm until relatively recently where the level is now in excess of 400 ppm. The seriousness of this increase has been strongly debated – in the long run it won't matter.

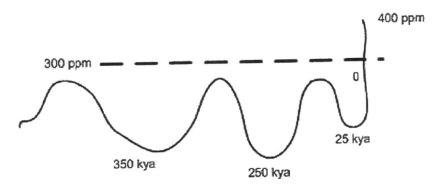

Figure 19-3 Carbon Dioxide variation over time

Of importance, the carbon dioxide level has been below 300 ppm until recently. The level is now at 400 ppm and climbing. The level is obviously changing dramatically and population growth and technological improvements are major contributors.

Coping with population growth and climate change must contend with two other features of our society:

- The reluctance to use genetically modified organisms (GMO) in food production.
- The futile attempt to replace fossil fuel generated electricity with wind and sun energy.to cope with climate change

To place the energy source situation in perspective, here is a chart illustrating the sources for US electricity generation in 2015[879]:

Energy Soure	Percent
Coal	33
Natural Gas	33
Nuclear	20
Hydropower	6
Wind	6
Solar	1
Other:	1

Table 19-2 US Electric Energy Sources in 2015

Thus, 66 percent of our electricity generation utilizes fossil fuel while 20 percent employs nuclear energy. Wind and solar provide a mere 7 percent. As a letter to the Wall Street Journal editor[880] pointed out:

> After the billions already spent and substantial subsidies that continue, wind and solar generated only 25,000 megawatts (MW) of electricity in 2015, or about 6% of U.S. demand.

In addition, both wind and sun are demonstrably unreliable. The sun doesn't shine at night and the wind doesn't blow reliably. Rotating turbines driven by steam created from fossil fuels or nuclear fission generate most of the electricity in the country 24/7 in a steady reliable manner. The rotating turbine is an extremely simple and reliable device.

Consequently, inverting the table is "rather difficult."

Demography, another significant constraint

Adding another "straw to the back of our future" demographers, who study the effects of population believe we have already exceeded the carrying capacity of the earth. Under the title *Even a killer plague wouldn't save the planet from us*, Demographers Corey Bradshaw and Barry Brook of the University of Adelaide in Australia have concluded that we have probably already exceeded Earth's carrying capacity by a considerable margin[881].

Resource exhaustion - the ultimate end?

It is difficult to tell which of these developments will have the largest impact on our future however the Earth is definitely finite. As noted previously, Archaeologist Ian Tattersall commented in his book *Masters of the planet* "we live on a finite world but believe in an infinite growth rate.[882]"

Accordingly, with our population increasing our consumption of resources will also increase. Eventually key resources will be exhausted. Due to the complex interaction between consumption of various resources, an accurate estimate of how long it will be until resource consumption becomes the determinant of our civilization's survival is difficult to ascertain.

Our house of cards

I regret ending this book on a somber note, but it is difficult to believe that we are not living in a house of cards. Unfortunately, the basic features of our civilization that have allowed us to proper and survive will probably bring our civilization to an end. Regrettably, there is relatively little we can do. There is an old saying that bad news never gets better. Our population already exceeds the planet's carrying capacity and practical/acceptable solutions to the growing temperature rise by trying to convert from fossil fuel to "green" fuel will devastate our economy causing more harm than good.

As this book was being readied for publication, one of earth's most respected scientists, Stephen Hawking issued a dire ultimatum: "start inhabiting extraterrestrial lands in the next century or prepare to face extinction[883]" Professor Hawking presumably means well, but mounting a trip to another, habitable planet within 100 years is merely science fiction.

Regarding the obvious question, "When will the axe fall?" Unfortunately, a significant downturn will occur suddenly and with little warning. The reason is the simple fact that the problems facing us are growing exponentially. To appreciate what this means, consider the example of the Lilly Pond introduced in *The Limits of Growth*. Imagine your neighbor has a lily pond. One day your neighbor places a small lily plant the pond. The lily doubles in size every day and begins to cover the pond. You ask your neighbor if your neighbor was concerned. The neighbor replies "Nah – I'm not going to start worrying until the plant covers half of the pond."

We are already seeing small harbingers of the future in the effect of severe storms. If relatively few people lived in Florida, a massive hurricane would not wreak the destruction such a hurricane causes now.

A question arises, when we do experience a significant decline, will the human race disappear from the planet? Total disappearance is quite unlikely. When the "shakeout" occurs after the unimaginable destruction, destruction which will make the bubonic plague seem like a picnic in the park, has occurred, some remnants of our species will remain. However, the magnificent civilization we currently have will be unattainable because the materials that allowed the formation of our civilization will no longer be available since we have consumed them all. Of course, materials of the Stone Age will still be available and that will be our civilization. We will return to and remain in a Stone Age.

Is it possible to escape the population increase by migrating to another planet? This question has been investigated rather thoroughly. Practical analyses of a manned Mars mission demonstrate that a significant percentage of the gross national product would be required to send even a few astronauts to Mars - transporting a significant number of citizens is pure science fiction.

The end of our sun and the frozen end of the universe

In the long run, all the items relative to our brief shining moment will not matter. In about 5 billion years our sun will have exhausted its supply of hydrogen and become a Red Giant like the star Betelgeuse in the Orion constellation, expanding until it reaches our orbit[884]. If there's anyone left on earth, they will be incinerated.

The progress of the universe will continue billions of years after our sun has become a toothless red giant. However, the universe has a finite amount of hydrogen (everything has limits). When the free clouds of hydrogen which can generate new stars are exhausted and all the stars existing at the end have consumed their hydrogen fuel, the universe will shut down to absolute zero and our universe will have completed its life cycle.

Chapter 19 Summary: The life cycle of our universe, from its fiery beginning to its frozen end

- The discussion began with our initial very primitive understanding of the universe
- Next Copernicus's startling discovery – we are not the center of the universe was reviewed
- Then Albert Einstein's mental leaps to the Special and General theories was introduced
- Russian cosmologist Alexander Friedman joined Einstein with a solution of his General theory – the possibility of an expanding universe
- Friedman's theory was corroborated by Edwin Hubble a few years later.
- The probable source of the expanding universe was next added with the discovery of radiation left over from the Big Bang
- George Gamow next predicted the type of radiation variation to be expected from a big bang:
- The Wilkinson Microwave Anisotropy mapping satellite confirms the predicted variation and reveals the universes 'beginnings which were tabulated by Nobel laureate Steven Weinberg in chapter 12.

- Of particular interest, after four hundred Myrs, stars emerged. Stars are central to the creation of elements beyond Helium and the possible creation of life
- About eight billion years ago the star we call the sun began to form surrounded by a disk within which our planet appeared.
- The development of life was recounted leading to the appearance our species H. sapiens
- H. sapiens, especially Europeans soon spread over the globe becoming the dominant primate.
- Three developments associated with our species success on the planet offer clues to our future: population growth, climate change and resource exhaustion:
  - o Beginning in the late 1800s, our population increased from less than one million to approximately 7.5 billion and is expected to grow to 8.5 billion in the next 20 years.
  - o Climate change is being exacerbated by explosive population growth and a dramatic increase in carbon dioxide to a level in excess of four hundred ppm and growing
  - o Finally and most serious, an increasing population will consume increasing quantities of resources both from sheer numbers and increased technical sophistication. A crude estimate of the life of known coal reserves is approximately three hundred years.
- Considering these few facts, it is difficult to not believe we are living in a house of cards, the collapse of which will make the bubonic plague seem like a picnic in the park. When "the dust settles" we will have regressed to the Stone Age;
- For those able to be philosophical; in the long run, all the items relative to our brief shining moment will not matter – the sun will exhaust its supply of Helium in about five billion years, become a Red Giant and the earth will be incinerated.
- Some uncountable billion years in the future, the last hydrogen in the universe will be consumed. Without a source of energy, the universe will have completed its life cycle: reduced to a few remnants at absolute zero.

GLOSSARY

a	Acceleration
AAAS	Am. Assoc. for the Advancement of Science
AMH	Anatomically Modern Human
AMS	Atomic Mass Spectrometer
BCE	Before Common Era - modern replacement for BC
CE	Common Era - modern replacement for AD
CERN	Center European Research Nuclear
CG	Center of Gravity
CRISPR	Collection of Regularly Interspersed Short Palindromic Repeats
DNA	Deoxyribonucleic Acid
E&M	Electricity and Magnetism
E/M	Electro-magnetic
ev	electron volt
Ga	(Giga) Billions of years ago
Gev	billions of electron volts
Gyr	billions of years
IQ	Intelligent Quotient
ka	Thousands of years ago
kyr	Thousands of years
l	wavelength
m	Mass
Ma	millions of years ago
mRNA	Messenger RNA
mtDNA	Mitochondrial DNA - DNA passed on by mother
Myr	millions of years
n	frequency

NMR	Nuclear Magnetic Resonance
PSI	Planetary Science Institute
RNA	Ribonucleic Acid
SD	Standard Deviation
tRNA	Transfer RNA
WMAP	Wilkerson Anisotropy Mapping Program

APPENDIX A

THE BOOK OF GENESIS[884]

[1:1] In the beginning when God created the heavens and the earth,

[1:2] the earth was a formless void and darkness covered the face of the deep, while a wind from God swept over the face of the waters.

[1:3] Then God said, "Let there be light"; and there was light.

[1:4] And God saw that the light was good; and God separated the light from the darkness.

[1:5] God called the light Day, and the darkness he called Night. And there was evening and there was morning, the first day.

[1:6] And God said, "Let there be a dome in the midst of the waters, and let it separate the waters from the waters."

[1:7] So God made the dome and separated the waters that were under the dome from the waters that were above the dome. And it was so.

[1:8] God called the dome Sky. And there was evening and there was morning, the second day.

[1:9] And God said, "Let the waters under the sky be gathered together into one place, and let the dry land appear." And it was so.

[1:10] God called the dry land Earth, and the waters that were gathered together he called Seas. And God saw that it was good.

[1:11] Then God said, "Let the earth put forth vegetation: plants yielding seed, and fruit trees of every kind on earth that bear fruit with the seed in it." And it was so.

[1:12] The earth brought forth vegetation: plants yielding seed of every kind, and trees of every kind bearing fruit with the seed in it. And God saw that it was good.

[1:13] And there was evening and there was morning, the third day.

[1:14] And God said, "Let there be lights in the dome of the sky to separate the day from the night; and let them be for signs and for seasons and for days and years,

[1:15] and let them be lights in the dome of the sky to give light upon the earth." And it was so.

[1:16] God made the two great lights - the greater light to rule the day and the lesser light to rule the night - and the stars.

[1:17] God set them in the dome of the sky to give light upon the earth,

[1:18] to rule over the day and over the night, and to separate the light from the darkness. And God saw that it was good.

[1:19] And there was evening and there was morning, the fourth day.

[1:20] And God said, "Let the waters bring forth swarms of living creatures, and let birds fly above the earth across the dome of the sky."

[1:21] So God created the great sea monsters and every living creature that moves, of every kind, with which the waters swarm, and every winged bird of every kind. And God saw that it was good.

[1:22] God blessed them, saying, "Be fruitful and multiply and fill the waters in the seas, and let birds multiply on the earth."

[1:23] And there was evening and there was morning, the fifth day.

[1:24] And God said, "Let the earth bring forth living creatures of every kind: cattle and creeping things and wild animals of the earth of every kind." And it was so.

[1:25] God made the wild animals of the earth of every kind, and the cattle of every kind, and everything that creeps upon the ground of every kind. And God saw that it was good.

[1:26] Then God said, "Let us make humankind in our image, according to our likeness; and let them have dominion over the fish of the sea, and over the birds of the air, and over the cattle, and over all the wild animals of the earth, and over every creeping thing that creeps upon the earth."

[1:27] So God created humankind in his image, in the image of God he created them; male and female he created them.

[1:28] God blessed them, and God said to them, "Be fruitful and multiply, and fill the earth and subdue it; and have dominion over the fish of the sea and over the birds of the air and over every living thing that moves upon the earth."

[1:29] God said, "See, I have given you every plant yielding seed that is upon the face of all the earth, and every tree with seed in its fruit; you shall have them for food.

[1:30] And to every beast of the earth, and to every bird of the air, and to everything that creeps on the earth, everything that has the breath of life, I have given every green plant for food." And it was so.

[1:31] God saw everything that he had made, and indeed, it was very good. And there was evening and there was morning, the sixth day.

APPENDIX B

ENCOUNTER IN SEDONA

The beautiful red rocks of Sedona are world renowned. The sandstone infused with iron oxide produces dramatic shades of red. The local authorities quite cognizant of the value/interest tourists would have in these rocks, have placed viewing stands as strategic places. The stands typically have a description of the rocks. Their geological descriptions in particular emphasize how old the rocks are.

One day, a few years ago, while driving along the road that winds through the rocks my wife and another couple and I paused at one of the roadside stands to take a look. My companions quickly returned to the car however I lingered to absorb the descriptive material. As I was doing so a man came running up waving his arms pointing at the display and pointing at the rocks shouting "They're all wrong! That's all wrong," he said pointing to the descriptive material – "All these rocks were created in 3 to 4 days!"

Taken aback by this I said "Excuse me sir I believe there are many, many geologists who would disagree". The man continued "But my God is stronger than their God!"

I would've liked to have continued the encounter however the glares from my companions indicated that this would be unwise. Besides I had gleaned enough in the brief encounter to realize that the gentleman was not even close to the beckoning bridge.

APPENDIX C

THE GEOLOGIC TIME SCALE[886]

EON	ERA	PERIOD	MYA
Phanerozoic	Cenozoic	Quaternary	1.6
		Tertiary	66
	Mezozoic	Cretacious	138
		Jurassic	205
		Triassic	240
	Paleozoic	Permian	290
		Pensylvanian	330
		Mississippian	360
		Devonian	410
		Ordovician	435
		Silurian	500
		Cambrian	570
Proterozoic		Ediacarran	630
			2500
Archean			3800?

APPENDIX D

TIME LINE FOR THE APPEARANCE OF FOSSILS IN ROCKS

Species	First appeared	Became extinct
Humans	4-5 Ma.	
Primate	30 Ma.	
Mammals	100Ma. – 65 Ma.	
Dinosaurs	230 Ma.	65 Ma.
Reptiles	320 Ma.	
Amphibians	420 Ma.	
Fish	500 Ma.	
Ediacaran Multi-celled animals	650	540 Ma.
Ediacaran Bacteria	650	– 540 Ma.
cyanobacteria	3.5 Billion years ago	

APPENDIX E

COMPARISON OF SPECIES CHARACTERISTICS

Species	Warm/ cold blooded	Where lives	How reproduces	Num Heart Chambers	Brain and CNS
Fish	Cold	Water exclusively	Female lays eggs Male fertilizes	2	limited
Amphibian	Cold	Water – land	Female lays eggs Male fertilizes	2	limited
Reptiles	Cold	Land	Fertilization in female, embryo in shell	3	Reticular
Mammal	Warm	Land	Fertilization in female, live birth	4	Limbic
Primate	Warm	Land	Fertilization in female, live birth	4	Cortex, small
Human	Warm	Land	Fertilization in female, live birth	4	Neocortex

APPENDIX F[887]

BASIC ORGANIZATION OF LIFE

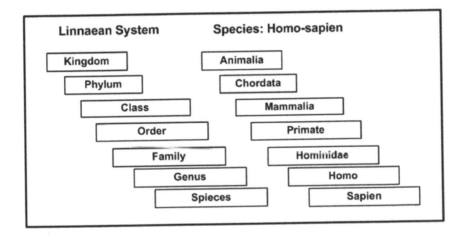

INDEX

REFERENCES

1   A person whose expertise spans a significant number of different subject areas

2   www.google.com/webhp?gws_rd=ssl#q=copernicus (accessed 3/14/16)

3   De revolutionibus orbium coelstium (Accessed 3/14/16)

4   www.webexhibits.org/calendars/year-text-Copernicus.html (accessed 8/31/16)

5   Ibid

6   The Age of Reason Begins, Will and Ariel Durant, pg. 608, Simon and Shuster, 1961

7   www.vexen.co.uk/religion/christianity_astronomy.html (accessed 10/15/16)

8   en.wikipedia.org/wiki/Ptolemy (accessed 4/16/16)

9   A system of repressive means, issued by ecclesiastical and civil authorities, to protect religious orthodoxy and social order threatened by doctrines of heresy (reaccessed 10/10/16)

10 en.wikipedia.org/wiki/Heresy (accessed 5/15/16)

11 Ibid 6

12 https://www.jstor.org/topic/scientific-revolution/

13 en.wikipedia.org/wiki/Galilean_moons

14 www.space.com/21950-who-invented-the-telescope.html (accessed 9/16/16)

15 Ian Cheny; constructionlitmag.com/culture/nicolaus-copernicus-reorganizes-the-map-of-the-universe/ (accessed 10/9/16)

16 Gallup Poll (5/10/16)

17 ka is the Geological Society of America standard abbreviation for thousands of years (reaccessed 10/10/16)

18 W. Maxwell Reed, The Earth for Sam, Harcourt, Brace & Co. New York, 1930

19 Ibid

20 Paradigms on Pilgrimage, Creationism, Paleontology, and Biblical Interpretation, Stephen J. Godfrey and Christopher R. Smith, Clements Publishing, Toronto, 2005

21 The Daemon Haunted World.. Carl Sagan, Random House, New York NY, 1996

22 Paper given at the 2013 annual meeting of the Pacific Division, American Association for the Advancement of Science

23 Paper given at the 2011 annual meeting of the Pacific Division, American Association for the Advancement of Science

24 The original name attached to the first evidence of our ancestor discovered at the convergence of a tal (the German name for stream) and the Neander river is Neandertal - despite the addition of h, I will use the name Neandertal; moreover, this name is becoming increasingly common

25 Masters of the Planet, Ian Tattersall, Macmillan, 2012

26 Ibid *Science and Religion – Are They Compatible? Paul* Kurz, Prometheus Books, Amherst NY, 2003

27 Why Is Creationism So Persistent?" Lawrence Wood, Free Inquiry, Vol. 34 May 14, 2014

28 en.wikipedia.org/wiki/Creationism (accessed 9/24/16)

29 Geology: Evidence of life in Earth's oldest rocks, Abigail C. Allwood, Nature, Vol 537, pp 500-501, 22 September, 2106

30 https://en.wikipedia.org/wiki/Arthur_Holmes

31 https://en.wikipedia.org/wiki/Radioactive_decay (accessed 6/12/16)

32 Ibid 29

33 en.wikipedia.org/wiki/Cyanobacteria (accessed 7/18/16)

34 en.wikipedia.org/wiki/Prokaryote (accessed 7/18/16)

35 en.wikipedia.org/wiki/Shark_Bay (accessed 7/18/16)

36 https://en.wikipedia.org/wiki/Robert_Hooke (accessed (4/21/16)

37 www.science-of-aging.com/timelines/images/hooke-cork-cells.jpg (accessed 12/23/16)

38 http://geoscienceworld.org/content/gspaleobio/26/3/386?download=true (accessed 5/4/16)

39 en.wikipedia.org/wiki/Zygote (accessed 9/10/16)

40 Result of Google search April 2016

41 www.encyclopedia.com/topic/protein.aspx (accessed 9/10/16)

42 biology.about.com/of/molecularbiology/a/aa101904a.htm (accessed 8/15/16)

43 https://en.wikipedia.org/wiki/Genetic_code

44 https://en.wikipedia.org/wiki/Messenger_RNA (accessed 8/15/16)

45 https://www.dnalc.org/view/15549-transcrition-translation-exons-and-introns.html (accessed 8/15/16)

46 en.wikipedia.org/wiki/Phillip_Allen_Sharp (accessed 10/29/16)

47 https://www.nobelprize.org/nobel_prizes/medicine/laureates/1993/roberts-bio.html (accessed 10/29/16)

48 www.nobelprize.org/nobel_prizes/medicine/laureates/1993 (accessed 10/29/16)

49 Alternative splicing and evolution, Stephanie Boue et al, Wiley Periodicals, 2003

50 Ibid

51 Ibid

52 www.sigmaaldrich.com/technical-documents/articles/biology/crispr-cas9-genome-editing.html (accessed 8/15/16)

53 CRISPR helps evo-devo scientists to unpick the origins of adaptations, Nature, 536, 249, 18 August 2016

54 www.broadinstitute.org/what-broad/areas-focus/project-spotlight/crispr-timeline (accessed 8/20/16)

55 www.nature.com/news/2010/100623/full/news.2010.315.html

56 Ibid 27

57 http://www.ucmp.berkeley.edu/vendian/ediacaran.php (accessed 8/6/16

58 the primary subdivision of a taxonomic (a scheme of classification) kingdom, grouping together all classes of organisms that have the same body plan. (reaccessed 10/10/16)

59 https://en.wikipedia.org/wiki/Cambrian_explosion (accessed 9/10/16)

60 What sparked the Cambrian explosion? Doug Fox, Nature 16 Feb 2016

61 http://www.queensu.ca/geol/narbonne (reaccessed 10/10/16)

62 en.wikipedia.org/wiki/Evolution_of_fish (accessed 9/10/16)

63 Master's of the Planet, Ian Tattersall, Palgrave MacMillan, 2012

64 Systems neuroscience: Yeo & Eickhoff A modern map of the human cerebral cortex, Nature 536, 152–154, 11 August 2016

65 Where to put then next billion people, Nature Vol. 537, 608–611 29 September 2016

66 http://www.worldometers.info/ (accessed 10/14/16)

67 Your body is younger than you think, Nichola Wade, August 2, New York Times

68 www.cdc.gov/nchs/fastats/leading-causes-of-death. (accessed Sep 20, 2016)

69 Variation in cancer risk among tissues can be explained by the number of stem cell divisions, C. Tomasetti and B. Vogelstein, Science 02 Jan 2010 Vol. 347, pp. 78-81 (accessed 10/1/16)

70 https://en.wikipedia.org/wiki/Afterlife (accessed 11/5/16)

71 http://www.salon.com/2012/04/21/near_death_explained (accessed 11/5/16)

72 www.google.com/webhp?gws_rd=ssl#q=rubaiyat+quotes (accessed 11/5/16)

73 en.wikipedia.org/wiki/Johann_Carl_Fuhlrott (accessed Oct 25 2016)

74 en.wikipedia.org/wiki/Hermann_Schaaffhausen (accessed 9/18/16)

75 The organization of relationships between various animal and plant groups first established in 1735by Linnaeus is ahown in Appendix tbd (accessed 7/15/16)

76 www.conservapedia.com/The_immutability_of_species (accessed 9/5/16)

77 Ibid 103

78 Ibid, Simon Winchester

79 Ibid

80 Population genetics: A map of human wanderlust, Serena Tucci & Joshua M. Akey, Nature Vol. 538, 13 Oct,2016

81 humanorigins.si.edu/evidence/human-fossils/fossils/engis-2 (accessed 9/9/16)

[82] en.wikipedia.org/wiki/Neanderthal1, Wikipedia (accessed 9/9/16)

[83] https://en.wikipedia.org/wiki/Gibraltar_1 (accessed 9/10/16)

[84] Ibid 90

[85] Ibid 52

[86] Ibid 91

[87] en.wikipedia.org/wiki/William_King_(geologist) (reaccessed 10/10/16)

[88] en.wikipedia.org/wiki/Louis_Lartet (accessed 7/14/16)

[89] en.wikipedia.org/wiki/Homo_erectus

[90] www.perfettaletizia.it/archivio/infomazione/evoluzionismo/inglese/Homo/ Homo_erectus.htm (accessed 7/14/16)

[91] en.wikipedia.org/wiki/Peking_Man (accessed 7/14/16)

[92] en.wikipedia.org/wiki/Otto_Schoetensack (reaccessed Oct 15 2016)

[93] *Der Unterkiefer des Homo Heidelbergensis aus den Sanden von Mauer bei Heidelberg. Ein Beitrag zur Paläontologie des Menschen. Leipzig, 1908, Verlag von Wilhelm Engelmann (retrieved from Wikipedia (2016)*

[94] H. G. Wells, *A short History of the World, www.bartleby.com/86/*

[95] en.wikipedia.org/wiki/Homo_heidelbergensis (reaccessed 10/10/16)

[96] various references to heidelbergesis

[97] /www.britannica.com/place/Altamira (reaccessed 10/10/16)

[98] Ibid 110

[99] http://www.strangescience.net/holmes.htm (reaccessed 10/10/16)

[100] archaeologyinfo.com/australopithecus-afarensis (accessed 7/14/16)

[101] humanorigins.si.edu/evidence/human-fossils/species/australopithecus-afarensis (reaccessed 10/10/16)

[102] en.wikipedia.org/wiki/Taung_Child (accessed 7/14/16)

[103] Info about L & M Leakey

[104] *https://en.wikipedia.org/wiki/The_Sign_of_the_Four* (accessed 9/10/16)

[105] Missionaries were one reason Europeans ventures to "Darkest Africa» (reaccessed 10/10/16)

[106] Info re Louis L parents (acessed 5/5/16)

[107] en.wikipedia.org/wiki/Louis_Leakey (accessed 5/5/16)

[108] en.wikipedia.org/wiki/Out_of_Asia_theory (accessed 5/5/16)

[109] *Canon Leakey also was a naturalist and must have been a significant model, as Louis wished originally to pattern his life after his father's. Canon Leakey was one of the original founders of the East Africa and Uganda Natural History Society, according to Louis' Memoirs, Chapter 8*

[110] The Acheulian hand axe (accessed 10/18/15)

[111] https://en.wikipedia.org/wiki/Acheulean (accessed 10/18/15)

[112] archaeologyinfo.com/homo-habilis (accessed 6/14/16)

[113] en.wikipedia.org/wiki/Homo_habilis (accessed 10/18/15)

[114] en.wikipedia.org/wiki/Richard_Leakey (accessed 5/5/16)

[115] en.wikipedia.org/wiki/Omo_remains (assessed 5/7/16)

[116] Ibid

[117] *Mcdougall, Ian; Brown, FH; Fleagle, JG (2005). "Stratigraphic placement and age of modern humans from Kibish, Ethiopia". Nature. **433** (7027): 733–736.*

[118] Ian McDougall, Francis H Brown, John G Fleagle *Sapropels and the age of hominins Omo I and II, Kibish, Ethiopia.* Journal of Human Evolution (2008) Volume: 55

[119] http://www.talkorigins.org/faqs/homs/15000.html (reaccessed 10/10/16)

[120] Ibid 126

[121] en.wikipedia.org/wiki/Lucy_(Australopithecus) (accessed 4/21/16)

[122] Perimortem fractures in Lucy suggest mortality from fall out of tall tree *Nature* Vol 537, pp 503–507 22 September 2016 (accessed 10/14/16

[123] ScienceDaily. 29 October 2015, retrieved from Wiki, May 2016

[124] https://en.wikipedia.org/wiki/John_T._Robinson (accessed 4/21/16)

[125] An early and enduring advanced technology originating 71,000 years ago in South Africa *Nature*, Pages: 590–593, 22 November 2012

[126] Sharpening the mind, Sally McBrearty, Nature, Pages: 531–532, 22 November 2012

[127] Cattelain, P. in Projectile Technology (Ed. Kneck, H) 213 -240 Plenum 1997

[128] General ref to Atapurca

[129] "Archaeological Site of Atapuerca". UNESCO World Heritage Centre. Retrieved November 29, 2015.

[130] DNA from Neandertal relative may shake up human family tree, Ann Gibbons, Science, Sep. 11, 2015.

[131] Nuclear DNA sequences from the Middle Pleistocene Sima de los Huesos hominins, Meyer, Nature, 24 March, 2016, pp 504-50

[132] DNA from Neandertal relative may shake up human family tree Ann Gibbons, Science, Sep. 11, 2015

[133] a group of organisms that consists of a common ancestor and all its lineal descendants, and represents a single "branch" on the "tree of life" (from Google)

[134] smithsonianmag.com/hominids/files/2012/11/picresized_1353865922_Homo_antecessor.jpg (accessed 9/18/16)

[135] archaeology.about.com/od/gterms/qt/gran_dolina.htm (accessed 4/21/16)

[136] Earth and Planetary Science Letters March 1996, Pages 47–61

[137] Definition from Dictionary.com

[138] Meat-Eating Among the Earliest Humans American Scientist, March – April pp 110

[139] https://en.wikipedia.org/wiki/Archaeological_record (accessed 7/18/16)

[140] Nov. 20012 Nature Magazine

[141] The Holocene is a geological epoch which began at the end of the Pleistocene, approximately 12 to 11.5 ka, and continues to the present (accessed 7/25/16)

[142] Brown et al, Early and Enduring Technology - 71 Ka… Nature 590.pp Nov 2012

[143] Poster presentation by UNLV Masters student Amber Ciravolo AAASPD mtg, June, 2013

[144] Tattersall Ibid

[145] Cognition definition – Google search

[146] WSJ May 21, 2015, Warren Buffet article

[147] From Steppes to Deserts, during the Aurignacian, Marcel Otte, 18 November 2015

[148] http://www.efossils.org/site/atapuerca (accessed 4/20/16)

[149] Ibid 128

[150] en.wikipedia.org/wiki/Louis_Agassiz (accessed 4/21/16)

[151] en.wikipedia.org/wiki/Cro-Magnon (4/6/16)

[152] Ibid 91

[153] Ancient DNA pinpoints dawn of Neanderthals, Edwin Callaway, Nature news, 17 Mar, 2016, p 2816

[154] The timing and spatiotemporal patterning of Neanderthal disappearance, Tom Higham, Nature, 21 August 2014

[155] The earliest evidence for anatomically modern humans in northwestern Europe, Tom Higham, Nature, 24 November, 2011

[156] An early and enduring advanced technology originating 71,000 years ago in South Africa *Nature* Kyle S. Brown, Volume:491, 22 November 2012

[157] Lethal weapons may have given early humans edge over Neanderthals, the Guardian, Ian Sample, science correspondent Wednesday 7 November 2012

[158] Throwing in the Middle and Upper Paleolithic: inferences from an analysis of humeral retroversion,", Jill A. Rhodes and Steven Churchill, *Journal of Human Evolution, Jan 2009* (retrieved from Wiki, Jan 2016).

[159] *Neandertal Epigenome* Archeology Monday, June 09, 2014, Zach Zorach.

[160] https://en.wikipedia.org/wiki/DNA_methylation

[161] The genetic history of Ice Age Europe, May 2, 2016 Nature

[162] Ibid

[163] Tenfold Population Increase in Western Europe at the Neandertal–to–Modern Human Transition, P. Mellars, Vol. 333 Science 29 July 2011:

[164] www.tested.com/science/life/454072-why-bigger-neanderthal-brains-didnt-make-them-smarter-humans (accessed 11/22/16)

[165] www.smithsonianmag.com/science-nature/science-shows-why-youre-smarter-than-a-neanderthal-1885827/

[166] American History, Oxford Research Encyclopedia, Genocide and American History, Jeffrey Ostler, Mar, 2015

[167] en.wikipedia.org/wiki/Homo_erectus (accessed 3/19/16)

168 American Heritage® Dictionary of the English Language, Fifth Edition. S.v. "type site." Retrieved December 8 2015 from probability) across Europe

169 Ibid from steppes

170 A History of the Ancient Word, C. Starr, Oxford University Press New York, 1991

171 "Discovering Lascaux", Brigette and Giles Delluc, free at cave, 1990

172 Ibid 200

173 Ibid 148

174 Personal communication with Professor Marcel Otte

175 response from Prof. Otte re use of his quote: oui, bien sur, très honore (yes, of course, I am honored)

176 Blackfeet Indian Stories, G. B. Grinnell, Riverbend Publishing, Helena, Mn, 1913

177 Ibid 204

178 Personal conversation with a Blackfoot native, August 2016

179 en.wikipedia.org/wiki/Animism (reaccessed 10/10/16)

180 en.wikipedia.org/wiki/Timeline_of_religion (accessed 9/15/16)

181 en.wikipedia.org/wiki/Lake_Mungo_remains

182 Ibid 155

183 en.wikipedia.org/wiki/Venus_of_Hohle_Fels (accessed Oct 25 2016)

184 en.wikipedia.org/wiki/Gravettian (accessed 7/29/16)

185 Le Solutrian, Janusz K. Kozlowski, Marcel Otte Supplment a la Revue Archeologique cu Centre de la France

186 www.google.com/wikipedia/magdalenian (accessed 7/29/16)

187 Ibid 174

188 see Appendix II for an explanation dating techniques.

189 https://en.wikipedia.org/wiki/Emile_Cartailhac

190 https://en.wikipedia.org/wiki/Chauvet_Cave accessed (2015)

191 www.visual-arts-cork.com/prehistoric/aurignacian-art.htm (accessed 7/29/16)

192 much of the material in this section is derived from "Chauvet-Pont D'Arc Cave, The First Masterpiece of Humanity - text by Pedro Lima, Pub by Synops. Purchased at the cave, Sept 2015

193 https://www.britannica.com/topic/Eliette-Brunel-Deschamps (accessed 10/29/16

194 http://plus.lefigaro.fr/tag/christian-hillaire (accessed 10/29/16)

195 http://www.grottechauvet-pontdarc.com/pages/page1gb.htm (accessded 10/29/16)

196 en.wikipedia.org/wiki/Venus_of_Hohle_Fels (accessed 7/29/16)

197 en.wikipedia.org/wiki/Minotaur

198 Chauvet-Pont d'Arc cave. The first Masterpiece of humanity, 2012, Editions Synops

199 https://en.wikipedia.org/wiki/Lascaux accessed (2015)

200 selections from Lascaux book

201 Ibid 177

202 The Shamans of Prehistory Hardcover, 1998 Jean Clottes and David Lewis-Williams Harry N. Abrams Publishers;

203 *jameseyerman.com/.../magdalenian-grottes-kalahari-san-people.htm*

204 copy obtained from author, at the Niax cave, France, September 2015

205 en.wikipedia.org/wiki/Le_Mas-d'Azil

206 en.wikipedia.org/wiki/André_Leroi-Gourhan (reaccessed 10/10/16)

207 en.wikipedia.org/wiki/Guns,_Germs,_and_Steel

208 en.wikipedia.org/wiki/Neolithic_Revolution (Acessed 3/6/16)

209 Ibid

210 https://en.wikipedia.org/wiki/Wheat#Origin (accessed 7/25/16)

211 Ibid 150

212 www.smithsonianmag.com/science-nature/what-is-the-anthropocene-and-are-we-in-it?

213 *GMOs Are a Necessity—for Farmers and the Environment,* Robert T. Fraley, WSJ. Oct. 3, 2016

214 The three ancestral tribes that founded Western civilization, Colin Barras, New Scientist, July 1

215 Ibid

216 Ibid

217 Ibid

218 Genetic Discontinuity Between Local Hunter-Gatherers and Central Europe's First Farmers, B. Bramanti, M. G. Thomas, et al, Science 02 Oct 2009: Vol. 326

219 Ibid

220 Ibid 241

221 Ancient human genomes suggest three ancestral populations for present-day Europeans, Losif Lazaridis, Nature, 17 September, 2014

222 Ibid

223 https://en.wikipedia.org/wiki/Yamna_culture#Physical_characteristics (accessed 10/3/16)

224 https://en.wikipedia.org/wiki/Corded_Ware_culture (accessed 10/3/16)

225 Ibid 195

226 en.wikipedia.org/wiki/Juan_Pizarro_(conquistador) (accessed 10/3/16)

227 Ibid 242

228 https://en.wikipedia.org/wiki/Battle_of_Hastings (accessed 10/2/2016)

229 Ibid 191

230 Ibid 88

231 en.wikipedia.org/wiki/Aristarchus_of_Samos

232 *"Stone Pages Archaeo News: Ancient metal workshop found in Serbia".* stonepages. com. *Retrieved 26 August 2015.*

233 https://commons.wikimedia.org/wiki/File:Metallurgical_diffusion.png

234 Ibid George Grinnell

235 en.wikipedia.org/wiki/History_of_writing (accessed Apr 10, 017

236 https://en.wikipedia.org/wiki/History_of_writing

237 When the Ancient Greeks began to Write, Eric Powel, Newly Discovered Inscriptions help explain how literacy spread, Archeology, Feb, 2017

238 Private communication

239 richarddawkins.net/2016/07/is-god-a-silverback, David Barash

240 https://en.wikipedia.org/wiki/Polygyny

241 oracc.museum.upenn.edu/amgg/listofdeities/marduk (accessed 10/20/16

242 https://www.google.com/webhp?gws_rd=ssl#q=aphrodite (accessed 10/20/16

243 www.ancient-origins.net/myths-legends/ancient-pagan-origins-easter

244 The Ghost Dance The Origins of Releigion, Westen La Barre, Dell Publcations, NY, NY, 1970

245 Apollo Christmas at the moon (accessed 9/18/16)

246 en.wikipedia.org/wiki/Documentary_hypothesis (accessed 9/17/16)

247 Ibid

248 Ibid 243

249 Ibid 243

250 en.wikipedia.org/wiki/Babylonian_captivity (accessed 9/16/16)

251 www.google.com/webhp?gws_rd=ssl#q=supernatural+Spirit%2C+God+or+Gods (reaccessed 10/10/16)

252 Ibid 7

253 Proof of Heaven, Eben Alexander M.D. Simon and Shuster, NY, 2012

254 https://en.wikipedia.org/wiki/Aristarchus_of_Samos (accessed 9/15/16)

255 en.wikipedia.org/wiki/Leucippus (reaccessed 10/10/16)

256 en.wikipedia.org/wiki/Democritus

257 "A History of Western Philosophy",Bertrand Russell, Simon and Shuster, NY NY. 1945

258

259 Quote from personal copy

260 The Living Universe: Gods and Men in Virgil's Aeneid by Agathe Thornton, 1976

261 en.wikipedia.org/wiki/Benjamin_Franklin#Inventions_and_scientific_inquiries (reaccessed 10/10/16)

262 en.wikipedia.org/wiki/Amber

263 The accepted scientific term of BCE for years instead of the religious term BC, as well as CE instead of AD will be employed throughout the book.

264 Thales (c.625-546 BC) From in2greece.com/english/historymyth/history/ancient/thales.htm

265 www.glasslinks.com/newsinfo/phoenician.htm

266 en.wikipedia.org/wiki/Magnetite (reaccessed 10/13/16)

267 dictionary.reference.com/browse/lodestone

268 www.smith.edu/hsc/museum/ancient_inventions/compass2.html (reaccessed 10/10/16)

269 en.wikipedia.org/wiki/Girolamo_Cardano

270 https://acmrs.org/publications/catalog/de-subtilitate-girolamo-cardano

271 The term E&M will generally be used when discussing electricity and magnetism

272 en.wikipedia.org/wiki/De_Magnete

273 Ibid 263

274 rack1.ul.cs.cmu.edu/is/gilbert (reaccessed 10/10/16)

275 en.wikipedia.org/wiki/Otto_von_Guericke13

276 www.srbrowne.com/booklet/page01.html

277 www.thefreedictionary.com/Vitreous+electricity

278 en.wikipedia.org/wiki/Electric_charge#History (reaccessed 10/10/16)

279 Ibid 265

280 Ibid en.wikipedia.org/wiki/Benjamin_Franklin#Inventions_and_scientific_inquiries

281 en.wikipedia.org/wiki/Leyden_jar

282 en.wikipedia.org/wiki/Electroscope (reaccessed 10/10/16)

283 physics.kenyon.edu/EarlyApparatus/Static_Electricity/Electroscope/Electroscope.html

284 en.wikipedia.org/wiki/Torsion_balance#Torsion_balance

285 en.wikipedia.org/wiki/Charles-Augustin_de_Coulomb

286 www.geocities.com/neveyaakov/electro_science/watson.html (reaccessed 10/10/16)

287 www.britannica.com/biography/Luigi-Galvani

288 en.wikipedia.org/wiki/Galvanic_cell

289 en.wikipedia.org/wiki/Alessandro_Volta (reaccessed 10/10/16)

290 en.wikipedia.org/wiki/Voltaic_pile

291 www.ushistory.org/franklin/info/kite.htm (reaccessed 10/10/16)

292 en.wikipedia.org/wiki/Thomas-Fran%C3%A7ois_Dalibard (accessed 10/24/16)

293 Ibid

294 www.fi.edu/history-resources/franklins-lightning-rod

295 en.wikipedia.org/wiki/Hans_Christian_Orsted (reaccessed 10/10/16)

296 en.wikipedia.org/wiki/Michael_Faraday (reaccessed 10/10/16)

297 en.wikipedia.org/wiki/William_Sturgeon (reaccessed 10/10/16)

298 en.wikipedia.org/wiki/Nicholas_Callan (reaccessed 10/10/16)

299 Maxwell, James Clerk, *"A Dynamical Theory of the Electromagnetic Field"*, Philosophical Transactions of the Royal Society of London 155, 459-512 (1865).

300 It is one of the unfortunate facts of the universe we inhabit, that the behavior of most phenomenon is described by second order differential equations – a reason for the emphasis on mathematics in science education.

301 As will be discussed in Chapter 7, the velocity of light was determined in 1680, by Danish Astronomer Olaf Roëmer to be 186,000 miles/sec. thus Maxwell had an experimental value to compare with.

302 www.livescience.com/3919-human-eye-works.html (reaccessed 10/10/16)

303 en.wikipedia.org/wiki/Heinrich_Rudolf_Hertz (accessed 9/20/16)

304 Ibid 294

305 Ibid 266

306 en.wikipedia.org/wiki/Geissler_tube (accessed 9/20/16)

307 en.wikipedia.org/wiki/Crookes_tube (accessed 9/20/16)

308 en.wikipedia.org/wiki/G._Johnstone_Stoney (accessed 9/20/16)

309 Introduction to Atomic Spectra, Harvey E. White, McGraw-Hill, NY, 1934

310 Ibid 248

311 Ibid www.in2greece.com/english/historymyth/history/ancient/thales.htm

312 ww.iep.utm.edu/a/anaximen.htm

313 en.wikipedia.org/wiki/Heraclitus

314 www.abu.nb.ca/courses/GrPhil/EmpedoclesText.htm (reaccessed 10/10/16)

315 Ibid 248

References for Chapter 2

316 http://en.wikipedia.org/wiki/Alchemy (accessed 8/20/16)

317 en.wikipedia.org/wiki/Occult

318 en.wikipedia.org/wiki/Philosopher's_Stone (accessed 8/20/16)

319 Ibid 310

320 Ibid 310

321 en.wikipedia.org/wiki/Robert_Boyle (accessed 8/20/16)

322 en.wikipedia.org/wiki/Jan_Baptist_van_Helmont

323 http://www.britannica.com/biography/Paracelsus

324 https://www.grc.nasa.gov/www/k-12/airplane/boyle.html (reaccessed 10/13/16)

325 www.infoplease.com/encyclopedia/science/element-the-elements-through-ages.html

326 *Beginnings of Modern Science*, Holmes, Boynton Ed. Classics Club, Walter J. Black, Roslyn NY, 1945, pg 209

327 en.wikipedia.org/wiki/Discovery_of_the_chemical_elements (reaccessed 10/13/16)

328 scienceworld.wolfram.com/biography/Lavoisier.html

[329] http://www.britannica.com/science/phlogiston

[330] http://www.britannica.com/topic/Elementary-Treatise-on-Chemistry

[331] Seems like the development of improved explanations required many fathers.

[332] By now, you must noted that I emphasize the empirical method used to deduce facts because the empirical method explains what, but not how and why which, for matter, is the province of quantum mechanics

[333] en.wikipedia.org/wiki/John_Dalton

[334] Dalton, John, 1766-1844; Wollaston, William Hyde, 1766-1828; Thomson, Thomas, chemist, 1773-1852

[335] https://en.wikipedia.org/wiki/Law_of_multiple_proportions

[336] Ibid 325

[337] en.wikipedia.org/wiki/Dmitri_Mendeleev

[338] https://www.google.com/#q=periodic+table&spf=384

[339] Introduction to Atomic Spectra, Harvey E. White, McGraw-Hill, NY, 1934

[340] Google - Hydrogen spectrum

[341] en.wikipedia.org/wiki/Thomas_Young_(scientist)

[342] en.wikipedis.org/wiki/electromagnetic spectrum

[343] en.wikipedia.org/wiki/Johannes_Rydberg

[344] en.wikipedia.org/wiki/Balmer_series (reaccessed 10/10/16)

[345] Ibid

[346] en.wikipedia.org/wiki/J._J._Thomson#Cathode_rays

[347] tudy.com/academy/lesson/jj-thomsons-cathode-ray-tube-crt-definition-experiment-diagram.html

[348] www.google.com/charge to mass ratio (accessed 5/28/16)

[349] https://en.wikipedia.org/wiki/George_Johnstone_Stoney

[350] en.wikipedia.org/wiki/Wilhelm_Conrad_Roentgen

[351] **https://en.**wikipedia.org/wiki/X-ray

[352] https://en.wikipedia.org/wiki/Chest_radiograph

[353] https://en.wikipedia.org/wiki/William_Henry_Bragg

[354] https://en.wikipedia.org/wiki/Braggs_law

[355] nobelprize.org/nobel_prizes/physics/laureates/1914/laue-bio.html (reaccessed 10/10/16)

[356] hyperphysics.phy-astr.gsu.edu/hbase/quantum/bragg.html

[357] https://en.wikipedia.org/wiki/X-ray_scattering_techniques

[358] en.wikipedia.org/wiki/Henri_Becquerel (reaccessed 10/13/16)

[359] https://en.wikipedia.org/wiki/Radioactive_decay

[360] https://en.wikipedia.org/wiki/Radium,_and_other_radioactive_substances

[361] https://en.wikipedia.org/wiki/Geiger_Marsden_experiment (reaccessed 10/10/16)

[362] https://en.wikipedia.org/wiki/Alpha_particle

[363] Ibid 353

364 en.wikipedia.org/wiki/Ernest_Rutherford

365 https://en.wikipedia.org/wiki/Atomic_nucleus

366 https://en.wikipedia.org/wiki/Max_Planck

367 en.wikipedia.org/wiki/Black_body

368 Ibid 358

369 https://en.wikipedia.org/wiki/Heinrich_Hertz

370 https://en.wikipedia.org/wiki/Albert_Einstein

371 https://en.wikipedia.org/wiki/Photon#Physical_properties

372 *Annalen der Physik*, 17(1905), [5], pp. 132-148.

373 en.wikipedia.org/wiki/Niels_Bohr (reaccessed 10/10/16)

374 https://en.wikipedia.org/wiki/Daltons_law (reaccessed 10/10/16)

375 https://en.wikipedia.org/wiki/Hydrogen_spectral_series

376 https://en.wikipedia.org/wiki/Bohr_model

377 https://en.wikipedia.org/wiki/Periodic_table

378 https://en.wikipedia.org/wiki/Louis_de_Broglie

379 Ibid 370

380 Clinton J. Davisson & Lester H. Germer, "Reflection of electrons by a crystal of nickel", *Nature*, V119, pp. 558-560 (1927).

381 https://en.wikipedia.org/wiki/Davisson_Germer_experiment (reaccessed 10/10/16)

382 https://en.wikipedia.org/wiki/Stern Gerlach_experiment (accessed 10/20/16)

383 https://en.wikipedia.org/wiki/Otto Stern

384 https://en.wikipedia.org/wiki/Walter_Gerlach

385 Ibid

386 https://en.wikipedia.org/wiki/Spin_(physics)

387 https://en.wikipedia.org/wiki/Uncertainty_principle (reaccessed 10/10/16)

388 https://en.wikipedia.org/wiki/Wave_equation

389 en.wikipedia.org/wiki/Quantum_tunneling

390 https://en.wikipedia.org/wiki/Integrated_circuit (reaccessed 10/10/16)

391 https://en.wikipedia.org/wiki/Proton

392 www.davidparker.com/janine/twins.html (reaccessed 10/10/16)

393 https://en.wikipedia.org/wiki/Discovery_of_the_neutron (Rutherford predicts neutron)

394 en.wikipedia.org/wiki/Atomic_mass_unit

395 https://en.wikipedia.org/wiki/James_Chadwick

396 en.wikipedia.org/wiki/Beta_decay (reaccessed 10/10/16)

397 https://en.wikipedia.org/wiki/Isidor_Isaac_Rabi

398 https://en.wikipedia.org/wiki/Felix Bloch

399 en.wikipedia.org/wiki/Nuclear_magnetic_resonance

400 https://en.wikipedia.org/wiki/List_of_Swiss_inventors_and_discoverers (reaccessed 10/10/16)

[401] www.answers.com/topic/isotope (reaccessed 10/10/16)

[402] en.wikipedia.org/wiki/Deuterium

[403] en.wikipedia.org/wiki/Tritium

[404] en.wikipedia.org/wiki/Quantum_chromodynamics (reaccessed 10/10/16)

[405] en.wikipedia.org/wiki/Mark_Oliphant

[406] https://en.wikipedia.org/wiki/Nuclear_fusion

[407] https://en.wikipedia.org/wiki/Nuclear_fission (reaccessed 10/13/14)

[408] https://en.wikipedia.org/wiki/Otto_Hahn

[409] https://en.wikipedia.org/wiki/Binding_energy

[410] https://answersingenesis.org/geology/carbon-14/doesnt-carbon-14-dating-disprove-the-bible/

[411] http://www.cs.unc.edu/~plaisted/ce/deception.html

[412] hyperphysics.phy-astr.gsu.edu/hbase/nuclear/alptun.html

[413] Ibid 384

[414] https://en.wikipedia.org/wiki/Electroweak_interaction

[415] nobelprize.org/nobel_prizes/physics/laureates/1979 (reaccessed 10/10/16)

[416] www.nde-ed.org/EducationResources/HighSchool/Radiography/subatomicparticles.htm

[417] https://en.wikipedia.org/wiki/Hadron

[418] https://en.wikipedia.org/wiki/Murray_Gell-Mann (accessed 10/20/16)

[419] https://en.wikipedia.org/wiki/George_Zweig (accessed 10/20/16)

[420] https://en.wikipedia.org/wiki/Lepton

[421] https://home.cern/about/updates/2015/09/atlas-and-cms-experiments-shed-light-higgs-properties

[422] https://en.wikipedia.org/wiki/Quark#Etymology

[423] http://hyperphysics.phy-astr.gsu.edu/hbase/particles/qevid.html

[424] https://en.wikipedia.org/wiki/Peter_Higgs (accessed 10/20/16)

[425] http://www.jupiterscientific.org/sciinfo/fundmass.html (reaccessed 10/10/16)

[426] http://home.cern/about/experiments/atlas (reaccessed 10/10/16)

[427] **ATLAS (A Toroidal LHC ApparatuS**

[428] https://en.wikipedia.org/wiki/Standard_Model

[429] https://en.wikipedia.org/wiki/Gordian_Knot

[430] http://www.reformation.org/stationary-earth.html (hilarious - chk it out)

[431] http://www.iep.utm.edu/anaxagor/

[432] http://eclipse.gsfc.nasa.gov/solar.html (reaccessed 10/10/16)

[433] https://en.wikipedia.org/wiki/Heraclides_Ponticus (accessed 9/15/16)

[434] Ibid

[435] https://www.google.com/#q=trigonometry

[436] https://www.google.com/#q=lunar+eclipse

[437] www.universetoday.com/36487/difference-between-geocentric-and-heliocentric (reaccessed 10/10/16)

438 https://en.wikipedia.org/wiki/Aristotle

439 en.wikipedia.org/wiki/Alexander_the_Great

440 http://philosophy.stackexchange.com/questions/23009/why-is-russell-so-critical-of-aristotle

441 https://en.wikipedia.org/wiki/Celestial_sphere (accessed 10/20/16)

442 csep10.phys.utk.edu/astr161/lect/retrograde/aristotle.html (reaccessed 10/10/16)

443 en.wikipedia.org/wiki/Ptolemy

444 https://en.wikipedia.org/wiki/Almagest

445 Ibid 426

446 Ibid https://en.wikipedia.org/wiki/Bertrand_Russell

447 Ibid 2

448 https://en.wikipedia.org/wiki/History_of_optics

449 https://en.wikipedia.org/wiki/History_of_the_telescope (reaccessed 10/10/16)

450 http://www.space.com/21950-who-invented-the-telescope.html

451 en.wikipedia.org/wiki/Galileo_Galilei

452 https://en.wikipedia.org/wiki/Moons_of_Jupiter

453 http://www.hps.cam.ac.uk/starry/tychoastrol.html (reaccessed 10/10/16)

454 en.wikipedia.org/wiki/Johannes_Kepler

455 http://galileoandeinstein.physics.virginia.edu/lectures/tycho.htm

456 http://ffden-2.phys.uaf.edu/212_fall2003.web.dir/Beth_Caissie/eccentricity.htm (reaccessed 10/10/16)

457 http://www.astronomynotes.com/gravappl

458 Barker and Goldstein, "Theological Foundations of Kepler's Astronomy", pp. 112–13. (reaccessed 10/10/16)

459 https://en.wikipedia.org/wiki/Isaac_Newton

460 http://www.themiddleages.net/plague.html

461 en.wikipedia.org/wiki/Robert_Hooke

462 http://csep10.phys.utk.edu/astr161/lect/history/newtongrav.html

463 http://www.physicsclassroom.com/Physics-Tutorial/Newton-s-Laws

464 http://www.storyofmathematics.com/17th_newton.html

465 http://www.britannica.com/biography/Edmond-Halley

466 *Philosophiae Naturalis Principia Mathematica* (reaccessed 10/10/16)

467 https://en.wikipedia.org/wiki/Pierre-Simon_Laplace (reaccessed 10/13/16)

468 Ibid

469 http://www.eoht.info/page/Napoleon+Laplace+anecdote

470 https://en.wikipedia.org/wiki/Special_relativity

471 https://en.wikipedia.org/wiki/General_relativity

472 Stephen Hawking "A Brief History of Time", Bantam Dell Publishing Group, 1988

473 *Dark matter: What's the matter?* Jeff Hecht *Nature* 637 29 September, 2016

474 www.geocities.com/ganesha_gate/galileo.html (reaccessed 10/10/16)

475 https://en.wikipedia.org/wiki/Eratosthenes

476 en.wikipedia.org/wiki/Giovanni_Domenico_Cassini

477 http://tonic.physics.sunysb.edu/~dteaney/F12_mystery/lectures/l6notes.pdf (reaccessed 10/10/16)

478 https://en.wikipedia.org/wiki/Ole_Roemer

479 http://scienceworld.wolfram.com/biography/Roemer.html

480 https://en.wikipedia.org/wiki/Michelson_Morley_experiment

481 Ibid

482 Ibid

483 en.wikipedia.org/wiki/Luminiferous_aether

484 en.wikipedia.org/wiki/Interferometry

485 https://en.wikipedia.org/wiki/George_Biddell_Airy

486 https://en.wikipedia.org/wiki/Cosmology

487 https://en.wikipedia.org/wiki/Parallax

488 http://hyperphysics.phy-astr.gsu.edu/Hbase/astro/para.html

489 en.wikipedia.org/wiki/John_Goodricke

490 https://en.wikipedia.org/wiki/Cepheid_variable

491 *Annals of the Astronomical Observatory of Harvard College* (reaccessed 10/11/16)

492 Miss Leavitt in Pickering, Edward C. "Periods of 25 Variable Stars in the Small Magellanic Cloud." *Harvard College Observatory Circular 173* (1912) 1-3

493 cosmology.berkeley.edu/Education/Projects/Desktop_Stars/DTS/ISQ/Discussion.html (reaccessed 10/11/16)

494 universeadventure.org/fundamentals/light-magnitude.htm

495 en.wikipedia.org/wiki/Lowell_Observatory

496 Vesto Melvin Slipher, "The radial velocity of the Andromeda Nebula", the inaugural volume of the Lowell Observatory Bulletin, pp.2.56-2.57, September 17, 1912.

497 en.wikipedia.org/wiki/Alexander_Friedmann

498 http://www.physicsoftheuniverse.com/scientists_friedmann.html (reaccessed 10/11/16)

499 en.wikipedia.org/wiki/Edwin_Hubble

500 antwrp.gsfc.nasa.gov/diamond_jubilee/1996/sandage_hubble.html (reaccessed 10/11/16)

501 http://earthsky.org/clusters-nebulae-galaxies/andromeda-galaxy-closest-spiral-to-milky-way

502 https://en.wikipedia.org/wiki/Andromeda_Galaxy

503 Ibid 501

504 en.wikipedia.org/wiki/George_Gamow

505 "The Origin of Chemical Elements" Physical Review, April 1948

506 https://en.wikipedia.org/wiki/Arno_Allan_Penzias

507 www.bell-labs.com/project/feature/archives/cosmology/

508   hyperphysics.phy-astr.gsu.edu/hbase/astro/bbang.html (reaccessed 10/11/16)
509   space.wikia.com/wiki/Wilkinson_Microwave_Anisotropy_Probe
510   https://en.wikipedia.org/wiki/Cosmic_microwave_background
511   Long-Awaited Data Sharpen Picture of Universe's Birth, Science Vol. 311 24 March, 2006
512   http://map.gsfc.nasa.gov/news/
513   Ibid 493
514   en.wikipedia.org/wiki/Star_formation
515   Ibid
516   Ibid 496
517   firstgalaxies.ucolick.org/cosmos.html
518   en.wikipedia.org/wiki/Milky_Way (reaccessed 10/11/16)
519   http://www.space.com/22471-red-giant-stars.html
520   *Red Giants and White Dwarfs*, Robert Jastrow, Harper and Row, 1967 NY. NY
521   https://en.wikipedia.org/wiki/Supernova
522   Ibid
523   http://www.space.com/17884-universe-expansion-speed-hubble-constant.html
524   Ibid 503
525   Ibid *502*
526   A Jupiter-mass companion to a solar-type star" Mayor, Michael; Queloz, Didier Nature vol 378 (1995).
527   Science News, July 5, 2008, pp 16-25
528   Planetary System Formation, Science Vol. 321 8 August, 2008
529   www.geology.wisc.edu/zircon/Valley2002Cool_Early_Earth.pdf (reaccessed 10/11/16)
530   en.wikipedia.org/wiki/Zircon#cite_note-2
531   geoscience.wisc.edu/geoscience/people/faculty/john-valley
532   A Cool Early Earth, John W. Valley, William H. Peck, et al *Geology* 30: 351–354 2002
533   Planetary System Formation, Science Vol. 321 8 August, 2008
534   www.cst.cmich.edu/users/dietr1rv/basalt.htm (reaccessed 10/11/16)
535   https://en.wikipedia.org/wiki/Granite
536   Ibid 462
537   https://en.wikipedia.org/wiki/Basalt (reaccessed 10/11/16)
538   Livingston, D. E., Brown, E. E., and Malcolm, C., 1974, Rb-Sr whole rock isochron ages for "older" Precambrian plutonic and metamorphic rocks of the Grand Canyon, Arizona: Geological Society of Am. Abstracts with Programs, v. 6, n. 7, p. 848.
539   goaustralia.about.com/od/wa/f/stromatolites.htm (reaccessed 10/11/16)
540   en.wikipedia.org/wiki/Banded_iron_formation (reaccessed 10/11/16)

541 www.emc.maricopa.edu/faculty/farabee/biobk/BioBookmito.html (reaccessed 10/11/16)

542 Ibid, 460

543 scijinks.jpl.nasa.gov/atmosphere-formation

544 www.eurekalert.org/pub_releases/2008-06/uow-ams061308.php (verified 10/11/16)

545 www.lpl.arizona.edu/faculty/drake_papers/CampinsDrake2006.doc

546 Ibid

547 Ibid 525

548 "Early Life Recorded in Archean Pillow Lavas", H/ Furnes et al, Science vol. 304, 23 Apr. 2004

549 How did Earth get its water? The answer lies in deuterium ratios and a theory called the Grand Tack Christopher Crockett, Science News May 6, 2015

550 www.lpl.arizona.edu/faculty/drake_papers/CampinsDrake2006.doc

551 en.wikipedia.org/wiki/Origin_of_water_on_Earth (reaccessed 10/11/16)

552 https://en.wikipedia.org/wiki/Carbonaceous_chondrite

553 Ibid

554 A. Morbidelli et al. Meteoritics & Planetary Science 35, 2000, S. 1309–1329

555 Ibid 465

556 http://www.simonwinchester.com/

557 *The Map that Changed the World,* Simon Winchester, Simon and Shuster, 2001

558 Ibid

559 http://www.naturaltreasure.com/genfossils.htm

560 http://www.ucmp.berkeley.edu/history/ancient.html (reaccessed 10/11/16)

561 Ibid Aristotle

562 en.wikipedia.org/wiki/Origin_of_life#Spontaneous_generation

563 http://necsi.edu/projects/evolution/evidence/remains/evidence_remains.html

564 Rick Steves travel information series on PBS (reaccessed 10/11/16)

565 "The First Fossil Hunters: Paleontology in Greek and Roman Times" A. Mayor, Princeton University Press, 2001, Princeton N. J.

566 http://www.biography.com/people/leonardo-da-vinci-40396 (reaccessed 10/11/16)

567 http://www.da-vinci-inventions.com/

568 https://en.wikipedia.org/wiki/Apennine_Mountains

569 https://en.wikipedia.org/wiki/Codex_Leicester

570 *Leonardo's Mountain of Clams and the Diet of Worms,* Stephen Jay Gould, Harmony Books, 1998 pg 26

571 http://www.stephenjaygould.org/ (accessed 10/16/16)

572 Ibid 562

573 "Ibid pp 22-29

574 www.answersingenesis.org/get-answers

575 *The Map that Changed the World,* Simon Winchester, Simon and Shuster, 2001

576 www.answersingenesis.org/articles/nab/catastrophic-plate-tectonics

577 Ibid 22

578 www.pantheon.org/articles/d/deucalion.html (reaccessed 10/11/16)

579 Bretz's Flood, John Soennichen, Sasquatch Books, Seattle, Wa 2008

580 Ibid

581 U.S. National Park Service Website, Ice Age Floods, 2002 http://vulcan.wr.usgs.gov/Glossary/Glaciers/IceSheets/description_lake_missoula.html

582 http://gsahist.org/gsat2/pardee.htm accessed (10/10/16)

583 Montana Joseph Thomas Pardee, Unusual currents in glacial Lake Missoula; Geological Society of America Bulletin; November 1942; v. 53; no. 11; p. 1569-1599

584 Mathew Roberts (Icelandic Meteorological Office) (accessed 10/16/16)

585 With Glaciers Atop Volcanoes, Iceland Zooms In on Signs of Unrest, NY Times article By Amanda Leigh Haag, January 17, 2006

586 Channeled Scablands: Overview, by Steven Dutch, Natural and Applied Sciences, http://www.uwsp.edu/geo/projects/geoweb/participants/dutch/vtrips/Scablands.HTM

587 https://en.wikipedia.org/wiki/Igneous_rock

588 https://en.wikipedia.org/wiki/Sedimentary_rock (reaccessed 10/11/16)

589 https://en.wikipedia.org/wiki/Metamorphic_rock

590 http://www.geolsoc.org.uk/

591 en.wikipedia.org/wiki/Neptunism

592 en.wikipedia.org/wiki/Siberian_Traps (reaccessed 10/11/16)

593 en.wikipedia.org/wiki/Plutonism

594 en.wikipedia.org/wiki/Catastrophism

595 http://www.killerasteroids.org/impact.php (reaccessed 10/11/16)

596 Ibid

597 Ibid 586

598 /www.james-hutton.org.uk/

599 http://www.heraldscotland.com/life_style/13211202.Joanna_Blythman_review__Slighhouse__Edinburgh/

600 James Hutton the Farmer." James Hutton.org (reaccessed 10/11/16)

601 www.strangescience.net/hutton.htm

602 Return to Slighhouses and Farm Improvement." James Hutton.org.

603 https://www.ieee.li/pdf/essay/life_of_maxwell.pdf (accessed 10/16/16)

604 The Birth of Plenty, How the Prosperity of the Modern World was Created, William J. Bernstein, McGraw-Hill, NY, NY 2004

605 Professor of natural philosophy at the University of Edinburgh. (reaccessed 10/11/16)

606 *The Theory of the Earth.* James Hutton.org

[607] Ibid 515

[608] American Museum of Natural History (2000). "James Hutton: The Founder of Modern Geology."

[609] https://www.royalsoced.org.uk (reaccessed 10/11/16)

[610] en.wikipedia.org/wiki/Jean_de_Charpentier

[611] en.wikipedia.org/wiki/Karl_Friedrich_Schimper

[612] en.wikipedia.org/wiki/Bill_Bryson

[613] en.wikipedia.org/wiki/A_Short_History_of_Nearly_Everything, 2005 (reaccessed 10/11/16)

[614] http://www.ucmp.berkeley.edu/history/agassiz.html

[615] Ibid

[616] http://ocp.hul.harvard.edu/expeditions/agassiz.html *History of the Freshwater Fish of Central Europe.*

[617] https://archive.org/details/etudessurlesgla00agasgoog (2010) (reaccessed 10/11/16)

[618] en.wikipedia.org/wiki/William_Buckland

[619] en.wikipedia.org/wiki/Roderick_Murchison

[620] en.wikipedia.org/wiki/Adam_Sedgwick (accessed 6/11/16)

[621] http://www.britannica.com/science/Devonian-Period (accessed 6/11/16)

[622] en.wikipedia.org/wiki/Silurian

[623] www.geo.ucalgary.ca/~macrae/timescale/timescale.html (reaccessed 10/11/16)

[624] https://en.wikipedia.org/wiki/Stratigraphic_column

[625] en.wikipedia.org/wiki/Charles_Lyell (Accessed 6/11/16)

[626] en.wikipedia.org/wiki/Uniformitarianism (Accessed 6/11/16)

[627] https://en.wikipedia.org/wiki/Serapeum (Accessed 6/12/16)

[628] https://en.wikipedia.org/wiki/Ammianus_Marcellinus (Accessed 6/14/16)

[629] www.mnsu.edu/emuseum/information/biography/klmno/lyell_charles.html (Accessed 6/18/16)

[630] *Principles of Geology* 1st vol. 1st edition, Jan. 1830 John Murry, London).

[631] https://www.google.com/#q=metamorphic+rock+definition&spf=582

[632] Adams, Frank D. *The Birth and Development of the Geological Sciences.* Dover Publications, Inc., 1938.

[633] Bailey, Edward 1962. *Charles Lyell.* Nelson, London.

[634] Bower, Peter J. (1975). *The Changing Meaning of "Evolution"* in *Journal of the History of ideas* 36: 95-114

[635] Ibid 596

[636] Ibid 515

[637] Ibid 515

[638] https://www.google.com/#q=vishnu+schist

[639] en.wikipedia.org/wiki/Earth%27s_internal_heat_budget#Radiogenic_heat

[640] Ashe, Thomas (1813). *History of the Azores, or. Western islands.* Oxford University

641 Ibid

642 Ibid 611

643 www.mariner.org/educationalad/ageofex/ (reaccessed 10/11/16)

644 Ibid 37

645 https://en.wikipedia.org/wiki/Pangaea

646 Alfred Wegener. *The Origins of Continents and Oceans* (4th edition) Courier Corp 12/14/2001

647 Ibid 615

648 en.wikipedia.org/wiki/Trilobite

649 Ibid

650 www.google.com/#q=tectonic (reaccessed 10/11/16)

651 Claire Mallard, et al, Subduction controls the distribution and fragmentation of Earth's tectonic plates, Nature, 7 July, 2016

652 Ibid, 583

653 en.wikipedia.org/wiki/Harry_Hammond_Hess

654 http://www.geolsoc.org.uk/Plate-Tectonics/Chap3-Plate-Margins/Divergent/Mid-Atlantic-Ridge (verified 10/11/16)

655 www.waterencyclopedia.com/St-Ts/Submarines-and-Submersibles.html

656 www.infoplease.com/ce6/sci/A0814954.html

657 www.platetectonics.com/book/page_15.asp (reaccessed 10/11/16)

658 http://www.sanandreasfault.org/

659 http://www.pnsn.org/outreach/about-earthquakes/plate-tectonics (reaccessed 10/11/16)

660 http://americastectonics.weebly.com/north-american-plate.html

661 en.wikipedia.org/wiki/Subduction

662 https://www.google.com/#q=hutton's+unconformity&spf=68

663 en.wikipedia.org/wiki/Orogenic

664 www.sierrahistorical.org/archives/geology.html (reaccessed 10/11/16)

665 en.wikipedia.org/wiki/Seismology

666 https://en.wikipedia.org/wiki/Wave_propagation

667 Ibid

668 Ibid 341

669 https://www.google.com/webhp?gws_rd=ssl#q=Beno+Gutenberg (accessed 10/9/16)

670 www.enotes.com/earth-science/richter-charles-f (reaccessed 10/11/16)

671 http://www.bbc.co.uk/schools/gcsebitesize/science/21c/earth_universe/seismic_wavesrev1.shtml

672 pubs.usgs.gov/gip/interior/ (reaccessed 10/11/16)

673 https://en.wikipedia.org/wiki/Tomography

674 www.uh.edu/engines/epi144.htm

675 https://answersingenesis.org/ (accessed 5/31/16)

676 Clocks in the rocks http://hyperphysics.phy-astr.gsu.edu/hbase/nuclear/clkroc.html (reaccessed 10/11/16)

677 www.talkorigins.org/faqs/faq-age-of-earth.html

678 https://en.wikipedia.org/wiki/Age_of_the_Earth (age of the Earth, meteorite dating) Accessed 10/12/16

679 https://en.wikipedia.org/wiki/Isotopes_of_lead

680 www.noanswesingenesis.au/as_old_as_time_plimer.htm

681 Ibid

682 http://www.nasa.gov/topics/earth/features/2012-poleReversal.html (reaccessed 10/11/16)

683 https://en.wikipedia.org/wiki/Chemical_process_of_decomposition

684 http://www.clinchem.org/content/47/9/1688.full (reaccessed 10/11/16)

685 http://www.astro.ucla.edu/~wright/age.html (reaccessed 10/11/16)

686 Ibid

687 Ibid

688 en.wikipedia.org/wiki/Accelerator_mass_spectrometry

689 Peter Manseau "Dating the shroud of Turin", Wall Street Journal (Books Review) April 11, 2009

690 http://evolution.berkeley.edu/evolibrary/article/history_06

691 An Historical Sketch Of The Progress Of Opinion On The Origin Of Species (understanding before modern science) (Accessed 7/20/16)

692 http://www.buffon.cnrs.fr/ice/ice_book_detail-en-text-buffon-buffon_hn-34-7.html (reaccessed 10/11/16)

693 http://evolution.berkeley.edu/evolibrary/article/history_06

694 www.ucmp.berkeley.edu/history/buffon2.html

695 en.wikipedia.org/wiki/Jean-Baptiste_Lamarck

696 Gould, Stephen Jay (2002). *The Structure of Evolutionary Theory*. Harvard: Belknap Harvard, pp 170-197 as quoted in wiki (reaccessed 10/11/16)

697 Coleman, William L. (1977). *Biology in the Nineteenth Century: Problems of Form, Function, and Transformation*. Cambridge: Cambridge University Press, pp1-2 (reaccessed 10/11/16)

698 https://www.google.com/webhp?gws_rd=ssl#q=philosophie+anatomique+saint+hilaire

699 www.victorianweb.org/science/cuvier.html (reaccessed 10/11/16)

700 https://embryo.asu.edu/pages/essay-cuvier-geoffroy-debate (reaccessed 10/11/16)

701 https://archive.org/details/theoryofeessayon00cuvirich (reaccessed 10/11/16)

702 http://www.macroevolution.net/cuvier.html

703 https://en.wikipedia.org/wiki/Polygenism

704 http://usslave.blogspot.com/2011/10/black-bodies-white-science-louis.html (reaccessed 10/11/16)

705 www.ucmp.berkeley.edu/history/haeckel.html

706 en.wikipedia.org/wiki/Charles_Darwin (accessed 5/14/16)

707 http://lunarsociety.org.uk/

708 en.wikipedia.org/wiki/Second_voyage_of_HMS_Beagle (accessed 5/14/16)

709 www.gct.org/intro.html

710 Secular Humanism, The force behind the Creation-Evolution Debate, Patrick Vosse, 2010, Holy Fire Publishing

711 en.wikipedia.org/wiki/John_Gould (accessed 6/14/16)

712 Ibid

713 lilt.ilstu.edu/gmklass/foi/readings/creativity.htm (reaccessed 10/11/16)

714 Ibid

715 Ibid

716 en.wikipedia.org/wiki/Thomas_Malthus (accessed 9/17/16)

717 *Geological Evidences of the Antiquity of Man* 1 vol. 1st edition, Feb. 1863 (John Murray, London) (verified 10/11/16)

718 Info regarding Darwin in ask.com

719 en.wikipedia.org/wiki/Alfred_Russel_Wallace

720 en.wikipedia.org/wiki/Wallace_Line (accessed 7/30/16)

721 Ibid 648

722 Ibid 648

723 en.wikipedia.org/wiki/The_Origin_of_Species (accessed 6/11/16)

724 Ibid 393

725 https://www.google.com/#q=intelligent+design+definition&spf=440

726 Wall Street Journal, Dec 20, 08. page 1

727 Ibid 394

728 www.accessexcellence.org/RC/AB/BC/Gregor_Mendel.html (accessed 6/11/16)

729 http://www.etymonline.com/index.php?allowed_in_frame=0&search=gene (accessed 10/30/16)

730 Ibid

731 en.wikipedia.org/wiki/Carl_Correns (accessed 6/11/16)

732 en.wikipedia.org/wiki/Erich_Tschermak_von_Seysenegg (accessed 6/13/16)

733 en.wikipedia.org/wiki/Hugo_De_Vries

734 https://en.wikipedia.org/wiki/Cell_theory#Microscopes - probably should be Ibid from ch 1

735 microbiology.suite101.com/article.cfm/anthony_van_leeuwenhoek (accessed 6/13/16)

736 en.wikipedia.org/wiki/Theodor_Schwann (accessed 6/13/16)

737 en.wikipedia.org/wiki/Matthias_Jakob_Schleiden (accessed 6/13/16)

738 Ibid 405

739 Ibid 406

740 Schleiden, Matthias Jakob 1839, "Contributions to Phytogenesis" (accessed 6/13/16)

[741] porpax.bio.miami.edu/~cmallery/150/unity/cell.text.htm (accessed 7/2/16)

[742] en.wikipedia.org/wiki/Cell_theory (accessed 6/13/16)

[743] www.genome.gov/26524120/chromosomes-fact-sheet

[744] en.wikipedia.org/wiki/Walther_Flemming (accessed 6/14/16)

[745] /en.wikipedia.org/wiki/Meiosis (reaccessed 10/11/16)

[746] Ibid

[747] en.wikipedia.org/wiki/Edouard_Van_Beneden (accessed 6/14/16)

[748] /en.wikipedia.org/wiki/Friedrich_Miescher (8/1/16)

[749] http://www.dnaftb.org/15/bio.html

[750] www.microbiologyprocedure.com/deoxyribosenucleic-acid-DNA/history-of-nucleic-acids.htm

[751] Fischer, E. *Berichte der Deutschen Chemischen Gesellschaft* 1899, *32*, 2550.

[752] /en.wikipedia.org/wiki/Richard_Altmann (8/1/16)

[753] en.wikipedia.org/wiki/Base_pair

[754] www.answers.com/topic/albrecht-kossel (8/1/16)

[755] en.wikipedia.org/wiki/Phoebus_Levene

[756] Levene P, (1919). "The structure of yeast nucleic acid." *J Biol Chem* 40 (2): 415–24.

[757] https://earthlingnature.wordpress.com/2012/09/29/why-thymine-instead-of-uracil/#comments

[758] en.wikipedia.org/wiki/Robert_Feulgen (8/1/16)

[759] en.wikipedia.org/wiki/Frederick_Griffith (8/1/16)

[760] en.wikipedia.org/wiki/William_Astbury (8/1/16)

[761] en.wikipedia.org/wiki/Oswald_Theodore_Avery (8/1/16)

[762] Hershey A, Chase M (1952). "Independent functions of viral protein and nucleic acid in growth of bacteriophage" (PDF). *J Gen Physiol* 36 (1): 39–56. doi:10.1085/jgp.36.1.39. PMID 12981234

[763] porpax.bio.miami.edu/~cmallery/150/gene/DNAdiscovery.htm

[764] Watson J.D. and Crick F.H.C. (1953). "A Structure for Deoxyribose Nucleic Acid" (PDF). *Nature* 171: 737–738. doi:10.1038/171737a0. PMID 13054692.

[765] James D Watson *The Double Helix: A Personal Account of the Discovery of the Structure of DNA* Touchstone, Rockefeller Center, 1230 Avenue of the Americas, NY, NY, 1968

[766] A Reader's Guide to The Double Helix

[767] en.wikipedia.org/wiki/Base_pair

[768] https://en.wikipedia.org/wiki/Genetic_code (accessed 11/3/016)

[769] en.wikipedia.org/wiki/Crick,_Brenner_et_al._experiment (reaccessed 10/11/16)

[770] "The evolutionary landscape of alternative splicing in vertebrate species". *Science*, 2012 Dec 21;338(6114):1587-93. (accessed 5/15/13)

[771] https://en.wikipedia.org/wiki/DNA_methylation (accessed 11/3/016)

[772] en.wikipedia.org/wiki/Epigenetics

773 https://en.wikipedia.org/wiki/The_Language_of_God

774 Venter, JC, et al (2001). "The sequence of the human genome.". *Science* 291: 1304–1351.

775 Ki-67 acts as a biological surfactant to disperse mitotic chromosomes, Sara Cuylen, Claudia Blaukopf et al, Nature vol. 535, 14 July 2016

776 www.storyofmathematics.com/19th_gauss.html

777 Nature Volume: 537, Pages: 152–155 08 September 2016

778 Ibid

779 Makel et al, Psychol Sci, 27. 1004-1018, 2016

780 https://en.wikipedia.org/wiki/Extinction (accessed 10/26/16)

781 Sid Perkins "The chemistry of minerals preserved in Australian rocks suggests tectonic activity for Earth's earliest eon", January 3rd, 2009; Vol. 175 #1

782 Named by Plate tectonics "discoverer", Alfred Wegener (reaccessed 10/11/16)

783 en.wikipedia.org/wiki/Paleomagnetism (reaccessed 10/11/16)

784 en.wikipedia.org/wiki/Magnetic (reaccessed 10/11/16)

785 Ibid, 476

786 www.peripatus.gen.nz/Paleontology/Rodinia.html

787 en.wikipedia.org/wiki/Cryogenian (reaccessed 10/11/16)

788 www.ucmp.berkeley.edu/vendian/vendian.html

789 www.asgp.pl/2004/74_3/257-265.html

790 McMenamin, Mark A.; Diana L. McMenamin [1990-01-15]. «The Rifting of Rodinia», *The Emergence of Animals*.

791 Ibid, 477

792 www.pbs.org/wgbh/evolution/library/03/4/l_034_02.html

793 en.wikipedia.org/wiki/Animals#Deuterostomes

794 Buckland, W. (1841). *Geology and Mineralogy Considered with Reference to Natural Theology*. Lea & Blanchard.

795 Ibid - Origen of species, pgs 315-316

796 What sparked the Cambrian explosion? Doug Fox, Nature 16 Feb 2016

797 en.wikipedia.org/wiki/Prehistoric_fish

798 Ibid

799 en.wikipedia.org/wiki/Devonian

800 http://www.amnh.org/exhibitions/water-h2o-life/life-in-water/surviving-in-salt-water/

801 Edward B. Daeschler, Neil H. Shubin and Farish A. Jenkins, Jr (6 April 2006). A Devonian tetrapod-like fish and the evolution of the tetrapod body plan. *Nature* 440: 757–763

802 Jennifer A. Clack, *Scientific American, Getting a Leg Up on Land* Nov. 21, 2005. (accessed 5/16/16)

803 en.wikipedia.org/wiki/Tiktaalik (accessed 5/16/16)

804 Shubin, Neil (2008). *Your Inner Fish*. Pantheon. (accessed 5/16/16)

[805] en.wikipedia.org/wiki/Neil_Shubin (accessed 5/16/16)

[806] Ibid

[807] www.backardnature.net/amphibs.htm

[808] en.wikipedia.org/wiki/Carboniferous

[809] en.wikipedia.org/wiki/Amniote (accessed 7/13/16)

[810] https://en.wikipedia.org/wiki/Sauropsida (accessed 7/13/16)

[811] Ibid

[812] en.wikipedia.org/wiki/Edwin_Stephen_Goodrich (reaccessed 10/18/16)

[813] en.wikipedia.org/wiki/Reptile (accessed 7/13/16)

[814] en.wikipedia.org/wiki/Archaeothyris

[815] Ibid 788

[816] Ibid

[817] The term "**reptilian**" refers to our primitive, instinctive **brain** function that is shared by all reptiles and mammals, including humans. It is the most powerful and oldest of our coping **brain** functions since without it we would not be alive.

[818] www.crystalinks.com/reptilianbrain.html

[819] The global decline of reptiles, deja' vu amphibians, J. Whitfield Gibbons, Butler University Libraries, 2000

[820] biology.about.com/library/organs/brain/blhippocam.htm

[821] en.wikipedia.org/wiki/Permian

[822] Ibid

[823] en.wikipedia.org/wiki/Archosaurs

[824] en.wikipedia.org/wiki/Cynodonts

[825] biology.about.com/library/organs/brain/blhippocam.htm

[826] en.wikipedia.org/wiki/Permian

[827] Ibid

[828] en.wikipedia.org/wiki/Archosaurs

[829] en.wikipedia.org/wiki/Cynodonts

[830] Jin YG, Wang et al, "Pattern of Marine Mass Extinction Near the Permian–Triassic Boundary in South China." *Science* 289 (5478): 432–436.

[831] Production Manager: Yolanda Ayres. "What Really Killed the Dinosaurs." BBC Horizon.

[832] en.wikipedia.org/wiki/Triassic.

[833] en.wikipedia.org/wiki/Pangaea

[834] A near-Earth object (NEO) is any small Solar System body whose orbit brings it into proximity with Earth

[835] Ibid

[836] Ibid

[837] en.wikipedia.org/wiki/Archosaur

[838] Ibid 734

[839] http://www.enchantedlearning.com/subjects/dinosaurs/dinofossils/First.shtml

840 Ibid

841 en.wikipedia.org/wiki/Dinosaur

842 Wang, S.C., and Dodson, P. (2006). "Estimating the Diversity of Dinosaurs." *Proceedings of the National Academy of Sciences USA* 103 (37): 13601–13605.

843 Bakker, R. T., Galton, P., 1974. Dinosaur monophyly and a new class of vertebrates. *Nature* 248:168-172. ref in http://en.wikipedia.org/wiki/Dinosaur

844 https://www.google.com/#q=kt+extinction

845 Alvarez, L. W., et al. 1980. Extraterrestrial cause for the Cretaceous-Tertiary extinction. *Science* 208: 1095-1108.

846 Pope KO, Ocampo AC, Kinsland GL, Smith R (1996). "Surface expression of the Chicxulub crater." *Geology (journal)*, 24 (6): 527–530.

847 en.wikipedia.org/wiki/Deccan_Traps#cite_note-mantleplumes-1

848 en.wikipedia.org/wiki/Mammal

849 Ibid

850 en.wikipedia.org/wiki/Limbic_system#cite_note-Conn-1

851 Ibid

852 en.wikipedia.org/wiki/Eocene

853 H.G. Stehlen, 1910. «Remarques sur les faunules de Mammifères des couches eocenes et oligocenes du Bassin de Paris,» in *Bulletin de la Société Géologique de France*, 4'.9, pp 488-520

854 Goodman, M., et al. (1990). "Primate evolution at the DNA level and a classification of hominoids." *Journal of Molecular Evolution* 30: 260–266

855 New Perspectives on anthropoid origins – PNAS, Sept 22, 2009

856 en.wikipedia.org/wiki/Haplorhini (accessed 9/28/16)

857 en.wikipedia.org/wiki/Strepsirrhini (accessed 9/28/16)

858 en.wikipedia.org/wiki/Hominidae (accessed 9/28/16)

859 https://www.newscientist.com/round-up/instant-expert-general-relativity (accessed April 16, 2017)

860 en.wikipedia.org/wiki/Alexander_Friedmann

861 en.wikipedia.org/wiki/George_Gamow

862 https://en.wikipedia.org/wiki/Arno_Allan_Penzias

863 space.wikia.com/wiki/Wilkinson_Microwave_Anisotropy_Probe

864 https://en.wikipedia.org/wiki/Cosmic_microwave_background

865 Long-Awaited Data Sharpen Picture of Universe's Birth, Science Vol. 311 24 March, 2006

866 *Population genetics: A map of human wanderlust* Serena Tucci et al, Journal name: *Nature* Volume: 538, 13 October 2016

867 www.sciencedaily.com January 16, 2017 Université de Montréal

868 Ibid

869 Steven R. Holden et al, A 130,000-year-old archeological site in southern Ca. Nature, Vol 544, 27 April 2017

870 *The Limits of Growth* MIT study sponsored by The Club of Rome, Dr. Dennis L. Meadows, Director, 1968

871 *The Birth of Plenty-How the Prosperity of the Modern World was Created,* William Bernstein, McGraw-Hill, NY, NY 2004

872 Ibid

873 https://www.google.com/#q=cures+childhood+illness+in+the+1800s

874 Ibid

875 *where to put the next billion people, Richard Foreman, Nature, 28 Sep 2016*

876 *Feeding the Ten Billion: Plants and Population Growth,* Lloyd T. Evans, 2016

877 *Scientists must have a say in the future of our cities, Nature* Volume: 538, 13 October 2016

878 https://en.wikipedia.org/wiki/Milutin_Milankovi%C4%87

879 www.eia.gov/tools/faqs/faq.cfm?id=427&t=3 (accessed Dec 30, 2016)

880 Wind and Solar Can't Replace Coal and Gas, George F. Steeg, WSJ. Jan 2, 2017

881 *A killer plague wouldn't save the planet from us,* www.newscientist.com/article/mg22429934-100-a-killer-plague-wouldnt-save-the-planet-from-us (accessed Jan 1, 2017)

882 Ibid *Masters of the Planet*

883 Colonize or become extinct, Stephen Hawking, Science, May 22, 2017

884 https://en.wikipedia.org/wiki/Betelgeuse

885 http://www.vatican.va/archive/bible/genesis/documents/bible_genesis_en.html

886 www.ucmp.berkely.edu/help/timefor.pho

887 en.wikipedia.org/wiki/Linnaean_taxonomy77

TRUE DIRECTIONS

An affiliate of Tarcher Perigee

OUR MISSION

Tarcher Perigee's mission has always been to publish
books that contain great ideas. Why? Because:

GREAT LIVES BEGIN WITH GREAT IDEAS

At Tarcher Perigee, we recognize that many talented authors, speakers,
educators, and thought-leaders share this mission and deserve to be published –
many more than Tarcher Perigee can reasonably publish ourselves. True
Directions is ideal for authors and books that increase awareness, raise
consciousness, and inspire others to live their ideals and passions.

Like Tarcher Perigee, True Directions books are designed to do three things:
inspire, inform, and motivate.

Thus, True Directions is an ideal way for these important voices to
bring their messages of hope, healing, and help to the world.

Every book published by True Directions– whether it is non-fiction, memoir,
novel, poetry or children's book – continues Tarcher Perigee's mission to publish
works that bring positive change in the world. We invite you to join our mission.

For more information, see the True Directions website:

www.iUniverse.com/TrueDirections/SignUp

Be a part of Tarcher Perigee's community to bring positive change in this
world! See exclusive author videos, discover new and exciting books, learn
about upcoming events, connect with author blogs and websites, and more!
www.tarcherbooks.com

TRUE DIRECTIONS
AN AFFILIATE OF TARCHER PERIGEE